Conflict in
Central America

KEESING'S PUBLICATIONS

Other titles currently available in the Keesing's International Studies series (all published by Longman Group UK Limited):-

China and the Soviet Union 1949–84, compiled by Peter Jones and Sian Kevill (1985)

From the Six to the Twelve: the Enlargement of the European Communities, by Frances Nicholson and Roger East (1987)

The Keesing's Reference Publications (KRP) series (all published by Longman Group UK Limited) includes the following currently available titles:-

Border and Territorial Disputes, edited by Alan J. Day (1982); a second edition is to be published in late 1987

Political Dissent: An International Guide to Dissident, Extra-Parliamentary, Guerrilla and Illegal Political Movements, compiled by Henry W. Degenhardt (1983); a revised and updated version, *Revolutionary and Dissident Movements*, is to be published in late 1987

Political Parties of the World (2nd edition), edited by Alan J. Day & Henry W. Degenhardt (1984)

State Economic Agencies of the World, edited by Alan J. Day (1985)

Maritime Affairs: A World Handbook, compiled by Henry W. Degenhardt (1985)

Latin American Political Movements, compiled by Ciarán Ó Maoláin (1985)

Communist and Marxist Parties of the World, compiled by Charles Hobday (1986)

OPEC, Its Member States and the World Energy Market, compiled by John Evans (1986)

Treaties and Alliances of the World (4th edition), compiled by Henry W. Degenhardt (1986)

Peace Movements of the World: An International Directory, edited by Alan J. Day (1986)

Keesing's Record of World Events (formerly *Keesing's Contemporary Archives*), the monthly worldwide news reference service with an unrivalled reputation for accuracy and impartiality, has appeared continuously since 1931. Published by Longman Group UK Limited on annual subscription; back volumes are also available.

Conflict in Central America

KEESING'S INTERNATIONAL STUDIES

by Helen Schooley

Longman

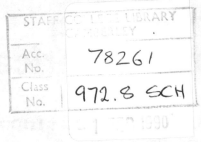

CONFLICT IN CENTRAL AMERICA
Published by **Longman Group UK Limited**, Longman House,
Burnt Mill, Harlow, Essex, CM20 2JE, UK

© Longman Group UK Limited 1987

First published 1987

British Library Cataloguing in Publication Data
Schooley, Helen
  Conflict in Central America.—(Keesing's
  international studies)
  1. Central America—History—1951–
  I. Title   II. Series
  972.8'052   F1439
  ISBN 0–582–90274–6

Typeset by The Word Factory, Rossendale, Lancashire, BB4 6HN, UK
Printed in Great Britain at The Bath Press, Avon.

CONTENTS

Section Six: Central American Peace Initiatives

6.1 International Declarations and Initiatives
    6.1.1   Introductory   275
    6.1.2   UN Resolutions   275
    6.1.3   The Socialist International   276
    6.1.4   The OAS   276
    6.1.5   The Non-Aligned Movement   277
    6.1.6   Spain   277

6.2 Regional Efforts
    6.2.1   Mexico, Venezuela and Panama   279
    6.2.2   The CDC   280
    6.2.3   The Forum for Peace and Democracy   280

6.3 Nicaraguan Peace Proposals
    6.3.1   Proposals Involving the United States, 1981–83   282
    6.3.2   The Manzanillo Talks   283
    6.3.3   Discussions with Miskito Leaders   284
    6.3.4   Contra Proposals   285

6.4 Negotiations on El Salvador
    6.4.1   Attempts to Open Political Dialogue (1981)   287
    6.4.2   The Apaneca Pact   288
    6.4.3   Stone's Peace Efforts   289
    6.4.4   FMLN–FDR Initiatives in 1984   289
    6.4.5   The La Palma Talks (1984)   290
    6.4.6   Abortive Attempt to Resume Talks (1986)   292

6.5 The Contadora Group
    6.5.1   Formation of the Group and Initial Meetings   294
    6.5.2   The Programme for Peace in Central America   296
    6.5.3   The Act for Peace and Co-operation in Central America   297
    6.5.4   US Attitude to the Contadora Process   301

Appendices, Select Bibliography and Indexes

INTRODUCTION

Central America consists of half-a-dozen small states, with few natural resources, a total population of only 23,000,000 (in 1985) and a record of natural disasters, social and economic backwardness and chronic political instability —the prototype "banana republics". Although political violence is hardly a new phenomenon in the region, there has been a marked escalation since the mid-1970s, involving the threat of inter-state hostilities, the outbreak of guerrilla war against government forces and government repression against any manifestations of political dissent (making Guatemala and El Salvador in particular among the foremost violators of human rights in the world). It is this three-fold conflict, estimated to have claimed at least 150,000 lives since 1978 (mostly civilian), which forms the subject of this book.

While there may be no disagreement that such a conflict exists, given the constant reports of armed engagements, military manoeuvres, death-squad assassinations and disappearances, there are widely different perceptions of the identity of the main combatants and the underlying causes of the political violence in Central America. According to some, the origins are to be found in the vast social, economic and political inequalities of the region, where most of the productive land, the manufacturing sector and commerce, and all political power, is held by a small, oligarchic minority, who have sought (through the armed forces) to suppress the growing political awareness of a largely landless, semi-literate and malnourished rural and urban working class. From this point of view, the countries' most urgent need is seen as social reform, ending the power of the oligarchies and introducing the necessary social and economic structures to make democracy a viable system; this programme sums up the declared aims—and some would say the achievements—of the Sandinista revolution in Nicaragua. Others, while not denying the existence of a measure of inequality, maintain that attempts at social change do not spring out of domestic concerns, but are necessarily inspired by communist infiltration from Cuba and (by extension) the Soviet Union, and insist that priority must be given to dealing with "communist subversion" even over the introduction of moderate reform.

It is this difference of perception of the nature of the conflict which has made peace efforts so hard to conduct, as the parties involved approach possible negotiations from such disparate standpoints. While the Contadora Group (Mexico, Colombia, Panama and Venezuela), Nicaragua and the Salvadorean and Guatemalan guerrillas have argued broadly along the political, social and economic line, the governments of Guatemala, Honduras, El Salvador and—perhaps more crucially—the United States, have portrayed the region's problems in terms of the "cold war" and the broader East-West conflict.

US political and economic influence have been dominant in the Central American region at least since the beginning of the 20th century. More recently (notably since the Cuban missiles crisis of 1962) its military presence and capability have risen sharply, with successive administrations describing the area as one of strategic importance. The isthmus has often been seen as vital to US interests, not least because of the commercial and strategic importance of the Panama Canal. (This has become especially obvious under the presidency of Ronald Reagan, a long-standing opponent of the relinquishment to Panama of any US jurisdiction over the canal or the surrounding territory.)

With the overthrow of the Arbenz government in Guatemala and the formation of Condeca, the main US role was to give economic and military support to the region's governments in their campaigns against internal dissent, but the nature of the conflict changed with the Sandinista triumph of 1979. By 1985 the US administration found itself supporting the elected government of El Salvador against Salvadorean guerrillas, but working against the elected government of Nicaragua through the agency of Nicaraguan guerrillas.

The point about US backing for a guerrilla movement in one country and efforts against a guerrilla movement in another illustrates the problem of political labels, which are widely used but not always with the same meaning. Some parties use the word "communist" to mean a strict Marxist-Leninist policy, while others use it to describe those who call for social change and do not adhere to US policy in the region. For some the term "socialist" means a political system based on a welfare state and a measure of state intervention in the economy, while for others it denotes a one-party system and close ties with the Soviet Union. The most ambiguous label of all, perhaps, is "democratic", which all parties in the conflict have claimed to be, but which has been used in the titles of organizations as different as Orden and the FDR in El Salvador. The Caracas Declaration of 1954 contained "a reiteration of 'the faith of the peoples of America in the effective exercise of representative democracy', which the representatives of dictatorial governments signed without turning a hair".[1]

In some respects the crisis of democratic ideals came in the early 1930s, after the Wall Street Crash and the great depression seemed to cast doubt on the efficacy of liberal democracy, and contributed to the rise of fascism in Europe and the not dissimilar dictatorships of Ubico, Carias, Martínez and Somoza in Central America. However, as these leaders and their successors generally had US support, the use of the words "democratic" and "socialist" came to be seen more in the foreign policy terms of pro-US or pro-Soviet than as descriptive of domestic politics.

The ambiguity of political terminology helps to explain why the regional crisis has not been substantially alleviated by political change within the separate countries. In the crucial year 1979 only Costa Rica had a government both elected and civilian; by mid-1986 all countries could claim to have civilian elected governments and yet inter-state rivalry and internal fighting continued unabated. Modification of the national constitutions and forms of administration has apparently made little impact on either social and economic structures on the one hand or foreign allegiance on the other.

Although an attempt has been made in this book to give some historical background in the first section, the bulk of the material concentrates on events since the late 1970s. The chapters on El Salvador and Nicaragua are necessarily more detailed because of their centrality in the conflict and as a reflection of the availability of information. Belize has been mentioned only briefly in the context of Guatemalan foreign policy, because it is not otherwise connected with the conflict (having a very different history and a geographical location on the more remote Atlantic coast). Panama, which also had a different colonial past from the rest of Central America, is directly involved in the conflict only to the extent of the controversial US military presence there and its membership of the Contadora Group; it has been included in the historical section in some detail because of the importance of the Panama Canal and the negotiation of the canal treaties.

Section 2 expands on the themes of the social and economic structures of Central American society, including two of the most powerful institutions — the Roman Catholic Church and the armed forces. Section 3 examines the origins of the guerrilla conflict and the extent to which internal troubles have involved other Central American states, and Section 4 deals with the humanitarian issues of refugees, human rights and the treatment of ethnic minorities. Not all the countries are mentioned in the separate chapters of Sections 2, 3 and 4, in particular Costa Rica, which has no army, no major guerrilla groups, no widespread abuse of human rights and fewer ethnic problems, suggesting that in some ways the country's involvement stems more from its geographical position than from internal factors.

Section 5 looks at foreign involvement in the region, chiefly by the United States and—to a lesser extent—by Cuba and the Soviet Union. The latter has been more speculative and has appeared not to have expanded, either financially or militarily, to the same proportion as US influence. The involvement of other countries, however, is minimal in comparison with both US and Cuban and Soviet participation.

The final section covers the variety of statements made on the conflict by international organizations and the peace initiatives made by the parties involved and outside mediators. The most widely acclaimed of these efforts is the Contadora process, but the absence to date (October 1986) of any agreement on the draft treaty drawn up by the Group in 1984 indicates the extent of the divisions between the parties and the complexity of the conflict.

There is a problem involved with the sources of material available on the region, as most people who have visited the countries—especially if they have served there in any capacity—tend to become advocates for one side and are accordingly condemned by the other as biased. The present book aims to present information from several different sources, concentrating where possible on sources present in the region, but also making extensive use of *Keesing's Record of World Events* (formerly known as *Keesing's Contemporary Archives*) and its editorial resources. Every effort has been made to achieve *Keesing's*-style objectivity and balance in the book's coverage.

Bristol, October 1986   *HS*

Note

1. Salvador de Madariaga, *Latin America between the Eagle and the Bear*, Hollis and Carter, London, 1962, p. 125.

LIST OF MAPS

LIST OF ABBREVIATIONS

International

AI — Amnesty International
AIFLD — American Institute for Free Labour Development
ALCOA — Aluminum Company of America
AWACS — airborne warning and control systems
BCIE — Central American Bank for Economic Integration
CACM — Central American Common Market
CBI — Caribbean Basin Initiative
CDC — Central American Democratic Community
CIA — Central Intelligence Agency
Condeca — Central American Defence Council
EEC — European Economic Community
ICJ — International Court of Justice
ICRC — International Committee of the Red Cross
IMF — International Monetary Fund
IUF — International Union of Food and Allied Workers
MAP — Military Assistance Program (US)
OAS — Organization of American States
ODECA — Organization of Central American States
PLO — Palestine Liberation Organization
SI — Socialist International
UFCO — United Fruit Company (US)
UN — United Nations
UN ECLA — UN Economic Commission for Latin America
UNHCR — UN High Commissioner for Refugees
UPEB — Union of Banana Exporting Countries
USAID — US Agency for International Development

Guatemala

CACIF — Co-ordinating Committee of Agricultural, Commercial,
        Industrial and Financial Associations
CAN — National Authentic Central
CAO — Organized Arañista Central
CCP — People's Co-ordinating Committee
CDP — Slum Dwellers' Committee
CETE — Council of State Workers' Organizations
CGUP — Guatemalan Committee of Patriotic Unity
CNT — National Workers' Central
CNUS — National Council for Trade Union Unity
CUC — Peasant Unity Committee
EGP — Guerrilla Army of the Poor
EGSA — Embotelladora Guatemalteca S.A. (Coca-cola bottling plant)
EM — Squadron of Death
ESA — Secret Anti-communist Army

FAR — Rebel Armed Forces
FDG — Guatemalan Democratic Front
FDCR — Democratic Front Against Repression
FERG — Revolutionary Students' Front
FP–31 — January 31 Popular Front
Frenu — National Unity Front
FTG — Federation of Guatemalan Workers
FUN — Front of National Unity
FUR — United Revolutionary Front
GAM — Mutual Support Group
M–13 — November 13 Revolutionary Movement
MDN — National Democratic Movement
MLN — National Liberation Movement
MRP — People's Revolutionary Movement
NOR — Revolutionary Workers' Nuclei
OCAS — Peasant Social Action Organization
ORPA — Organization of the People at Arms
PAAC — Aid Programme for Areas in Conflict
PAC — civilian armed patrol
PCG — Guatemalan Communist Party
PDCG — Christian Democratic Party
PGT — Guatemalan Labour Party
PID — Democratic Institutional Party
PNR — National Renewal Party
PR — Revolutionary Party
PRN — National Reconciliation Party
PSD — Democratic Socialist Party
PUA — Anti-communist Unification Party
UCN — Union of the National Centre
UNO — National Opposition Union
URNG — Guatemalan National Revolutionary Unity
USAC — University of San Carlos

Honduras

APROH — Association for the Progress of Honduras
Codeh — human rights commission
Cofadeh — Committee of the Relations of the Disappeared
Conadi — National Investment Corporation
DNU — United National Directorate
FMLH — Morazanist Front for the Liberation of Honduras
FPH — Honduran Patriotic Front
FRP — Popular Revolutionary Forces
FUTH — United Federation of Honduran Workers
INA — National Agrarian Institute
MPLC — Cinchonero Popular Liberation Movement
MUR — Revolutionary Unity Movement
PCH — Communist Party
PCH–ML — Marxist–Leninist Communist Party
PDC — Christian Democratic Party

PINU — Innovation and Unity Party
PL — Liberal Party
PN — National Party
PRTCH — Central American Workers' Party of Honduras
PUN — National Union Party
UNC — National Peasants' Union
URP — Revolutionary People's Union

El Salvador

AD — Democratic Action
AGEUS — General Association of Salvadorean University Students
ANDES — National Teachers' Association
ANEP — National Association of Private Enterprise
Arena — National Republican Alliance
BPR — People's Revolutionary Bloc
CCE — Central Election Council
CRM — Revolutionary Co-ordinating Council of the Masses
CUS — Trade Union Co-ordinating Committee
CUANES — Christian Urgent Action Network for El Salvador
DRU — Unified Revolutionary Directorate
ERP — People's Revolutionary Army
ESA — Secret Anti-communist Army
FAPU — United People's Action Front
FARN — Armed Forces of National Resistance
FDR — Democratic Revolutionary Front
Feccas — Christian Federation of Salvadorean Peasants
FMLN — Farabundo Martí National Liberation Front
FPL — Popular Liberation Forces
FUDI — Democratic United Front
FUR–30 — Revolutionary Forces
ISTA — Salvadorean Institute of Agrarian Transformation
LP–28 — People's Leagues – 28 February
Merecen — Stable Republican Centrist Movement
MLP — Movement for Popular Liberation
MNR — National Revolutionary Movement
MPSC — Social Christian Popular Movement
MUSYGES — United Movement of Salvadorean Trade Unions and Associations
Orden — National Democratic Organization
PAIS/PAISA — Salvadorean Authentic Institutional Party
PAR — Party of Renewal Action
PCN — National Reconciliation Party
PCS — Salvadorean Communist Party
PDC — Christian Democratic Party
PDS — Social Democratic Party
POP — Popular Orientation Party
PPS — Salvadorean Popular Party
PRTC — Central American Workers' Party
PRUD — Revolutionary Party of Democratic Union

RN — National Resistance
UCS — Salvadorean Communal Union
UDN — National Democratic Union
UDP — Popular Democratic Union
UGB — White Warriors' Union
UNO — National Opposition Union
UPT — Slum Dwellers' Union
UR–10 — Revolutionary Union of Students
UTC — Farmworkers' Union

Nicaragua

ANDEN — National Teachers' Association
Arde — Democratic Revolutionary Alliance
ATC — Rural Workers' Association
BOS — Southern Opposition Bloc
CAUS — Centre for Trade Union Action
CD — Democratic Co-ordinating Board
CDS — Sandinista Defence Committee
CEPAD — Evangelical Committee for Development
CGT–I — Independent Confederation of Workers
Cosep — Higher Council for Private Enterprise
CSN — Nicaraguan Trade Union Co-ordinating Committee
CST — Sandinista Workers' Confederation
CTN — Nicaraguan Workers' Central
CUS — Confederation for Trade Union Unification
ELN — National Liberation Army
EPS — Sandinista People's Army
FAD — Democratic Armed Forces
FAO — Broad Opposition Front
FDN — Nicaraguan Democratic Front
Fetsalud — Health Workers' Association
FO — *Frente Obrero* (Labour Front)
FPN — Nicaraguan People's Front
FPR — Patriotic Front of the Revolution
FRS — Sandinista Revolutionary Front
FSDC — Christian Democratic Solidarity Front
FSLN — Sandinista National Liberation Front
GPP — Prolonged Popular War (FSLN tendency)
INDE — Nicaraguan Development Institute
INRA — National Agrarian Reform Institute
KISAN — Nicaraguan Indigenous Communities Union
M–3V — 3rd Way Movement
MAP–ML — Marxist–Leninist Popular Action Movement
MDN — Nicaraguan Democratic Movement
Milpas — People's Anti-Somozist Militias
Misurasata — Miskito, Sumo, Rama, Sandinista, All Together
MLC — Constitutionalist Liberal Movement
MPS — Sandinista Popular Militias
MPU — United People's Movement

PCD — Democratic Conservative Party
PCN — Communist Party
PLI — Independent Liberal Party
PLN — National Liberal Party
PPSC — Popular Social Christian Party
PSCN — Social Christian Party
PSD — Social Democratic Party
PSN — Socialist Party
TP — Proletarian Tendency (FSLN tendency)
Udel — Democratic Liberal Union
UDN/FARN — National Democratic Union/Nicaraguan Revolutionary
           Armed Forces
UNIR — Nicaraguan Unity for Reconciliation
UNO — Nicaraguan Opposition Unity
Upanic — Union of Agricultural Producers
UPN — Journalists' Union

Costa Rica

CP — Communist Party
MNR — New Republican Movement
MRP — Revolutionary People's Movement
PAD — Alajuela Democratic Party
PAS — Social Action Party
PD — Democratic Party
PDC — Christian Democratic Party
PLN — National Liberation Party
PPC — People's Party
PRC — Calderonist Republican Party
PRD — Democratic Renewal Party
PRN — National Republican Party
PSD — Social Democratic Party
PU — People United
PUN — National Unification Party
PUSC — Social Christian Unity Party
PVP — Popular Vanguard Party

Panama

ADO — Opposition Democratic Alliance
CPN — National Patriotic Coalition
Frampo — Broad Popular Front
Freno — United Opposition Front
MAI — Independent Lawyers' Movement
Papa — Popular Action Party
PDC — Christian Democratic Party
PP — Panamanian Party
PPA — Authentic Panamanian Party
PPP — Panamanian People's Party
PRD — Democratic Revolutionary Party
Unade — National Democratic Union

COUNTRY PROFILES

Guatemala:　Capital: Guatemala City
Area: 108,899 sq km
Population: 8,181,403 (1984 estimate)
GDP: $9,775 million (1984)
Foreign Debt: $2,100 million (end 1985)
Army: 51,600 (1984)†
President: Vinicio Cerezo (took office January 1986)

Honduras:　Capital: Tegucigalpa
Area: 112,087 sq km
Population: 4,092,000 (mid-1983)
GDP: $2,940 million (1983)
Foreign Debt: $2,300 million (end 1985)
Army: 23,000 (1984)†
President: José Simón Azcona del Hoyo (took office January
1986)

El Salvador:　Capital: San Salvador
Area: 21,393 sq km
Population: 4,913,000 (1983)
GDP: $3,548 million (1982)
Foreign Debt: $1,968 million (December 1984)*
Army: 51,150 (1984)†
President: José Napoleón Duarte (took office June 1984)

Nicaragua:　Capital: Managua
Area: 148,006 sq km
Population: 3,163,000 (1984 estimate)
GDP: $3,918 million*
Foreign Debt: $4,450 million (December 1984)*
Army: 61,800 (1984)†
President: Daniel Ortega Saavedra (took office January 1985)

Costa Rica:　Capital: San José
Area: 50,899 sq km
Population: 2,460,226 (mid-1984)
GNP: $3,189 million (1982)
Foreign Debt: $4,250 million (end 1985)
President: Oscar Arias Sánchez (took office May 1986)

Panama:　Capital: Panama City
Area: 77,082 sq km
Population 2,134,000 (1984 estimate)
GNP: $4,381 million (1983)
Foreign Debt: $3,700 million (mid-1985)
President: Eric Arturo del Valle (took office September 1985)

* Preliminary figures.
† Figures from the Council for Hemispheric Affairs, Washington.

SECTION ONE

POLITICAL HISTORY

1.1: THE REGION

1.1.1: General Chronology

1821   Declaration of independence from Spain
1822   Annexation to Mexico
1823   Independence from Mexico as United Provinces of Central America
        Pronouncement of Monroe Doctrine
1826   Ratification of Treaty of Friendship and Commerce with USA
        Outbreak of civil war
1829   Guatemala City falls to Morazán's forces
1830   Morazán becomes president and introduces radical liberal reforms
1837   Peasants' revolt led by Carrera
1838   Dissolution of federation into five states
        Return to conservatism under domination of Carrera
1840   First moves to re-establish religious orders in the region
1842   Morazán takes Costa Rica in effort to re-establish federation, but is
        executed
1850   Clayton-Bulwer Treaty between USA and Britain (abrogated 1901)
1855   Completion of Panama Railway (begun in 1850)
1860   US troops land in Panama to restore order and protect railway
1879   Panama Canal Company (of France) begins construction of canal
1885   US forces sent to Panama
1889   Panama Canal Company forced into liquidation
1898   Outbreak of Spanish–American war
1899   Outbreak of 1,000 days war in Colombia
        Formation of UFCO
1901   Cuba gains independence from Spain with US military aid
        US troops return to Panama
1903   Hay-Herrán Treaty between USA and Colombia (*January*)
        Panama gains independence from Colombia with US help (*November*)
        Conclusion Hay-Bunau-Varilla Treaty (*November*)
1904   Roosevelt Corollary
1906   Marblehead Pact
1907   Formation of Central American Court of Justice (closed 1918)
1910   Mexican revolution
1912   US marines arrive in Nicaragua, withdrawn briefly 1925–26 and finally
        withdrawn 1933
1915   US marines land in Haiti (withdrawn 1934)
1916   US marines land in Dominican Republic (withdrawn 1924)
1924   Formation of Standard Fruit and Steamship Company
1933   Establishment of Trujillo dictatorship in Dominican Republic
        Coup in Cuba brings Batista to power
1936   First revision of Canal treaties by USA and Panama (ratified 1939)
1948   Formation of OAS
1951   Formation of ODECA under Charter of San Salvador
1954   Caracas Declaration
1955   Second revision of Canal treaties by USA and Panama

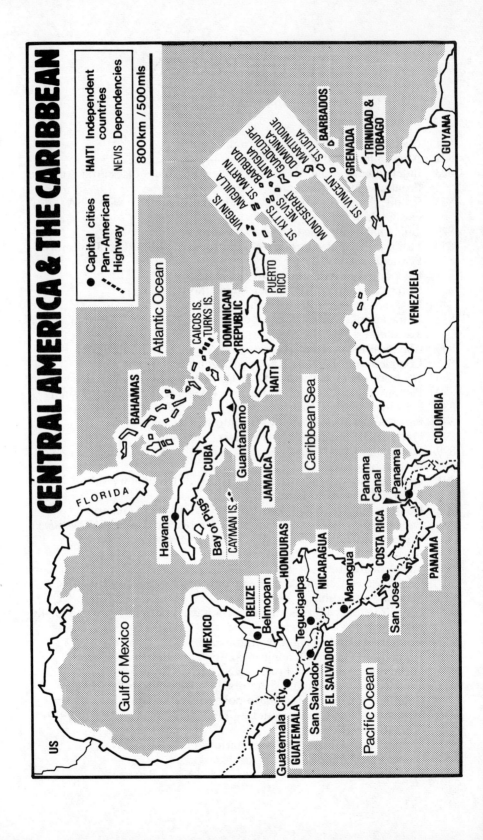

CENTRAL AMERICA & THE CARIBBEAN

Capital cities ●
Pan-American Highway ----

HAITI Independent countries
NEVIS Dependencies

800km / 500mls

us

Gulf of Mexico

FLORIDA

Atlantic Ocean

BAHAMAS

MEXICO

Havana

CUBA

Bay of Pigs

CAYMAN IS.

Guantanamo

JAMAICA

Caribbean Sea

BELIZE

Belmopan

HONDURAS

Guatemala City

GUATEMALA

Tegucigalpa

San Salvador

EL SALVADOR

NICARAGUA

Managua

Pacific Ocean

COSTA RICA

San Jose

Panama Canal

Panama

PANAMA

CAICOS IS.

TURKS IS.

DOMINICAN REPUBLIC

HAITI

PUERTO RICO

VIRGIN IS

ANGUILLA

ST. MARTIN

BARBUDA

ST KITTS

NEVIS

ANTIGUA

GUADELOUPE

MONTSERRAT

DOMINICA

MARTINIQUE

ST LUCIA

ST. VINCENT

BARBADOS

GRENADA

TRINIDAD & TOBAGO

COLOMBIA

VENEZUELA

GUYANA

1958   Visit of Milton Eisenhower to Central America
1959   Overthrow of Batista regime in Cuba by Castro
1960   Formation of CACM
1961   Abortive attempt to overthrow Castro in Bay of Pigs (*April*)
        Launch of Kennedy's Alliance for Progress (*August*)
1962   Cuba excluded from OAS (*February*)
        Cuban missiles crisis (*October*)
        Re-establishment of ODECA (*December*)
1963   Declaration of Central America
        Formation of Condeca
1964   Anti–US rioting in Panama
1965   Civil war in Dominican Republic; arrival of US marines
1968   Del Monte company enters banana trade
        Latin American bishops' conference in Medellín (Colombia) denounces "institutionalized violence"
1969   Outbreak of football war between Honduras and El Salvador
1970   Withdrawal of Honduras from CACM
        UFCO merges to become United Brands
1972   Formation of UPEB
1973   Withdrawal of Honduras from Condeca
1974   Imposition of tax on banana exports by UPEB
        Declaration of Guayana
1975   Passage of Freedom of Action resolution by OAS on Cuba
        Declaration on Co-operation
        Passage of Harkin Amendment by US Congress linking foreign military aid to human rights performance
        United Brands sell lands in Panama and Costa Rica
1976   US congressional hearing on human rights in Nicaragua, Guatemala and El Salvador
1977   Negotiations of new Canal treaties (signed 1978, ratified 1979)
        Cancellation of US military aid to Guatemala and El Salvador
1978   US ban on arms sales to Guatemala and El Salvador
1979   NJM coup in Grenada led by Bishop (*March*)
        Somoza overthrown by Sandinistas in Nicaragua (*June*)
        Revolution in El Salvador by reformist officers (*October*)
1980   San José agreement (*August*)
        Conclusion of peace treaty between Honduras and El Salvador (*October*)
        Start of border incidents between Nicaragua and Honduras
1981   Launch of FMLN "final offensive" (*January*)
        Resumption of "lethal" US aid to El Salvador (*January*)
        Inauguration of President Reagan (*January*)
        Suspension of US aid to Nicaragua (*January, confirmed in April*)
        US White Paper on arms supply to FMLN (*February*)
        Visit by Gen. Walters to Argentina and Chile to ask for military assistance to Central America (*February*)
        Mexican–Venezuelan peace initiative (*March*)
        SI peace initiative (*April*)
        Enders' visit to Nicaragua (*August*)
        Franco–Mexican declaration recognizing FMLN–FDR as representative political force (*August*)

1982   First use of certification process by US administration in granting aid
       to El Salvador (*January*)
       Formation of CDC (*January*)
       Launching of Reagan's Caribbean Basin Initiative (*February*)
       Mexican attempt to arrange negotiations between USA, Nicaragua
       and Cuba (*February*)
       Honduran peace proposal advanced by Paz Bárnica (*March*)
       Panamanian peace proposal (*June*)
       Establishment of Forum for Peace and Democracy (*October*)
       Reagan's visit to Central America (*December*)
       Passage of Boland Amendment by US Congress banning use of funds
       for destabilizing Nicaragua (*December*)
1983   Formation of Contadora Group (*January*)
       Pope John Paul's visit to Central America (*March*)
       Appointment of Stone as special envoy (*March*)
       Soviet officials suggest possibility of placing missiles in Central
       America (*April*)
       Formation of Kissinger Commission (*July*)
       Opening of US training base at Puerto Castilla (Honduras) (*July*)
       Ortega's peace initiative (*July*)
       Start of US–Honduran Big Pine II military and naval manoeuvres
       (*August*)
       Enactment of (US) Caribbean Basin Economic Recovery Bill (*August*)
       Publication of Contadora 21-point programme for peace (*September*)
       Revival of Condeca (*October*)
       Nicaraguan multilateral peace proposal (*October*)
       US military intervention in Grenada to remove NJM (*October*)
       Reagan's veto of the certification process (*November*)
       US Congress approves $24,000 aid to contras (*November*)
       Stone's meeting in Panama with contra leaders (*December*)
1984   Publication of Kissinger Commission report (*January*)
       Announcement by US administration of new five-year aid programme
       (*January*)
       Agreement on revised Contadora treaty (*January*)
       US–Honduran Grenadier exercises (*April*)
       Publication of Contadora Act for Peace and Co-operation in Central
       America (*June*)
       Manzanillo talks between Nicaragua and USA (*June-November*)
       After conference with Central American officials in San José
       European Community decides to increase aid to region (*September*)
       Announcement by Nicaraguan government of willingness to sign Con-
       tadora treaty (*September*)
       Honduras, El Salvador and Costa Rica demand changes in Contadora
       treaty (*October*)
       US Congress approves $28,000 aid to contras (*October*)
       "MiGs crisis" in Nicaragua (*November*)
1985   Suspension of Manzanillo talks by USA (*January*)
       Boycott of Contadora negotiations by Costa Rica (*February*)
       Big Pine III joint manoeuvres (*February-April*)
       Ortega's offer of a ceasefire (*April*)

US Congress rejects administration's request on funding for contras
(*April*); agreement to exclude CIA direction of funds (*June*)
Ortega's visit to Moscow (*April*)
Imposition of US trade embargo on Nicaragua (*May*)
Formation of Lima Group (*July*)
Presentation of revised draft Contadora Act (*September*)
Nicaraguan rejection of revised draft (*November*)
Postponement of negotiations on draft until mid-1986 (*December*)
1986   Blazing Trail US joint exercises in Honduras and Panama
(*January–June*)
ICJ ruling in favour of Nicaragua's complaint against the United States
(*June*)
Indefinite delay of signature deadline for Contadora draft (*June*)
US Congress approves \$100,000,000 aid to contras (*August*)

1.1.2: Colonization

The first Spaniards to arrive in Central America were Rodrigo Bastidas and
Vasco Núñez de Balboa in 1500, and over the next three decades the isthmus
was gradually explored and claimed by settlers from Panama City to the south
and Mexico City to the north. The Maya civilization, which had been
dominant in the region since about 300 AD, had declined by the 11th century
and the Mayans were conquered by the Toltecs and later by the Aztecs. The
Aztecs remained in the vicinity of Mexico City, leaving small ethnic groups
further south, including the Pipil in El Salvador, the Lenca in Honduras and
the Suma and Miskitos in Nicaragua.

Central America was ruled through the *Audiencia* (the high court which
also held executive power) established at Guatemala in 1543. In 1549 the
whole region was designated the Kingdom of Guatemala, although it continued to be governed directly from Madrid by the Spanish monarch. The
Kingdom comprised the provinces of Guatemala, Honduras, Chiapas (now
part of Mexico), Nicaragua and Panama (until 1751—see section 1.7.2); El
Salvador did not gain status as a separate province until the 18th century. In
order to maintain its control the Spanish government deliberately exploited
the local rivalries of the region, particularly over the concentration of power
in Guatemala.

The strong centralization of the Spanish empire caused severe difficulties
for the colonies during the rapid decline of the Spanish monarchy in the 17th
century. After the war of the Spanish Succession, which was concluded in
1713 by the Treaty of Utrecht and confirmed the accession to the Spanish
throne of the Bourbon Philip V, a series of reforms (the Bourbon reforms)
was introduced in the 18th century covering administration, economic
practice and naval defence policy (to counter the British threat to trade). Also
introduced were new anti-clerical measures to curb the influence of the
Roman Catholic Church.

1.1.3: Independence

As elsewhere in Spanish America the revolt in Central America was sparked
off by the 1820 revolution in Spain and encouraged by the Mexican de-

claration of independence in February 1821. Under the leadership of José Cecilio del Valle the Kingdom of Guatemala issued its own declaration on Sept. 15, 1821, and at the invitation of the Mexican ruler Agustín de Iturbide (who later assumed the title of Emperor Agustín I) Central America was annexed to Mexico in January 1822. After Iturbide abdicated several months later, the general congress of the Central American provinces met on June 24, 1823, and declared their independence as a federation known as the *Provincias Unidas del Centro de América*. (Chiapas remained within Mexican territory.) Mexico acknowledged the secession in 1824 and Spain finally recognized their independence in 1850. All five provinces promulgated republican constitutions in 1824.

From its earliest stage the federation was politically divided between two factions: the conservatives, who favoured unitary states (and were particularly strong in Guatemala), and the liberals, who supported the principle of federation. In 1826 civil war broke out in the form of a revolt led by Fernando Morazán in El Salvador, which was soon joined by Honduras, Nicaragua and Costa Rica. Morazán took Guatemala City in 1829, installed Pedro Molina as president, becoming his successor in 1830, and made San Salvador the new federal capital in 1834. He introduced liberal reforms which aimed to destroy the traditional Spanish politcal and social patterns of state and replace them by a US or British model; they included measures to control the power of the Church.

The radical liberal measures were blamed by the conservatives for the federation's economic problems and alienated the rural masses who resented the attack on their traditional way of life. In 1837 their hardship was increased by the outbreak of a cholera epidemic and they rose in revolt under the leadership of the Guatemalan Rafael Carrera; to some extent the conflict became a race war of the creole (i.e. of European extraction) and *mestizo* (mixed blood, or *ladino*) liberals against the traditionalist Indians. Carrera's revolt was successful and in 1838 Nicaragua, Honduras, El Salvador and Costa Rica seceded, leaving Carrera as ruler in Guatemala. The last act of the federal congress allowed each province to choose its own form of government.

The civil war led to the downfall—and in some cases to the massacre—of the liberals and assured the dominance of conservatism in each country for several years to come. The conservative-liberal feud continued in each state as the conservatives overturned Morazán's reforms and restored the power of the Church. The liberals regained power in the 1870s as New Liberals or Positivists, committed to the development of the national economy and infrastructure; however, this concentration on economic rather than political liberalization accentuated the existing tendency towards dictatorship and strengthened the political role of the armed forces.

1.1.4: Attempts to Resume the Federation

Morazán, who had gone into exile after being defeated by Carrera in 1838, returned to Central America in 1842 and overthrew the Costa Rican dictator Braulio Carrillo. As president he tried to rebuild the federation but within months he was defeated and shot.

A series of further unsuccessful attempts to renew the union were made, including proposals for El Salvador and Guatemala in 1845, for El Salvador, Nicaragua and Honduras in 1847, 1849 and 1862, and for all five states in 1876; the last plan failed when war broke out between Guatemala and El Salvador. In 1885 the liberal President Barrios of Guatemala was overthrown while working for union and in 1895 a project for a partial federation between Nicaragua, El Salvador and Honduras collapsed when the Salvadorean government fell. A Nicaraguan politician, Salvador Mendieta, organized the Central American Unionist Party in 1899, with the aim of getting members elected in each country, but the party never gained a mass following and only achieved power briefly in Guatemala in 1920–21 (see section 1.2.2).

1.1.5: Growth of US Interest in Central America

Although Central America gained its political independence from Spain the states came under increasing foreign economic domination. The first British settlers to reach the region arrived in 1642, and one of the principal contributions of British buccaneers was to increase smuggling, thereby undermining the economy (which before the Bourbon reforms suffered from the traditional Spanish disdain for trade). During the 19th century the United States challenged the British control of trade and by 1900 had wrested commercial domination for itself, although Britain, France and the Netherlands still had major trading interests in the region because of their Caribbean colonies.

The Anglo-American trade rivalry focused in particular on the search for a transisthmian route to link the Atlantic and Pacific Oceans. In 1850 the two powers signed the Clayton-Bulwer Treaty, in which they agreed that neither would hold exclusive control over the route currently favoured, running along the southern border of Nicaragua (and incorporating Lake Nicaragua). The treaty was abrogated in 1901 and two years later the United States negotiated an exclusive canal treaty with the newly-independent Republic of Panama (see also sections 1.5.2 and 1.7.3).

1.1.6: The Monroe Doctrine—Roosevelt's "Good Neighbour" Policy

The United States had revealed its interest in Central (and South) America as early as 1823 when on Dec. 2 President James Monroe enunciated "a principle in which the rights and interests of the United States are involved, that the American continent, by the free and independent condition which they have assumed and maintain, are henceforth not to be considered as subjects for future colonization by any European powers". The Monroe Doctrine, as this principle came to be known, was extended in 1904 by President Theodore Roosevelt (in the Roosevelt Corollary): "Chronic wrongdoing or an impotence which results in a general loosening of the ties of civilized society, may in America, as elsewhere, ultimately require intervention by some civilized nation, and in the Western Hemisphere the adherence of the United States to the Monroe Doctrine may force the United States, however reluctantly, in flagrant cases of such wrongdoing or impotence, to the exercise of an international police power."

Roosevelt's successor, William Taft, in 1912 made an even more outspoken statement of what he regarded to be his country's rights and responsibilities:

"The day is not far distant when three Stars and Stripes at three equidistant points will mark our territory: one at the North Pole, another at the Panama Canal and third at the South Pole. The whole hemisphere will be ours in fact, as by virtue of superiority of race, it already is ours morally."

US intervention had already occurred in the Spanish–American war of 1898–1902. During this episode Cuba gained independence from Spain in 1901 (with a constitution containing the Platt Amendment granting the United States the right of intervention in Cuban affairs—see also section 5.3.2) and Puerto Rico was ceded to the United States as a "non-incorporated territory which belongs to, but is not a part of, the United States". Subsequently, US marines were sent to Panama in 1902–03 (see section 1.7.3), to Nicaragua in 1912–33 (see section 1.5.4), to Haiti in 1914–34 because of economic collapse and political instability and to the Dominican Republic in 1916–24 because of the outbreak of civil war. (US forces also entered the Dominican Republic in the civil war of 1965.) A US State Department memorandum of 1927 stated "Our ministers accredited to the five little republics . . . have been advisers whose advice has been accepted virtually as law. . . . We do control the destinies of Central America and we do so for the simple reason that the national interest absolutely dictates such a course. . . . Until now Central America has always understood that governments which we recognize and support stay in power, while those we do not recognize and support fall."[1]

The policy of open intervention was replaced in 1933 by the "good neighbour" policy of President Franklin Roosevelt, which was pursued until after the Second World War. In 1947 President Truman said that the United States would "support free peoples who are resisting attempted subjugation by armed minorities or by outside pressure"—a statement of intent directed primarily against Soviet-inspired communism (or even the possibility of it under socialist governments). The first full implementation of this policy in Latin America came in 1954 with the overthrow of the Arbenz government in Guatemala (see section 1.2.5).

1.1.7: US Involvement in Regional Disputes

In the early part of the 20th century, the United States also attempted to use its influence to resolve disputes between the Central American states arising from one state interfering in the internal affairs of a neighbour. Such interference sometimes took the form of direct military action, but more usually concerned one government aiding the exiled rebels of another state.

In 1906 war broke out when El Salvador (later joined by Honduras) gave support to Guatemalan exiles working to overthrow the Guatemalan dictator Manuel Estrada Cabrera. President T. Roosevelt tried unsuccessfully to negotiate a ceasefire and then, along with President Porfirio Díaz of Mexico and the Costa Rican government, sponsored the Marblehead Pact which bound all five states to stop hostilities and end the abuse of political asylum. A conference was convened in San José (Costa Rica) to sign agreements on the harbouring of exiles, the establishment of a Central American tribunal to settle future disputes and the adoption of US and Mexican mediation in the recent war. The agreements were signed by all states except Nicaragua, whose ruler, José Santos Zelaya, refused to accept that the United States had any right to intervene in Central American affairs.

Later in 1906 Honduran forces invaded Nicaragua, claiming that the Zelaya government was giving support to Honduran exiles plotting against President Policarpo Bonilla of Honduras (see also section 1.3.3). Both states refused to declare a ceasefire and in 1907 the Central American Tribunal announced that it had failed to achieve a solution. At the instigation of the Roosevelt administration a further conference was held at which a Central American Court of Justice was formed, to be based at Cartago (Costa Rica), composed of one judge from each of the five countries; the Court closed in 1918.

1.1.8: Organization of Central American States

Representatives from all five states met in November 1951 and signed the Charter of San Salvador, establishing the Organization of Central American States (ODECA), although a Nicaraguan proposal for political union received no response. Guatemala withdrew briefly in 1953–54 (see section 1.2.4). The body achieved little in its first 10 years and in November 1962 it was agreed that a new ODECA should be formed. Accordingly the New Charter of San Salvador was signed (in Panama City) in December 1962 providing for the establishment of councils of the heads of state, foreign ministers and defence ministers, an executive council (based in San Salvador), legislative, economic and cultural and educational councils and a Central American court of justice. Panama was invited to join ODECA but declined on the grounds of "international commitments and economic problems". The executive council met on July 2, 1973, and agreed to form a special commission for the restructuring of the organization in view of the current political and financial crisis, but no progress was made.

1.1.9: Organization of American States

At the OAS conference held in Caracas (Venezuela) in March 1954 (against a background of rising US anxiety over the Arbenz government in Guatemala) the United States put forward a proposal on regional co-operation against communism, which was passed by 17 votes to one (Guatemala) with two abstentions (Argentina and Mexico). Known as the Caracas Declaration it stated inter alia: "The domination or control of the political institutions of any American state by the international communist movement, extending to this hemisphere the political system of an extracontinental power, would constitute a threat to the sovereignty and political independence of the American states, endangering the peace of America and would call for a meeting of consultation to consider the adoption of appropriate action in accordance with existing treaties." John Foster Dulles (then US Secretary of State) worked hard to ensure the passage of the declaration, "twisting arms, threatening to withhold aid from non-co-operative nations and repeating his sermons on the communist peril".[2]

At the meeting of OAS foreign ministers held in Santiago (Chile) on Aug. 14–20, 1959 (seven months after the Cuban revolution, for which see section 5.3.2), a declaration was issued with a preamble proclaiming "the general aspiration of the American peoples to live in peace under the protection of democratic institutions, free from all intervention and all totalitarian influence". The declaration upheld the rule of law and the choice of government by free elections, stated that perpetuation in power without a fixed term and the "systematic use of political proscription" were "contrary to American democratic order", and called on members to ensure individual freedom and social justice, the protection of human rights by effective judicial procedures and the freedom of the press, information and expression in order to "achieve just and humane living conditions for their peoples."

The OAS conference held in Punta del Este (Uruguay) on Jan. 22–31, 1962, was dominated by the general question of Cuba and the "communist threat". Central American representatives were at the forefront of demands for collective action against Cuba. Among the resolutions passed was one excluding Cuba from the inter-American system (see section 5.3.2).

1.1.10: Central American Common Market

Honduras, Guatemala, El Salvador and Nicaragua signed two treaties on Dec. 13, 1960, to establish the Central American Common Market (CACM). The treaties had been drawn up in 1954 under the aegis of the UN Economic Commission for Latin America (ECLA) and created a free trade area and a system of regional industries in Central America. (Costa Rica joined CACM under a protocol signed on July 23, 1962.) The Central American Economic Integration Treaty immediately removed tariff restrictions on a number of goods (which together accounted for about half of the trade in the region); it also provided for the abolition of all tariffs within five years, and promised the free movement of labour and capital. The other treaty, the Charter of Central America, provided for the setting up of a regional development bank to fund regional integration programmes; the bank's headquarters in Tegucigalpa (Honduras) opened in March 1961 with initial contributions of US$10,000,000 from the United States and $4,000,000 from each member country. Trade between members rose at an annual rate of 32 per cent from 1961 until 1968.

By the early 1970s CACM faced difficulties in implementing its integration policies (especially after the withdrawal of Honduras in 1970 following the outbreak of the "football war" with El Salvador—see section 1.3.7). In 1972 Costa Rica's balance-of-payments problems forced its government to adopt protectionist policies against other CACM members, even though in October of that year they had advanced a $25,000,000 line of credit to Costa Rica and made import concessions.

An unsuccessful attempt to replace CACM was made in 1976. On May 16 of that year the text of a draft treaty was published in Nicaragua providing for the formation of a Central American Economic and Social Community (CESC). The treaty would have abolished all customs duties on inter-regional trade, and Panama was to be given the option of joining at a later date.

1.1.11: The Alliance for Progress

The Alliance for Progress was launched by President Kennedy on Aug. 5, 1961, when he promised over $1,000 million in US development assistance to Latin America for the year beginning March 13, 1961 (the date on which it was first proposed), as "only the first step in our continuing and expanding effort to help build a better life for the people of the hemisphere". The basic principle of the Alliance was that "only under freedom and through the institutions of representative democracy can man best satisfy his aspirations, including those for work, home and land, health and schools". It was generally seen as an attempt to prevent the spread of the Cuban revolution by offering controlled reform under the auspices of US aid.

The programme's aims were set out by the US Treasury Secretary, Douglas Dillon, as being "long-term national programmes of economic and social development", which "recognize the right of all the peoples to share fully in the fruits of progress", and "industrialization to help modernize our economies and provide employment for our rapidly growing urban populations". It would also seek to abolish "the social and economic injustice which undermines free political institutions", giving specific attention to the eradication of disease, slum housing and illiteracy, and a reform of fiscal administration. He added that the question of economic and social development should be "brought to bear on military expenditures in considering the competing demands of development and inter-American defence". (The Alliance envisaged an improvement in internal security by strengthening local military and police forces, and to this end several training schemes for military and security personnel were introduced; this aspect of the programme was eventually to prove the most successful and lasting.)

The Alliance was approved at the August 1961 Punta del Este conference of the OAS (from which Cuba was excluded), which at its close on Aug. 17 issued the Declaration to the Peoples of America. The signatories undertook to "accelerate economic and social development, to encourage proofs of comprehensive agrarian reform . . . with a view to replacing latifundia and dwarf holdings by an equitable system of property . . ., to assure fair wages and satisfactory working conditions, to wipe out illiteracy, to reform tax laws, demanding more from those who have most, to punish tax evasion severely and to redistribute the national income to benefit those who are most in need, to maintain monetary and fiscal policies which, while avoiding the disastrous effects of inflation or deflation, will protect the purchasing power of the many, to stimulate private enterprise, to accelerate the integration of Latin America".

In the year 1961–62 US allocations of aid to Central America under the Alliance were as follows: Guatemala $3,669,000, Honduras $5,076,000, El Salvador $23,514,000, Nicaragua $10,729,000 and Costa Rica $17,899,000.

President Kennedy arrived in San José on March 18, 1963, for talks with the Central American heads of state (including President Chiari of Panama), which were reported to have concentrated on allegations of Cuban infiltration and subversion in Central America. A Declaration of Central America was issued on March 19, in which the Central American presidents agreed on joint measures to restrict the movement of nationals to and from Cuba and the flow of material, propaganda and funds from Cuba, while President Kennedy promised US co-operation and strong financial support for integration policies.

The Alliance for Progress lost much of its impetus after Kennedy's assassination in November 1963, not least because under President Johnson the major foreign policy issue became US involvement in Vietnam.

1.1.12: Central American Defence Council

The Central American Defence Council (Condeca) was formed in December 1963 by Guatemala, Honduras, El Salvador and Nicaragua; Costa Rica and Panama (which had abolished their national armies) were offered observer status, but only Panama accepted, resisting subsequent pressure by the United States to upgrade its status to full membership. (Earlier that year, on Sept. 30, the presidents of Honduras, El Salvador, Costa Rica and Nicaragua had signed a declaration condemning the military overthrow of constitutional regimes and undertaking not to recognize any future military government without prior consultation with each other.) The Council had substantial US backing with an emphasis on co-ordinated military action against guerrilla activity. After 1964 over a dozen counter-insurgency operations organized by Condeca were held between Guatemala, El Salvador and Nicaragua.

The attempt to achieve military co-ordination was hampered by the withdrawal of Panama in 1968, of Honduras in 1973 and of Nicaragua in 1979, Honduras' decision arose out of the football war with El Salvador, which Condeca made no effort to solve although one of its founding principles had been to eliminate rivalries and antagonisms between national armies. The withdrawal of Nicaragua after the Sandinista revolution was an even greater blow, as the Nicaraguan National Guard established by the US forces in the 1930s (see section 1.5.4) had formed what one writer has described as the "lynchpin of Condeca's system of regional repression".[3]

Gen. Somoza of Nicaragua was believed to have attempted to use the Condeca framework in his regime's war against the Sandinistas. In mid–1976 Condeca manoeuvres were held in Nueva Segovia (where anti-Somoza guerrillas were very active) under the aegis of the US Southern Commands forces based in Panama. According to the Sandinistas these manoeuvres involved 1,100 US troops, excluding other US counter-insurgency experts, and Brazilian and South Korean troops, but not Honduran, Panamanian or Costa Rican security forces. At Condeca's seventh annual conference in August 1976 a declaration was issued, stating: "The Council is prepared to act wherever member states need [such action] to oppose subversive activities in the Central American isthmus provoked by international communism or any other subversive force."

In December 1978 Somoza met with Gen. Lucas García of Guatemala and Gen. Romero of El Salvador (and Gen. Paz García of Honduras), and it was alleged by some sources that these countries had sent secret military assistance to Nicaragua. The Sandinistas claimed on June 5, 1979, to have captured a Guatemalan colonel in the city of León, who was said to be in command of about 150 Guatemalan troops fighting along with Salvadorean troops in support of the Nicaraguan National Guard.

The downfall of the Somoza regime made more evident some of Condeca's weaknesses and focused US attention on Honduras. Many observers suggest that the conclusion of the Honduras–El Salvador peace treaty in 1980 and the return to civilian rule in Honduras in the same year—both supported, if not instigated, by the US administration—were directly related to US military policy in Central America.[4] (According to the *Latin America Weekly Report* of Aug. 27, 1982, a US State Department secret briefing paper described Honduras as a state where "dictatorship has been replaced by a democratically elected government willing to co-operate in the struggle against the guerrillas in El Salvador and against anti-democratic forces [i.e. the Sandinista government] in Nicaragua". In the course of one of a series of visits to Washington in mid–1982 President Suazo was assured by Reagan that "the people of Honduras should be able to rely on their friends for help . . . and they can count on us".) From 1981 growing tension between Honduras and Nicaragua and the opposition of the Honduran authorities (especially Gen. Alvarez) to the Salvadorean left-wing guerrillas encouraged the Honduran and Salvadorean armies to work toward greater military co-operation (see section 3.3.6).

Condeca was revived in 1983 by El Salvador, Honduras and Guatemala with the aim of reaching a joint approach by all three armed forces to what they termed "an extra-continental aggression of a Marxist-Leninist character". The United States gave its support in an attempt to isolate Nicaragua (see also section 5.1.3).

1.1.13: 1975 Declaration on Co-operation

The five Central American presidents met in Jalapa (Nicaragua) on Feb. 3, 1975, and signed the Declaration on Co-operation. The principles outlined in the document were (i) the resumption of relations between El Salvador and Honduras to strengthen the Central American community; (ii) an agreement on frequent meetings between the heads of state on CACM affairs, economic and social integration and international issues; (iii) that the economic ministers should plan food and energy programmes and adopt a common stance to the international food crisis; and (iv) that agriculture should be given the highest priority in economic planning.

1.1.14: Central American Democratic Community

The Central American Democratic Community (CDC) was founded at a meeting held in San José on Jan. 19, 1982, between the foreign ministers of Costa Rica, El Salvador and Honduras, with the aims of promoting security and democracy in the region, mutual solidarity in the face of external aggression against a member country and economic development (especially in the private sector). Support for the CDC was expressed by the US Assistant Secretary of State for Inter-American Affairs, Thomas Enders, on Jan. 27, and the United States, Venezuela and Colombia were given observer status. In a statement issued on Jan. 21 the US embassy in San José described the formation of the CDC as "a very positive step towards the resolution of the serious problems predominating in the region", and said the United States "fully supports the new initiative and will help where it is feasible and appropriate".

Nicaragua, Panama and Guatemala, who were not invited to participate, protested against the move, which the Nicaraguan broadcasting station Radio Sandino described on Jan. 20, 1982, as "an instrument of the reactionary minorities of Central America". The Sandinista National Directorate said on Feb. 15 that the CDC was "anti-democratic" in nature and simply "another manoeuvre" by the Reagan administration in preparation for "greater aggression" against Nicaragua. Guatemala was later invited to join the CDC and became a full member on July 6, 1982.

Notes

1. Quoted in Robert Armstrong and Janet Shenk, *El Salvador—The Face of Revolution*, London, Pluto Press, 1982, pp.225–226.
2. Stephen Schlesinger and Stephen Kinzer, *Bitter Fruit: The Untold Story of the American Coup in Guatemala*, Sinclair Browne, London, 1982, p.143.
3. George Black, *Triumph of the People—The Sandinista Revolution in Nicaragua*, London, Zed Press, 1981, pp.47–49.
4. Richard Lapper, *Honduras: State for Sale*, London, Latin America Bureau, 1985, Chapter 5; Jenny Pearce, *Under the Eagle*, London, Latin America Bureau, 1981 (revised edition 1982), p.157; Armstrong and Shenk, *op. cit.*, pp.214–218; Black, *op. cit.*, pp.351–352.

1.2: GUATEMALA

1.2.1: Chronology

1865 Death of Carrera
1871 Liberals come to power under Barrios
1885 Barrios assassinated
1898 Estrada Cabrera becomes dictator
1920 Overthrow of Estrada Cabrera
      Election of Central American Unionist Party government
1921 Military coup installs military government
1931 Election of Ubico, beginning of purge of left-wing elements
1944 Ubico overthrown in military coup, leading to civil war
      Victory gained by revolutionary forces and elections held
1945 Arévalo inaugurated president and new constitution promulgated
1949 Assassination of Araña triggers abortive military coup
1950 Arbenz elected president
1952 Introduction of land-reform programme
1953 Expropriation of UFCO lands
1954 Arbenz overthrown by US–backed forces led by Castillo Armas
      Constitution abrogated
1955 Castillo Armas confirmed as president
1956 New constitution promulgated
1957 Castillo Armas assassinated
      Presidential elections held and then annulled, and military junta takes
      control
1958 Ydigoras elected for six-year term
1960 Unsuccessful left-wing uprising starts guerrilla war
1962 Formation of M–13 and FAR guerrilla groups
1963 Military coup installs Peralta and abrogates constitution
1965 New constitution promulgated
1966 Méndez Montenegro of PR elected president
      Opening of counter-insurgency campaign led by Araña Osorio
      Appearance of White Hand and other extreme right-wing death
      squads
1970 Araña Osorio of MLN elected president
1971 Formation of ORPA
1972 Relative lull in guerrilla activity
      Formation of EGP (secret until 1975)
1974 Laugerud García wins narrow election victory over Ríos Montt
1976 Earthquake kills over 20,000 and partially destroys capital
      Resurgence of guerrilla activity
1977 Cancellation of US military aid
1978 Election of Lucas García of PR–PID–CAO
1979 Formation of FDR
1980 Spanish embassy siege leads to formation of FP–31 (*January*)
      Resignation of Vice-President Villagrán Kramer (*September*)

1981   Belize granted independence from Britain, but not recognized by
        Guatemala (*September*)
        IMF agreement (*November*)
1982   Formation of URNG and CGUP (*February*)
        Presidential election overturned by military coup led by Ríos Montt;
        formation of junta (*March*)
        Imposition of state of siege (*July*)
        Formation of Council of State (*September*)
1983   Resumption of supply of spare military parts from USA (*January*)
        State of siege lifted (*March*)
        Ríos Montt overthrown in military coup led by Mejía Victores (*August*)
        Suspension of IMF agreement (*September*)
1984   Constituent elections give MLN–CAN the largest number of seats in
        the Assembly (*July*)
        First session of Constituent Assembly (*September*)
        Resumption of full US military aid (for fiscal 1985) (*October*)
1985   Presidential and congressional elections, presaging a return to civilian
        government, are dominated by right-wing and conservative formations
        (*November*)
        Vinicio Cerezo Arévalo (Christian Democrat) wins run-off poll for
        presidency (*December*)
1986   Inauguration of civilian government under Cerezo (*January*)
        Promulgation of new constitution (*January*)

1.2.2: Early History

The 1837 peasants' revolt led by Rafael Carrera did not cause a social
revolution in Guatemala, but merely restored the traditional Spanish
structures of government and society, and in particular strengthened the
Roman Catholic Church. Carrera dominated Guatemalan politics for nearly
30 years, being made perpetual president of the country in 1854 until his
death in 1865. Led by Justo Rufino Barrios, the liberals came to power in
1871 and promoted the cause of the liberals in neighbouring Honduras (see
section 1.3.2). President Barrios' attempts to renew the Central American
federation were brought to an abrupt end with his assassination in the revolt
of 1885 (see also section 1.1.4).

In 1898 Manuel Estrada Cabrera came to power and became one of the
longest ruling dictators in the region, surviving a Salvadorean- supported
uprising against him in 1906 (see section 1.1.7), until in 1920 he was replaced
by an elected government. The winning party, the Central American Unionist
Party, launched a tripartite unification initiative with El Salvador and Honduras which failed when the next year the government was overthrown in a
military coup, starting a decade of military rule.

In 1931 Jorge Ubico was elected president; a militant anti-communist, he
organized a purge of left-wing elements, especially among trade unions, and
by 1934 he had disbanded the unions and effectively neutralized the left-wing
political parties. He maintained his control by close association with the
country's coffee and banana plantation owners, by support from the United
States and by an economic strategy which increased government control over

labour. Active opposition to his rule began slowly to regroup and in 1941 university students started staging demonstrations against him, at a time when his own political position was weakened by the prevailing anti-Nazism of the Second World War.[1] In 1944 he suspended constitutional guarantees, seeking to use the armed forces to maintain control. However, a wave of strikes forced his resignation, and he handed over to a three-man junta under Federico Ponce Vaides, who restored the constitutional guarantees.

1.2.3: Victory for Revolutionary Forces—Election of Left-wing Government—Introduction of Land-reform Programme

The junta's concessions did not, however, satisfy left-wing activists among the opposition to Ubico, who marched on the capital and installed a government under their own broad-based junta of Francisco Araña, Jacobo Arbenz Guzmán and Jorge Toriello Garrido (all members of the progressive sector of the armed forces). The elections held in December were won by the progressive Juan José Arévalo Bermejo, who took office in March 1945, and in that year a new constitution was promulgated which incorporated for the first time the right of illiterates (then some 27 per cent of the population) to vote.

During Arévalo's six-year term of office many political, social and economic reforms were introduced, and industrial wages increased by over 80 per cent. The trade unions generally expanded their strength and influence, becoming dominated by communist and other left-wing elements (although the Communist Party itself had only limited influence in national politics, its membership never exceeding 4,000 in a population of nearly 3,000,000). These reforms gave rise to opposition, notably from Col. Araña (the army Chief of Staff), who declared his intention of contesting the next presidential election and was also rumoured to be plotting a coup. His assassination in July 1949 sparked off an unsuccessful rebellion by officers loyal to him. According to some reports the assassination was personally instigated by Arbenz; others claimed that his death had occurred during an attempt to arrest him.[2]

The November 1950 elections were won with an absolute majority by Arbenz, with the support of the Party of Revolutionary Action and the National Regeneration Party, against nine other candidates, and he was sworn into office in March 1951. The Arbenz government extended the reforms of the previous administration, introducing its most controversial policy (and the one which was to ensure US antagonism) on June 17, 1952, when a new law was passed giving the government the authority to expropriate large landed estates (for details see section 2.3.2). In February 1953 the government gave a warning to the United Fruit Company (UFCO—a US concern founded in 1899 and dominant in the Central American cultivation and marketing of bananas) that much of its land would be confiscated, and despite protests from UFCO and the US government the expropriation went ahead. Also subject to the new law was the International Railway of Central America, an Anglo-US concern of which UFCO was the largest shareholder, whose land was expropriated on Oct. 10, 1953.

Several members of the US administration had direct or indirect financial links with UFCO. Secretary of State John Foster Dulles (whose brother Allen headed the CIA) had represented UFCO as a company lawyer when the company's contract with the Guatemalan government had been negotiated. Moreover, the brother of John M. Cabot, the Assistant Secretary of State for Latin American Affairs, had been a director and former president of UFCO. Against this background, the US government equated Guatemala's attack on US interests with the harbouring of Soviet sympathies. In a speech made on Oct. 14, 1953, Cabot accused Guatemala of "openly playing the communist game" by introducing the land-reform programme. Subsequently, President Eisenhower himself said that by his actions Arbenz "soon created the strong suspicion that he was merely a puppet manipulated by the communists".[3]

1.2.4: Deterioration of Relations with Neighbouring States

Meanwhile on April 7, 1953, Guatemala had withdrawn from ODECA on the grounds that the other member countries were allegedly giving assistance to Guatemalan "reactionaries" trying to overthrow the government. At the same time the government had protested to the United Nations against what it termed the "systematic press campaign by US newspapers to represent Guatemala as a tool of Moscow and an outpost of Soviet communism on the American continent". In a speech on May 1 Arbenz repeated an earlier denial that Guatemala had become a communist country, but there continued to be concern among right-wing neighbours and the United States. The Guatemalan authorities claimed on Jan. 29, 1954, that the governments of Nicaragua, El Salvador, the Dominican Republic and Venezuela and "the government of the north" were planning to invade Guatemala by land, sea and air, and specifically (i) that this plan was being directed from Managua (Nicaragua) with the active support of Gen. Somoza, (ii) that UFCO had supplied arms and commando training to the assembling forces, and (iii) that anti-Guatemalan broadcasting stations had been established in Honduras and Nicaragua. Guatemalan anxiety over imminent invasion was increased further by the Caracas Declaration made by the OAS in March (see section 1.1.9), which was later invoked by Dulles on May 25, when he said: "The important question is whether Guatemala is subject to communist colonialism. . . . The extension of communist colonialism to this hemisphere would, in the words of the Caracas Declaration, endanger the peace of America."

1.2.5: Overthrow of Arbenz Government by Col. Castillo with US Assistance

The factor precipitating the 1954 coup, code-named by the US Central Intelligence Agency (CIA) "Operation Success"[4] was the US State Department announcement of March 17 that "an important shipment of arms from communist-controlled territory" (namely Szcezecin in Poland) had arrived at the Guatemalan port of Puerto Barrios. Two days later President Eisenhower said that it would be "a terrible thing if the communist dictatorship established an outpost on this continent", and Nicaragua broke off diplomatic relations with Guatemala on the grounds of its supposed "communist tendencies" and of allegations that it had tried to spread communist propaganda in Nicaragua. The US State Department said on May 24 that US arms supplies were being flown to Nicaragua and Honduras under military assistance pacts made with the two countries on May 20 and April 23 respectively, although their delivery had been accelerated in view of the Polish shipment.

In the face of statements and activities in the United States and other Central American countries, Arbenz on June 8 suspended constitutional guarantees for 30 days, and on June 18 insurgent forces headed by Col. Carlos Castillo Armas crossed into Guatemala at several points on the Honduran border; according to several reports these forces included US marines and members of the CIA. The government accused Honduras and Nicaragua, in conjunction with the United States, of "open aggression" and protested to the UN Secretary-General over the violation of Guatemalan airspace by aircraft from the direction of Honduras, distributing leaflets "inciting the Guatemalan army to rise against the legitimate and constitutional government of our country". The protest was referred to the OAS on June 20, but no decision was taken pending the report of a fact-finding team, which did not arrive in Guatemala until June 30—after the Arbenz government had fallen; the slowness of the OAS to act on this occasion was attributed to member states' disaffection with Guatemala. (The CIA's use of bases in Honduras and Nicaragua, and particularly of radio stations, served as a model in the Bay of Pigs campaign seven years later[5]—see section 5.3.2.)

1.2.6: Formation of Government under Col. Castillo—Constitutional Changes

Arbenz declared martial law on June 21, 1954, but six days later he was forced to resign in favour of the head of the armed forces, Col. Carlos Díaz, who formed a junta with Gen. Elfego Monzón and Col. José Angel Sánchez; Castillo had meanwhile on June 21 established his own government at Chiquimula. One of the first acts of the junta was to outlaw the Communist Party (PCG), as the National Vanguard had been called since 1949. This measure did not satisfy Castillo, who on June 28 demanded that the junta should arrest all "communists" in the former government and start negotiations with him. When he received no reply to his demands his forces bombed certain military targets close to the capital, and negotiations opened on June 30 in San Salvador. As a result a new five-man junta was formed, including Castillo.

On July 21 the new junta formed the National Committee for Defence against Communism, giving it authority to suppress all manifestations of communism and to keep a register of all people engaged in communist activity. The 1945 constitution was abrogated on Aug. 11 and replaced by a temporary political statute providing for rule by junta (illiterates had been disenfranchised by decree on July 6). The junta also halted the land-reform programme and abolished the agricultural co-operatives formed by the previous government to administer the sequestered large estates. In December 1954 UFCO's lands were restored to the company.

By September 1954 four of the junta members had resigned, leaving Castillo in sole control, and in October a plebiscite was held in which the electorate was asked "Do you wish Col. Castillo Armas to continue as President of the Republic for a period to be fixed by the National Assembly?" There were 485,693 yes votes to only 400 against, and on Nov. 6 Castillo was installed as president until March 15, 1960. In simultaneous elections the new National Anti-communist Party won 63 out of 66 seats in a constituent assembly, which approved a new constitution on Dec. 30 (with effect from March 1, 1956) banning any communist activity as a criminal offence and granting juridical status to religious organizations. In the legislative elections of December 1955 all seats were won by the pro-government National Electoral Alliance.

A new electoral law was passed in April 1956 making voting compulsory for literate adults and optional for illiterates, and requiring that parties should have at least 5,000 members in order to gain legal recognition. The government declared a state of emergency on June 24, claiming that there had been communist plans "to spread panic and disorder in the country and thus prepare a propitious atmosphere for the development of subversive intentions", but constitutional guarantees were restored on Aug. 25.

1.2.7: Assassination of Col. Castillo—Disputed Election of Col. Ydigoras

President Castillo was assassinated on July 26, 1957, by one of his presidential guards (Romeo Vásquez Sánchez, who immediately committed suicide); Vice-President Luis Arturo González López became provisional president. The presidential election held on Oct. 20 was contested by three conservative candidates only, as the new left-wing (but anti-communist) Revolutionary Party (PR) was denied registration by the provisional government on the grounds that it had allegedly been infiltrated by communist elements. In the preliminary results announced on Oct. 21 Sr Ortiz Passarelli of the National Democratic Movement (MDN) gained 198,931 votes against 128,323 for Col. Manuel Ydigoras Fuentes of the extreme right-wing National Reconciliation Party (PRN) and 26,452 for Miguel Asturias Quiñónez (a moderate). Ydigoras accused the government of electoral manipulation and organized a demonstration by his supporters in Guatemala City on Oct. 23, to which the provisional government responded by declaring a state of siege. (Ydigoras had held a provincial governorship under Ubico and had been one of the leaders of the 1954 coup, but because of disagreement with Castillo had been appointed ambassador to Colombia instead of joining the new government.)

The army high command announced on Oct. 24, 1957, that the provisional government had been replaced by a military junta consisting of Col. Oscar Mendoza Azurdia, Col. Gonzalo Yurrita Novoa and Col. Roberto Lorenzana. After negotiations with the junta Ydigoras agreed on Oct. 25 to call off the demonstration and on the following day the junta issued a decree invalidating the Oct. 20 elections on the grounds that "the citizens had no full guarantee of the exercise of their rights". In line with the constitution, the Second Vice-President, Guillermo Flores Avendano, was asked to form an interim administration (the First Vice-President having headed the first provisional government), and he was sworn into office on Oct. 27.

Fresh presidential elections were held on Jan. 19, 1958, contested by Ydigoras for the PRN, Col. José Luis Cruz Salazar of the MDN, Mario Méndez Montenegro of the PR and Col. Enrique Ardón Fernández of the small National Liberal Union. Ydigoras gained less than 40 per cent of the vote cast (with a further five per cent declared invalid) but he was approved as president in a congressional run-off election between him and Col. Cruz, and was sworn into office for a six-year term on March 2. There was, however, considerable opposition to him, involving protests against the continuance in force of the state of siege, an abortive coup attempt against him in November 1960, and allegations of fraud by the government in the December 1961 congressional elections.

During 1962 there was a brief revolt in the northern part of the country in February, student riots in March, and on Nov. 25 air force units staged an unsuccessful coup, which Ydigoras claimed had originated from the "Castro-communist" regime. It appeared, however, that one of the most immediate causes of the military rebellion was the imposition of more stringent income tax laws, introduced and approved by Congress on Nov. 24.

1.2.8: Overthrow of Col. Ydigoras—Growth of Guerrilla Opposition

A successful bloodless coup was staged on March 30, 1963, by Col. Enrique Peralta Azurdia (the Defence Minister), in whose name the armed forces issued a declaration saying that they had acted because they considered Guatemala to be "on the brink of an internal conflict as a result of subversion promoted by pro-communist sectors". Peralta became head of state pending elections, but the sudden reappearance in the capital of ex-President Arévalo (secretly returned from exile in Mexico) caused such a disturbance in the election campaign that Peralta suspended the constitution, dissolved the Congress, banned all political activity and extended the state of siege.

The "subversion" mentioned by the armed forces was a reference to the activities of guerrilla groups, including many left-wing leaders who had been forced underground after the 1954 coup. Although the fortunes of these groups fluctuated, the guerrillas became a permanent armed opposition to the military-dominated government. (For army counter-insurgency campaign, see section 3.3.2; for growth of guerrilla organizations, see section 3.1.2; for human rights issues, see section 4.2.2.)

1.2.9: Introduction of New Constitution—Intensification of War against Guerrillas

The next presidential elections, held on March 6, 1966, were won by Julio César Méndez Montenegro of the PR (chosen by the PR to replace his brother Mario, who had been shot the previous October by unidentified assailants). The other parties contesting the election were the right-wing National Liberation Movement (MLN) and the right-wing Democratic Institutional Party (PID). The election was held within the provisions of a new constitution, promulgated on Sept. 15, 1965, which reduced the presidential term of office from six years to four, established a Council of State and declared communism and other forms of totalitarianism illegal. President Méndez' term of office was marked by a sharp increase of violence from left- and right-wing groups. Although he lifted the state of siege soon after taking office, it was subsequently reintroduced for brief periods, notably after the kidnapping of Archbishop Casariego by a paramilitary group on March 18, 1967, and after the assassination on Aug. 28 of the US ambassador, John Gordon Mein.

In the election of March 1, 1970, Col. Carlos Araña Osorio of the MLN, who had been at the forefront of the army's anti-guerrilla operation, defeated the candidates of the PR and the Christian Democratic Party (PDCG), in an electoral campaign characterized by violence. The PDCG had been formed in 1968 as an anti-communist party favouring "reform in depth of the national, social and economic structure", and had some support from left-wing groups, although most of them boycotted the election. In collusion with other senior officers Araña had in 1968 sent President Méndez an ultimatum to resign in favour of a military government, but he had refused and Araña had been posted as ambassador to Nicaragua, returning to contest the election on a platform to uphold law and order and eradicate Marxism. At the beginning of March his election was ratified by Congress and he took office on July 1.

Within months of his inauguration he intensified the war against the guerrillas, with hundreds of arrests and detentions in late 1970; by 1972 guerrilla activity had declined as many leaders had been killed or silenced. The right-wing paramilitary groups continued their actions against left-wing sympathizers and killed several prominent members of the Guatemalan Labour Party (PGT) in 1972–74. By early 1977 the guerrillas had regrouped in the mountains and resumed their armed operations.

1.2.10: Disputed Elections—Civil Disturbances

The presidential election of March 3, 1974, was won by Gen. Kjell Eugenio Laugerud García, the candidate of a coalition between the MLN and the PID; after ratification by Congress he was sworn in on July 1. The other candidates in the contest were Gen. Efraín Ríos Montt and Col. Ernesto Paiz Morales of the PR–FDG (Guatemalan Democratic Front). Ríos Montt claimed that the poll had been fraudulent and called for a general strike in protest, but the electoral commission confirmed Laugerud's victory.

Gen. Fernando Romeo Lucas García, the candidate of the PR–PID–CAO (Organized Aranista Central), emerged as the leading candidate in the March 5, 1978, election over Col. Peralta of the MLN and his nephew Gen. Ricardo Peralta Méndez of the centre-left National Unity Front (Frenu, comprising the PDCG, the Authentic Revolutionary Party and the Popular Participation Front). Congress ratified Lucas Garcia's victory on March 13 and along with Vice-President Francisco Villagrán Kramer he was sworn into office on July 1. In the simultaneous congressional election the MLN gained 20 seats, the PID 17, the PR 14, the PDCG seven and the CAO three.

The MLN leader, Mario Sandoval Alarcón, attempted unsuccessfully to get the presidential count nullified on the grounds of alleged fraud and intimidation. A general lack of faith in the electoral process was evident in the turnout rate which fell in 1978 to only 36 per cent (from 59 per cent in 1958), even though voting was compulsory and penalties for failing to vote were theoretically strict. The intransigence of the military rulers of the 1970s, the widespread abuse of human rights and the general level of political violence in the country helped to prevent the growth of a strong moderate voice and left many disillusioned with constitutional solutions. As Villagrán Kramer said in 1979: "The people do not care about elections because of their experiences in the past. We cannot talk about an electoral method of change."[6]

The new presidential term of office was greeted by a resurgence of violence from left and right. It was estimated that 130 people lost their lives in this violence in January 1979 alone, with hundreds more being killed in the next few months. Responsibility for the assassination on March 22 of Manuel Colom Argueta, the leader of the social democratic United Revolutionary Front (FUR, which had been granted legal registration only a few days before), was generally attributed to one of the right-wing death squads (see section 3.2.2). In what appeared to be a retaliatory act the Chief of Staff, Gen. José David Cancinos Barrios, was killed on June 10, probably by left-wing activists. There were also several attacks on trade union leaders by paramilitary groups, and especially on members of the National Workers' Central (CNT).

In late 1978 the CNT had organized a strike in the capital—together with the National Council for Trade Union Unity (CNUS) and the Council of State Workers' Organizations (CETE)—in protest against the doubling of bus fares in October. The government was forced by this strike to reach a compromise by giving a subsidy to the privately-owned bus company and by undertaking to form a state-owned national transport service. In addition there was an increase in student protests and in land seizures by rural workers, often resulting in violence, which the authorities said were incited by priests. (For relations between church and state, see section 2.4.4.)

Villagrán Kramer announced in February 1979 that he would resign unless there were an end to violence and unless investigations were opened into political assassinations which had already taken place. He tried to initiate an inter-party debate on how to bring peace to the country, but the only parties willing to attend such a debate were the MLN and the National Authentic Central (CAN—as the CAO was renamed). He submitted a letter of resignation in January 1980, but withdrew it after reportedly receiving death threats from paramilitary groups if he were to leave office. He finally resigned on Sept. 1, as the only member of the government who accepted international criticism of the regime for its human rights abuses.

1.2.11: Formation of FDCR

In March 1979 about 70 organizations joined to form the Democratic Front against Repression (FDCR), whose objectives were to denounce all repressive actions against opponents of the regime and to provide aid for the widows and orphans of such violence; it subsequently developed close links with the guerrilla Organization of People at Arms (ORPA). The political violence of 1979, which included the murders of Colom Argueta and of Alberto Fuentes Mohr, the leader of the Democratic Socialist Party (PSD), escalated in 1980 when 10 FUR officials were killed. In mid–1980 the PDCG closed all its offices throughout the country because of the attacks on its members, and between April 1980 and April 1981 76 leading party members were killed, while there had also been an attempt on the life of the secretary-general, Vinicio Cerezo Arévalo. Other prominent victims of the right-wing death squads were the staff and students of San Carlos University (USAC).

In February 1982 the FDCR joined the Guatemalan Committee of Patriotic Unity (CGUP) which, while denying any direct links with the guerrillas, endorsed the basic programme adopted by the co-ordinated guerrilla command, the Guatemalan National Revolutionary Unity (URNG), also formed in February. This programme advocated popular revolutionary war as the only path remaining for the accomplishment of political change.

1.2.12: Military Coup by Gen. Ríos Montt—Improved Relations with the USA

In the presidential election held on March 7, 1982, Gen. Angel Aníbal Guevara of the Popular Democratic Front—a coalition of the PR, the PID and the right-wing Front of National Unity (FUN) founded in 1977—gained 38.9 per cent of the vote, well ahead of Sandoval Alarcón of the MLN, Gustavo Anzueto Vielman of CAN and Alejandro Maldonado of the centrist National Opposition Union (UNO), a coalition of the National Renewal Party (PNR) and the PDCG. The FUR refused to participate after one of its leaders, Guillermo Alfonso Rodríguez Serrano, who had been nominated as the candidate of a moderate left-wing coalition, was murdered in Guatemala City on Feb. 21.

Gen. Guevara was prevented from taking office by a bloodless military coup on March 23, 1982, led by Ríos Montt and a group of young officers, who claimed that the elections had been fraudulent and that they aimed to restore "authentic democracy". The coup apparently received the support of the MLN, which had disputed the election results, and of several sectors of the ruling class which resented Lucas García's amassing of wealth while in power. It was also claimed that the United States had favoured the coup and had even lent it some assistance; certainly the US administration was quick to recognize the new regime and military aid, cut off in 1977, was restored in 1983 (see section 5.2.2).

A three-man junta was established, consisting of Ríos Montt, Brig.-Gen. Horacio Maldonado Schaad and Col. Francisco Gordillo Martínez, and also a six-member Advisory Council of Young Officers. The new government announced that it would aim to bring respect to the rule of law and an end to hunger and misery brought about by "a corrupt minority through terror". It urged security forces "still at the service of corruption" to surrender their arms and put themselves at the disposal of the army. Ríos Montt also accused the previous government of "dishonesty and inefficiency"; promised that "no longer will corpses be thrown on the roadside or piled into trucks"; and called on the guerrillas to lay down their arms—"If not we shall take them from you" and "we will shoot anyone who breaks the law".

On the day after the coup Congress was closed, the constitution abrogated, political parties suspended and the March 7 elections declared null and void. The MLN, PDCG, PNR and CAN expressed their support for the new government, organizing rallies in favour of the coup, and talks were started with party and church leaders, academics and other prominent national figures. Ríos Montt announced on June 9 that he had assumed sole executive and legislative functions as President and C–in–C and intended to stay in power at least until the end of 1984.

Ríos Montt, who had since 1978 belonged to the Protestant fundamentalist California-based Church of the Complete Word (which had about 800 members in Guatemala), stated in mid–May 1982 that he had been offered several million dollars by Christian organizations in the United States to develop a new social, political and economic system, called "communitarianism". The avowed aim of this system was to build model villages, each with a school and community health centre and each peasant owning his own house; however, the original ideal was apparently subsumed in the continuing war against the guerrillas, and the model villages established by the army were strongly criticized as being based on fear and intimidation (see section 3.3.2). The ascendancy of this militantly protestant sect under the Ríos Montt government made the Roman Catholic Church still more outspoken against the excesses of the government (see section 2.5.2).

1.2.13: Introduction of State of Siege—Growing Opposition to Ríos Montt Government

A state of siege was imposed on July 1, 1982, lasting until March 23, 1983, in response to criticism of the military authorities by the press, which was adjured to "sacrifice sensationalism in favour of the good of the nation". In addition, political and trade union activities were banned, the death penalty decreed for "disturbing the public order" (such offences to be tried in secret by three-man tribunals specially appointed by the President), and the government acquired the authority to mobilize into civil defence units all men aged 18–30 who had performed military service (see section 3.2.2). The government issued a decree on Aug. 17 providing for the formation of a 34-member advisory Council of State, which was installed on Sept. 15, even though only the FUR agreed to take part, while the four parties which had originally given their support to Ríos Montt refused, calling the Council a "mask" for the government.

The MLN, which had its own private army of about 5,000, became involved in a number of coup attempts against the government along with several other disaffected sectors. Senior army officers resented the prominence given to younger officers (especially with the formation of the Advisory Council of Young Officers); the private sector objected to the new government's economic policies, especially the introduction on Aug. 1, 1983, of a 10 per cent value-added tax and a new agricultural programme; and the Roman Catholic Church protested against the anti-Catholic stance of the new government and also against the continued large-scale abuse of human rights. The US administration claimed that under Ríos Montt human rights had improved in Guatemala, but according to other reports such an improvement had extended only to the capital, while severe abuses continued in the rural areas, particularly under the rural pacification and resettlement programme (see sections 3.3.2 and 4.2.2).

In an attempt to appease the opposition Ríos Montt announced in July 1983 that the Advisory Council of Young Officers had been dissolved and that elections would be held in 12 months' time in preparation for a return to democratic rule by 1985, and he suspended 10 death sentences currently pending from the hearings of the secret tribunals. (For operation of tribunals and national and international protest over death sentences, see section 4.2.2)

1.2.14: Overthrow of Ríos Montt

In August 1983 President Ríos Montt was overthrown in a coup led by Brig.-Gen. Oscar Humberto Mejía Victores, the Minister of Defence, who said that the army had "resumed the responsibility for the return to civilian life", and that elections would be held in mid–1984 as planned. The army high command issued a statement saying: "A religious, fanatical and aggressive group, taking advantage of the positions of power held by its highest members, has used and abused the means of government for its own benefit. . . . We affirm our commitment to Guatemala to fight, by all means available, to eradicate the Marxist-Leninist subversion which threatens our freedom and sovereignty."

Four days after the coup (Aug. 12) Mejía Victores declared a 90-day amnesty for left-wing guerrillas (subsequently extended until June 1984), signed a decree guaranteeing the legal rights of detainees and formally dissolved the secret tribunals. However, in a warning suggesting that the army hoped to keep control of the political process for at least the duration of the new constituent assembly to be elected in 1984, Mejía Victores asserted that "the politicians must understand that the elections constitute an opportunity that the army is graciously offering", and that if the assembly should go beyond certain limits "they will see what will happen, if they want a dictator, they shall have one".

1.2.15: 1984 Constituent Elections—Preparations for Presidential Elections

The constituent elections of July 1, 1984, were contested by 17 newly-registered parties (of over 30 groups which had applied for legal recognition) and the allocation of seats was: MLN–CAN 23, the centre-right Union of the National Centre (UCN) 21, PDCG 20, PR 10, PNR five, PID five, and one each for the Anti-communist Unification Party (PUA), FUN and the (Indian) Peasant Social Action Organization (OCAS). The PDCG had polled the highest number of votes—269,372 as against 245,514 for the MLN–CAN—but had failed to gain more seats as its strength lay in the urban areas which had larger constituencies. The FUN deputy later defected to the MLN, but was killed on Oct. 26. The PR and PNR formed an alliance in July and the MLN–CAN coalition was joined by the PID in September; the PR-PNR coalition staged a protest walk-out at the Assembly's first session.

Voting was still compulsory in the elections, and there were reports of people who failed to vote being threatened with fines, loss of employment, prison and even—in some rural areas—death. Nevertheless, the turnout was only about 53 per cent of some 3,500,000 people eligible to register to vote (about 1,000,000 failed to do so, while a further 500,000 votes were spoilt or blank). The campaign had been marked by violence, which the president of the Supreme Electoral Tribunal, Arturo Herbruger, said on Feb. 13 posed a threat to the entire election process, with 12 political kidnappings in the capital in the previous 48 hours alone. By March 13 it was reported that about 300 people had "disappeared" during the campaign.

The new Assembly convened on Aug. 1 to draft the country's fourth new constitution in 40 years, but one of the first matters to be decided by the delegates was their own salary, which was set at $3,000 per month, pegged to the presidential salary of $12,000 per month. (By contrast the average professional salary was between $800 and $1,500 per month and an average worker's wage between $100 and $200 per month.)

Debate on the new constitution was protracted, and amid rumours of a coup and of the Assembly disrupting the political and electoral timetable Mejía Victores announced on May 20, 1985, that deputies would be imprisoned if the Assembly declared itself a Congress. The final draft was completed by the deadline of May 31, and in fact contained only minor alterations to the two previous constitutions, including an extension of the presidential mandate from four years to five.

1.2.16: Election of Civilian Government

In the presidential and legislative elections held on Nov. 3, 1985, the PDCG emerged as the leading party with 38.7 per cent of the vote and 51 of the 100 seats in Congress, followed by the UCN with 20.2 per cent. Since the PDCG presidential candidate, Vinicio Cerezo Arévalo, gained less than the necessary 50 per cent of the vote, a run-off election between him and UCN candidate, Jorge Carpio Nicolle, was held on Dec. 8, which was won by Cerezo with 55 per cent of the vote. Cerezo and a new civilian government were inaugurated on Jan. 14, 1986, when the new constitution was promulgated.

Earlier in 1985 the right wing had fragmented when the PR and PNR left the coalition with the UCN, thus weakening Carpio. He had previously been expected to win the presidential election, being reputed to have the backing of the military command and of the US administration (although he denied allegations that the UCN was being funded by the CIA). Of the 14 parties which gained official recognition and contested the first-round election, all were centre-right or right-wing except the PSD, whose candidate, Mario Solorzano, gained 3.4 per cent of the vote. Prior to the ballot Archbishop Próspero Peñados del Barrio asserted that the elections, hailed by the government as a "democratic opening", were likely simply to produce a "militarized civilian government". For their part, the guerrilla movements contested the validity of the elections and made persistent efforts to discourage the population from voting.

There was further internal party trouble soon after the inauguration of the new government, and the PDCG lost its overall majority when in February four of its deputies defected to the opposition. The opposition, however, also faced division, notably with the emergence of a new faction within the MLN in March.

1.2.17: Guatemala's Role in Central American Conflict

Guatemala has not been directly involved in the conflict engulfing El Salvador, Honduras and Nicaragua, but many observers suggest that it will become more so, both because of its polarized internal politics and as US military ties have strengthened since the re-establishment of Condeca (see section 1.1.12). In March 1982 the then US Secretary of State, Alexander Haig, commenting on El Salvador, said: "It's a matter of weeks or months before you see—perhaps even more consequential in terms of potential damage to United States interests—a similar situation developing in Guatemala. It is a clear, self-influencing sequence of events which could sweep all of Central America into a Cuba-dominated region and put a very fundamental threat on Mexico in the very predictable future."[5]

A similar stance was taken by Gen. Wallace Nutting (head of the US Southern Command 1979–83), as follows: "The political implications of a

Marxist takeover in Guatemala are a lot more serious than in El Salvador. . . . [The US] Congress does not realise the historic importance of the competition in Central America."[6] In 1984 the Kissinger Commission (see section 5.1.4) concluded in its report: "In terms of regional and US security interests, Guatemala, with its strategic position on the Mexican border, the largest population in the Central American area and the most important economy, is obviously a pivotal country."

1.2.18: Belize Issue

For the last 20 years a central issue of Guatemala's foreign policy has been Belize, to which Guatemala has laid claim since the mid–19th century. A British settlement since the 17th century, it became a colony called British Honduras in 1862 and changed its name to Belize in 1973. Both Guatemala and Mexico had claimed the territory when they gained independence from Spain in 1821, and Britain acquired the Mexican interest in 1826 (although Mexico did not finally renounce its claims until 1896). By the Anglo-Guatemalan Agreement of 1859 Guatemala agreed to recognize the settlement's borders, and in exchange Britain undertook to contribute to the construction of a road from Guatemala City to the Caribbean coast; however, the British did not fulfil this condition and Guatemala never ratified the agreement.

The Guatemalan claim became more insistent after 1964 when the colony was granted internal self-government, and then sought independence, which was approved by the UN and finally achieved on Sept. 21, 1981. Tripartite negotiations between Guatemala, Belize and Britain began in 1976 without any immediate result, and a new round of talks which opened in January 1983 broke down after Belize refused a Guatemalan proposal under which Guatemala would have renounced its claim to the entire territory in exchange for a slice of southern Belize to extend its Caribbean seaboard. Informal discussions were held in May and July 1984, with a new session of talks beginning on Feb. 12, 1985, at which Britain was an observer.

The territorial dispute is not directly linked to the main conflict in Central America, except in so far as it concentrates Guatemalan interest away from its southern neighbours and as the withdrawal of British authority has made Belize look more to the United States in defence matters. There were indeed signs of possible progress towards resolution of the dispute with the omission in the new Guatemalan constitution of May 1985 of any explicit claim to Belize and with the restoration of consular relations between Britain and Guatemala in August 1986 and full diplomatic relations in December.

Notes

1. Ralph Lee Woodward, *Central America: A Nation Divided*, New York, OUP, 1976. Woodward points out that such propaganda was harmful to all current Central American dictators (Carias in Honduras, Martínez in El Salvador and Somoza in Nicaragua), who were nominally on the side of the Allies but politically closer to European fascism.
2. Schlesinger and Kinzer, *op. cit.*, pp.43–45.
3. Peter Wyden, *Bay of Pigs—The Untold Story*, London, Jonathan Cape, 1979.
4. Quoted in George Black, *Garrison Guatemala*, London, Zed Press, 1984, p.48.
5. Quoted in Pearce, *op. cit.*, p.274.
6. Quoted in Black, *op. cit.*, p.159.

1.3: HONDURAS

1.3.1: Chronology

1840   Liberal revolt fails to unseat conservatives

1848   New constitution promulagated

1852   Liberal government elected

1855   Liberal government removed at Carrera's instigation

1865   New constitution promulgated

1876   Liberals regain power

1880   New constitution promulgated
       Tegucigalpa declared the national capital

1891   Election of conservative government

1894   New constitution promulgated

1906   New constitution drafted and implemented, but overturned by Dávila in 1908 (with support of Zelaya in Nicaragua)

1907   Policarpo Bonilla overthrown by rebels with Nicaraguan backing and replaced by Dávila

1910   Dávila deposed by US mercenaries and replaced by Manuel Bonilla

1923   Presidential election won by Carias of PN, who is prevented from taking office

1924   Carias' forces take Tegucigalpa
       Fresh presidential election won by Paz Baraona of PN

1925   New constitution promulgated

1932   Carias elected president, remaining in office without further ballot

1936   New constitution promulgated

1948   Resignation of Carias
       Gálvez of PN elected (taking office in 1949)

1954   General strike
       Presidential election won by Villeda Morales of PL
       Vice-President Lozano seizes power, dissolves Congress and abrogates constitution

1956   Constituent elections held, but overturned in military coup

1957   Villeda Morales elected president
       PL gains majority in Congress
       New constitution promulgated

1959   Abortive military coup

1960   Resolution of border dispute with Nicaragua on Atlantic coast, leading to creation of Cape Gracias a Dios

1961   Introduction of land-reform programme

1963   Elections pre-empted by military coup
       López Arellano declared head of state by decree

1965   López Arellano elected president by new constituent assembly
       New constitution promulgated

1969   Four-day football war with El Salvador

1971   Cruz of PN elected president

1972   Bloodless coup installs López Arellano as head of state

1974 Hurricane causes severe damage to banana crop and infrastructure
1975 United Brands bribery scandal
      Overthrow of López Arellano by reformist officers led by Melgar Castro
      Acceleration of land-reform programme
      Abolition of special privileges for foreign banana companies
1978 Military coup replaces Melgar Castro by junta under Paz García
1980 Constituent elections won by PL (*April*)
      Signing of peace treaty with El Salvador officially ends football war (*October*)
      First US military trainers arrive (*October*)
1981 IMF agreement (*June*)
      Suazo Córdova of PL wins presidential election (*October*)
1982 Suazo Córdova takes office (*January*)
      New constitution promulgated (*January*)
      Appointment of Alvarez as Head of the Armed Forces (*January*)
      Passage of new anti-terrorist laws (*April*)
      IMF agreement (*November*)
1983 Opening of US training base at Puerto Castilla (*July*)
      Start of Big Pine II military and naval manoeuvres with USA (*August*)
1984 Dismissal of Alvarez and accession of López Reyes (*March*)
      Grenadier joint exercises (*April*)
      Honduran army halts Salvadorean training at Puerto Castilla (*July*)
1985 Big Pine III joint exercises (*February–April*)
      Constitutional crisis over the appointment of judges (*April–May*)
      PL wins general elections (*November*)
1986 Azcona inaugurated as president (*January*)
      Blazing Trail US joint exercises (*January–June*)
      Resignation of López Reyes and replacement by Regalado Hernández (*February*)

1.3.2: Early History

For the first 10 years after the dissolution of the Central American federation in 1838 Honduras was ruled by Francisco Ferrera (an associate of Rafael Carrera of Guatemala), who survived a brief liberal revolt in 1840. He was succeeded in 1847 by another conservative, Juan Lindo Zelaya, who introduced a new constitution in 1848 restoring the bicameral legislature and changing the presidential term of office to four years (under the 1839 constitution there had been a unicameral legislature and the president had held office for only two years). He established sufficient political order to enable a peaceful handover of power in 1852 after the liberals had won the election, and José Trinidad Cabañas became president.

Conservative rule was restored by Carrera in 1855 under Santos Guardiola, who was assassinated in 1862 and was succeeded by José María Medina, president in 1863–68 and 1870–72. Under Medina a new constitution was promulgated in 1865, which restored the single chamber legislature and extended the power of the executive head of state. Under President Barrios, Guatemala intervened in Honduran politics in 1873, establishing the liberal Ponciano Leiva as president, who was followed in 1876 by Marco Aurelio

Soto. The new constitution of 1880 restored many rights to the legislative arm of government, in particular increasing its control over the government's finances. After a series of differences with Barrios, Soto resigned in 1881 and was replaced (at Barrios' instigation) by Luis Bográn Baraona; Barrios' influence was so strong in boosting the Liberals that after his assassination in 1885 the Honduran Liberals lost control in 1891.

After their electoral defeat of 1891 the liberals looked to José Santos Zelaya in Nicaragua for support. Two years later Policarpo Bonilla was elected president, taking office in 1895 under a new constitution drafted in 1894. Bonilla's nominee, Terencio Sierra, succeeded him in 1899, and Bonilla regained office in 1903. He drafted a new constitution in 1906 which was overturned by the next president in 1908.

1.3.3: "Banana Republic"

From the mid-19th century the history of Honduras has been dominated by the cultivation and export of bananas, the main economic activity. There was also some mineral prospecting, chiefly for silver, which dictated the choice of Tegucigalpa as capital in 1880, but the expansion of the banana industry was a decisive factor in politics and in the country's infrastructural development. As the banana companies constructed 1,162 km out of Honduras' total railway network of 1,261 km, Tegucigalpa (which has little direct connection with the banana industry) became the only capital in Latin America not to be served by a railway.

Towards the end of the 19th century many presidents and government officials gained foreign backing by generous concessions of land to growers, either as gifts or at only nominal rents, while the foreign (mostly US) investors favoured Honduras because of its proximity to US ports, its low labour costs and the reported ease with which many local officials could be bribed. Moreover, the government was politically weak and lacked even a strong military arm. The first banana concession was granted in 1899 to the Vaccaro brothers, who later formed the Standard Fruit Company, and from 1912 UFCO acquired some 175,000 acres (nearly 71,000 hectares) of prime agricultural land with no straight cash payment being made. It also became recognized practice for the government to hand over between 250 and 500 ha. of land to the fruit companies for every kilometre of railway they built.[1]

In 1907 President Bonilla was overthrown by another liberal, Miguel Dávila, who had been supported by the Nicaraguan government since the previous year (see section 1.1.7). Dávila provoked US antagonism by trying to halt the indiscriminate concessions of land, and in 1910 a US citizen, Sam Zemurray (accompanied by some US mercenaries) invaded Honduras and replaced Dávila by the more pliant Manuel Bonilla; Zemurray himself later became C-in-C of the Honduran army and managing director of UFCO in 1933.[2] At that time about one-half of the national banana production was in the hands of local growers, who were gradually dispossessed, and thereafter Zemurray's Cuyamel Fruit Company (which was absorbed by UFCO in 1929) gained large tracts of land with exemption of payment for 25 years, and by 1946 UFCO (through its wholly-owned subsidiary the Tela Railroad Company) had gained nearly 170,000 ha. of land, although only a small fraction of this area was put under cultivation.

1.3.4: Disputed Election of 1923—Eventual Assumption of Presidency by Carias

The presidential election of 1923 was won by Gen. Tiburcio Carias Andino of the National Party (PN), which had initially grouped conservatives and was called the Democratic National Party in 1919 before being reorganized in 1923 by Carias and renamed. The Congress refused to ratify his election and so he gathered his soldiers around him and by 1924 he held the capital and most of the outlying regions. After negotiations, in which the United States acted as a mediator, Carias agreed to the selection of his vice-presidential candidate, Miguel Paz Baraona, who was duly elected with the full support of Carias. In the 1928 elections Carias was unexpectedly beaten by Vicente Mejía Colindres of the Liberal Party (PL).

Carias won a decisive majority in the 1932 presidential election against Angel Zúñiga Huerte of the PL, and took office for a four-year term, with no immediate re-election allowed. A constituent assembly was elected in January 1936 and a new constitution promulgated in March, which included provisions for the president and vice-president to stay in office until January 1943; it also made voting compulsory for all adult males, while women were still denied citizenship, and in its sections on industry and labour made no reference to the growing labour organizations. Carias gave a measure of internal political stability to the country, with opponents of the regime bound by an agreement to abstain from revolution, conspiracy or clandestine anti- government activities, and in particular inaugurated a road building programme (with over 1,600 km of roads laid by 1945) and achieved a balanced budget (except during the war years).

Carias continued in office until the end of 1948, under a constitutional measure of December 1939 further extending his term, and in the election of October the PN candidate Juan Manuel Gálvez was elected unopposed, taking office on Jan. 1, 1949. Gálvez was committed to honest and open government and continued Carias's road programme and economic measures, but he was similarly conservative in his approach to organized labour.

1.3.5: General Strike—Inconclusive Election

A political and economic crisis erupted in April 1954 when dock workers at Tela refused to load ships at the UFCO wharves, demanding pay at double rate for Sunday working. As the dispute escalated into a general protest against the UFCO management, Gálvez sent troops to Puerto Cortes on April 28, but by May 3 the strike had spread to all the four UFCO divisions at Tela, Puerto Cortes, La Lima and El Progreso. The workers demanded a reduction of their working week and a wage rise of at least 50 per cent. By mid-May Standard Fruit Company workers had joined the action, taking the number on strike to nearly 50,000. The strikers' case was supported by Guatemala, fuelling allegations in Honduras and among the US banana companies that the strike was "communist" inspired, and at one time there was general anxiety that there might be war with Guatemala. The strikers became divided in their demands and over the conduct of negotiations, and in July eventually agreed

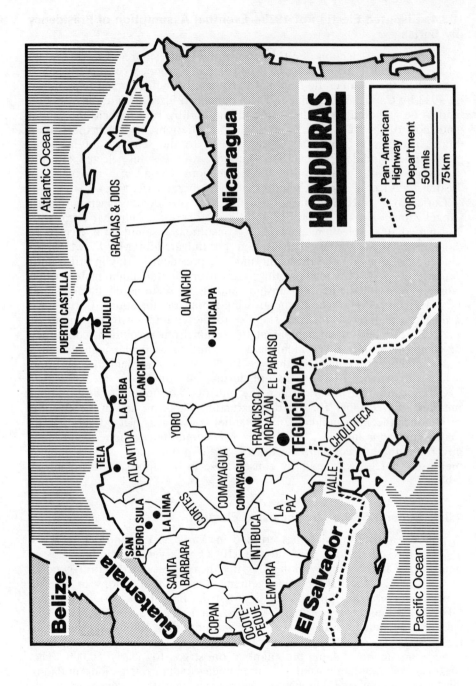

to return to work after compromising on their demands. The fruit companies had been especially worried as the strike had occurred at harvest- time, and UFCO and Standard Fruit lost nearly $15,000,000 between them; the Honduran government lost about $1,000,000 in customs revenue and the workers lost over $2,000,000 in wages.

The civilian unrest aroused by the strike became still more evident in the campaign for the October 1954 election, which was contested by Ramón Villeda Morales of the PL, Carias of the PN and Gen. Abraham Williams Calderón (who had been Vice-President under Carias) of the Reformist Party, which had broken away from the PN in 1953. The campaign was acrimonious, with further disturbance caused by severe flooding in the country in September, and in the poll there was no clear winner as Villeda Morales gained only 48 per cent of the vote (the required minimum being 50 per cent). Moreover, Gálvez was taken ill and handed over to Vice-President Julio Lozano Díaz. Congress convened on Dec. 6 to choose the next president, but as it was inquorate Lozano dissolved it and then proceeded to declare himself head of state, formed an all-party Council of State and promised to convene a constituent assembly to draft a new constitution.

In February 1955 Lozano called on all the political parties to abstain from "activities encouraging a climate of unrest" and in March the police reported that a communist plot had been discovered, designed to bring down the government. He became unpopular when he announced tax changes, including a rise in the rate of income tax from 15 to 30 per cent, and when the preparations he guaranteed for future elections proved to be extremely slow. In July Villeda Morales was arrested and sent into exile along with two other PL members, provoking an abortive military coup in August.

When the constituent elections were held on Oct. 7, 1956, the National Union Party (PUN, founded by Lozano in 1955) claimed all 56 seats in the new assembly, leading to allegations by the PL and PN of fraud, backed up by reports of intimidation in polling stations and police attacks on PL members. Lozano was overthrown on Oct. 20 in a bloodless military coup, and a junta was formed by Col. Héctor Caraccioli, Maj. Roberto Gálvez (son of the former president) and Gen. Roque Rodríguez. The junta declared a political amnesty, formed a new coalition cabinet, abrogated the recent elections and called new constituent elections. The new regime's commitment to a return to constitutional government was indicated when in July 1957 Gen. Rodríguez was dismissed from the junta for interfering in politics.

In the constituent elections held in September 1957 the PL gained 37 seats, the PN 18 and the Reformist Party three. At its first session the new assembly voted in favour of Villeda Morales as president, who was sworn into office on Jan. 1, 1958. In the new constitution the presidential term of office was set at six years with no re-election and universal suffrage was for the first time extended to women.

1.3.6: Overthrow of Civilian Government in Military Coup—Domination by Col. López Arellano

President Villeda Morales introduced a series of economic and social reforms, including the passage in 1959 of labour legislation and of measures to establish a state social security system. (Honduras was the last country in Central

America to adopt a state benefit system.) His relatively moderate reforms posed a threat to the traditional ruling class, and in February 1959 there was an abortive military coup, with fighting continuing for several months. A successful coup was staged in October 1963 (pre-empting the scheduled elections) under the leadership of Col. Oswaldo López Arellano, the Defence Minister and Head of the Armed Forces. Villeda Morales and Vice-President Modesto Rodas Alvarado went into exile in Costa Rica; Rodas, who as the candidate of the PL in the forthcoming election had been expected to win, had declared during the campaign that if elected he would seek to exert stronger control over the armed forces.

Col. López issued a decree naming himself as president, and announced the immediate imposition of a state of siege, the dissolution of Congress and the proscription of all political activity. In response to the coup the United States broke off diplomatic relations and suspended all except humanitarian aid. However, relations were resumed in December because of the new government's verbal commitment to an electoral timetable and its assurances of respect for full civil and political rights.

Elections to a new constituent assembly took place in February 1965, resulting in 35 seats for the PN against 29 for the PL, which then boycotted it. The Assembly held its first session in March and elected Col. López to serve as president for a six-year term with effect from June, when it was redesignated a full legislative assembly.

President López announced in November 1970 that general elections would be held the following March, and in advance of the poll the PL and PN concluded a pact of national union under which each party would have 32 seats, so that in any debate the president would have the casting vote. The predominant election issue was the question of the continued membership of CACM, suspended in 1970 because of the war with El Salvador (see below); the PN favoured withdrawal, arguing that Honduras had suffered as a result of being the least industrialized member of the Community. In the presidential ballot, which recorded a 60 per cent turnout, Ramón Ernesto Cruz of the PN gained a narrow majority over Jorge Bueso Arias of the PL.

1.3.7: The Football War

The conflict between El Salvador and Honduras now known as the "football war" broke out in July 1969, when incidents after two football matches led to full-scale hostilities. The first match, in the elimination round of the World Cup, was played in Tegucigalpa on June 8, with Honduras winning 1–0; afterwards Salvadorean supporters complained that they had been ill-treated by Hondurans. Similar claims were made by Honduran supporters against Salvadoreans after the return match played in San Salvador on June 15, which El Salvador won 3–0. (The deciding match, played in Mexico City on June 28, was won by El Salvador by three goals to two.) In the wake of the second match many Salvadoreans living in Honduras began returning home, saying that their possessions had been forfeited. On June 24 the Salvadorean Foreign Minister, Francisco José Guerrero, said in a radio broadcast that nearly 12,000 Salvadoreans had been expelled from Honduras and called on the OAS to investigate charges against Hondurans of rape, plunder, oppression and mass expulsion.

In recent years an estimated 300,000 Salvadoreans had gone to Honduras to find work, and their increasing role in the Honduran economy had led to resentment among the Honduran workforce. Even before the football matches there had been attacks on Salvadoreans in Honduras and tension had risen after the introduction of agricultural legislation designed to dispossess Salvadoreans by limiting ownership of land to Honduran nationals. Salvadoreans had moved northwards since the 1920s because of demographic pressure; the population density in El Salvador was 137 people per sq km compared with 20 per sq km in Honduras. (For economic causes of war, see also section 2.2.2.)

The Salvadorean government declared a state of emergency on June 24, ordering its soldiers to report to barracks; two days later it broke off diplomatic relations with Honduras, which itself broke relations on June 27. In an attempt to resolve this dispute the foreign ministers of Guatemala, Nicaragua and Costa Rica (respectively Alberto Fuentes Mohr, Lorenzo Guerrero and Fernando Lara) arrived in Tegucigalpa on June 27 and tried unsuccessfully to find a solution. On the same day the Secretary-General of the OAS, Galo Plaza Lassa, sent members of the OAS human rights commission to both countries. After a fortnight of border incidents full-scale hostilities broke out on July 14 when Salvadorean forces crossed the border into Honduras and quickly gained the military advantage because of their superior military equipment. Most of the people who died in the fighting, estimated at between 2,000 and 4,000, were Hondurans.

After OAS mediation a ceasefire was adopted on July 18, 1969, but El Salvador refused to withdraw its troops without what it considered adequate guarantees for Salvadoreans still in Honduras, which insisted on troop withdrawal as a priority. On July 23 the OAS declared El Salvador responsible for failing to comply with the terms of the ceasefire and threatened to levy diplomatic and economic sanctions, while on July 28 the OAS foreign ministers received a report from the area containing allegations of grave excesses by Salvadorean troops in Honduras. A compromise settlement was reached on July 30 which provided for (i) the immediate withdrawal of all Salvadorean forces; (ii) guarantees for Hondurans and Salvadoreans living in El Salvador and Honduras respectively under the supervision of the OAS; and (iii) the formation of a special OAS commission to ensure that the settlement was not breached.

At a meeting of the five Central American foreign ministers in San José on June 4, 1970, under the auspices of the OAS, it was agreed that a demilitarized zone should be established on the border and that Guatemala, Nicaragua and Costa Rica would provide security patrols to operate within the zone.

The war had serious effects in the two countries, not least because both virtually lost their small air forces. Whereas Honduras felt the greater economic impact from the expense of the war and the loss of skilled manpower, El Salvador's resources were strained by a sudden influx of some 25,000 refugees. The economic damage to both countries was exacerbated by the continued closure of the border, restricting their trade within the region. (For Honduran withdrawal from CACM and Condeca after the war, see sections 1.1.10 and 1.1.12.)

Negotiations for a full peace treaty began in 1976, but the final draft was not signed until Oct. 30, 1980, being formally ratified by both sides on Dec. 10. The treaty reopened the border, demarcating two-thirds of the frontier and committing both sides to resolving within five years the remaining sections, which were pockets of land (known as *bolsones territoriales*) included in the 1970 demilitarized zone. An undertaking was made that if no resolution had been achieved by 1985 the dispute would be referred to the International Court of Justice (ICJ) at The Hague.

The delay in the peace negotiations had been caused by the Honduran insistence that the border should be finalized before any settlement could be reached, but this condition had been dropped in April 1980, apparently in response to US pressure (see section 3.3.6). The US administration was anxious to heal the rift between the Honduran and Salvadorean armies in order to co-ordinate the military campaign against the Salvadorean guerrillas, some of whom operated within the *bolsones*. By 1984 (after the fall of Alvarez—see below) Honduras was reported to be attempting to exert pressure on El Salvador by threatening to close the US training base for Salvadorean soldiers at Puerto Castilla (see below and section 5.2.7), and also with regard to the refugee situation (see section 4.1.4).

1.3.8: Emergence of Young Officers' Movement—United Brands Scandal

The government of President Cruz was overthrown in a bloodless coup led by Gen. López Arellano on Dec. 4, 1972. The president was accused of taking the country into "economic chaos" and was placed under house arrest, while the Defence Council (composed of members of the commands of the three branches of the armed forces) took over all executive functions. López was confirmed in power as head of state for at least five years, and as C.–in–C. of the Armed Forces he enjoyed virtual independence of any civilian authority. At the time of the coup the Cruz government had been weakened by a split in the PL–PN coalition, especially when in October 1972 the PN had disputed that the original agreement had assured the PL of a certain proportion of government appointments.

The López government also ran into economic problems which eroded its control, after a serious hurricane hit the country in 1974 (see section 2.2.2). In March 1975 a group of young dissident officers managed to instigate a purge in the higher ranks of the army, forcing over 40 colonels into retirement and replacing López by Col. Juan Alberto Melgar Castro as C.–in–C. The same group of officers, led by Melgar Castro, staged a coup against López on April 22, also seizing control of the Supreme Council of the Armed Forces. Announcing that they had acted to "safeguard the integrity and honour of the country", they promised to make extensive changes in the public administration and to give priority in their government programme to land reform, adding that in order to achieve these objectives they would retain power "as long as is necessary". (A further 29 senior officers were retired from active service in late June.)

The young officers' movement had originated in the football war, when they had been critical of the lack of preparation for military engagement on the part of the senior command and also of the extent of corruption apparent in the higher ranks. The army had also been slow to act after the 1974 hurricane and in several cases young officers had taken over command of battalions in the relief programme. The allegations of corruption became more serious after the publication of an article in the *Wall Street Journal* on April 9, 1975, which reported that López had in 1974 received bribes totalling $1,250,000 from the US company United Brands (as UFCO had become after a merger in 1970) to reduce the banana tax, recently imposed by the Union of Banana Exporting Countries (UPEB), of $1.00 per 64 kg box. On the same day the US Securities Exchange Commission filed a suit against United Brands, charging the company with issuing false accounts to conceal a bribe to Honduran officials.

The investigation into United Brands' dealings had begun in February 1975 after the company's chairman, Eli Black, jumped to his death from the 44th floor of a New York building. Although López refused permission for the investigatory commission to examine his foreign bank accounts, the commission's findings implicated him and the Economy Minister, Abraham Bennaton Ramos. The commission's report found that Black had personally handed $1,250,000 to Bennaton, half the amount agreed, and estimated that the UPEB tax would have cost United Brands $77,400,000 between mid–1974 and the end of 1975. When the case against United Brands was brought on July 19, 1978, the company pleaded guilty to the charge of conspiracy to pay a bribe of $2,500,000 and was fined the maximum sum of $15,000.

1.3.9: Opposition to Political and Economic Reforms

The new government faced considerable opposition to its land-reform programme (for which see section 2.3.3), and the opposition increased in January 1976 when President Melgar Castro said that the army would retain political power at least until 1979 in order to implement the policies it had promised. Elections would be held in 1979 and the newly-elected government would be advised on policy by a council of state, whose members would be drawn from trade unions, student movements, political parties and private business. The Supreme Council of the Armed Forces approved a new electoral law on Dec. 27, 1977, in preparation for these elections, providing for the full resumption of political activity (banned since 1972). There had earlier, on Oct. 21, 1977, been an unsuccessful attempted coup by right-wing civilian and military elements opposed to the government's reforms.

President Melgar Castro was overthrown in a right-wing coup on Aug. 7, 1978, by the C.–in–C., Gen. Policarpo Paz García, who then headed a junta which also included Lt.-Col. Amilcar Zelaya Rodríguez, the chief of the public security forces, and Col. Domingo Alvarez Cruz, the Air Force commander. The junta promised to guarantee the "process of constitutionalization of the country which has already begun", and specifically to continue the land-reform programme; however, elections were delayed for a year until 1980 and the land-reform programme was later dropped. Immediately before the coup a number of senior officers in the armed forces, including both Melgar Castro and Paz García, had been named in allegations of involvement with drug smuggling and accused of having links with organized crime.

1.3.10: Return to Civilian Elected Government

The constituent elections of April 20, 1980, resulted in a surprise win for the PL, which gained 52 per cent of the votes and 35 of the 71 seats in the new assembly, while the PN gained 33 seats and the new Innovation and Unity Party (PINU, founded in 1978) gained three. The turnout was 75 per cent in spite of a call for a boycott made by the Honduran Patriotic Front (FPH), a group of nearly 50 left-wing parties which were either unable to stand—such as the Christian Democratic Party (PDC), banned on a technicality—or were illegal—notably the pro-Soviet and pro-Chinese communist parties. The junta formally handed over legislative powers to the new Assembly on July 20, and on July 25 the Assembly voted overwhelmingly in favour of Paz García continuing in office as provisional president, pending presidential and congressional elections in 1981, for which it drafted a new electoral law.

The presidential contest of Nov. 29, 1981, was won by Roberto Suazo Córdova of the PL, who defeated Ricardo Zúñiga Augustinus of the PN, Miguel Andonie Fernández of the PINU and Hernán Corrales Padilla of the PDC. President Suazo, who had been the PL leader since 1979 and was known to be pro–US, anti-communist and generally conservative, was sworn into office on Jan. 27, 1982, and a new constitution was promulgated.

The congressional elections were contested by several parties, including the FPH, and the allocation of seats in the new Assembly was: PL 44, PN 34, PINU three and PDC one. The PL nearly lost its majority in January 1983 when six PL deputies defected to the PN–PINU–PDC opposition, but the government maintained its control by persuading two of the dissidents and a PN deputy to leave the opposition.

At its first session on Jan. 27, 1982, the Assembly appointed the hardline police chief, Gen. Gustavo Adolfo Alvarez Martínez, as Head of the Armed Forces. This move confirmed the continued hold of the military over political life, in line with a pact made a month before the elections, in which the two front runners—Suazo and Zúñiga—had agreed with the senior command that the armed forces would retain their power of veto over cabinet appointments and their responsibility for national security, and also that there would be no investigation into cases of alleged corruption on the part of members of the outgoing government.

The armed forces had been able to retain their prominence at least partly because of the rise in guerrilla activity (see section 3.3.7), which also pre-cipitated the passage of a new anti-terrorist law in April 1982, revoking some of the civil rights and guarantees stipulated in the new constitution pro-mulgated in January. A notable addition was the introduction of a sentence of 50 years' imprisonment for hijackers, kidnappers and "those who occupy public or private places even temporarily, with the purpose of pressurizing the authorities to a decision, or who distribute subversive literature, or exhort the people to revolt". It subsequently emerged that under Alvarez the army had launched a "dirty war" against suspected subversives, and several officers who served under his command were later dismissed for their part in the campaign (see section 4.2.3).

At the request of the armed forces the government announced a series of constitutional amendments on Nov. 24, 1982, under which the role of C.–in–C. was transferred to the Head of the Armed Forces (i.e. Alvarez), while the President, who had formerly been accorded the title, became Supreme Chief, a purely ceremonial function. Earlier in November Alvarez had announced plans to restructure the army high command, after which some of his close associates were appointed to senior commands; six months previously he had removed officers critical of his "authoritarianism".

1.3.11: Removal of Gen. Alvarez

Alvarez was dismissed as C.–in–C. on March 31, 1984, and replaced on April 15 by Brig.-Gen. Walter López Reyes.[3] Although this development was apparently an internal army matter (see section 2.5.3), Alvarez (who went into exile in Miami) was also accused of plotting a coup to overthrow the elected government and of corruption, chiefly through his links to the Association for the Progress of Honduras (APROH). Founded in January 1983, APROH's principal ideology was opposition to the Sandinista government in Nicaragua (which came to power in 1979) and it favoured US military intervention in Central America. It had also been severely criticized for its links with the Unification Church (a vehemently anti-communist sect led by the South Korean Sun Myung Moon and known as the "Moonies"), which gave APROH a donation of $5,000,000 in January 1983 to help it fight "subversives". The sect, which had tried to establish itself in other Latin American countries with right-wing governments (with considerable success in Uruguay), made advances in Honduras early in 1983 until denounced by the press and the Roman Catholic Church. (APROH was outlawed in November 1984.)

1.3.12: 1985 Constitutional Crisis

In a move apparently connected with the presidential election due in November 1985, the National Assembly dismissed the Chief Justice (Manuel Arita Palomo) and four other Supreme Court justices on March 29, 1985, and announced five new appointments. President Suazo demanded the reinstatement of the five justices (who were said to be his personal friends), arrested the new Chief Justice (Ramón Valladares Soto) and accused the other four appointees of treason. (The Supreme Court held considerable authority over the conduct of the forthcoming election, and it was rumoured that Suazo was hoping either to ensure the election of his own nominee or to alter the constitution to allow for his own re-election; there had already been division within the PL over the selection of the party's presidential candidate.)

By mid–April 1985 there were fears of a coup by the armed forces to resolve the crisis, but on April 14 López Reyes announced that in spite of pressure for a coup from "certain quarters", it would not be permitted to happen: "There is nothing to be gained by a coup . . . we are going to make sure that the president lasts until the November elections." On May 10 Suazo requested the armed forces to declare a state of siege and dissolve the Assembly, but they refused. The leader of the opposition in the Assembly, José Azcona del Hoyo, commented: "Since 1929 no civilian government in Honduras has been succeeded by another one. For the last year the armed forces have been trying to stay out of politics, but now the whole country is looking to them to resolve the crisis—but they are divided."

When the trade unions threatened to call a general strike for the end of May

1985 to demand electoral reforms, Suazo was reportedly summoned to army headquarters and informed by López Reyes that unless he agreed to the army's terms he would be forced to abandon the presidency on health grounds for the rest of his term of office. Eventually on May 21 Suazo announced that Valladares would be released and the four reinstated justices replaced; he added that in the election no party would be allowed to field an official candidate, but that all nominees would be included on the ballot and receive state funds for their campaigns.

In October 1985 there was another attempt to disrupt the electoral process when a PN deputy (belonging to a PN faction which supported Suazo) tried to introduce a bill to extend the President's term and convert Congress into a constituent assembly, effectively deferring the general elections for up to two years. The attempt failed when López Reyes issued a warning to Congress that anyone pursuing it would be tried for violation of the constitution.

1.3.13: 1985 General Elections

Presidential, legislative and municipal elections held on Nov. 24, 1985, were won by the PL, which gained 67 seats in Congress (now enlarged from 82 to 132 seats), although there was considerable confusion over the election system, leading to many allegations of fraud. Only eight hours before the polls opened the National Electoral Tribunal announced that the president would be elected not by simple majority but that the leading candidate of the party with the largest presidential vote would be declared the winner. This ruling was held to favour the PL, which had four presidential candidates, while the PN had only three; the only two other candidates allowed to stand were from the PDC and the PINU. Thus the leading PL candidate, José Azcona del Hoyo, with about 27 per cent of the votes, was declared duly elected, although the leading PN candidate, Rafael Leonardo Callejas, had gained 41 per cent. This was because the aggregate share of the PL candidates was 51 per cent, whereas the total PN vote was only 45 per cent.

Azcona, who was believed to be the candidate favoured by the US administration, defeated the "official" PL candidate (i.e. Suazo's choice), Oscar Mejía Arellano, who took only 20 per cent of the vote. There was little perceptible difference between the electoral platforms of Azcona and Callejas, as both were in favour of continued US military and economic support and campaigned on anti-corruption tickets with regard to internal politics. Azcona was sworn into office on Jan. 27, 1986, and undertook to lift the country out of its worst economic crisis for 50 years and to support the Contadora process.

1.3.14: Relations with USA

Under Alvarez, Honduras became more closely aligned with US policy in Central America, particularly in the measure of support given by Honduran and US troops to the Nicaraguan contras based in Honduras (see also section 3.4.2). The United States had been instrumental in ensuring the return to civilian rule in 1982 and in mid–1984 the US ambassador to Honduras, John D. Negroponte, described Honduras as "an important model for democracy and tranquility" in the region, adding: "We in the United States have a great interest in the success of its constitutional system". By 1984, however, the Suazo government was facing economic difficulties, divisions had appeared within both major parties and there were rumours of a possible military coup, so that US support became the single most important factor for the government's stability.

Nevertheless, after the dismissal of Alvarez the Honduran army began to assert a measure of independence from the US administration. In mid–1984 the government announced that it would halt the training of Salvadorean soldiers at Puerto Castilla on the grounds that the border dispute with El Salvador had still not been resolved (see above). Moreover, in August 1984 Honduras proposed that the existing military co-operation treaty with the United States, concluded in 1954, should be renegotiated, this being subsequently coupled with a request for increased US economic and military aid. Talks on these matters were complicated by disagreement over the continued presence on Honduran soil of Nicaraguan contras, concerning whom Honduras demanded a guarantee that they would be flown out of Honduras if they ran out of money or if they were defeated in an attempted invasion of Nicaragua. Exchanges on such matters intensified following President Reagan's re-election in November 1984 and in May 1985 President Suazo paid an official visit to Washington. This resulted in the signature of a number of annexes to the 1954 treaty, in which context President Reagan gave an undertaking to "defend Honduran sovereignty and territorial integrity".

Notes

1. For further details see Norman Lewis, "Portrait of a Banana Republic", quoted in Pearce, *op. cit.*, pp.14–15.
2. For further details see Schlesinger and Kinzer, *op. cit.*, pp.68–70; Lapper, *op. cit.*, pp. 25–27.
3. See Lapper, *op. cit.*, pp. 104–09 for details of ousting of Alvarez.

1.4: EL SALVADOR

1.4.1: Chronology

1859   Brief rule by liberals

1863   Conservative rule restored after Carrera's intervention

1871   Liberal revolution

1880   Beginning of abolition of communal land ownership (completed by 1918)

1922   Formation of National Guard

1923   Formation of first permanent trade union

1929   Formation of the Society for the Defence of Coffee by leading plantation owners

1930   Formation of PCS

1931   Formation of reformist government by Araújo (*March*)
Military coup installs Martínez (*December*)

1932   Abortive peasants' revolt led by Farabundo Martí, crushed in *La Matanza*

1944   Martínez forced to resign; replaced by Castañeda

1948   Formation of PRUD
Castañeda ousted in military coup led by Osorio

1950   Presidential election won by Osorio of PRUD
New constitution promulgated

1956   Presidential election won by Lemus of PRUD, virtually unopposed

1959   Communists disenfranchised

1960   Introduction of state of siege (*September*)
Lemus overthrown and replaced by civilian-military directorate (*October*)

1961   Directorate replaced by military junta led by Rivera
In constituent elections all 54 seats gained by PCN (renamed from PRUD)
Formation of PDC
Formation of Orden by Medrano

1962   Presidential election won by Rivera of PCN unopposed
New constitution promulgated

1964   Duarte elected mayor of San Salvador
In legislative elections PCN loses overall majority in Congress
Formation of Feccas

1965   Formation of MNR

1967   Presidential election won by Sánchez of PCN

1968   Formation of UCS

1969   Four-day football war with Honduras
Formation of UNO
Formation of UDN

1970   In legislative elections PCN reverses losses of 1967
Formation of FPL–FM

1971   Formation of ERP

1972   Molina of PCN declared winner of disputed election

Attempted coup resulting in arrest and exile of Duarte (the defeated UNO candidate)

1974 In legislative elections no results given, but all PCN candidates elected
Formation of FAPU

1975 Introduction of moderate land-reform programme
ERP and FPL become active
Split within ERP results in murder of Roque Dalton
Formation of BPR and FARN
Establishment of *Socorro Jurídico*

1976 Formation of ISTA

1977 Mgr Romero consecrated Archbishop (*February*)
Murder of Grande (*March*)
Inauguration of Gen. Romero of PCN (boycotted by Church) (*June*)

1978 Formation of LP–28
Legislative elections boycotted by UNO; PCN gains 50 seats and PPS 4

1979 Formation of MLP
Gen. Romero overthrown by moderate young officers (*October*)
Formation of civilian-military junta (*October*)
USA offers military and economic assistance (*October*)

1980 Formation of second junta (*January*)
Formation of CRM (*January*)
Announcement of land-reform programme and nationalization of banks (*February*)
Mgr Romero's letter to Carter (*February*)
Assassination of Mgr Romero (*March*)
Formation of FDR (*April*)
Attempted coup by d'Aubuisson (*May*)
White's unsuccessful attempt to arrange negotiations between FDR and government (*October*)
Formation of FMLN (*October*)
Formation of FMLN–FDR (*November*)
Murder of six FDR leaders (*November*)
Murder of four US missionaries (*December*)
Reorganization of junta (*December*)
Inauguration of Duarte as president (*December*)

1981 Launch of FMLN "final offensive", and announcement of seven-member diplomatic-political commission to form a democratic revolutionary government (*January*)
Resumption of US "lethal" military aid (*January*)
Murder of ISTA president Viera and US officials Hammer and Pearlman (*January*)
FMLN–FDR declares its willingness to enter negotiations without preconditions (*June*)
Franco-Mexican recognition of FMLN–FDR as representative political force (*August*)
Formation of Arena by d'Aubuisson (*December*)

1982 First use of certification process on US aid (*January*)
Constituent elections give PDC largest number of seats, but majority held by right-wing parties (*March*)
Murder of four Dutch journalists (*March*)

Magaña elected president by Assembly (*April*)
Magaña announces Apaneca Pact (*August*)

1983   Ochoa rebellion (*January*)
Replacement of Defence Minister García by Vides Casanova (*April*)
Murder and suicide of FPL leaders "Ana María" and Carpio (*April*)
Murder of US naval officer Schaufelberger (*May*)
Formation of MUSYGES (*May*)
Talks between Zamora and Stone held in Bogotá (*July*)
Introduction of National Campaign Plan (*August*)
Reagan's veto of the certification process (*November*)
FDR moves office from Managua to Mexico City (*November*)
Promulgation of new constitution, effectively ending land-reform programme (*December*)

1984   First round presidential election (*March*)
Run-off election between Duarte and d'Aubuisson won by Duarte (*May*)
Conviction of five guardsmen for murder of four US missionaries (*May*)
Inauguration of Duarte as president (*June*)
Revocation of Phase III of land-reform programme (*June*)
Duarte government and FMLN–FDR meet for talks at La Palma (*October*)
Second round of talks (*November*)

1985   Municipal elections result in unexpected victory for PDC (*March*)
Duarte's daughter kidnapped by "Pedro Pablo Castillo Front", and released in exchange for 22 guerrillas (*September–October*)

1986   Abortive attempt to resume talks between government and FMLN–FDR at Sesori (*September*)
Earthquake in San Salvador (*October*)

1.4.2: Early History—Rise of the 14 Families

Although El Salvador[1] had for a while, under Francisco Morazán, been the political centre of the united provinces (see section 1.1.3) and therefore had strong links with federalism, like the other Central American states it came under the control of Carrera, who in 1840 installed a fellow conservative, Francisco Malespin, as president. The conservatives held power after Malespin's assassination in 1846, but in 1859 the first of the "new liberals" in Central America, Gerardo Barrios, became president. Only four years later Carrera invaded El Salvador and replaced Barrios with the conservative Francisco Dueñas. The latter stayed in power until the liberal revolution of 1871, when he was replaced by Santiago González.

In the later part of the 19th century El Salvador became increasingly dependent on its prime product and export, coffee. The amassing of land, wealth and political influence by an elite led to the country coming under the dominance of 14 families, who have controlled the country ever since. While giving the country a measure of political stability, this concentration of power in the hands of a few was rarely exercised through government office, added to which El Salvador experienced the regionally typical rise of the military to political influence. These developments weakened respect for elected government, especially as the results of many of the elections held were foregone conclusions. Moreover, the relative political stability from the 1890s to the 1920s concealed growing social problems, the main one being the vastly inequitable distribution of land.

1.4.3: Establishment of Dictatorship by Gen. Martínez—Peasants' Revolt—La Matanza

The presidential election of 1931 was won convincingly by Arturo Araujo of the Salvadorean Labour Party, the only candidate to advocate a policy of political change, including land-reform. He took office in March, with Gen. Maximiliano Hernández Martínez (another candidate in the election, who had withdrawn just before voting began) as vice-president, but his government lacked experience and soon appeared very corrupt. It also failed to meet the demands of the rural workers who wanted the immediate implementation of the promised reforms. In the face of peasant protests and demonstratíns the government imprisoned the peasant leader, Agustín Farabundo Martí, but was later forced by popular pressure to release him.

In December 1931 the army ousted the Araujo administration and installed Gen. Martínez as provisional president. The municipal elections due in January 1932 were held as scheduled, but when the Salvadorean Communist Party (PCS, formed in 1930) registered large gains the government refused to certify the results. The PCS accordingly prepared for a popular insurrection to begin on Jan. 22. The plan was discovered by the authorities and Martí was arrested on Jan. 18, but attempts to stop the insurrection failed, so on Jan. 22 a group of peasants marched on Sonsonate (a commercial centre for the coffee region in the western part of the country) and in the ensuing clash about 100 people were killed. Directed by Martínez, the army defeated the rebels and then launched a systematic purge of the left wing, eliminating PCS members and sympathizers (identified by the election lists). Martí was shot by firing squad on Feb. 1 and it is generally estimated that about 30,000 Salvadoreans were murdered in a campaign which because of its ferocity (and despite more recent atrocities) is still known as *La Matanza* (The Massacre).

Gen. Martínez then introduced an autocratic system of government, incorporating some elements of contemporary European fascism, including the following measures: (i) prohibition of immigration by Arabs, Hindus, Chinese and Blacks; (ii) laws to discourage further industrialization (to destroy the worker and peasant alliances of January 1932) and to increase the hold of the coffee growers on the national economy; (iii) the introduction of compulsory identity cards; and (iv) the placing of all print shops under government supervision. His strong economic policies, including the declaration of a moratorium on all debt, the encouragement of cotton cultivation and manufacture along the coast and the establishment of a central bank helped to stabilize the economy, but his rule was also characterized by repression and torture.

Martínez was also famous for his eccentricities, his interest in the occult and his radio broadcasts of his own singular philosophy. As the Salvadorean poet Roque Dalton recorded: "On the occasion of the outbreak of a measles epidemic in El Salvador, General Maximiliano Hernández Martínez refused to put into practice any of the modern measures for controlling epidemics or

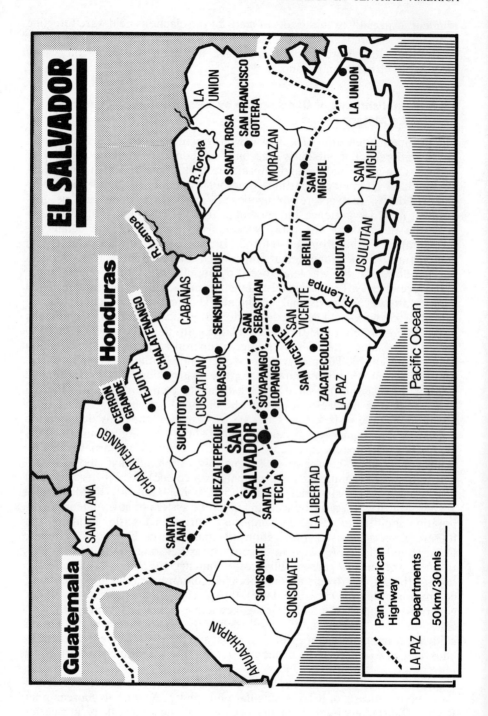

to accept the aid of international health organizations. He simply ordered that the street lights be wrapped in coloured cellophane, concluding that the multi-coloured light would be enough to purify the air and wipe out the pestilence."[2]

1.4.4: Resignation of Martínez—Election of Castañeda—Military Coup

Early in 1944 a number of discontented officers attempted to oust Martínez, but were defeated and executed. Serious opposition to the government erupted in April in the form of a general strike, during which a permanent vigil was held outside the National Palace. When the son of a US immigrant, José Wright Alcaine, was shot dead by the national police on May 7, the US government demanded an explanation, but none was forthcoming. Two days later Martínez resigned and left the country.

The high command took control and to counter a wave of strikes and demonstrations calling for political reforms, they imprisoned many labour leaders and exiled several left-wing politicians. In 1945 Gen. Salvador Castañeda Castro was elected president, taking office on March 1. A general strike called in 1946 with the intent of overthrowing him failed and the growing union organizations were forced to operate in secret. (A major influence on the Salvadorean and other right-wing Central American governments at this time was the perceived "communist threat" posed by the left-wing Arévalo government in Guatemala and by the growth of militant trade unionism in that country—see section 1.2.3.)

A split in the ruling class between those who favoured the traditional economic pattern (as encouraged by Martínez) and technocrats who wanted to modernize the economy came to a head in December 1948 when Lt.-Col. Oscar Osorio led a coup against President Castañeda and brought the modernizers to power. He repealed the anti-industry legislation and introduced strong incentives for investors in new manufacturing and commercial sectors. He also founded the Revolutionary Party of Democratic Union (PRUD) —which developed an extensive national network closely linked to the military authorities—and was elected president as the PRUD candidate in March 1950. The constitution promulgated in the same year incorporated the right to organize unions, under strict limitations, the right to strike, the establishment of a minimum wage and the introduction of social security benefits and subsidized housing, although all these rights extended only to industrial workers (in order not to antagonize the coffee plantation owners). In September 1952 Osorio declared a state of siege on the grounds of an alleged communist plot to overthrow him, and over 1,200 "left-wing extremists" were accused of belonging to communist cells and arrested. Several of them, including Salvador Cayetano Carpio (later to lead one of the major guerrilla groups), were also tortured.

1.4.5: Lemus elected President—Military Intervention—Return to Elective Government

In the presidential election of March 4, 1956, Lt.-Col. José María Lemus of the PRUD was elected virtually unopposed, as all the leading opposition candidates withdrew from the contest on Feb. 29, claiming that there had been intimidation and fraud on the part of the PRUD. Lemus took office in September and continued the right-wing policies of Osorio, disenfranchising communist adherents in December 1959. In response to disturbances by supporters of the new Cuban revolutionary leader, Fidel Castro, by students and by other government opponents, he imposed a state of siege in September 1960; the protests related to charges of corruption in the administration, the detention and torture of many government opponents and the country's poor economic performance. Lemus was removed from office on Oct. 26, 1960, in a bloodless coup, and replaced by a six-member civilian-military directorate, which charged him with having "governed out- side the law, trampled on the constitutions and the rights of citizens, com- mitted illegal acts and created a climate of general discontent".

The directorate, which consisted of junior officers and independent pro- fessionals linked to the San Salvador Catholic University, promised prompt and free elections and proposed a nationwide literacy programme. It enjoyed broad support and several demonstrations were staged in backing the re- forms, several people being killed and a number of Castro supporters arrested. However, it was ousted by a group of officers led by Col. Julio Adalberto Rivera in January 1961.

The US administration recognized the new military-civilian junta almost immediately and announced plans to send economic aid; President Kennedy subsequently expressed his approval of the Rivera coup when he said that "governments of the civil-military type of El Salvador are the most effective in containing communist penetration in Latin America", while Col. Rivera for his part was an ardent supporter of Kennedy's Alliance for Progress. It was alleged that the United States had in fact contributed to the success of the Rivera coup in order to contain what it viewed as the threat of communism spreading from Cuba.[3]

The new junta, which promised to be "constitutional, anti-communist and anti-Osorist", drafted a new electoral law and constituent elections were held in December 1961 in which all seats were won by the National Reconciliation Party (PCN), a reorganized version of the PRUD. In the presidential elec- tions of April 29, 1962, Col. Rivera was elected unopposed, polling 370,000 votes out of a total electorate of 800,000, with the other papers blank or spoiled. The opposition parties, which had participated in December 1961, boycotted the presidential contest, claiming that the government had given financial assistance to the PCN. On the abolition of the junta the constituent assembly became the National Assembly and promulgated a new con- stitution.

1.4.6: Emergence of New Political Groups—Continued Domination of PCN

The other four parties to contest the December 1961 elections were the anti- communist Authentic Constitution Party, the moderate left-wing Party of Renewal Action (PAR), the newly-formed anti-communist Christian Demo- cratic Party (PDC) and the right-wing Social Democratic Party (PDS). (The PAR, PCD and PDS had stood together as the United Democratic Party coalition.) One of the PAR leaders was Fabio Castillo, a member of the directorate of October 1960, while the PDC leaders included José Napoleón

Duarte, who was elected mayor of San Salvador in 1964. Another party formed in the 1960s was the left-wing National Revolutionary Movement (MNR), led by Guillermo Ungo.

The military hold on political life was greatly extended by the formation in 1961 of the rural vigilante National Democratic Organization (Orden), which became notorious for its treatment of anyone with left-wing connections, however remote. Orden's founder, Gen. José Alberto Medrano, said that its aim was to organize "the peasantry in order to indoctrinate them to carry out an ideological campaign on behalf of representative democracy and the free world against the dictatorial communist world". In return for their political allegiance and co-operation the organization's members received economic perks—such as employment—and the network reached so far that by the late 1970s the total membership was estimated at between 50,000 and 100,000.

The opposition parties made gains in the legislative elections of 1964, although in the 1967 presidential election the PCN candidate, Col. Fidel Sánchez Hernández, defeated Abraham Rodríguez of the PCD and the candidates of the PAR and the right-wing Salvadorean Popular Party (PPS). The outbreak of the football war against Honduras in July 1969 (see section 1.3.7) caused a surge of popularity for the government and the electoral gains for the opposition parties were reversed in the 1970 legislative elections, which left the PCN with an absolute majority in Congress (holding 30 of the 52 seats).

1.4.7: The 1972 Elections—Abortive Coup

By 1972 the excitement over the football war had abated and it appeared that the PCN might lose power to a united opposition. The outlawed PCS had formed an electoral front called the Nationalist Democratic Union (UDN) which joined with the MNR and the PDC in the National Opposition Union (UNO), with Duarte and Ungo as presidential and vice-presidential candidates respectively. In the course of the campaign UNO supporters were reportedly beaten up by Orden and by national guards; there were also allegations of corruption when some ballot boxes were found to contain not a single opposition vote. Duarte based his campaign on the slogan "a popular demand for change", promising social justice, land reform and economic policies to combat employment, while the PCN candidate, Col. Arturo Molina, concentrated mainly on denouncing Duarte as a "communist".

The Central Election Board announced on Feb. 22, 1972, firstly that Molina had won by 314,000 votes to 292,000 and then that Duarte had gained a slight majority of 321,000 against 315,000. After a three-day news blackout victory was finally given to Molina; Gen. Medrano of the right-wing Independent Democratic United Front (FUDI) and the PPS candidate gained less than five per cent of the vote between them. It was later discovered that the voting figures for some rural provinces had been tampered with by the authorities.[4]

Duarte accused the government of denying him victory fraudulently and on March 25 troops commanded by Col. Benjamin Mejía arrested President Sánchez Hernández on charges of violating the constitution. Once the coup attempt was under way Duarte allied himself with Mejía, but the two of them failed to rouse sufficient civilian support. Although Mejía had substantial backing in the army, the air force remained largely loyal to the government. In the fighting up to 200 soldiers and civilians were killed, and after Mejía's forces were defeated Col. Sánchez Hernández announced on March 28 that 53 soldiers and 25 civilians would be tried by a military tribunal. Later, on April 3, the Congress declared a state of siege. Duarte, who had fled to the Venezuelan embassy only to be seized by Salvadorean soldiers and beaten up in prison, was threatened with trial for sedition, but eventually went into exile in Guatemala (later travelling on to Venezuela). According to Fabio Castillo, the Salvadorean armed forces received assistance from Condeca and the United States to crush the rebellion.[5]

Under the Molina government, which took office in July, 1972, a deliberate attempt was made to break up the opposition and on July 19 troops arrested 800 teachers and students at the National University (15 of whom—including Fabio Castillo—were exiled), and the university was closed for two years. Allegations of government manipulation of elections increased when in the 1974 legislative elections the Central Electoral Board issued no results but simply declared all PCN candidates duly elected.

1.4.8: Formation of Guerrilla and Other Opposition Groups

The widespread disillusionment with the existing political process caused by the 1972 elections and the "disappearance" of many UNO supporters after the 1974 poll encouraged many of the government's opponents to look for alternative ways to achieve political reform. The secretary-general of the PCS, Salvador Cayetano Carpio, left the party in 1969 in protest against its support for the war against Honduras and its decision to participate in the 1972 election. He subsequently founded the Popular Liberation forces (FPL) in 1970 (for FPL and other guerrilla groups, see section 3.1.3).

There was also evidence of growing political awareness among trade unions and students. The announcement by President Molina in May 1974 of a project to build a hydroelectric dam at Cerrón Grande, flooding the homes of 15,000 rural workers, led to the formation of the United People's Action Front (FAPU) to protect the workers' rights. The main components of the group were the Christian Peasants' Federation (Feccas) and other unions, students, church organizations and teachers, as well as political parties, although there was initial disagreement over the front's purpose: some members wanted it to be a new form of grassroots mass movement, whereas the PCS, PDC and MNR wanted it to keep within the electoral system. As a result of this division FAPU in its first manifestation collapsed in less than six months.

In June and July 1975 student protests broke out in the capital over the holding of the Miss World beauty contest there at a time when the country faced such severe economic problems. Students began a protest march on July 30, after troops had invaded the National University campus at Santa Ana, but were surrounded by soldiers who opened fire. At least 20 people were taken away in ambulances (some still alive) and were never seen again, and in a strong outcry against the armed forces several hundred people occupied the metropolitan cathedral.

The events of 1975 encouraged the formation of another popular opposition movement, the People's Revolutionary Bloc (BPR), leading in turn to the reorganization of FAPU, which then established a strong base in the countryside (where poverty was greater and land reform a pressing issue). Between November 1974 and May 1975 the National Guard killed 13 peasants involved in protests over the government's land-reform programme (see section 2.3.3). The growing unrest among the rural labourers caused a sharp reaction among the wealthy landowners, especially when on Dec. 5, 1976, a group of peasants marched on the house of the Orellana family (one of the 14 families), complaining that the Orellanas had been adequately compensated for their land submerged in a dam project, whereas the peasants had received nothing. Two members of the family appeared outside the house and in a moment of confusion one of them was shot (although precise responsibility could not be attributed). The landowner took reprisals against Feccas and "communist priests", accusing them of fomenting rebellion (for campaign against rural priests, who identified with the peasants' cause, see section 2.4.5).

1.4.9: Election of Gen. Romero

The presidential elections of Feb. 20, 1977, were won by the PCN candidate, Gen. Carlos Humberto Romero (who as Defence Minister since 1972 had direct responsibility for Orden), with the slogan "democracy or communism". When it was announced that Gen. Romero had gained 812,281 votes against 394,661 for the UNO candidate, Col. Ernesto Claramount Rozeville, out of a total electorate of about 1,800,000, the UNO claimed that 400,000 names on the electoral register were false (other sources set the number at 150,000) and a week of demonstrations in the capital broke out, involving nearly 50,000 people. The government sent in the National Guard on Feb. 28 to clear the demonstrators with water cannon and tear gas, and many were reportedly shot dead as troops sealed off the main square.[6] Claramount was deported to Costa Rica and a state of siege imposed for nine months. In commemoration of those who died a new guerrilla organization was formed, the People's Leagues—28 February (LP–28).

The unrest continued, especially after the murder on Sept. 16, 1977, of the rector of the National University, Carlos Alfaro Castillo, by the FPL. On the following day the General Association of Salvadorean University students (AGEUS) issued a statement describing Castillo as "a hated landlord, oligarch, author of countless outrages and insults against students, teachers and university workers". Carlos Humberto Siguenza was appointed his successor on Sept. 19, but the next day he resigned after receiving death threats and left the country.

In an attempt to improve El Salvador's image abroad and to stop the flow of information to foreign human rights organizations, a new public order law was introduced on Nov. 27, 1977, prohibiting demonstrations, strikes which "prejudice the national economy", "subversive" meetings, and propaganda which "threatens the social order". The law also made it a crime to "spread at home or send abroad, by word of mouth, writing or by any other means, false or tendentious news or information destined to disturb the constitutional legal order, the tranquility and security of the country, the economic or monetary system or the stability of its value or public effects", and granted the authorities powers to detain people adhering to "totalitarian" ideals.

In the campaign for the legislative election of March 12, 1978, political rallies were banned, and there was a low level of participation (under 50 per cent) as only the PCN and the PPS took part. The PCN won 50 seats and the PPS, which had presented candidates in only seven of the country's 14 departments, took four, claiming that the electoral tribunal was biased in favour of the PCN. The boycott by the PCD was also supported by the FPL, which launched a sabotage campaign against the election.

1.4.10: The 1979 Revolution—Formation of First Junta

By early 1979 it was clear that the nation was seriously divided and that if civil war were to be averted there was a need for immediate concessions from the government. In February 1979 the public order law of November 1977 was repealed, while in March the National Association of Private Enterprise (ANEP), Gen. Romero's main civilian support, called for peace and for the correction of "errors which have been committed". In a television broadcast of May 17 Gen. Romero called for a national dialogue to be held with the moderate opposition, excluding the BPR; however, the UNO refused because of what it termed "the contradiction between the declaration of an opening of dialogue and the reality of the repression which the country is suffering". A state of siege was imposed on May 23 after the murder of the Education Minister, Carlos Herrera Rebollo of the PDC, by gunmen claiming to belong to the FPL.

Gen. Romero lifted the state of siege on July 24, 1979, and on Aug. 16 announced a general amnesty for political exiles. He gave an undertaking that the status of political prisoners would be reviewed, and invited the OAS to supervise the legislative election due in 1980. These measures, however, did not go far enough to satisfy the opposition and between August and October there was a sequence of anti-government protests. Moreover, the tide of political violence continued to rise, claiming the lives of about 550 people in the first nine months of the year, while the victory of the Sandinistas in Nicaragua in July made a compromise solution seem yet more remote.

Amid rumours of an imminent coup by right-wing elements, a group of young moderate officers led by Col. Jaime Abdul Gutiérrez and Col. Adolfo Arnoldo Majano took over on Oct. 15, 1979, and ordered Gen. Romero to leave, whereupon the latter departed for Guatemala along with a few other leading politicians and senior officers. Gutiérrez and Majano described El Salvador as being in a state of "true economic and social disaster", and on Oct. 17 they established a "revolutionary junta". The latter body included two progressive politicians, namely Ungo (of the MNR) and Román Mayorga Quiroz (a university rector), as well as a representative of the private sector (Mario Antonio Andino), apparently at the insistence of the United States. None of the junta members had any previous political experience.

The junta dissolved Congress and suspended the Supreme Court, and promised free elections, an amnesty for all political prisoners and exiles, freedom to form a political party of any complexion, respect for trade union liberties and the dismantling of Orden (although this last undertaking remained largely a nominal measure and Orden continued to operate without restraint). The junta also appealed to extremists on both left and right to end the violence and abide by the will of the majority. The cabinet formed on Oct.

23 included representatives of the PCS and PDC as well as a former political prisoner. One of the PCS ministers, Gabriel Gallegos Valdes (labour and social security), said that his party (which was still illegal) supported the junta "because we believe it is going to comply with its promises and open the possibility of democratizing the country".

The new government was generally well-received, in particular by the PDC leader, José Antonio Morales Erlich. It also received qualified support from the Archbishop of San Salvador, Mgr Oscar Arnulfo Romero y Galdames, who said: "We recognize the junta's good will, but this government can deserve the confidence and collaboration of the people when it shows that its beautiful promises are not dead letters, but rather real hope that a new era has begun for our country." In contrast, the left-wing formations protested over the continuation of military rule, especially when on Oct. 16 the armed forces stormed five factories occupied by BPR members since the week before the coup, killing 18 and detaining a further 78 (some of whom were reportedly tortured). In another incident immediately after the coup members of the security forces opened fire on a demonstration organized by FAPU, BPR and LP–28 calling for higher wages, lower prices for consumer goods, land reform, public trials of Romero's officers and disclosure of the whereabouts of the "disappeared". Within three days of the coup at least 28 people had lost their lives in political violence, which continued after the government on Oct. 23 lifted a state of siege and a curfew declared on Oct. 16.

The junta was caught between the demand for immediate reforms made in the popular demonstrations and the antagonism from the traditional ruling class to change, even to moderate reforms such as the raising of the minimum wage for fieldworkers by 30 per cent to $4.50 a day. The young officers were neither as radical nor as strong as, for example, the Sandinistas in Nicaragua; wary of fullscale revolution and lacking any real power base, they came increasingly under the influence of the more hardline officers, especially Col. Guillermo García (the new Defence Minister) and Col. Carlos Eugenio Vides Casanova (who succeeded García in the defence portfolio in April 1983 after the Ochoa military rebellion (see section 2.5.4).

In a realignment of the country's foreign policy the government said that measures should be taken to increase ties with Nicaragua and to re-establish relations with Cuba (which had been broken in 1961). On Nov. 28, 1979, diplomatic relations with South Africa were severed.

1.4.11: Formation of Second Junta

The junta disintegrated in January 1980 when on Jan. 1 it failed to meet an ultimatum presented by the cabinet that it show concrete proof of willingness to initiate political and economic reforms, halt its swing to the right and take full control of the security forces. The ministers also demanded the expulsion from the junta of Andino, who as the representative of private enterprise was regarded as being partly responsible for this rightwards shift. Salvador Samayoa (Minister of Education) and Enrique Alvarez Córdova (Minister of Agriculture) had resigned on Dec. 29, 1979, declaring: "We see now that this political project was, from the very beginning, a manoeuvre against the people. But we do not regret having participated in this government, having put all our efforts and skills towards a different outcome. But now that everything is clear, we would regret for the rest of our lives any further collaboration."[7] Ungo and Mayorga then issued their own ultimatum and resigned on Jan. 3, while Andino resigned the next day. Four days afterwards Samayoa announced that he intended to join the FPL. The collapse of the junta was followed on Jan. 11 by the formation of a united opposition, the Revolutionary Co-ordinating Council of the Masses (CRM), by the BPR, LP–28, FAPU, Nationalist Democratic Union (UDN) and the Movement for Popular Liberation (MLP).

After hastily-conducted negotiations the PDC agreed to join a new junta on the condition that changes were made in the security forces, that a dialogue was opened with the left-wing guerrillas and that all private business representatives were excluded from the government. The second junta was formed on Jan. 9 with Morales Erlich, Héctor Dada Hirezi (hitherto Foreign Minister) and José Ramón Avalos Navarrete (nominally an independent) replacing Ungo, Mayorga and Andino. The same day Majano and Gutiérrez issued a new programme of economic and social reforms dealing with education, health services and housing. They promised that elections would be held as soon as possible and undertook to enter into "constructive dialogue" with the left.

After the decision by its party leadership to join the junta, the PDC began to divide into two tendencies, with a right-wing faction under Duarte and a more left-wing group more committed to dialogue. A prominent member of the left-wing tendancy, Mario Zamora Rivas (the Attorney-General), was murdered on Feb. 23, when gunmen burst into his home and shot him dead; only a few days earlier, Maj. Roberto d'Aubuisson Arrieta (who had recently retired from the army but was closely associated with the activities of right-wing paramilitary groups, especially the death squads) had denounced Zamora in a television broadcast as a clandestine member of the guerrillas. The PDC publicly accused d'Aubuisson of responsibility for the murder but no arrests were made and d'Aubuisson was not even interrogated. Disillusioned with the party, Zamora's brother Rubén (Minister of the Presidency) and other leading party members resigned, and with about 20 per cent of the PDC membership formed the Social Christian Popular Movement (MPSC) in March.

The division within the party, exacerbated by Zamora's assassination, extended to the junta when on March 3 Dada Hirezi resigned in protest and left the country, stating as his reasons: "We have not been able to stop the repression, and those committing acts of repression in defiance of the junta go unpunished. . . . The promised dialogue with the popular organizations fails to materialize, and the chances for enacting reforms with the support of the people are receding beyond reach."[8]

Despite the announcement on March 6 of a new land-reform programme and the nationalization of the banking system, the junta continued to lose support within El Salvador, especially as the political violence continued to rise with a death toll of 10 a day by March. In such circumstances, the junta had to rely increasingly on its main strength, namely US economic and military assistance and political solidarity.

1.4.12: Assassination of Archbishop Romero

The most celebrated victim of the violence during this period was Archbishop Romero, who was shot dead by unknown assailants on March 24, 1980, while saying mass in the metropolitan cathedral. Although no-one was brought to trial, it was widely held that the murder had been instigated by d'Aubuisson. (White, the US ambassador, told the Senate Foreign Relations Committee in April 1981 that he had "compelling if not 100 per cent conclusive evidence" of d'Aubuisson's responsibility. Duarte ordered the major's arrest in 1981, but he fled to Guatemala, returning later in the year to contest the 1982 election.) The judge in charge of the murder investigation, Atilio Ramírez Amaya, was himself threatened with assassination and fled the country.

When appointed to the archbishopric in 1977 Mgr Romero (no relation to Gen. Romero) was regarded as a conservative, but he gradually became more and more outspoken against social injustice and human rights violations, and the cathedral developed into a focal point for the defence of human rights (see also sections 2.4.5 and 4.2.4). It was apparently his denunciation of the death squads which led to his death; in his sermon on the day before he died he spoke in defence of the CRM and addressed the soldiers and security forces with the following words: "Brothers . . . we are the same people. The peasants you kill are your own brothers and sisters. . . . It is time that you come to your senses and obey your conscience rather than follow a sinful command. . . . In the name of God, stop the repression."[9]

The killing caused deep shock both at home, where a three-day period of national mourning was decreed, and internationally. The funeral, which took place in the cathedral on March 30 was charged with emotion, and as Romero's body was carried out there was a shout of one of the left-wing slogans: "The people united shall never be defeated" (*El pueblo unido jamás será vencido*). Simultaneously a bomb exploded at the National Palace and the crowd outside tried to enter the cathedral for safety. There was also gunfire, and in the resultant stampede 26 people died and about 200 were wounded.

1.4.13: Formation of United Political Opposition Front—Further Splits within Government

Early in April 1980 the MNR and MPSC joined with nine trade union organizations and the two universities (National and Catholic) to form the Democratic Front. The Front united with the CRM on April 18 in the Democratic Revolutionary Front (FDR) led by Alvarez Córdova (for its political platform, see appendix 1). Like the CRM in January, the FDR was launched on the campus of the National University, which operated as a refuge for government critics and housed offices for all the popular organizations. In November 1980 the FDR joined in a political-military front with the new guerrilla united command, the Farabundo Martí National Liberation Front (FMLN—see section 3.1.4). In the same month Alvarez Córdova and four other FDR leaders were murdered (ibid.) and Ungo became FDR secretary-general.

It was reported in the first week of May 1980 that d'Aubuisson had led an unsuccessful coup attempt against the junta, having previously circulated a video tape to military garrisons denouncing Majano and Morales Erlich as communists. Majano issued an order for the major's arrest on May 8, but found himself facing the opposition of the senior command, which on May 9 voted to replace him as C.–in–C. by Col. García. D'Aubuisson was released on May 13 when the authorities announced that they had insufficient evidence to keep him in detention.

The government encountered another blow to its fading prestige when the US administration suspended all aid after the discovery near San Salvador of the bodies of four US missionaries on Dec. 4; they had apparently been raped and then killed by members of the security forces (for attempts to trace and prosecute those responsible, see section 4.2.4). This suspension of aid precipitated a reorganization of the junta: Majano was dismissed, and on Dec. 22 Duarte and Gutiérrez were sworn in as president and vice-president respectively. US economic aid was restored on Dec. 17 (although military aid was still withheld), after the murders had been denounced by Duarte and Morales as a "strategic crime" intended to destabilize the country. The removal of Majano was the culmination of a growing division between him and the more right-wing Gutiérrez; other prominent right-wing figures included García and the deputy Defence Minister, Col. Nicolás Carranza.

In protest over the imposition of a state of siege in March 1980 after the occupation of the Venezuelan embassy in San Salvador (see section 3.3.3) the FDR staged strikes on June 24–25 and Aug. 13–15 which succeeded in closing up to 90 per cent of businesses. In response to a strike by 1,500 power workers on Aug. 21 (as a demonstration against government policy) the government declared a state of national emergency on Aug. 23 and placed the supply and communications network under military control. By August the government had taken preventive measures against industrial unrest by amending the criminal code to make the occupation of public buildings such as churches a "terrorist crime". Throughout the actions there was a heavy police presence wherever the strikers rallied.

The strike of Aug. 13–15 had originally been scheduled to take place in July but had been postponed after the National University was closed; on June 27 the government ordered the army to enter the university (which they did using tanks), claiming that it was being used as a guerrilla training ground. In the ensuing clashes 16 students were killed and the popular movements suffered a severe blow to their communications network, for which the university had been the main centre.

1.4.14: Beginning of Civil War

The FMLN launched its first major military offensive against the government forces on Jan. 10, 1981, when fighting broke out in the departments of Chalatenango, San Vincente and Morazán. A strike was called for Jan. 15 to enable people to declare their sympathy with the guerrillas and 20,000 public employees walked out; however, the action faded with many union leaders imprisoned and some later appearing on army mortality lists as "subversives killed in combat". By the end of January the offensive, which had hardly touched any urban areas, had been turned back, with the guerrillas suffering from a lack of experience and equipment; nevertheless, they regrouped after retreating and by late 1981 it was evident that the Salvadorean armed forces would be unable to gain an outright victory relying solely on its own resources and manpower.

The FMLN had announced its intention of beginning hostilities in December 1980 in order to consolidate the opposition before President Reagan took up his first term of office in January 1981. The election of Reagan was clearly regarded as a boost by the right wing, and on election night in November 1980 a mutilated body was found in the streets of San Salvador bearing the sign: "With Reagan we will eliminate the miscreants and subversives in El Salvador and Central America."

The FDR formally announced from its base in Mexico City on Jan. 14, 1981, that it had formed a seven-member diplomatic-political commission to seek to establish a "democratic revolutionary government"; members of the commission included Ungo, Samoyoa and Ruben Zamora. The FDR also called for direct negotiations with the United States, which it believed carried a "quota of responsibility" for the crisis in the country, had been "demonstrated to be the power behind the Salvadorean throne", and had "contributed to the radicalization and polarization of the process". The US administration refused to enter negotiations and advised the FDR to speak directly to the Salvadorean government. (This debate over who was responsible was to figure prominently in the future discussions and attempts at dialogue between the two sides—see section 6.4.1.)

The announcement made on Aug. 28, 1981, by the French and Mexican governments that they recognized the FMLN–FDR as a "representative political force" originally prompted new hope for a political settlement as the junta had so far refused to negotiate with the guerrillas, and also drew the question of El Salvador further into the international arena. The junta, however, rejected the Franco–Mexican initiative on Aug. 30 as interference in the country's internal affairs.

1.4.15: 1982 Constituent Elections

The junta announced on Oct. 15, 1980, that constituent elections would be held in 1982 in preparation for a handover to an elected government in 1983. On March 5, 1981, Duarte created a three-man electoral commission to oversee the process and in July the government approved measures on the registration and participation of political parties. All four existing legal parties—i.e. the PDC, the PCN, the PPS and the Popular Orientation Party (POP) led by Gen. Medrano—would be able to apply for registration; the FDR would also be eligible if it agreed to break its links with the FMLN.

Two additional right-wing parties were founded in late 1981: one was the National Republican Alliance (Arena), formed by d'Aubuisson after his return from Guatemala; the other was Democratic Action (AD) led by Rene Fortín Magaña, which grouped business interests favouring limited land reform and was committed to the maintenance of private property. The formation of AD reflected a disaffection for the Duarte government on the part of the private sector, which the President had described in July as being the greatest threat to the government's reform programme. A group of nine businessmen announced on July 30 the conclusion of a "national unity pact" to press for changes in government policy and for a greater voice for the business community in government decision-making.

Meanwhile the political violence continued to grow from both sides and the toll for violent deaths in 1981 was given by the independent Salvadorean human rights commission as 16,276 (although the US embassy in San Salvador asserted that the figure was only 6,116). The country had again earned international notoriety with the murder on March 17 of four Dutch journalists (Jacobus Andries Koster, Jan Kuiper, Johannes Willemsen and Hans ter Laan), apparently at the hands of the armed forces. The journalists had been in El Salvador to film a guerrilla group, and according to the Dutch parliamentary report they had "either run coincidentally into an army patrol or had been lured into an ambush by the army patrol". Duarte said that he was "perfectly satisfied" that the deaths were accidental, but this declaration was decried by those who pointed out that on the very same day one of the death squads—the Maximiliano Hernández Martínez Anti-communist Alliance—had issued a death list with the names of 34 journalists (mostly foreign, although not including the four Dutchmen).

The election campaign opened on Jan. 28, 1982, in preparation for the voting on March 28, but was boycotted by all left-wing groups. In December 1981 the FMLN had announced that although it was prepared to enter dialogue it would not suspend its military activities for the elections. To allow campaigning to take place the government lifted the curfew and eased restrictions imposed under the state of siege in October 1981, but the curfew and the restrictions were reimposed a month after the election on April 28. Members of the armed and security forces were forbidden to vote and the official rate of abstention was given as 26 per cent.

The elections received substantial backing from the United States. The US ambassador, Deane Hinton, said on March 16 that the continuance of US aid depended on commitments by the new government for social and economic reforms, while on March 29 Secretary of State Haig described the elections as an indication of "the Salvadorean people's commitment to the power of the Salvadorean democratic vision". The elections were, however, wide open to abuse; since the electoral registers were out of date citizens were allowed to vote on production of their identity cards; moreover, there were reports of people being stopped just before voting and deprived of the identity cards by various armed groups. Lord Chitnis, acting as an independent observer for the British Parliamentary Human Rights Group, stated: "My conclusion is that the election in El Salvador is so fundamentally flawed as to be invalid. The election complicated the political problems of the country, made life worse for the people in it, and has caused the deaths of people who, without the election, would still be alive."

Although the PDC gained the largest number of seats, winning 24 against 19 for Arena, 14 for the PCN, two for the AD and one for the PPS, it did not gain a majority and lost any hope of being the dominant party in the new assembly when the five right-wing parties signed an agreement on March 30 to form a "government of national unity". This agreement specified (i) a rejection of "communism" as the model of society proposed—as they claimed—by the PDC; (ii) support for parliamentary democracy and free enterprise; (iii) a commitment to human rights and social justice; (iv) a continuation of the reforms begun by the previous government; and (v) an undertaking that there would be no revenge or retribution for acts of political violence. Duarte insisted that the PDC should have some role in the new government and on April 2 d'Aubuisson (who had increased his political influence in the election) said that the right-wing parties would allow the PDC to participate in the government but would not let Duarte continue as president. On April 20 the US Senate foreign relations committee warned that any Salvadorean government excluding the PDC would not be seen as credible by the United States (for US policy, see section 5.1.2).

1.4.16: Formation of Magaña Government—Apaneca Pact

The new Assembly met for its preliminary session on April 22, 1982, and elected d'Aubuisson as its president. The Assembly formally opened on April 26, but was boycotted by the PDC, the junta and the armed forces, who were worried that the limited role given to the PDC would make the United States less willing to maintain its economic—and more particularly its military—aid to the country. The Assembly decided to adopt the 1962 constitution for reference pending the draft of a new document and effectively abandoned the second phase of the land-reform programme (in direct contravention of the strict terms of the national unity pact).

Three days later the Assembly met to vote on the three candidates for the national presidency nominated by the armed forces. Alvaro Magaña, leader of the moderate AD and thus effectively politically independent, was elected by 36 votes to 17, ahead of the Arena and PCN candidates. D'Aubuisson accused Gutiérrez of imposing on the Assembly "his personal decision to put Alvaro Magaña in the presidency" in spite of a "categorical no" from the Arena deputies. Magaña was sworn into office on May 2, and on May 17 he became C.-in-C. replacing Gutiérrez who was forced into retirement. In the cabinet formed by Magaña on May 14 the PDC was given three portfolios (foreign affairs, education and labour and social welfare), while Arena and the PCN gained four portfolios each and two independents were included (in addition to García, who continued as Defence Minister).

President Magaña launched a political initiative on Aug. 3, 1982, called the Apaneca Pact (after the town where it was signed), drawn up by him and signed by representatives of the PDC, Arena, PCN, AD and PPS, providing for the establishment of (i) a political commission to prepare for further elections and the consequent transfer of power; (ii) a human rights commission (the first such official body); and (iii) a peace commission to draft an amnesty proposal. The pact did not, however, unite the parties, which differed chiefly over the question of negotiations with the FMLN. Although the government claimed to be open to the possibility of negotiations, it nevertheless moved against the left-wing, and it was reported on Oct. 22, 1982, that five leaders—Luis Menjívar (MPSC), Jorge Herrera, David Elias Guadrón and Mauricio Domenech Velásquez (MNR) and Carlos Molina of the National University—had been arrested. Three days later the Ministry of Defence said that eight men (including Menjívar, Domenech and Molina) had been detained and would be tried "for being leaders of terrorist delinquent groups which have brought pain to the Salvadorean family".

There was a realignment of the parties in October 1982 when a major part of the PCN split from the main party to form the more right-wing Salvadorean Authentic Institutional Party (PAIS/PAISA), leaving those in favour of negotiations with a very slender majority (i.e. PDC 24, PCN 5, AD 2) over those opposing any compromise with the FMLN (Arena 19, PAISA 9 and PPS one).

The political commission failed to meet its deadline of Sept. 30, 1982, for setting an election date; although the US administration pressed for a date as early as possible, Magaña said that it would not be feasible to hold elections before 1984. The Salvadorean government also said that there would be difficulties in financing the poll and in compiling a new electoral register. The United States promised to help in both of these matters.

Magaña announced on Feb. 23, 1983, that an amnesty commission had been formed "to create the conditions for social and political justice and a programme for peace as soon as possible"; a new amnesty bill passed into law on May 4. The law covered any political prisoner or civilian involved in the fighting (although not deserters from guerrilla units), specifying that if such persons applied within 60 days they would be issued with special identity cards or passports to enable them to leave the country. Human rights groups censured the plan, claiming that possession of the special identity cards could be virtual death warrants to the holders from either the guerrillas or the armed forces, while the FMLN denounced the whole scheme as a propaganda gesture because of the visit of Pope John Paul II to the country in March (see section 2.4.2). It was reported in mid-August 1983 that 1,114 people had been amnestied, and that half of them had been political prisoners while the other half were described as "persons in arms or collaborators".

1.4.17: Promulgation of Constitution—Presidential Elections

By mid-June 1983 the commission formed to draft a new constitution had completed its work except for the matters of the date of transfer to an elected government and land-reform—the two most crucial political issues. The new constitution was finally approved on Dec. 14, taking effect on Dec. 20, and officially ended the state of siege in operation almost continuously since 1980. The matter of elections had been controversial as the PDC, Arena and PAISA had all wanted immediate presidential elections, whereas the smaller parties (PCN, AD and PPS) wanted simultaneous presidential, legislative and local elections; it was not until Nov. 22 that the larger parties had prevailed and settled on the date of March 25, 1984, for sole presidential elections. The land-reform issue was not resolved until Dec. 13, when the programme was effectively halted by the acceptance of an Arena proposal (for further details, see section 2.3.4).

The candidates in the first round of the 1984 presidential election were Duarte for the PDC (selected as early as April 1983 in preference to Foreign Minister Fidel Chávez Menz), d'Aubuisson for Arena, Francisco José Guerrero for the PCN, Fortín of AD, Francisco Quiñónez Avila of the PPS, Col. Roberto Escobar García of PAISA, Gilberto Trujillo of POP and Juan Ramón Rosales of a new party, the Stable Republican Centrist Movement (Merecen). Duarte had the support of the centrist Popular Democratic Union (UPD)—a trade union federation with about 400,000 members, which received considerable financial assistance from the United States—and based his campaign on a call for a new political structure to replace that of the military domination which, he claimed, lay at the root of the country's current crisis. D'Aubuisson based his campaign on denouncing the PDC as communist, referring disparagingly to "poor mad Duarte, a willing tool of Moscow". For his part, Guerrero claimed to be a moderate with the support of much of the private sector (and was thought to have the backing of the high command and of the United States).

In the poll Duarte gained 43 per cent, d'Aubuisson 30 per cent, Guerrero 19 per cent and the other candidates less than 10 per cent between them, forcing a run-off election on May 6 between Duarte and d'Aubuisson. In the first round the voting turnout was about 55 per cent, and of the 1,400,000 votes cast over 100,000 were declared void. The process did not run smoothly, with many polling stations reporting that they had no papers or no boxes; the Central Election Council (CCE) said that 760 of the 6,598 boxes issued had not been used because of maladministration or civil disturbance. Although the United States had supplied a computerized register at the cost of $10,000,000 (the old one having been found to contain 92,000 errors), many of the staff did not know how to use it and at 3.00 pm on March 25 the CCE announced that officials would be allowed to revert to the former system of identity cards. The new register was used in the second round on May 6 and the voting was generally reported to be far less chaotic, with a turnout of nearly 80 per cent, although the number of municipalities in which voting was disrupted by guerrilla sabotage was put at 45 by the army and 91 by the guerrillas out of the total 261.

In the run-off Duarte gained 53.6 per cent of the vote and was declared the winner. Arena had hoped that Guerrero would transfer his support to d'Aubuisson to ensure a right-wing victory, to which end d'Aubuisson offered the PCN four portfolios in an Arena government; however, Guerrero said that he regarded Arena's policies as "too radical, too intransigent" and on April 16 declared himself neutral. The army high command backed Duarte in the second round, fearing that if d'Aubuisson were elected he might try to take personal control of the armed forces and that the United States might suspend aid because of d'Aubuisson's notoriety; in April the officers sent both candidates a letter warning that whoever won the election the army would retain military authority. The FMLN called the election a farce and refused to halt hostilities, and Archbishop Arturo Rivera y Damas (Mgr Romero's successor) remarked shortly before the vote that "this is not a process headed towards democracy".

Arena claimed that the election had been fraudulent and alleged that the CIA had worked against d'Aubuisson; it was unofficially reported in Washington on May 11, 1984, that the CIA had given $960,000 to the PDC and $437,000 in a bid to prevent d'Aubuisson's election, although President Reagan denied that "any agency" of the US government had interfered. The election resulted in a split in Arena, with a substantial section breaking away under the leadership of Hugo Barrera (d'Aubuisson's running-mate in the 1984 presidential election), who in May 1985 formed a new party called Free Fatherland (*Patria Libre*). Increasingly reported as a liability because of his notoriety, d'Aubuisson resigned as Arena leader in September 1985 (becoming honorary president) and was replaced by Alfredo Cristiani.

1.4.18: Inauguration of President Duarte—Negotiations with FMLN-FDR

Duarte was inaugurated on June 1, 1984, and pledged his government to the elimination of the death squads and to "humanizing" the war to curb the complaints of human rights abuses committed by the armed forces. Archbishop

Rivera y Damas gave a very qualified welcome to these undertakings, saying: "People's expectations are very high, and their frustrations will be all the greater if mechanisms are not speedily set in motion to convert these promises and fine words into reality." During the campaign Duarte had been criticized by the right wing for what they saw as his conciliatory line towards the guerrillas, but in his inaugural speech he moderated this stance when he called on all Salvadoreans to "acknowledge that our homeland is immersed in an armed conflict which . . . has gone beyond our borders and has become a focal point in the struggle between the big world power blocs, [so that] with the aid of Marxist governments like Nicaragua, Cuba and the Soviet Union an army has been trained and armed and has violated our homeland".

Under pressure from the UPD and the United States Duarte announced on Oct. 8, 1984, that he was prepared to enter negotiations with representatives of the FMLN-FDR (having in June rejected a guerrilla proposal for a ceasefire). The UPD had become more outspoken and critical since Duarte's victory and was calling for dialogue with the guerrillas as the only way to solve the country's economic and social problems, while the US administration wanted to present the new government in a favourable light to the US Congress in order to gain its approval for extra military aid. (Early in 1986 the UPD withdrew its support for Duarte because of his failure to implement promised social reforms and became the main component of a new centre-left labour organization, the National Unity of Salvadorean Workers—UNTS.) During the subsequent talks, however, both the armed forces and the guerrillas were eager to prove that they were talking from a position of strength and there were a number of armed incidents (for further details, see section 6.4.5; for details of US debate over military aid, see sections 5.1.2 and 5.2.4).

After the first round of talks Duarte faced the scepticism of the left wing, which said that his stance offered nothing new, while the right wing and the army high command totally opposed any negotiations. D'Aubuisson even toured the army barracks to speak against the talks, which he called "a smokescreen to deceive the people". The main domestic support for the dialogue came from the unions, the church and human rights groups, which held a special joint "pilgrimage" for peace in San Miguel.

By January 1985 the immediate prospects for substantive negotiations had faded, as the government delayed further rounds, ostensibly waiting (for the outcome) of the legislative and municipal elections due in March (see section 6.4.5). These elections resulted in a surprise victory for the PDC, giving them 33 seats in the Assembly and control of 156 of the 262 municipalities. In the election campaign the PDC accused Arena (which formed a temporary coalition with the PCN) of financing itself with receipts from the drug trade, while Arena claimed that the recent murder of some right-wing politicians had been carried out not by the guerrillas as generally held but by "the green squads" (i.e. the PDC). When the results were declared Arena declared them fraudulent and called for a new election, accusing the armed forces of manipulating the electoral process; however, in a broadcast on May 1 the entire army high command stated that the will of the voters would be respected.

1.4.19: Increased Political Violence

There was an increase in the activity of the death squads from late 1984, in response to the death in November in an aircrash of Lt.-Col. Domingo Monterosa (see also section 3.3.5). A plea by Archbishop Rivera y Damas for a Christmas truce was accepted by the guerrillas, who declared a unilateral ceasefire over the Christmas and New Year holidays. Overall military activity, however, did not decline, and the armed forces gained the military initiative in the first part of the year in a series of sweeping exercises, while the guerrillas intensified their sabotage campaign (see section 3.3.5).

Notes

1. Joan Didion, *Salvador*, London, Chatto and Windus, 1983, p. 72, records that El Salvador was so uncertain of its identity at independence that it petitioned for full admission to the United States, but was refused.
2. Quoted in Armstrong and Shenk, *op. cit.*, p.31.
3. *Ibid.*, pp.41–43.
4. *Ibid.*, p.62.
5. Pearce, *op. cit.*, p.216.
6. Armstrong and Shenk, *op. cit.*, p.88.
7. *Ibid.*, p.130.
8. *Ibid.*, p.141.
9. *Ibid.*, p.149; see also William Purcell, *Martyrs of Our Time*, Oxford, Mowbray, 1983, pp.153–60.

1.5: NICARAGUA

1.5.1: Chronology

1852   Managua becomes capital
1855   Invasion by Walker to aid liberals
1857   Walker overthrown; conservative rule restored
1860   Under Treaty of Managua Britain given protectorate of Mosquito coast
1893   Zelaya comes to power
1894   Last British intervention on Mosquito Coast
1906   Britain relinquishes all claims to Mosquito Coast
1909   Revolt led by Estrada
1910   Estrada takes Managua, replaces Zelaya as president
1911   Estrada resigns; conservative rule restored by Diaz
       Knox-Castillo Treaty places country under US protection
1912   US marines arrive
1916   Bryan-Chamorro Treaty confirms status as US protectorate
       Conservative Emiliano Chamorro elected president
1921   Conservative Diego Manuel Chamorro elected
1925   Conservative Solorzano elected
       US marines withdrawn
       Left-wing revolt led by Moncada
1926   US marines return
       At US instigation Diaz made president
1927   Tipitapa agreements provide basis for US occupation and election of 1928
1928   Liberal Moncada elected president
       Sandino launches guerrilla warfare
1932   Liberal Sacasa elected president
1933   Withdrawal of all US troops after establishing National Guard under Somoza
1934   Murder of Sandino
1936   Sacasa removed by Somoza's forces
       Presidential election won by Somoza of PLN
1938   Somoza takes office for an eight-year term
1947   Argüello elected president; replaced by Lescayo
       Román y Reyes elected
1950   Death of Román y Reyes; Somoza re-elected
       New constitution promulgated
1956   Assassination of Somoza; National Assembly votes in favour of his son Luis completing term of office until 1957
1957   Luis Somoza elected president
1960   Resolution of border dispute with Honduras
1961   Formation of FSLN by Fonseca Amador, Borge and Mayorga
1963   Schick of PLN elected president
1966   Death of Schick; term completed by Guerrero

1967 Anastasio Somoza of PLN elected
      Death of Luis Somoza
1971 Congress dissolves itself, abrogates the constitution and transfers
      executive power to Somoza, pending new constitution
1972 Constituent elections; new constitution drafted (*February*)
      Somoza succeeded by triumvirate and named Supreme Army Comman-
      der (*May*)
      Earthquake followed by declaration of martial law (*December*)
      Somoza appointed chairman of National Emergency Committee
      (*December*)
1974 Promulgation of new constitution (*April*)
      Formation of Udel (*mid-year*)
      Somoza re-elected (*September*)
      FSLN raid in Managua (*December*)
1977 Martial law lifted (*September*)
      Formation of Group of 12 (Los Doce) (*October*)
      FSLN offensive (*October*)
1978 Murder of Pedro Joaquín Chamorro halts proposed dialogue (*January*)
      Troops sent in to break national strike (*January*)
      Formation of MDN (*April*)
      Formation of FAO (*July*)
      FSLN commando occupies National Palace (*August*)
      National strike (*August-September*)
      FSLN launches insurrection, holding Masaya, León, Chinandega and
      Estelí for several days (*September*)
1979 Formation of FPN (*January*)
      FSLN takes León and Matagalpa and marches on Managua (*June*)
      IMF agreement (*June*)
      Managua falls to FSLN; junta forms new government (*July*)
      Nicaragua admitted to non-aligned movement (*August*)
      IMF agreement suspended (*August*)
      Start of border incidents with Honduras (*October*)
      Start of talks on renegotiation of foreign debt (*December*)
1980 Introduction of Plan 80 to revive the economy (*January*)
      Inauguration of militias under Pastora (*February*)
      Signing of aid agreement with Cuba (*February*)
      Official visit to Soviet Union and Eastern Europe (*March*)
      Formation of FPR (*July*)
      Somoza assassinated in Asunción (Paraguay) (*September*)
      Conclusion of debt talks, allowing Nicaragua a five-year grace period on
      part of foreign debt (*September*)
1981 Imposition of US economic sanctions and suspension of aid (*January,
      confirmed in April*)
      Junta reduced from five members to three, with Daniel Ortega as Co-
      ordinator (*March*)
      Formation of CD (*July*)
      Introduction of land-reform legislation (*July*)
      Enders' visit to Managua (*August*)
      Introduction of state of economic and social emergency (*September*)
      Formation of FDN (*November*)

1982   Evacuation of Miskito population from the north (*January*)
       Declaration of state of emergency after FDN sabotage (*March*)
       Formation of Arde (*September*)
       Passage of Boland Amendment in US Congress, banning US funding of
       efforts to destabilize Nicaragua (*December*)
1983   Passage of law on political parties and of controversial military service bill
       (*August*)
       Contra attack on port of Corinto (*October*)
       Formation of M–3V (*October*)
       Amnesty decree and election decree (*December*)
1984   Contra mining of Corinto and Puerto Sandino (*March*)
       Resignation of Pastora from Arde leadership (*May*)
       Assassination attempt against Pastora (*May*)
       Visit of government delegation led by Ortega to Soviet Union (*June*)
       Relaxation of state of emergency (*July*)
       Formation of Misatán (*July*)
       Unification of FDN and Arde (except FRS) in UNIR (*September*)
       Lifting of state of emergency except in "war zones" (*October*)
       Rivera announced would enter talks with government (*October*)
       General elections won by FSLN (*November*)
       MiGs crisis (*November*)
       1,200 Cubans leave (*end-1984*)
1985   Ortega sworn in as president (*January*)
       Inauguration of new assembly (*January*)
       Postponement of talks with Rivera (*January*)
       Introduction of austerity measures (*February*)
       100 Cuban military advisers asked to leave (*February*)
       Ortega's visit to Moscow (*April*)
       Imposition of US trade embargo (*May*)
       Talks with Rivera held in Bogotá, but collapse (*May*)
       Formation of UNO (*June*)
       Formation of BOS (*August*)
       Formation of KISAN (*September*)
       Reintroduction of state of emergency (*October*)
1986   Closure of Radio Católica (*January*)
       Formation of Atlantic Coast Commission for Justice, Peace and Unity
       (*March*)
       Attempts to unite BOS and UNO (*March*) and Arde and FARN (*May*)
       Closure of *La Prensa* newspaper (*June*)
       Expulsion of leading church officials (*June–July*)
       Capture and conviction of alleged CIA agent Hasenfus (*October–
       November*)

1.5.2: Early History—Anglo–US Rivalry

Nicaragua had an extremely turbulent post-independence history, with the
political divide between liberals and conservatives being focused on the towns of
León (liberal) and Granada (conservative). It was not until 1852 that the two
factions agreed to the adoption of Managua as the national capital and political
centre.

Nicaragua also had uncertain borders because of a conflict with British settlers on the eastern coast. In 1816 the British protectorate of this area, known as the Mosquito Coast, was re-established and the Mosquito king George Frederick II was crowned in Belize. The British continued military activities in the region, occupying San Juan del Norte in 1848–50 and renaming it Greytown. Under the Treaty of Managua signed in 1860 Britain gave up its claim to be protector, but it was not until 1894 that Britain ceased to intervene on the east coast and that the region was fully incorporated into Nicaragua. Only in 1906 did Britain finally relinquish all claims to the coast.

In order to resist the British influence (by far the most powerful foreign interest in the mid-19th century), Nicaragua turned to the United States; consequently US political and military intervention was more marked there than elsewhere in Central America from the late 19th century until 1979. In

1894 Nicargua reached agreement with a US company for a Nicaraguan transisthmian canal and the following year the Clayton-Bulwer Treaty was signed (see section 1.1.5).

When the French Panama Canal Company went bankrupt in 1889 (see section 1.7.2) a company was formed in the United States to construct a canal across Nicaragua, and in 1901 the Second Hay-Pauncefote Treaty abrogated the Clayton-Bulwer Treaty, leaving the United States free to develop the route unilaterally. Even after the Panama Canal opened in 1914 the feasibility of a Nicaraguan canal continued to be studied.

1.5.3: Walker Invasion and Brief Liberal Rule—Zelaya Dictatorship

In 1855 a US adventurer, William Walker, landed in Nicaragua with a group of mercenaries to assist the liberals against the conservatives. Walker gained control of the army and became president in 1856, but his rule was opposed by the other Central American states and in May 1857 he was overthrown by a joint Central American force (with British support). He made three further invasion attempts, each of which was foiled by US officials, and in 1860 he was captured and executed in Nicaragua. This liberal interlude was followed by conservative domination, which lasted until José Santos Zelaya came to power in 1893.

Zelaya was one of the New Liberals and his rule alienated not only many Nicaraguans but also foreign investors who found him difficult to deal with. (For his opposition to US and Mexican involvement in Central America and his war with Honduras, see sections 1.1.7 and 1.3.2.) In 1909 an internal revolt started at Bluefields led by the conservative Juan Estrada, who had foreign backing, and the next year his forces captured Managua and overthrew Zelaya; Estrada's de facto seizure of power was then ratified in a presidential election.

1.5.4: US Military Occupation, 1912–33

In the face of a possible military revolt against him, Estrada resigned in 1911 and was replaced by Vice-President Adolfo Díaz, who adopted far more traditional conservative policies to reverse the changes under Zelaya (including the restoration of the privileged position of the Roman Catholic Church). He applied to the US administration for support and under the Knox-Castillo Treaty Nicaragua became a US protectorate. The treaty included an understanding that in return for loans of $14,000,000 the US government would be accorded the right to protect US financial interests in Nicaragua and to arbitrate in any dispute in which Nicaragua became involved. In addition a number of private loans were advanced, increasing Nicaragua's economic dependence on the United States.

The signing of the Knox-Castillo Treaty generated opposition protests from both liberals and disaffected conservatives (who were led by Gen. Emiliano Chamorro Vargas), with the result that in 1912 units of US marines landed at Corinto and took over the running of the railway and of the main cities. Under US auspices an election was held which confirmed Diaz as president. Nicargua's protectorate status was further defined in the Bryan–Chamorro Treaty of 1916, by which the United States gained the exclusive and perpetual right to construct and operate an inter-oceanic canal between the San Juan river and Lake Nicaragua, while in return Nicaragua received $3,000,000 to help meet its foreign debt. In the 1916 presidential election the liberals were barred from standing and Gen. Chamorro was elected unopposed after US officials had persuaded Díaz's candidate, Carlos Cuadro Pasos, to withdraw from the contest.

Another member of the Chamorro family (one of the most prominent political families in the country since the beginning of the century, although often in opposition to the government), Diego Manuel Chamorro, was elected to the presidency in 1921, again with US support. After the transfer of power to another conservative, Carlos Solorzano, in the 1925 election, the US government withdrew the marines, and immediately fresh anti-government revolts erupted. The US administration, alarmed by the discovery that the Nicaraguan rebels were receiving arms from Mexico (where there had been a violent left-wing revolution in 1910), sent the marines back in 1926 because it wanted to "protect American lives and propety". It also feared the threat of "Mexican-fostered Bolshevik hegemony between the United States and the Panama Canal".

Solorzano was ousted by Gen. Chamorro in 1926, but the latter was in turn opposed by Vice-President Juan Bautista Sacasa, a liberal. A settlement was negotiated by the US State Department and Diaz was installed again as president, but in order to cope with the continued civil unrest the US military presence was increased. The basis for this military occupation of Nicaragua was laid down in the Tipitapa agreements of 1927, which also provided for the holding of an election the following year.

The liberal army chief, José María Moncada, who had been actively opposed to the US military presence, won the election and tried to end the protectorate; in 1931 a gradual US withdrawal began. However, Moncada's acceptance of presidential office while US forces were still in the country alienated many of his supporters, the most famous of whom, Lt. Augusto César Sandino, took to the hills around Matagalpa and launched military operations in the north-east of the country. In this guerrilla war Sandino and his followers proved too quick and well-trained (and familiar with the terrain) for the 4,000 marines, even though the US forces used aerial bombing in their counter-insurgency campaign.

The last US-supervised election, held in 1932, was won by Sacasa and the following year the last of the US troops were withdrawn. The US occupation left three important legacies: US economic domination, the guerrilla war with Sandino and the formation and training of the specially selected National Guard under the command of Gen. Anastasio Somoza García. In February 1934 Sacasa arranged a meeting with Sandino to work out a peace agreement in good faith, involving gradual disarmement; but Sandino was murdered by members of the National Guard, allegedly on the orders of Somoza (who was reported to have prevented the prosecution of the suspects). (Sandino became a folk hero and it was after him that the FSLN was named—see below.)

1.5.5: Establishment of Somoza Rule

For the next four decades Nicaragua was ruled by the Somoza family by means of the National Liberal Party (PLN) and the National Guard, either directly or through their nominees. As with the 14 families in El Salvador (see section 1.3.2), the Somozas also held power through their broad-based economic activities and social links. Although the United States gained considerable economic and financial concessions, the Somozas monopolized most economic concerns (see also section 2.2.4).

Gen. Somoza forced Sacasa to resign in June 1936 and in the ensuing election the general's candidate, Carlos Buenes Jarquín, defeated the only other contender, who was fighting the campaign from exile. Under this interim government traditional liberal policies were followed in disestablishing the Roman Catholic Church and improving public health facilities; but it was also characterized by a controlled press and closer friendship with the United States, while the conservative party became a loyal opposition. Somoza himself won the election of December 1936 with a total of 107,201 votes (against 169 for the conservative candidate, Leonardo Argüello) and took office in May 1939 for an eight-year term.

Argüello was elected with Somoza's support in February 1947, but when he tried to implement some of his own policies he was removed in less than four weeks. Benjamín Lescayo Sacasa became provisional president, but he too disagreed with Somoza and was in turn replaced by V. M. Román y Reyes (Somoza's uncle). In May 1950 Somoza was re-elected (in preference to the conservative Emilio Chamorro Bernard) and he took office a year later.

1.5.6: Assassination of Gen. Somoza—Continuation of Somoza Rule through his Sons

During a visit to León on Sept. 21, 1956, Gen. Somoza was shot and mortally wounded. President Eisenhower immediately dispatched US medical specialists to Nicaragua and arranged for the general to be flown to a US military hospital in the Panama Canal Zone, but he died on Sept. 29. His assassin, Rigoberto López Pérez, who was instantly gunned down by the presidential guards, had recently returned from El Salvador where he had met Nicaraguan exiles, but there was no evidence of a well-planned conspiracy to overthrow the government (see also section 3.4.1).

A state of siege was declared and the National Assembly voted unanimously in favour of the general's son, Col. Luis Somoza Debayle, completing his father's term of office until May 1957, while his other son, Anastasio, took over command of the National Guard. Luis Somoza was elected president by a massive majority in 1957, beating Eduardo Amador of the conservatives. A constitutional amendment passed in 1955 had allowed the president to serve a third term and had removed the ban on the election of a new president standing within four degrees of blood relationship to the outgoing president. (Later, in August 1959, Luis Somoza approved a law banning the immediate re-election of the president and also preventing all blood relatives of the president from standing.)

In the February 1963 election Rene Schick Gutiérrez of the PLN defeated Diego Manuel Chamorro of the mainstream conservative party; the conservatives had split and the faction led by Fernando Agüero Rocha, called the Traditional Conservative Party, boycotted the election. President Schick permitted the press to operate freely and sought to improve the national economy by encouraging foreign capital investment in the country and through fuller participation in the Central American Common Market (CACM). He died in office in August 1966 and his term was completed by Vice-President Lorenzo Guerrero Gutiérrez.

1.5.7: Election of Anastasio Somoza—Abrogation of Constitution—Establishment of Triumvirate

In the February 1967 election Gen. Anastasio Somoza Debayle gained a victory over Alejandro Abaunza Marenco of the conservative party and Agüero, standing for the National Opposition Union; the Union was co-ordinated by Pedro Joaquín Chamorro, the editor of the opposition newspaper, *La Prensa*, and included the Christian Democrats led by Eduardo Rivas Gasteazoro. Somoza took office in May (his brother Luis having died in April). Prior to the election the opposition had staged a mass demonstration (of about 60,000 people) outside the presidential palace on Jan. 23, hoping to initiate a nationwide movement to remove Somoza. The demonstrators were fired upon by the National Guard and Chamorro and other leaders were imprisoned. The death toll, officially set at 201, was reported by other sources to have been as high as 600.[1]

While the demonstration had been organized by the mainly conservative opposition, other opponents had begun to separate themselves from the political process and to seek the armed overthrow of the Somoza government as the only way to achieve political change. Among such movements, the Sandinista National Liberation Front (FSLN) was formed in 1961 by Carlos Fonseca Amador, Tomás Borge Martínez and Silvio Mayorga, becoming active in 1963. Although by early 1967 many of its early leaders had been killed, it regrouped in the northern hills, and by 1970 it had renewed its guerrilla activities and had gained the support of left-wing students.

Early in 1971 the Social Democrats and other left-wing parties formed the National Civic Alliance with a view to contesting the 1972 elections. However, the constitutional process was interrupted when in August 1971 the Congress voted its own dissolution, abrogated the constitution and transferred all executive and legislative powers to Somoza pending the drafting of a new constitution. Somoza (whose term was due to expire in May 1972) in March 1971 concluded an agreement with the conservatives that between 1972 and 1974 the country would be governed by a triumvirate of two liberals and one conservative. The agreement, which was reported to have been inspired by the current US ambassador in Managua, Turner Shelton,[2] was hailed by Somoza as the "debut of a democratic revolution in Nicaragua". It provided that Somoza would stand for re-election in 1974, and also established that in the new constituent assembly to be elected in February 1972 the stronger party would hold 60 per cent of the seats and the weaker 40 per cent. In the event the liberals polled 534,171 against 174,897 for the conservatives, while the opposition groups—including some anti-Somoza liberals and conservatives together with the Social Christian Party (PSCN), founded in 1957—staged a boycott, with the support of the Roman Catholic Church.

Executive power was transferred to the trumvirate of Gen. Robert Martínez Laclayo, Alfonso Lobo Cordero and Agüero on May 1, 1972, for a term to last until Dec. 31, 1973. Somoza himself became Supreme Army Commander.

1.5.8: 1972 Earthquake

A violent earthquake occurred in Nicaragua on Dec. 23, 1972, virtually destroying Managua and leaving about half of the city's population of 300,000 homeless; the death toll was officially set at 12,000 but some sources put the figure as high as 20,000. (In his book *Triumph of the People* George Black describes the earthquake as "a pivotal movement in the disintegration of *Somocismo*", because of its effects on the country's economic and social structure.[3]) The earthquake did, however, extend Somoza's political and economic authority as he was appointed chairman of the National Emergency Committee.

1.5.9: Promulgation of New Constitution—Formation of Udel

The 100-member constituent assembly, which had convened in April 1972, formally dissolved itself in March 1974 and was replaced by a bicameral National Congress of 70 deputies and 30 senators elected six months later. The constitution which it had drafted, promulgated in April, barred any serving military officer from standing for the presidency and made a boycott of the elections illegal. (In order to comply with the first of these provisions Somoza gave up being directive head of the National Guard and became its Supreme Head, a purely administrative post.)

Despite the constitutional ban nine opposition parties called for a boycott of the September 1974 elections and 27 leaders were arrested and deprived of their political rights until March 1975. The parties continued to protest and filed charges with the Supreme Electoral Tribunal accusing the government of fraud, bribery and coercion and constitutional violation. Some of the 27 leaders were members of the newly-formed Democratic Liberation Union (Udel), led by Pedro Joaquín Chamorro, who was later replaced as leader by Rafael Córdova Rivas. In a statement issued on Oct. 7, 1977, Udel demanded the introduction of democracy, a general amnesty, guarantees for the freedom of expression, Udel participation in government and freedom of assembly for trade unions.[4]

1.5.10: Chamorro's Assassination

The possibility of a compromise political settlement virtually disappeared when on Jan. 10, 1978, Pedro Joaquín Chamorro was shot dead in Managua, responsibility for the murder being generally attributed to the National Guard. Udel immediately cancelled the negotiations with the government scheduled for February and directed its energies into demands for Somoza's resignation. In support of its demand for a full investigation into the killing Udel called for a general strike on Jan. 23 and was backed by the major trade union bodies. The government responded by imposing a news blackout on the strike, and closing private radio stations which attempted to defy the ban. However, an alternative source of information was found when the church began to express its opposition to the government more forcibly by delivering strike bulletins from its own pulpits.

Although an inquiry was set up into the Chamorro killing, little progress was made. On the first anniversary of Chamorro's death some 30,000 demonstrators gathered at a rally in Managua and called a general strike in protest over what the Nicaraguan Development Institute (INDE, led by Alfonso Robelo Callejas), described as "very grave injustices" in the murder investigations.

Gen. Somoza reactivated the 1972 National Emergency Committee on Jan. 28, 1978, and National Guard units were sent in to break the strike, which had the support not only of many workers but also of some anti-Somoza businessmen. After a limited strike on Feb. 7 the Guard were called out again on Feb. 21–23 to deal with Indian and student demonstrators. Somoza announced on Feb. 26 that a programme of political and social reforms was being prepared and would be presented to Congress in April; however, no substantial political changes were made and a student strike broke out in April, closing colleges and schools all over the country. The students' protest was a broad anti-government one, although specific demands included improved treatment for political prisoners, and as the strike spread there were clashes with the National Guard in which several people were killed. The second general strike of the year took place on July 19, 1978, staged in protest against the handling by the authorities of a demonstration at Jinotepe on July 9, and a further 26 people died in clashes with security forces.

1.5.11: Formation of FAO and MPU

Early in July 1978 Udel joined with the Nicaraguan Democratic Movement (MDN)—formed by Robelo in April—and the Group of 12 (*Los Doce*) —which had close links with the FSLN—to form the Broad Opposition Front (FAO) under the leadership of Córdova Rivas. Also included were small opposition parties and trade unions, as well as several businessmen, intellectuals and priests who had returned from Costa Rica on July 5, having gone there during the FSLN offensive of October 1977 (see below) to establish links with the FSLN.

The Group of 12 had first emerged in October 1977 when its members (all prominent professionals) put their signatures to a statement printed in *La Prensa* and asserting that there could be no solution to the country's political crisis without the full participation of the FSLN. The members included Ernesto Castillo Martínez and Joaquín Cuadra Chamorro (lawyers), Fr Fernando Cardenal Martínez and Fr Miguel d'Escoto Brockmann (priests), Carlos Tunnerman Bernheim (academic), Sergio Ramírez Mercado (writer), and Arturo Cruz (banker). In a press statement Cardenal said of the group that "none of us is a politician, none of us has even been in politics, none of us is interested in power".

The FAO's policies were supported by the Roman Catholic Church, from which the Archbishop of Managua, Mgr Miguel Obando y Bravo, called on Somoza to resign in favour of a government of national unity which would implement political reforms. In an apparently conciliatory gesture Somoza announced on Aug. 11 that 30 out of 35 commanding officers had been dismissed, but there was no accompanying political change and no positive response from the opposition.

At about the same time as the formation of the FAO the FSLN organized the United People's Movement (MPU), incorporating about 20 trade unions and student bodies, to project its political demands. The MPU issued an "immediate programme" for a new post-Somoza government, including promises of constitutional pluralism, abolition of the National Guard, a non-aligned foreign policy, economic and financial reorganization and land-reform, a new labour code and national education, health and housing programmes.

1.5.12: Emergence of FSLN—Seizure of National Palace—September 1978 Insurrection

The FSLN emerged as an important guerrilla force when on Dec. 27, 1974, it staged a surprise attack on a gathering of diplomatic and political officials at a house in the Los Robles area of Managua. The guerrillas demanded the release of FSLN prisoners (including Daniel Ortega Saavedra who was to lead the Sandinistas to victory some years later), a $2,000,000 ransom, the publication in the press and broadcasting on radio and television of a statement and an across-the-board wage rise. Their demands were met and they were flown out to Cuba, but the stage of siege imposed by the government made it possible for the authorities to increase repressive measures against the opposition, particularly in the censorship of the press and the establishment of permanent military courts. When the state of siege was lifted on Sept. 5, 1977, there was an explosion of popular demonstrations and for the first time barricades were erected in street protests. An uprising launched on Oct. 12–13, 1977, and apparently intended to spark off a general revolt involved a series of attacks on National Guard posts and fighting at San Carlos (near the Costa Rican border), Ocotal, Esquipulas, Masaya and the outskirts of Managua; however, FSLN forces were forced to withdraw on this occasion.

A group of 25 FSLN activists, disguised as members of the National Guard, occupied the National Palace in Managua, on Aug. 22, 1978, and took over 1,000 people hostage, including two of Somoza's relations. Most of the hostages managed to escape or were freed, but 70 continued to be held while the guerrillas demanded the release of 85 Sandinista prisoners (including Tomás Borge Martínez), a general amnesty for all political prisoners, a ransom of $10,000,000, safe conduct out of the country and the public issuing of a political statement. The group, calling itself the Rigoberto López Pérez Commando (after the assassin of Somoza in 1956—see above), was led by Edén Pastora Gómez, known as "Commandante Cero". On the next day a state of emergency was declared, the airports sealed off and the border with Costa Rica closed; after mediation by Mgr Obando y Bravo, however, the FSLN unit obtained all of its demands and left for Panama on Aug. 24 taking 58 Sandinista prisoners with them. (The other 27 listed were not accounted for by the authorities and appeared to have died while in prison.) Somoza claimed that the incident had been backed by Cuba and that the FSLN as such had been virtually eliminated.

The FAO and main union organizations called on Aug. 24, 1978, for a general strike to demand Somoza's resignation; and by the end of the month most shops and businesses had closed. The stoppage was supported by the Federation of Nicaraguan Chambers of Commerce and INDE, which were banned by the government on Aug. 28 and Sept. 3 respectively. In early September the National Guard arrested some 600 supporters of the strike, while in clashes in Matagalpa (where the National Guard was commanded by Col. Anastasio Somoza Portocarrero, the president's son) between 25 and 50 civilians were reported dead and up to 200 people injured, with many others arrested by the National Guard in house-to-house searches. While the strike continued the FSLN attacked and captured the towns of Masaya, León, Chinandega and Estelí on Sept. 9, but by Sept. 21 all four towns had been retaken by the National Guard. Fighting had also reached Managua and martial law was introduced on Sept. 13 (with full press censorship from Sept. 15), lasting until Oct. 9. According to the International Committee of the Red Cross (ICRC) about 5,000 people died in the violence of September 1978.

Following this military setback for the FSLN, the strike ended on Sept. 24, and shortly afterwards Somoza said that an amnesty would be offered to all those arrested, except those detained for terrorist offences. A few days later, on Oct. 4, he announced plans to double the National Guard from its current size to 15,000 and to make a corresponding increase in the state allocations on defence and security to 20 per cent of the national budget.

1.5.13: Attempts to Start Negotiations

The Nicaraguan government announced on Sept. 25, 1978, that it would accept the recent offer of mediation made by the United States and the OAS. The offer caused a split within the FAO, and at first it refused to co-operate with the OAS commission which arrived in Nicaragua in October, although some sections accepted the OAS proposal as a basis. All members of the FAO maintained that the FSLN should be represented in a new provisional government, and the talks which began on Oct. 16 broke down as Somoza refused to resign before the expiry of his mandate at the end of 1980. It has been suggested that it was the failure of those talks that finally convinced the US administration that Somoza "had to go" if a solution to the Nicaraguan problem were to be found.[5]

The Group of 12 withdrew from the talks on Oct. 26, claiming that the United States wanted a "docile government", and that the US political programme "would leave practically intact the corrupt structures of the Somoza apparatus" and would amount to "somozaism without Somoza". In a communiqúe issued on Oct. 27 the Group asserted that "we must tell the United States that no solution exists to this crisis unless the Somoza system is dismantled, unless the Somoza family is separated from power and unless the FSLN participates in any future stage of national life". The Nicaraguan Workers' Central (CTN) withdrew from the talks on Nov. 3, and shortly afterwards the Socialist Party (PSN) also withdrew. Before the talks had opened Cardenal had announced from Lisbon (Portugal) on Oct. 2 that the FAO had appointed a triumvirate to serve in the event of Somoza's resignation, consisting of Ramírez Mercado, Córdova Rivas and Robelo.

Somoza reiterated his defiance when on Nov. 10, 1978, he called for a plebiscite to determine the strength of the opposition within "the future government which I will organize as president". The entire FAO withdrew temporarily from the negotiations on Nov. 21, but provisional agreement was reached by both parties on a proposal made on Nov. 23 by the OAS commission, to the effect that there should be a plebiscite giving the choice of Somoza's continuance in power or his replacement by a government of national unity. Martial law was lifted on Dec. 7 and negotiations continued into January 1979, when Somoza refused to allow the plebiscite to be monitored by observers from the PLN, the FAO and political independents. The US State Department announced on Feb. 8 that in view of Somoza's rejection of the commission's proposals all military aid to Nicaragua had been cancelled and all economic aid for 1979, amounting to $10,500,000, had been frozen. Early in March Somoza again promised reforms, but made no significant concessions.

The split within the FAO over the negotiations was confirmed on Jan. 11, 1979 when the sections opposed to mediation—the Group of 12, the CTN, the Independent Liberal Party (PLI) and the Popular Social Christian Party (PPSC)—joined with the MPU and the (Maoist) Workers' Front (FO) to form the Nicaraguan People's Front (FPN). The new body issued a 22-point statement affirming its commitment to "national sovereignty, effective democracy, justice and social progress" and called for the resignation of Somoza and the dismantling of the entire regime.

1.5.14: FSLN Military Campaign

The FSLN announced in January 1979 that it would intensify its effort to overthrow Somoza, and specifically that it would increase attacks on National Guard targets and seek to occupy major towns. In the first three months of the year it stepped up military actions along the country's northern and southern borders and the death toll in this period rose to an average of five per day. In commemoration of the 45th anniversary of the murder of Sandino the FSLN staged on Feb. 21 a series of harrassment attacks against National Guard posts in Masaya, Managua, Granada, Diriamba (south of Managua) and León, and planted several hundred small explosive devices. On April 5 the FSLN issued a programme for national reconstruction, of which the main features were: (i) the formation of a provisional government of national unity in which "all the social and political forces in our country will have real participation"; (ii) a strategy to "save Nicaragua from the social, economic, political and moral catastrophe" it faced; (iii) the formation of a new national army to "defend the democratic process and national unity", excluding soldiers who were "corrupt and guilty of crimes against the people"; (iv) the adoption of a non-aligned foreign policy; and (v) the expropriation of "all the goods usurped by the Somoza family".

A group of 250 guerrillas penetrated the town of Estelí on April 9 and held it for five days despite aerial bombardment of the town and surrounding area by the National Guard. The town's food and water supplies were cut off and 5,000 of the inhabitants fled to avoid the National Guard's counter-offensive. After the town fell on April 14 it was reported that the National Guard had bombarded civilian homes with tanks, had conducted house-to-house searches and had, on April 12, entered the town's hospital and executed 40 young people, the hospital director, a doctor and a nurse. The National Guard claimed to have killed 70 FSLN fighters (although most apparently escaped to the mountains) and the FSLN claimed to have killed 120 guardsmen; the ICRC reported that nearly 1,000 people had been either killed or arrested. Later in the month the FSLN again made an assault on León, but were again driven back by the ground and aerial bombardment of the National Guard.

Somoza announced in late April 1979 that all May Day rallies would be banned except for the official one, which was addressed by him, and during which he promised a 15 per cent wage-rise and reform of the social security system. On May 1 the FSLN attacked a number of guard posts in Managua and the government arrested four prominent opponents: Elias Altamirano, the secretary general of the banned Communist Party (PCN), Alejandro Solorzano, leader of the Independent General Confederation of Workers (CGT–I), Córdova Rivas and Robelo. The seizure of the two FAO members caused a protest on May 4 from the US administration, which described them as "moderate critics" of the government wanting a "peaceful and democratic solution". The two were later released.

1.5.15: Foreign Pressure on Somoza Government

President José López Portillo of Mexico announced on May 20, 1979, that his government had broken diplomatic relations with Nicaragua because of what he described as the Somoza regime's "horrific genocide" against the Nicaraguan people; he called on other Latin American countries to "ratify the decision through the OAS". The next day the Panamanian ambassador to Nicaragua was summoned home "on urgent business", and diplomatic relations were broken on June 18. Other Latin American countries followed this lead, Ecuador on June 17, Brazil on June 25 and Peru on June 26, and on June 17 Colombia, Venezuela and Bolivia said that they recognized both sides as "belligerents", thereby giving the FSLN equal status as a representative of authority in Nicaragua.

1.5.16: Final Sandinista Assault—Formation of Provisional Junta

The FSLN launched a two-pronged offensive on May 28, 1979, from the Costa Rican border, near Rivas and Peñas Blancas, and in the north-east of the country at Puerto Cabezas, also attacking León, Matagalpa and National Guard posts in Managua. On May 30 the government closed Managua airport and banned all news broadcasts and the next day the FSLN called for a national insurrection, to begin with a general strike on June 4. The guerrillas were temporarily driven back at Rivas by Gen. José Somoza (the President's half-brother), but the offensive continued and on June 3 heavy fighting broke out in Managua. They took León on June 5 and were reported to be holding Matagalpa and the western sector of Masaya, and to be attacking Jinotepe, Diriamba, Chichigalpa, Chinandega and El Ostronal.

The government declared a state of siege on June 7, giving it powers of arrest and detention; but although its forces recaptured several towns, León and Matagalpa remained in FSLN hands and in the capital the population began to mobilize in support of the guerrillas, encouraged by broadcasts from the FSLN Radio Sandino station operating in Costa Rica. A curfew was imposed on June 7, when the FSLN was reported to be closing on the central part of the capital, and La Prensa was forcibly shut down. The Managua insurrection began on June 9 as the FSLN entrenched itself in the slum quarters of the city, which it described as "the liberated zones of free Managua", and withstood the Guard's aerial bombardment, during which the La Prensa offices were razed to the ground. The National Guard garrison at León, which had been under siege for several days, was finally evacuated on June 18 and the guerrillas increased their hold on other major towns, so that by the beginning of July they held over 20. The bombing of Managua intensified on June 23, resulting in civilian casualties estimated at between 10,000 and 12,000, and on June 28 the FSLN withdrew from the city to Masaya and León to avoid further civilian casualties. The FSLN took Jinotepe and San Marcos on July 6 and Santa Catarina two days later and then regrouped to move on Managua.[6]

It was later estimated that the civil war caused damage worth about $5,000 million, and that of a population of some 2,500,000 people, 60,000 died in the last two months of war, 250,000 fled their homes and 50,000 children were orphaned.

The FSLN announced in San José (Costa Rica) on June 16, 1979, that it had formed a "provisional junta of national reconstruction", consisting of Ramírez Mercado, Robelo, Daniel Ortega, Violeta Barrios de Chamorro (widow of Pedro Joaquín Chamorro) and Moisés Hassán Morales (a founder member of the MPU and the FPN). Three months earlier, on March 8, the Front had annnounced the formation of its Joint National Directorate, consisting of (i) Daniel Ortega, Humberto Ortega Saavedra (Daniel's brother) and Víctor Tirado, from the Insurrectionary or *Tercerista* tendency, (ii) Luis Carrión Cruz, Jaime Wheelock Román and Carlos Núñez Telles of the Proletarian tendency, and (iii) Borge, Henry Ruiz and Bayardo Arce Castaño of the Prolonged Popular War (GPP) tendency (see section 3.1.5).

1.5.17: Conciliation Efforts

The Nicaraguan government said on June 15, 1979, that it was prepared to accept the intervention of an OAS peace-keeping force and to negotiate with "whomever it was necessary" to stop the fighting, although when the Venezuelan and Ecuadorean foreign ministers (respectively José Alberto Zambrano and José Ayala Lasso) had arrived in Managua on June 11 on a peace mission Somoza had told them that the only possible solution would be found in elections and had reiterated his determination not to leave office before the end of his term. In any event, the proposal for a peace-keeping force, made by President Carter, was rejected by the OAS at a meeting on June 21–23, when a resolution was adopted calling for the resignation of Somoza as well as for the holding of free elections.

The US government launched a new mediation effort at the end of June 1979 in an attempt to reach a political settlement and the new US ambassador to Managua, Lawrence Pezzulo, arrived in Nicaragua on June 28 and tried to persuade Somoza to resign. The *Washington Post* published an interview with Somoza in its July 11 edition, in which the general said that he had told the US authorities that he would leave office and that the timing of his resignation depended on the US government, but he continued to insist on the "constitutional survival of the PLN and the National Guard". He added that the pressure being brought to bear on him made him like "a tied donkey fighting with a tiger".

It was reported on July 15 that the government and the guerrillas had reached an agreement in principle to end the war, containing three main conditions: (i) the resignation of Somoza, his departure from Nicaragua and his replacement by a constitutional president, (ii) a ceasefire, and (iii) the transfer of power to the provisional junta at Managua.

1.5.18: Somoza's Resignation and Flight

Somoza finally resigned on July 17, 1979, after the FSLN agreed to his final main condition that all the higher ranks of the National Guard would be included in the proposed new national army. Later the same day he left the bunker where he and several members of his government had taken refuge the previous month, and flew to Miami with his family. In resigning he also nominated as his successor the president of the National Assembly, Francisco Urcuyo, whose interim appointment was confirmed by Congress; Col. Federico Mejía was appointed Commander of the National Guard.

The fighting continued when it was discovered that Urcuyo wanted to complete Somoza's presidential term, causing the US to recall Pezzulo on July 18, on the grounds that the government had "gone back on" its agreement for the transfer of power. Under this pressure Urcuyo resigned and left Nicaragua on July 19. He announced in August 1980 his intention to form a government-in-exile in Guatemala, but nothing further was heard of this initiative, as by that time the Sandinista government was well-established and the opposition was grouping around figures of greater political influence such as Robelo (see below).

From Miami Somoza travelled to the Bahamas, but he was expelled on Aug. 4 and arrived in Paraguay 15 days later. The new Nicaraguan government announced that it intended to apply for the extradition of him and his family to stand trial in Managua; one of his sons, Col. Anastasio Somoza Portocarrero, who had gone to Honduras and tried to raise forces for a counter-attack, was on Jan. 15, 1980, formally charged in absentia of planning the murder of Chamorro in 1978 in complicity with 10 other National Guardsmen.

Somoza was shot dead by unknown assassins in the Paraguayan capital (Asunción), on Sept. 17, 1980, and his body was flown to Miami for burial. The Paraguayan police originally said that a group called the Argentine People's Revolutionary Army had been responsible, but on Oct. 1 Paraguay broke diplomatic relations with Nicaragua claiming it had evidence of Sandinista involvement in the murder, although the Nicaraguan government denied this charge.

1.5.19: Formation of New Government

The junta of national reconstruction announced on July 16, 1979, that it had named a provisional government council. On the next day the junta members arrived in Nicaragua along with the foreign ministers of the Andean Pact countries (Colombia, Venezuela, Ecuador, Peru and Bolivia), who had recently travelled to Costa Rica for talks with the junta. An understanding was reached that there would be no reprisals against members of the Somoza regime and that human rights would be upheld, while Mgr Obando y Bravo promised to give sanctuary to anyone wishing to leave the country. The Costa Rican government gave formal recognition to the junta on July 18 as the legitimate government of Nicaragua, which had meanwhile been established in León. FSLN units entered Managua on July 19, taking key installations, and the National Guard fled to Guatemala, leaving its new commander, Lt.-Col. Fulgencio Larga Espada, to broadcast the surrender.

The junta left León and arrived in Managua on July 20 and the provisional government was flown from Costa Rica in a Mexican aircraft; both were sworn into office on the same day. The ministers included Borge (interior), one of the few surviving founder members of the FSLN; it also included four members of the Group of 12, namely Fr Ernesto Cardenal (culture), d'Escoto (foreign affairs), Castillo (justice) and Cuadra (Fernando's brother— finance). The inclusion of d'Escoto and other priests in the government caused a split within the Church, broadly along hierarchical lines, as the bishops echoed the Pope's call for the resignation of the priests from political office and began to oppose the government, while the majority of priests continued to favour the Sandinistas (see also section 2.5.5).

1.5.20: Political, Economic, Social and Military Reforms

The new government announced the dissolution of the National Guard and of Congress, the abolition of the death penalty and of military courts, the abrogation of the constitution and the expropriation of the Somoza family assets. It restored all political, religious and human rights, pending the drafting of a new constitution, and announced the creation of a new national army and a separate police force. It promised legislative elections but estimated that it might be three or four years before these could be held. For economic reasons the government declared a state of emergency on July 24, 1979, in order to help the process of national reconciliation, under which the FSLN took control of all military installations and communications media, and prison terms ranging from three months to two years were introduced for offences such as disrupting transport or refusal to work. On July 25 a nationalization programme was announced for the finance, mining, fishing and forestry sectors (for further economic details, see section 2.2.4).

A Basic Statute was issued providing for the creation of a Council of State to serve as an interim legislative body and to draft a new constitution, and all parties except the PLN were allowed to participate in the Council. The Basic Statute was extended the next month when on Aug. 21, 1979, the government issued the Statute on Rights and Guarantees for the Citizens of Nicaragua, decreeing a wide range of democratic freedoms including the right to organize politically, to vote and stand for re-election, the prohibition of all forms of discrimination and of torture and slavery, and confirming the abolition of the death penalty, establishing 30 years imprisonment as the maximum sentence.

Press restrictions were lifted on Aug. 10, 1979, and *La Prensa* reappeared on Aug. 16 under the editorship of Xavier Chamorro (brother of Pedro Joaquín), gradually becoming a voice of opposition to the government (as it had been under Somoza). In April 1980 Chamorro and many of the editorial staff left the paper to form a new pro-government journal, *El Nuevo Diario*, which like the FSLN organ *Barricada*, failed to achieve as high a circulation as *La Prensa*, which was from then on edited by Pedro Joaquín Chamorro Barrios (Pedro Joaquín's son). Another press law also passed in August 1979 stipulated that all publications should display "legitimate concern for the defence of the conquests of the revolution, the reconstruction process and the problems of the Nicaraguan people" and be "vehicles for the development, cultural and educative process". It was also required that articles critical of the government should be constructive and based on "provable facts with which those concerned have been confronted" (which in practice meant that no economic articles could be written unless supported by official statistics). Also on Aug. 10 the government (i) announced that a new unified health service would be established under the aegis of the health ministry, to be financed by a new 9 per cent tax on earnings, and (ii) introduced a 15-point code of ethics for government officials.

The Sandinista People's Army (EPS) was established by decree on Aug. 22, out of the fighting force of the FSLN, and in February 1980 the Sandinista Popular Militias (MPS) were created under the leadership of Pastora to assist the armed forces in emergencies.

The trials of some 7,000 national guardsmen detained by the new government under ICRC supervision opened on Dec. 17, 1979, before nine special military tribunals; most of those charged were soldiers from the ranks as the officers had fled the country. Borge had announced in August 1979 that it was hoped that most of them would be freed and had promised that none of those found guilty of war crimes would be executed. The tribunals were finally dissolved on Feb. 20, 1981, and according to official figures 4,331 guardsmen had been sentenced to prison terms of between one and 30 years, 1,000 had been acquitted or pardoned and 979 released for lack of evidence; Córdova Rivas conceded that several had also been executed.

1.5.21: Foreign Relations

The United States and Nicaragua agreed on July 24, 1979, to continue relations; four days later Lawrence Pezzullo (the US Ambassador) returned to Managua. Panama and Grenada recognized the new government on June 22 and June 23 respectively; relations with Cuba, broken since 1961, were restored; and by April 1981 all Latin American countries had recognized the Sandinista government, although Bolivia severed relations in August 1980 after the García Meza coup and Paraguay in October 1980 after the assassination of Somoza (see above). Most East European countries established links with the new regime and the Soviet news agency Tass announced on Oct. 19, 1979, that full diplomatic relations had been established between the USSR and Nicaragua.

At the meeting of foreign ministers of the countries of the non-aligned movement in Havana on Aug. 30–Sept. 1, 1979, it was decided that Nicaragua's request for admission to the movement should be granted; accordingly, Nicaraguan representatives were able to participate in the sixth summit held in Havana on Sept. 3–9.

By the end of 1979 Nicaragua was receiving substantial economic, food and emergency aid from abroad, mostly from the United States, Mexico, Venezuela, Western Europe, the Soviet Union and Libya. During a visit by President López Portillo to Nicaragua on Jan. 24, 1980, agreement was reached on the delivery of 7,500 barrels per day of petroleum to Nicaragua with effect from April, and Mexico also offered industrial and mining technical assistance.

1.5.22: Government Consolidation by FSLN—Plots against Regime—Junta Changes

As the new government became established the Sandinistas gained increasing control of its apparatus, and its left-wing stance was enhanced both by foreign attitudes (especially as friendship with Cuba and the Soviet bloc made the United States suspicious that Nicaragua might adopt communism) and by the need to protect the revolution against the armed attacks of former guardsmen and other opponents grouping in Honduras (see below and section 3.4.2).

The government issued a decree on Sept. 13, 1979, limiting the use of the description "Sandinista" strictly to the FSLN and its organizations, giving the party the sole right to be the "defender and loyal interpreter of the principles and objectives of the Sandinista ideology". One of the first organizations to fall foul of this decree was the Social Democratic Party (PSD), officially constituted on Sept. 23 with Wilfredo Montalván as secretary-general, which wanted to describe itself as a Sandinista party but was refused permission to do so on the grounds that it did not share the FSLN's political aspirations and had not participated in the armed struggle against Somoza.

The entire cabinet resigned on Dec. 4, 1979, to allow the junta a free hand in the reorganization of the government with a view to accelerating "national reconstruction", and in the new ministerial team formed on Dec. 27 more Sandinistas were included, notably Henry Ruiz as Economic Planning Minister, Humberto Ortega as National Defence Minister (thus merging the ministry with the army command), and Carrión as deputy defence minister alongside Pastora.

Humberto Ortega succeeded Lt.-Col. Bernardino Larios, who was on Sept. 10, 1980, charged with complicity in a plot to assassinate the FSLN directorate, and was alleged by the government to be the commander of a new group, the anti-Sandinista Democratic Armed Forces (FAD). (In November 1980 he was sentenced to 14 years' imprisonment for links with the FAD and violation of the public order and security law, but was released on March 22, 1984, after his sentence had been annulled on a legal technicality.) Later in September 1980 the police reported the discovery of another plot against the junta and FSLN directorate, and in a raid killed the man they claimed was the ringleader. He was Jorge Salazar Argüello, the vice-president of the Higher Council for Private Enterprise (Cosep), the head of the Union of Agricultural Producers (Upanic) and Robelo's brother-in-law. According to the government the plot had involved former guardsmen, members of the political opposition and representatives of private enterprise, with links in other Central American countries, the Salvadorean junta and the United States. On Dec. 11 eight people received sentences of up to nine years for plotting against the government.

Within months of the July 1979 revolution divisions were beginning to appear within the forces which had combined to overthrow Somoza. In December 1979 Robelo urged the FSLN to be a multi-class party uniting all the anti-Somoza elements, but on April 22, 1980, he resigned from the junta in protest over the fact that his party, the MDN, had been allocated only one seat on the Council of State (see below); he also objected to what he saw as the domination of the Council by the FSLN and its associated bodies, especially the Sandinista Defence Committees (CDS), and accused the Sandinistas of imposing a new kind of dictatorship and of allowing Cuba an undue influence in the country. Robelo and Violeta Chamorro (who had resigned three days previously for health reasons) were replaced on the junta by Córdova Rivas and Arturo Cruz (from the Group of 12), who were sworn into office on May 18.

The government was also criticised from the left, and on Jan. 23, 1980, closed the FO organ, *El Pueblo* (which had a circulation of about 2,000) for violation of the public order law prohibiting "the written publication of proclamations or manifestos designed to harm popular interests". The FO had criticized Plan 80 (see section 2.2.4), demanding "active sabotage of the economic plan in order to bring power back into the hands of the people", and had called for the "replacement of the government with another truly capable of defending our self-determination in the face of attack".[7] The government stated that FO and its armed wing, the People's Anti-Somozist Militias (Milpas), were threatening production and provoking unrest (the police having found Milpas arms caches which were supposed to have been surrendered to the authorities after the revolution). On April 10 Ramírez Mercado said that the FO and the pro-Chinese PCN would not be allowed to participate in the Council of State. (The FO like the MDN had been in favour of the immediate establishment of the Council of State, excluding the popular organizations).

1.5.23: Formation of Council of State—Announcement of Election Timetable

In an attempt to overcome the crisis of confidence caused by the two resignations and to persuade the private sector to take part in the Council of State, the government made a number of concessions to the businessmen's demands, including the lifting of the state of emergency on April 28, 1980. At the same time it introduced judicial protection measures to counter such eventualities as arbitrary government rulings, undertook to cease land expropriations and to declare a date for municipal elections, and (on May 26) passed a law protecting private property.

The first session of the Council of State was held on May 4, 1980, but was boycotted by the Democratic Conservative Party (PCD) led by Adolfo Calero Portocarrero, the PSCN, led by Adán Fletes and the MDN, although the MDN representative eventually took his seat on June 10. The final allocation of seats was:

Political parties:	FSLN	6
	PLI	1
	PSN	1
	PPSC	1
	MDN	1
	PCD	1
	PSCN	1
Mass Organizations:	CDS	9
	Sandinista Youth	1
	Association of Nicaraguan Women	1
Trade Unions:	Sandinista Workers' Confederation (CST)	3
	Rural Workers' Association (ATC)	2
	CGT-I	2
	Centre for Trade Union Action and Unity (CAUS)	2
	CTN	1
	Confederation for Trade Union Unification (CUS)	1
	Health Workers' Federation (Fetsalud)	1

Cosep:	INDE	1
	Chamber of Industry	1
	Chamber of Construction	1
	Confederation of Chambers of Commerce	1
	Upanic	1
	Confederation of Professional Associations	1
Others:	EPS	1
	National Association of Clergy	1
	National Council for Higher Education	1
	Teachers' Union (ANDEN)	1
	Journalists' Union (UPN)	1
	Misurasata (Indian organization)	1
Total		47

At the instigation of the FSLN, the PLI, PPSC and PSN joined together on July 23, 1980, to form the Patriotic Front of the Revolution (FPR) to support the government's "patriotic and democratic" policy and to acknowledge the FSLN's vanguard position in the defence and promotion of the revolution along democratic lines. The CST, ATC, CGT-I, CAUS, Fetsalud, ANDEN and UPN all belonged to the Nicaraguan Trade Union Co-ordinating Committee (CSN), which also joined the FPR. In May 1981 membership of the Council of State was expanded from 47 to 51 to include a representative from the Constitutionalist Liberal Movement (MLC, formed by centrist elements of the former PLN) and three from other unions and associations. At the same time the MDN, PSCN, PCD, CUS, CTN and Cosep representatives were excluded, having resigned six months previously because the government had banned a political rally organized by the MDN (which was subsequently authorized but then cancelled by the MDN). Two members of the PSD, including party leader Montalván, were appointed to the Council in November 1981.

The private sector and several of the political parties expressed disquiet over the announcement made on Aug. 23, 1980, by Humberto Ortega that the present leadership would remain in power at least until 1985 as the process of reconstruction was being hampered by the country's "economic, social and moral backwardness". Maintaining that democracy "neither begins nor ends with elections" but instead began "when social inequalities begin to diminish, when the workers and peasants improve their standard of living", Humberto Ortega said that electoral preparations would begin in 1984 to chose "those who will carry on the revolution". On Aug. 27 the government issued one decree banning all election activity until 1984 and another controlling the reporting by the media of economic matters, such as shortages of staple goods.

The question of elections raised particular problems over the status of the FSLN, which could not contest elections unless it formally became a party, but could not retain its own army if it became a party. In November 1980 Cosep made the following attack on the party: "The FSLN, although de facto a political party, avoids defining itself as such, giving rise to a confusion between Government–Party–FSLN, with all that this implies—such as the unilateral use of confiscated television, radio and newspapers, the use of state economic resources for FSLN party ends . . ., the creation of parastatal Sandinista bodies which are granted state buildings and economic resources to realise political activities. . . . The army is the army of a party, not a national army."[8]

The FSLN was also accused of political indoctrination through its literacy campaign which began in March 1980, as the presence of a large number of Cubans among the teachers suggested to many of the government's critics that it was essentially a political programme (although 10 per cent of the total cost of the campaign—$20,000,000—was donated by USAID, the largest single foreign contributor). The literacy campaign, directed by Fernando Cardenal and undertaken by 95,000 volunteers (*brigadistas*), lasted five months and reduced the national illiteracy rate from 50.3 per cent to 12.3 per cent. (For Sandinista economic and social reforms, see section 2.2.4.)

1.5.24: Changes in Junta—Attempts at National Dialogue—Formation of CD

The junta announced on March 4, 1981, that its membership had been reduced to three (Daniel Ortega, Ramírez Mercado and Córdova Rivas) and that Daniel Ortega had been appointed Co-ordinator of the Junta; of the two members dropped, Cruz was named ambassador to Washington and Hassán became president of the Council of State. The continuation of rule by junta was criticized by several political parties and on March 23 the PSCN, PSD, MDN, PCD and MLC issued a joint declaration accusing the government of trying to impose a Marxist–Leninist dictatorship on the country and of violating the freedom of political and trade union organizations.

The FSLN leadership issued a communiqué on March 30, 1981, saying that in the interests of national unity it would begin a dialogue with the country's political, economic and social forces, and a meeting was held the next day. No formal conclusions were reached as the opposition parties insisted that solutions should be jointly agreed, that all productive sectors should participate in economic decisions and that there should be "true" non-alignment and democracy. Further attempts at dialogue were made in June, which ended in August with no result, and the PPSC call made in November for a "national reflection dialogue" by all parties was accepted by Montalván for the PSD but rejected by Robelo on behalf of the MDN.

In July 1981 the PSCN, PCD, PSD, MLC, Cosep, CUS and CTN united to form the Democratic Co-ordinating Board (CD), which later chose Rivas Gasteazoro as its president.

In response to increasing restiveness on the part of the private sector the government on Sept. 9, 1981, declared a state of "economic and social emergency" (for details see section 2.2.4). Cosep protested against this measure in a letter to the junta of Oct. 19, accusing the FSLN leadership of turning the revolution into a "Marxist–Leninist adventure". The government, for its part, claimed that Cosep had been spreading false information "tending to provoke alterations in prices, provisions and currency". Four leading Cosep members were charged with violation of the economic laws, and at a judicial hearing on Oct. 29 three of them were sentenced to seven months' imprisonment. At the same time four PCN members were convicted on the same charge after publishing a document on Oct. 6 denouncing the "serious economic crisis and the deviation of the Sandinista revolution" and criticizing the government for not being sufficiently radical. In a conciliatory gesture the government released the three Cosep members on bail in February 1982.

1.5.25: Relations with USA and Mexico

In January 1981 Managua's relations with the United States deteriorated sharply when the US administration levied economic sanctions against Nicaragua and stopped the delivery of a wheat purchase (see section 5.2.5). Behind this action was the onset of what was to become a crucial factor in US policy in Central America, namely the belief that the Sandinista government was supplying arms to the FMLN in El Salvador (see also section 5.3.6). From this point the rift between the two countries grew, especially after the visits of Thomas Enders and Alexander Haig in November 1981 (see also section 5.1.3).

The Nicaraguans' strongest supporters in the region were Cuba and Mexico, and during a visit to Mexico City by Daniel Ortega on May 6–8, 1981, President López Portillo said that his country would defend Nicaragua's cause "as though it were our own" and that he believed that Nicaragua contributed to the stability of the region. In a joint communiqué issued on May 7 the two leaders made an indirect reference to the US sanctions when they rejected the economic pressures being brought to bear to destabilize the "process of institutionalization of the revolutionary pluralistic Nicaraguan regime".

1.5.26: Formation of FDN and Arde—Introduction of State of Emergency—Passage of Law on Political Parties

During 1981 and 1982 several former supporters of the revolution left Nicaragua to join armed anti-government groups, so that the Sandinistas faced threats from US-backed guerrilla forces (whom they termed counter-revolutionaries or "contras") in Honduras to the north and in Costa Rica to the south. (For Nicaraguan relations with Honduras and Costa Rica, see sections 3.4.2 and 3.4.3.)

A secret radio broadcast from Honduras on Nov. 27, 1981, announced the formation of the Nicaraguan Democratic Force (FDN), and the first major encounter between EPS and FDN units took place on March 18, 1982 (see section 3.4.2). A sabotage campaign by the FDN had begun earlier in the year, culminating on March 14, 1982, with the bombing of two bridges in Chinandega and Nueva Segovia. The government responded to these bombings by declaring a state of emergency on March 15, in a decree which asserted that "the plans of aggression directed against our country are increasingly assuming more concrete forms and are intended to disturb the peace in our country, to destroy our system of production and our country's physical infrastructure, to prepare an escalation of counter-revolutionary military attacks, and consequently to replace people's power with a Somoza-style regime".

The state of emergency was initially introduced for 30 days, but it was repeatedly extended and was not to be lifted until 1984, and then only partially (see below). One of its most immediate effects was a clamp-down on the press, as radio stations were instructed to issue government-prepared news bulletins and revolutionary slogans four times a day; on June 22 the Justice Ministry expropriated three privately-owned radio stations. *La Prensa* became subject to "control" and was closed for short periods in August and November 1982, while *El Nuevo Diario*, which usually supported the government line, was suspended briefly on March 17 for making a reference to the "state of siege".

The state of emergency automatically suspended the current discussion by the Council of State of the draft political parties bill, which had begun in late 1981. The debate resumed in November 1982 but as an increasing number of parties and organizations boycotted the Council by mid-1983 the only non-Sandinista groups left in the debate were the PSCN, the MLC and the CUS. The law, which was finally approved on Aug. 17, 1983, permitted parties to form on the following conditions: (i) that their fundamental principles must be "popular, pluralistic, anti-imperialist and anti-racist"; (ii) that they submit details of their membership, leaders and election platform to the Council of State; and (iii) that they must be represented on the Council of State and abstain from "activities against public order and the stability of the institutions of the national reconstruction government". Pastora, who had resigned as deputy defence minister in mid-1981 and had been replaced as MPS chief by Humberto Ortega, left the country and announced at a news conference in San José (Costa Rica) on April 15, 1982, that he intended to launch the "struggle for the true Sandinist revolution". In September 1982 he announced the formation in Costa Rica of the Democratic Revolutionary Alliance (Arde), which was based on his own recently-formed party, the Sandinista Revolutionary Front (FRS), and included many members of the MDN, although the more left-wing elements of the MDN remained in Nicaragua as members of the CD. Robelo, who became a co-leader of Arde, had left Nicaragua in June 1982 after his estate had been confiscated under the agrarian reform programme, and his Gracsa oil production plant and his house in Chinandega were declared forfeit to the state because of his "aggressive activity".

Two other prominent figures defected in 1982 in protest against what they felt to be a more left-wing trend in the government's policies: Alfredo César Aguirre, the president of the Central Bank (with ministerial rank) went into voluntary exile in May, and Francisco Fiallos, the ambassador to the United States, joined Arde in December. Arde launched its first military offensive in April 1983 (see section 3.4.3; for attempts to unify all contra forces in 1984, 1985 and 1986, see section 3.1.5).

In 1983 the contras intensified their programme of economic sabotage culminating in the attack on Corinto on Oct. 10 (see section 3.4.4), widely believed to have been planned by and executed with the help of US military units which had begun joint military manoeuvres with Honduras two months earlier. The Nicaraguan fear of direct US intervention was accentuated by the military occupation of the island of Grenada later in October (see section 5.3.3).

1.5.27: Military Service Bill—December 1983 Decrees

The government faced strong criticism with the passage into law on Aug. 31, 1983, of its military service bill, making military service compulsory for all men aged 17–21 (while leaving it optional for women). Humberto Ortega, who presented the bill to the Council of State, said that it aimed to institutionalize the Sandinista revolution rather than prepare for any foreign engagement, and it was this aspect of the bill which provoked so much opposition. The PSCN boycotted discussion of the bill and the PCD denounced it on the grounds that it would be used to train men to fight for Sandinism rather than for the nation. Moreover, the Nicaraguan episcopal conference issued a statement on Aug. 31 saying that "no-one can be obliged to take arms in defence of a fixed ideology with which he does not agree, nor to give military service in the cause of a political party". (For further details of church reaction, see section 2.4.6.)

In the wake of the US-led invasion of Grenada the government introduced two decrees in December 1983 which, according to d'Escoto, removed a possible pretext for a US invasion of Nicaragua. The amnesty decree of Dec. 1 extended to all Miskitos (the east coast Indians, many of whom had joined the FDN because of their treatment by the Sandinista government—see section 4.3.3) and to all Nicaraguan citizens "involved in criminal actions because of the situation of aggression" in northern Zelaya. Those eligible were encouraged to return from Honduras with a promise of safe conduct, land and voting rights. The government maintained that the decree would cover all 307 Miskitos currently in prison convicted of political offences (although the Miskito leader, Steadman Fagoth Müller, claimed that this was only a fraction of the real number) but would exclude all members of Somoza's security forces and any contra leader who had appealed for foreign assistance (i.e. including Fagoth Müller).

It was announced in February 1984 that so far 806 contras had applied for amnesty and that the offer would be extended into May. Those taking up the amnesty included Carlos Coronel, an Arde political adviser, who returned to Managua on Sept. 10, 1983, to discuss reconciliation with the FSLN government (having broken with it in October 1981). Two days after the amnesty decree Wheelock Román announced a modification of the land-reform programme (see section 2.3.5) and Córdova Rivas said that certain prisoners convicted of politically-linked crimes would be released under special pardon laws.

The Dec. 4 decree promised that the Council of State would begin discussion of a draft electoral law on Jan. 31, 1984, and that a general election date would be fixed, the state of emergency lifted, full civil rights restored and press censorship relaxed. The opposition, however, did not welcome these plans. Rivas Gasteazoro claimed that the government was "not yet showing the will to make openings which would satisfactorily allow us to participate in the elections, while Clemente Guido of the PCD said that "we will not lend ourselves to a legitimization of totalitarianism" and that "the political space left us is now so small that we may soon have to dissolve the party and take up arms".

The main provisions of the electoral law, which was passed in March 1984, were that (i) armed contras taking advantage of the December 1983 amnesty would be able to take part in the process, although armed contra leaders and untried former National Guardsmen would be excluded; (ii) members of the armed forces would be allowed to vote, but not to campaign on behalf of any party, and would be eligible as candidates only if they gained leave of absence from their military duties; (iii) voting would be by means of proportional representation, with the country divided into 10 constituencies (with two to cover Managua), each of which would elect between one and 13 representatives; (iv) all people aged 16 and over would be obliged to register to vote, although voting would not be compulsory; (v) parties would be allowed to receive funds from abroad if these were registered with the Central Bank; (vi) parties would be allowed 15 minutes each day on television and 30 minutes on the radio for their broadcasts during the campaign, with private radio stations obliged to set aside 5–30 minutes a day for party political broadcasts; and (vii) candidates would be elected for a six-year term and the National Assembly draft a new constitution within two years.

1.5.28: 1984 Presidential and Legislative Elections

In preparation for the general elections on Nov. 4, 1984, the state of emergency was relaxed on July 19 (having been extended in May, when it was supposed to have been lifted, on the grounds that the country was "endangered by foreign aggression") and fully lifted on Oct. 20 except in "war zones" on the northern and southern border regions. An interim easing of restrictions on Aug. 6 included the restoration of the right to strike, and the first strike since 1979 occurred on Aug. 20–24 when workers at the state-owned Victoria Brewery walked out.

The CD's intended presidential candidate, Arturo Cruz, said in mid–1984 that the CD would participate in the elections only if there were a "national dialogue" including the contras and other concessions including the separation of the FSLN party organization from the state apparatus. FDN and Arde leaders pledged their support for Cruz and said they would consider a ceasefire if his demands were met. The demand for negotiation with the contras was dropped on Aug. 15. Talks between Arce Castaño (FSLN party leader) and Cruz on Oct. 1 broke down, preventing the signature of a pre-agreed document postponing elections until Jan. 13, 1985, if a ceasefire were declared by Oct. 10 and an end to hostilities called by the FDN and Arde before Oct. 25. The CD vice-presidential candidate, Fletes, said on Oct. 17 that the CD had decided to boycott the elections because of what it saw as the FSLN's "unwillingness to cede power".

The presidential election was won by the FSLN candidate, Daniel Ortega, with 66.9 per cent of the vote, against Clemente Guido of the PCD with 14 per cent, Virgilio Godoy Reyes of the PLI with 9.6 per cent, Mauricio Díaz of the PPSC with 5.6, and the PCN, PSN and Marxist–Leninist Popular Action Movement (MAP–ML) candidates with less than two per cent each. The turnout for the election was 75 per cent and foreign observers (including an all-party British parliamentary team) reported that the voting was free from intimidation and irregularities, although the US State Department called the elections a "farce" as "there was no meaningful opposition".

President Ortega and his vice-presidential running-mate, Ramírez Mercado, were sworn into office on Jan. 10, 1985, at a ceremony attended by only three foreign heads of state (from Yugoslavia, Vietnam and Cuba). In his inaugural speech Ortega said: "We are not guerrillas. We are not militants. Nicaragua will never be an aggressive country." In the new National Assembly, which replaced the Council of State and held its first session on Jan. 9 the FSLN held 61 seats, the PCD 14, the PLI nine, the PPSC six and the PCN, PSN and MAP–ML two each. The new government incorporated only two cabinet changes, but a new planning commission was created, headed by the president and directly responsible to him. In addition a new amnesty was announced which, unlike the offer of December 1983, was extended to contra leaders. It was officially rejected by the FDN and Arde, but those taking it up included an FDN commander, José Efren Martínez Mondragón, who decided to leave the FDN because of its human rights abuses (see section 4.2.5).

Ortega introduced an austerity package on Feb. 8, 1985, in support of the national war effort, including a devaluation and the abolition of state food subsidies (see section 2.2.4).

1.5.29: National Dialogue—Reintroduction of State of Emergency

The parties and organizations belonging to the Council of State met on Oct. 31, 1984, in a national dialogue, including the parties boycotting the election, which Arce Castaño said would still be allowed to exist even though their action rendered them illegal. At the first meeting the CD demanded a postponement of the elections and guarantees of a "free and fair" campaign, but these demands were ignored and the CD parties withdrew. According to Rivas Gasteazoro "there is no point, the national dialogue is dominated by the Sandinistas; we think that only genuine political parties should take part", and he also accused other non-Sandinista organizations of having "sold out". Pedro Joaquín Chamorro Barrios, (a leading member of the CD) left the country in December, stating that he would not return until the travel restrictions imposed on political opponents by the government were lifted, as he and some 30 other leading opposition members had experienced difficulty in gaining exit visas.

The government suspended the dialogue on Nov. 30, 1984, as not all parties had agreed to the drafting of a call to international organizations "to restrain the political, military and economic aggressions planned by the North American government". Various attempts were made to resume the dialogue, with the opposition parties hoping to exclude the FSLN, but in February 1985 Chamorro and Cruz announced that they were joining with contra leaders in an effort (which turned out to be unsuccessful) to force the government to resume the dialogue (see section 6.3.4).

Borge announced on Oct. 15, 1985, a renewal of the 1982 state of emergency because of new contra military efforts (made possible by new US funding—see section 5.2.5), and blamed the United States for creating what he described as a "truly extraordinary situation" for Nicaragua. The National Assembly voted on Oct. 30 to restore certain judicial freedoms including habeas corpus, although the suspension of other freedoms, including the right to strike, was ratified. Two days after the reintroduction of the state of emergency Borge announced that 134 people had been arrested on suspicion of aiding contras, and in the following weeks several dozen religious and political activists were reportedly detained and interrogated. The government clamped down particularly on church and opposition news media, closing Radio Católica on Jan. 1, 1986 (for failing to broadcast the president's new year message) and La Prensa on June 26 (for alleged disinformation and for being "an accomplice of the aggression which the Reagan administration is hurling against Nicaragua"). (For action against church leaders, see also section 2.4.5.)

1.5.30: Debate on Draft Constitution

In March 1986 a special constitutional committee (formed in June 1985 from all the parties represented in the National Assembly except the PLI, which had withdrawn) issued a draft document for public debate. It embodied democracy (defined as the construction of a society with the participation of the people) and political pluralism (i.e. the existence and involvement of all political organizations except those advocating a return to *Somocismo*). The state apparatus would comprise the legislature (an assembly), the executive, the judiciary and the electoral branch, and the national president would be both chief of state and head of the armed forces. With regard to the economy, work would be considered the principal source of wealth and the state would oversee economic activity to guarantee national development. The first public meeting on the draft was held on May 18, and it was anticipated that a revised version would be presented to the Assembly in time for the new constitution to be promulgated in January 1987.

The final debate in the Assembly opened on Sept. 16, 1986, despite a request for a two-month delay from the PLI, PPSC, PSN, PCD and PCN, which wanted the government first to reach "real agreement with democratic organizations in favour of national unity to face the crisis which is shaking the country", and to abide by the vote of Oct. 30, 1984, on civil liberties and specifically freedom of the press.

Notes

1. Black, *Triumph of the People*, pp. 43–44.
2. *Ibid.*, p. 58.
3. *Ibid.*, p. 59.
4. *Ibid.*, pp. 115–16. Black asserts that by early 1978 Udel was losing political ground because of the ineffectiveness of the bourgeois opposition, while failing to be sufficiently radical to attract mass support.
5. See for example Pearce, *op. cit.*, p. 125. Pearce also attributes the failure of the negotiations to the US rejection of an FAO proposal that a settlement could be reached if the whole Somoza family were excluded from political and military power and if the FAO formed a government.
6. For daily chronology for May 29–July 19 and maps on national offensive and Managua campaign, see Black, *op. cit.*, chapter 10.
7. *Ibid.*, pp. 336–38.
8. Black, *op. cit.*, p. 257.

1.6: COSTA RICA

1.6.1: Chronology

1835 San José becomes capital
1842 Conservative dictator Carillo ousted by Morazán
Morazán defeated and executed
1844 New constitution promulgated
1849 Establishment of conservative government under Mora
1859 Resignation of Mora; Montealegre family hold power until 1869
New constitution promulgated
1860 Mora leads abortive invasion and is executed
1869 New constitution promulgated
1870 Inauguration of liberal government under Guardia
1871 New liberal constitution promulgated
1889 Elections won by conservatives
1890 Inauguration of conservative government under Rodríguez
1894 Rodríguez's nominee Iglesias becomes president
1902 Election of liberal candidate Esquivel
1906 Inconclusive election: Congress chooses liberal González
1910 Election of conservative Jiménez Oreamuno
1914 Inconclusive election: Congress chooses non-contender González Flores
1917 Tinoco seizes power in coup and abrogates constitution
1919 Tinoco resigns
Constitution of 1871 restored
1924 Jiménez Oreamuno elected
1928 González elected
1930 Formation of CP under Mora Valverde
1932 Formation of PRN
Jiménez Oreamuno elected president
1936 PRN candidate Cortés elected
1940 PRN candidate Calderón gains landslide victory; Cortés later forms PD
1943 CP reorganized as PVP
1944 Election won by Picado of PRN–PVP coalition
1947 Formation of PRD by Carazo
1948 Election won by Ulate of PD–PSD–PUN coalition, although PRN gains majority in Congress, which annuls results (*February*)
Outbreak of civil war (*March*)
Picado overthrown by forces led by Figueres (*April*)
Formation of Junta of Second Republic (*May*)
Supporters of Picado stage unsuccessful invasion attempt from Nicaragua (*December*)
1949 Ulate inaugurated as president (*November*)
New constitution promulgated abolishing army and outlawing PVP (leading to formation of PAS) (*November*)
1951 Formation of PLN by Figueres

1953	Figueres wins presidential election as PLN candidate
1955	Further abortive invasion attempt by exiles based in Nicaragua
1958	PUN candidate Echandí elected president
1962	Election won by Orlich of PLN
	Formation of PDC
1966	Election won by Trejos of National Unification Coalition
1970	Figures wins election as PLN candidate
	Anti-government protest over US interest denounced by government as being provoked by "communist elements"
1974	Oduber of PLN elected president
1975	Government purchase of uncultivated land owned by United Brands
	PVP legalized
1976	Emergence of splits in PLN and PUN
	Formation of PRC by Calderón
1977	Restoration of consular relations with Cuba
1978	Formation of Unity coalition by PRD, PRC, PDC and PU
	Presidential election won by Carazo of Opposition Union
	In legislative election PVP–MRP gains three seats
1981	Report of parliamentary commission on government involvement in arms trafficking to the FSLN (*May*)
	Moratorium on debt payments (*September*)
1982	Election won by Monge of PLN
	Emergence of splits in PSC and MRP (which later changes name to MNR)
	IMF agreement (*December*)
1983	Division in PVP; Mora leaves to form PPC
	Unity renamed USC under leadership of Calderón
1984	Beginning of 10-week strike by banana workers (*July*)
	Cabinet reshuffle, indicating right-wing shift in government (*August*)
	IMF agreement (*September*)
1985	Arrival of US military training team (*May*)
1986	General elections won by PLN (*February*)
	Arrival of US military engineers for "Operation Peace Bridge" (*February*)
	Inauguration of Arias Sánchez (*May*)

1.6.2: Early History—Alternation of Liberal and Conservative Rule

During the years of the federation Costa Rica enjoyed a far greater degree of political stability than its neighbours to the north, especially during the the administration of Juan Mora Fernández in 1824–33. In 1835 the conservative dictator Braulio Carillo took power and in 1838 became the independent country's first ruler, proclaiming his rule for life in 1841. The following year, however, he was overthrown by Morazán in the latter's unsuccessful attempt to renew the federation, (see section 1.1.4), but Morazán was himself ousted later in 1842 and executed. Although Costa Rica had been one of the united provinces it tended to look southwards to Panama (then part of Gran Colombia—see section 1.7.2) for economic links rather than northwards to Nicaragua.

After the Morazán episode there followed several years of political disorder, during which a new constitution was promulgated in 1844, while a basic charter of January 1847 established the office of president with a six-year term; a further charter of November 1848 designated Costa Rica a republic. A measure of stability was achieved following the inauguration in 1849 of the conservative government of Juan Rafael Mora Porras (which helped in the overthrow of the Walker government in Nicaragua—see section 1.5.3), but soon after he started his third term of office in 1859 Mora was deposed. A new government was formed under José María Montealegre (and a new constitution promulgated, reducing the presidential tenure to three years) and Mora's abortive invasion of 1860 resulted in his execution. The Montealegre family retained power until 1869, when another constitution was introduced, restoring the six-year term of office.

Conservative rule ended in 1870 when the New Liberal Tomás Guardia became president, and a liberal constitution came into effect in 1871 (which was to become the longest-lasting constitution in Central America, surviving 75 years with a two-year interruption); it established a four-year term for the president and a unicameral congress and prohibited the re-election of the president. In order to bypass this stipulation Guardia stepped down in 1876, (while remaining chief military commander) and resumed the presidency in 1877 until his death in 1882. Liberal rule was continued under Bernardo Soto, elected in 1885 (to hold office 1886–90), who made efforts to counter illiteracy by introducing compulsory free education.

In the 1889 elections, which were largely free of government interference, the conservatives emerged as the winners and José Joaquín Rodríguez took office as president the next year. Rodriguez ensured his succession in 1894 by another conservative, Rafael Iglesias, who persuaded Congress to amend the constitution to allow for his re-election in 1898. Under Iglesias Costa Rica became more closely involved in the affairs of its northern neighbours because of a dispute with the Zelaya government in Nicaragua—although the dispute was eventually resolved by the Marblehead Pact of 1906. Because it had been less involved in previous regional disputes Costa Rica also came to be seen as a natural mediator for other Central American conflicts and as a home for exiled dissidents.

Iglesias agreed to give his support to the liberal Ascención Esquivel in 1902, but in the 1906 election no candidate gained a clear lead, and so Congress declared the liberal Cleto González the winner. He was succeeded in 1910 by the conservative Ricardo Jiménez Oreamuno, and when no winner emerged in the 1914 election Jiménez ensured that the Congress elected his nominee, Alfredo González Flores (who had not contested the election). González introduced a series of unpopular measures, including an increase in taxes, and also aroused opposition for his attempts to control the mid-term congressional elections.

1.6.3: 1917 Military Coup—Reorganization of Political Parties

In 1917 a military coup was staged by the Minister of War, Federico Tinoco Granados, who abrogated the constitution and prepared to draft a new one. However, he failed to gain recognition from abroad, most damagingly from the United States, and was forced to resign in 1919. The 1871 constitution was restored, and in 1920 Julio Acosta García was elected to the presidency, succeeded by Jiménez in 1924, with Cleto González being elected in 1928 and Jiménez again in 1932.

In the early 1930s several new political forces emerged, in particular the communists, who formed a party in 1930 under Manuel Mora Valverde called the Workers' and Peasants' Bloc. In 1934 two of the party's candidates were elected to seats in the national Congress and the party headed a strike in the banana zone of Limón which gained the workers a raise in the minimum wage (the practice of a minimum wage rate having been adopted by the government the previous year).

The 1936 presidential election was won by León Cortés Castro of the reformist National Republican Party (PRN), which had been formed in 1932, and moderate political and social changes were introduced. He was succeeded in 1940 by another PRN candidate, Rafael Angel Calderón Guardia, who gained a landslide victory and proceeded to implement radical reforms in public welfare and labour legislation with the support of the communists, who were renamed the Popular Vanguard Party (PVP) in 1943. The reforms caused a split within the PRN, with the more conservative members under Cortés breaking away to form the Democratic Party (PD).

The PRN and PVP formed a working coalition to contest the 1944 elections and its candidate, Teodoro Picado Michalski, defeated Cortés, while in Congress the PRN gained 28 seats, the PD 13 and the PVP four. The PVP deputies were very active, arousing opposition to what many feared was communist influence. The mid-term congressional elections of 1946 were contested by two new groups; (i) the conservative National Unification Party (PUN), led by Otilio Ulate (an opponent of Calderón), who accused the PRN of having links with Moscow and of fraudulent practices in the 1944 elections; and (ii) the Social Democratic Party (PSD), led by José Figueres Ferrer, who had gone into exile in Mexico in 1942–44. The two new parties each won a seat from the PRN.

1.6.4: Outbreak of Civil War—Formation of Junta of Second Republic —Inauguration of Ulate—Promulgation of New Constitution

The two candidates in the February 1948 presidential election were Ulate for the National Union (comprising the PD, PSD and PUN) and Calderón; Ulate was declared the winner. The PRN, however, retained its majority in Congress and voted in favour of the results being annulled. Ulate was briefly arrested and civil war broke out in March when forces led by Figueres took up arms against President Picado.

In April Figueres entered the capital and deposed Picado, and in May executive authority was assumed by the Junta of the Second Republic. (Calderón fled to Nicaragua, launching an abortive invasion attempt from there in December with the support of the Somoza government—see section 3.4.3) Agreement was reached that Figueres should head the junta as president for its duration until November 1949, when the assembly would acknowledge Ulate as the duly elected president for a four-year term. In the constituent assembly elections of December the PUN gained 33 seats, the new extreme right-wing Constitutional Party six, the PSD and others two; in the legislative election held 10 months later the PUN retained its majority while the PSD lost a seat. (The PSD was later reorganized in 1951 to form the National Liberation Party, still under Figueres' leadership.)

Ulate was inaugurated as president in November 1949 and a new constitution promulgated, which extended the franchise to women for the first time, abolished the national army (a measure begun by presidential decree in December 1948) and outlawed the PVP. Many communist supporters regrouped in the Socialist Action Party (PAS).

1.6.5: Elections, 1953–1970

Figueres gained a large majority in the presidential elections of July 25, 1953, and his National Liberation Party (PLN) also gained over half of the seats in Congress (against three for the PRN). Despite the abolition of the army the government managed to overcome a further invasion attempt by exiles in Nicaragua in 1955 (see section 3.4.3). The dominance of political life by Figueres as leader of the PLN and the strong mutual antagonism between him and Somoza helped to mould relations between the two countries until Somoza's downfall in 1979. (For use of Costa Rica as base for Nicaraguan rebels in 1959, ibid.) Figueres remained firmly anti-communist, but opposed any armed intervention in Guatemala in 1954, arguing instead in favour of political pressure on the Arbenz Government to moderate its more extreme left-wing policies.

In 1958 the PLN candidate, José Francisco Orlich, polled only 43 per cent of the vote, against 46 per cent for Mario Echandí Jiménez of the PUN; the PLN vote had been eroded when a dissident member, José Rossi Chavarría, decided to stand as a third candidate on an independent slate. In the concurrent congressional elections the PLN gained 20 seats, the PRN 11, the PUN 10, independents (supporting Rossi) three and the Revolutionary Civil Union one. It was speculated that Figueres might attempt to overturn the presidential result, but he said that the PLN would form a responsible opposition and was "not interested in creating difficulties for the new administration".

The PLN returned to power in 1962 when Orlich defeated Calderón of the PRN, Ulate of the PUN and Enrique Obregón of the PAS (which was specifically pro-Castro), while in the elections to an enlarged Congress the PLN gained 30 seats, the PRN 19 and the PUN eight, with none for the PAS. In preparation for the 1966 elections the PRN, PUN and Authentic Republican Union formed the National Unification coalition, whose candidate, José Joaquín Trejos Fernández, gained a majority of less than one per cent over Daniel Oduber Quiros of the PLN, while the PLN maintained its majority in Congress. (The PAS was barred from standing in these elections.)

Figueres was elected in 1970, defeating Echandí, while the other three contenders gained less than 4 per cent of the vote between them. In June 1966 there had been a proposal for a constitutional amendment to bar any former president from seeking a second term, but it had failed.

1.6.6: Involvement in Regional Political Conflicts

In the early 1970s there were signs of growing unrest, with the emergence of the Central American Revolutionary Commando (see section 3.1.6). On April 24, 1970, a group of over 200 demonstrators (mostly students) were arrested after trying to storm the legislature in protest over the signing by the government of a contract with the Aluminum Company of America (ALCOA), granting it the right to prospect for bauxite in Costa Rica. The protest had been organized by left-wing leaders who were concentrating on building up labour organizations rather than on political and electoral gains. The Minister of Public Security, Diego Trejas Fonseca, said in reference to the protest that the authorities had discovered a plan to overthrow the government, stirred up by "professional agitators" and "communist elements".

Figueres improved relations with communist countries, establishing diplomatic ties with Eastern Europe and allowing a Soviet embassy to open in San José. Nevertheless, during the electoral campaign of 1974 the issue of left-wing loyalties became so intense that the Supreme Electoral Tribunal banned the use of the words Marxist and communist. The PLN won 27 seats, the PUN 16 and the new right-wing National Independent Party (PNI) six, with the remaining eight distributed among the smaller parties. The presidential contest was won by Oduber of the PLN, the other candidates including Rodrigo Carazo Odio of the Democratic Renewal Party (PRD), who gained just under 10 per cent of the vote. Oduber continued the policy of friendly relations with communist countries, and on Jan. 14, 1975, the government announced that it had resumed trade relations with Cuba (full relations having been broken in 1962) and relations at consular level were restored in February 1977. (The government also became increasingly hostile to Somoza and favourable to the Sandinistas of Nicaragua—see section 3.4.3.) In 1975 the PVP was given legal status again, under the leadership of its secretary-general, Mario Solis; a land-reform programme was introduced and in October 1975 a national scheme was introduced including the takeover of the distribution of petroleum products (see section 2.3.6).

1.6.7: Party Realignments—1978 Elections

In 1976 the PLN split with Figueres heading a splinter group, leaving Oduber as party leader and Luis Alberto Monge Alvarez as secretary-general and presidential candidate. Figueres had been accused of financial irregularities while in office, and in particular of manipulating national laws in order to protect a friend of his, the US financier Robert Vesco, who was trying to avoid being forced to return to the United States to face charges of embezzlement. In the following month the PUN split when Calderón formed the Calderonist Republican Party (PRC).

The February 1978 elections were won by Carazo, the candidate of the Opposition Unity coalition (comprising the PRD, the Christian Democratic Party —PDC—and the Popular Union) with 49 per cent of the vote against Monge with 42 per cent. The remaining votes were cast for Rodrigo Gutiérrez Saenz of the People United (PU) coalition, comprising the PVP, the Socialist Party (PSC) and the Marxist Revolutionary People's Movement (MRP)—this last formation being reportedly a Sandinista support group. The PU gained three of the seats in the 57-member legislature.

1.6.8: Foreign Relations—1982 Elections

President Carazo was firmly anti-communist and his two major policy intentions were to fight corruption within the country and to scale down relations with communist countries. After a wave of strikes in August 1979 at the Atlantic port of Limón, during which clashes between strikers and the Civil Guard left two dead and some 100 injured, the President said in a television broadcast on Aug. 19 that three Soviet diplomats had been declared personae non gratae. He accused them of having interfered in the country's internal affairs and made references to "international agitators" and "anti-nationalist forces inside and outside the country". It had previously been suggested that the number of Soviet diplomats at the embassy in San José, which had grown to about 20, was excessive in view of the small scale of trading between the two countries. In November 1982 the government asked a further 17 Soviet diplomatic staff to leave, on the grounds that the original agreement made in 1970 provided for only eight staff and that a later protocol signed by the Costa Rican ambassador to Moscow raising the number to 25 was invalid. There were further strikes in December 1979 and January 1980 at the Standard Fruit and United Brands plantations in support of wage demands (see also section 2.2.5).

Consular relations with Cuba were broken on May 11, 1981, and the Costa Rican Foreign Minister claimed that Cuba had accused his government of "quite brazenly backing" a US "counter-revolutionary campaign" against Cuba. At the same time, however, Costa Rica was viewed by the right-wing Central American states and apparently also by the United States as too left-wing and was accused of involvement in supplying arms to left-wing guerrillas in the region.

On the domestic political front the dominant issue of 1981 was a disagreement over the conduct of negotiations with the IMF in the face of the country's deepening economic crisis (ibid). In April the Finance Minister, Hernán Saenz Jiménez, resigned when Carazo refused to support the IMF austerity programme; Saenz's successor also resigned very soon after taking office. During a visit to Washington in May 1981 Monge said that the PLN reserved the right to renegotiate the IMF agreement if it were elected in 1982. The economic crisis caused the government to move to the right, with an increased role for the private sector, and was used by the United States as an opportunity to impose its own Central American policy on Costa Rica. Although in 1981 the Costa Rican government refused US offers of military help against subversion after a few minor terrorist incidents, by 1984–85 circumstances had forced it into a closer relationship with Washington (see section 5.2.6).

Monge won the February 1982 election with 57 per cent of the vote against 33 per cent for Calderón of the Unity coalition (formerly the Opposition Union) and only 4 per cent for Echandí of the new conservative National Movement. In Congress the PLN gained 37 seats, Unity 18, PU four, National Movement one and the provincial Alajuela Democratic Party (PAD) one. Monge's campaign included the slogan "Return to the land", which became a programme designed to stimulate agricultural production and stem the rural exodus. He said that the country's democracy was threatened by the economic crisis and especially by the fall in the world coffee price.

In December 1983 the Unity coalition was formally registered as a single party under the name of the Social Christian Unity (PUSC) with Calderón as president. In July 1984 the Chamber of Commerce presented a 40-point US-backed plan recommending a break of relations with Nicaragua, full acceptance of the IMF economic reform proposals, imprisonment of trade union leaders who had called strikes and no negotiations with the banana workers who had just begun a strike that was to last three months (see section 2.2.5). The plan was denounced by President Monge as a "well-orchestrated and funded campaign to destabilize the government." In December 1984 Calderón was nominated the PUSC presidential candidate for the February 1986 elections, and the following month the PLN elected Oscar Arias Sánchez. Both nominations had been contested within the parties, although in the PUSC the other two contenders had withdrawn before the final ballot, and both reflected a right-wing drift in the parties, particularly as both candidates viewed the Sandinista government as a direct threat to Costa Rica.

1.6.9: Divisions in Left-wing Groups

The PSC was split in 1982 by splinter groups and in December 1983 the PVP divided when Mora left to form the People's Party (PPC), generally portrayed as a less hardline communist party, while Humberto Vargas became PVP leader. It was reported in February 1985 that the PVP had been excluded from the PU, although the PPC was allowed to rejoin, and that a split similar to that within the PVP had developed within the MRP, within the mainline party still led by Otto Castro, and the more moderate splinter group, called the New Republican Movement (MNR) under the leadership of Erick Ardón. According to Mora and Ardón the split within the ranks of the left in Costa Rica (and elsewhere in Central America) was instigated by the United States to render them ineffective. Soon after the inauguration of the Monge government the MNR was accused of having organized 4,000 armed men on the Atlantic coast in preparation for a coup. In a meeting with Ardón, Monge said that the government had taken the accusation seriously as it had been based on a US State Department document.

1.6.10: 1986 General Elections

In the general elections held on Feb. 2, 1986, the PLN lost four seats but narrowly retained its overall majority with 29 seats as against 25 for the PUSC and one each for the PU and the Popular Alliance (a recently formed left-wing coalition including the PVP) and one independent candidate. The PLN presidential candidate, Arias Sánchez, gained 52.3 per cent of the vote to defeat Calderón (with 45.8); while both men had campaigned chiefly on the issues of the Nicaraguan threat and the state of the national economy, Arias Sánchez had emerged as the more conciliatory to the Sandinistas and the less monetarist in economic policy, promising to uphold the welfare state while cutting public expenditure. In his victory speech he undertook to renegotiate the foreign debt and to ensure that in future no more than 25 per cent of foreign aid be devoted to debt service. He was inaugurated on May 8.

1.6.11: Relations with Nicaragua and United States

Costa Rica favoured the Sandinistas before the fall of Somoza and after 1979 tried to pursue a policy of neutrality in the general Central American conflict (see section 3.4.3). During a European tour in June 1984 Monge reiterated his government's commitment to neutrality as follows: "We are irrevocably opposed to war; our neutrality is unarmed neutrality as Costa Rica has no army and does not wish to have one . . . We are not ideologically neutral; we support democracy and oppose all dictatorship. . . . We remain convinced . . . that poor countries do not have resources for education and an army. We choose education, health and the welfare of our people."

There was, however, widespread opposition to US policy, and on May 15, 1984, the PLN organized a demonstration by up to 30,000 people in the capital to declare their support for neutrality with the slogan "No to armaments for Costa Rica" (see also section 5.2.6). The organizers expressly banned anti-US and pro-FSLN slogans, but there were calls for Pastora to cease using Costa Rica as a base for his armed activities against the Nicaraguan government.

The unpopularity of the economic austerity measures (see section 2.2.5) made the country more amenable to offers of US financial assistance, apparently made in exchange for greater and more tangible support for US policies.

In a cabinet reshuffle of August 1984 Angel Solano, the Minister of Public Security, who had strongly criticized any links between the Costa Rican authorities and the anti-Sandinista guerrilla group Arde, was replaced. At the end of August an agreement was signed between the US Information Agency (USIA) and the Costa Rican Information and Culture Association (ACIC) to provide for the transmission of Voice of America broadcasts by radio stations in northern Costa Rica with funds from the USIA. President Reagan claimed that "the radio stations would broadcast two firm voices invoking democratic ideals: that of Costa Rica and that of the United States", but the PLN criticized the agreement as "a violation of Costa Rican sovereignty in the north of the country". The government defended its decision by saying that the ACIC was a private association with the right to subcontract any agency, and that it therefore did not have final authority in the matter.

President-elect Arias Sánchez stated in February 1986: "We always claimed that choice in this election was between rifles and bread; the people have chosen bread." His government would enforce the country's neutrality and would not "tolerate abuses of our hospitality" by Nicaraguan contras, "but we will also not permit any action that endangers our sovereignty", and would retain neutrality while being "eternally grateful" for continued US financial assistance.

In his book on Costa Rica, published in 1984, Leonard Bird comments: "Since the Somoza dictatorship in Nicaragua was finally overthrown in July 1979, the situation in Costa Rica has not reverted to normal as we hoped. This is to a large extent due to the United States, which has sought to encourage and assist the Somozistas' endeavours to stage a counter-revolution and to dislodge the Sandinista government."[1]

Note

1. Leonard Bird, *Costa Rica*, London, Sheppard Press, 1984, p. 183.

1.7: PANAMA

1.7.1: Chronology

1821	Declaration of independence
1822	Unification with Gran Colombia
1830	Secession of Venezuela and Ecuador from Gran Colombia
1840	Revolt gives Panama brief independence until 1842
1846	US–New Granada Treaty
1850	Building of Panama Railway, completed by 1855
1859	Revolt led by Mosquera
1860	US troops restore order
1863	New Granada renamed Colombia
1878	French Panama Canal Company acquires right to dig canal
1879	Excavation work begins on canal
1885	Revolt leads to intervention by US forces to protect railway and US property
1889	French Panama Canal Company goes bankrupt
1899	Outbreak of civil war in Colombia
1903	Hay-Herrán Treaty (*January*)
	Panama gains independence from Colombia with US help (*November*)
	Hay-Bunau-Varilla Treaty (*November*)
1904	New constitution promulgated
	National army disbanded
1908–1912	National elections held under US supervision
1914	Panama Canal opened
1918	Constitutional crisis leads to US intervention; liberal Porras installed as president
1932	Election of Harmodio Arias
1936	Arosemana elected
	First revision of 1903 Canal Treaty, in which USA agrees to non-intervention
1939	Revised Treaty ratified
	Death of Arosemana; replaced by First Vice-President Boyd
1940	Arias Madrid of National Party elected unopposed
1941	New right-wing constitution promulgated
	Arias Madrid deposed in bloodless coup; replaced by Adolfo de la Guardia
1942	Defence agreement with USA on US stations and airfields in Panama
1943	Abortive plot against de la Guardia government
1945	Congress elect Jiménez president
1947	Resolution of controversy arising from 1942 defence agreement
1948	Constitutional crisis; Diaz Arosemana elected narrowly defeating Arias Madrid
1949	Death of President Diaz Arosemana; bloodless coup led by Remón installs Arias Madrid

1951 Arias Madrid overthrown; coalition government formed
1952 Remón elected president as candidate of Patriotic Coalition
1955 Assassination of Remón; inauguration of Guizado, who is then impeached and replaced by Arias Espinosa
Second revision of Canal Treaty
1956 Election of Ernesto de la Guardia of National Patriotic Coalition
1959 Abortive invasion by Cuban group, disowned by Castro
Anti–US riots over Canal Zone
1960 Election of Chiari of National Opposition Union
1964 Brief severing of diplomatic relations with USA; OAS called in to mediate
Robles elected president
1968 Constitutional crisis; Arias Madrid elected
Arias Madrid overthrown by Torrijos; formation of junta (*October*)
1969 Unsuccessful coup attempt against Torrijos
1972 Election of 505–member National Assembly of Community Representative on non-party basis
New constitution gives Torrijos executive power as Chief of Government
1973 US–Panama Declaration preparing for negotiation of new canal treaty
1974 Restoration of diplomatic relations with Cuba
1975 Joint Declaration on Zone
1977 Agreement in principle reached on new treaties, approved in Panama by referendum
1978 US Senate approves treaties
Legislative elections give majority to pro-government candidates
Formation of PRD
National Assembly elects Royo president
1979 Beginning of registration of political parties (*March*)
After amendments by US Senate, new Canal Treaties take effect (*October*)
Arrival of deposed Shah of Iran (*December*)
1980 Shah leaves for Egypt (*March*)
Partial elections to National Legislative Council (*September*)
1981 Torrijos killed in air crash (*July*)
1982 Resignation of President Royo under National Guard pressure, replaced by de la Espriella
1983 Constitutional amendments approved in referendum
1984 Resignation of de la Espriella, replaced by Illueca (*February*)
Election won by Ardito Barletta of PRD over Arias Madrid (*May*)
Inauguration of new government, with substantial majority in Assembly for Ardito's supporting coalition Unade (*October*)
1985 Resignation of Ardito and replacement by del Valle (*September*)
1986 Blazing Trail and Kindle Liberty exercises by US forces (*January–May*)

1.7.2: Early History

Although Panama is geographically part of Central America its early history after the Spanish conquest was more bound up with the South American mainland developments. Over the last hundred years, however, Panamanian

108

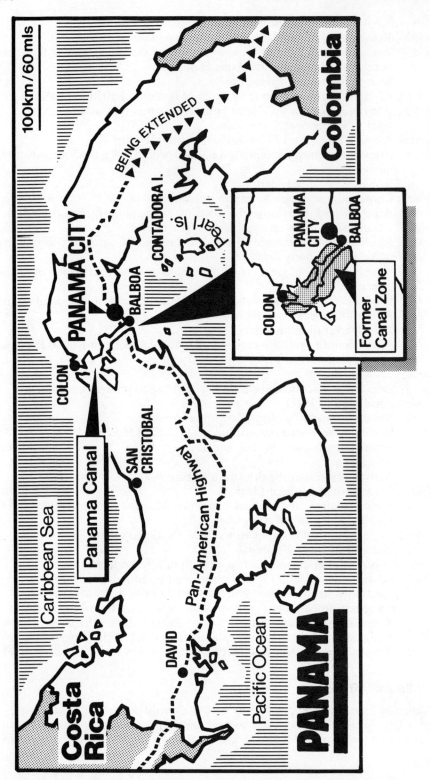

affairs have been dominated by the decision to cut the transisthmian canal through Panamanian territory. It is only more recently that Panama has become involved in Central American affairs, partly because US forces monitoring events in the region are stationed in the country (see section 5.2.7) and partly through the government's membership of the Contadora Group (see section 6.5.1).

Christopher Columbus arrived in present-day Panama in 1502, and 11 years later another explorer, Vasco Núñez de Balboa, crossed the isthmus to reach the Pacific. The first royal *Audiencia* at Panama City was established in 1533, to form the seat of government for an area extending as far south as Peru. The following year Charles V of Spain instructed officials to consider the construction of a canal across the land to facilitate the shipment of Peruvian mineral wealth back to Spain. This plan did not materialize and for the next three centuries, with the decline of the Spanish monarchy, the area was a focal point for European buccaneering activity. In 1751 Panama was placed under the jurisdiction of the government of Santa Fé de Bogotá in New Granada (Colombia).

Following the Mexican lead of a few months earlier, Panama declared its independence in November 1821, but the following year it opted for incorporation into Gran Colombia. This federation also included Venezuela and Ecuador, although these two countries seceded in 1830 while Panama remained under Colombia (under the constitution of 1831). A short-lived revolt against the Colombian authorities was staged in 1840 by Col. Tomás Herrera, but was overcome within two years and a new constitution promulgated in 1842 brought Panama under the greater control of a centralized government in Bogotá. A semi-federal system of government was introduced in the constitution of 1853, with further amendments to consolidate Panamanian regional autonomy in 1855 and 1858; however, the passage in 1859 of legislation restricting these measures of devolution provoked a new revolt, led by Gen. Tomás de Mosquera. Under the 1863 constitution Panama was granted independence as a province within Colombia, but 12 years later Colombian troops intervened in the provincial government, deposing the Panamanian president, Pablo Arosemana. After a revolt in 1885 a new constitution promulgated in 1886 placed more rigid controls over Panama.

1.7.3: US Role in Panama—1846 US–New Granada Treaty

The United States concluded a treaty with New Granada (Colombia) in 1846, in which Article 35 stated: "The United States guarantees, positively and efficaciously, to New Granada . . . the perfect neutrality of the isthmus, with the view that the free transit from one to the other sea may not be interrupted or embarassed in any future time while this treaty exists, . . . and the United States also guarantees . . . the rights of sovereignty and property which New Granada had and possesses over the said territory." The US interest in Panama as an important transit point increased with the California gold rush of 1849 and the building by a US concern of the Panama Railway in 1850–55. Under the 1846 treaty US forces restored order in Panama in 1860, 1873, 1885, 1901 and 1902 to protect the railway and US property, generally.

Initially the contract to construct a transisthmian canal was won by a French concern, the Panama Canal Company, and Ferdinand de Lesseps began work on the project in 1879. The company greatly underestimated the scale of the task and it is reported that between 16,000 and 20,000 men lost their lives on the project before operations were suspended in 1888. The company went bankrupt the following year, sparking off a political scandal in France. The collapse of the French company left the United States as the main contender for building the canal as the Clayton-Bulwer Treaty of 1850 applied only to the Nicaraguan route (see section 1.1.5).

1.7.4: Independence—Negotiation of First Canal Treaty

In January 1903 the US Secretary of State, John Hay, reached an agreement with the Colombian government (known as the Hay-Herrán Treaty), authorizing the Panama Canal Company to sell out to the United States. Under its provisions a strip of land six miles (9.6 km) wide along the proposed route of the canal would be leased to the United States for 100 years, although Colombia would retain sovereignty over the territory; in return the United States would pay $10,000,000 in gold as an initial payment and an annual rent of $250,000 from nine years after the conclusion of the agreement. The US Senate ratified the treaty, but its Colombian counterpart raised objections, precipitating a revolt in Panama on Nov. 3. (Panama had become increasingly restive during the "1,000 days" civil war in Colombia which lasted from 1899 until 1903).

Colombian forces were despatched to deal with the Panamanian revolt, but nine US ships were also sent, ostensibly to protect the railway, and US officials prevented the Colombian troops from crossing the isthmus. A new regime led by Manuel Amador Guerrero was recognized as the de jure government by the United States on Nov. 13, 1903, and a Frenchman, Philippe Bunau-Varilla (a member of the Panama Canal Company who helped to foster the revolt and subsequently became a minister in the new administration), immediately left for Washington to negotiate the sale of the company's holdings to the United States.

The Hay-Bunau-Varilla Treaty was concluded on Nov. 18, 1903, incorporating the terms of the Hay-Herrán agreement, except that the United States was granted the lease in perpetuity. The new treaty was drafted in such haste that it contained a highly ambiguous provision regarding the zone, granting Panama sovereignty and the US "sovereign rights", without explaining how this arrangement would operate in practice. The first major dispute to arise out of this clause came within a few months in 1904, when Panama objected to the US government's exercise of sovereignty in establishing ports of entry, customs houses, tariffs and post offices with the zone.

The US role in assuring Panama's achievement of independence from Colombia in 1903 was justified by the United States in terms of the 1846 US–New Granada Treaty; thereafter Washington continued to have close involvement in Panama's internal affairs. The elections of 1908 and 1912 were held under US supervision (the conservative José Domingo de Obaldía elected in 1908 being succeeded in 1912 by the liberal Belisario Porras). In 1918 US forces were sent to resolve a constitutional crisis, after which Porras became president again. In 1920 and 1924 the opposition candidates requested US electoral supervision in an attempt to counter the influence of Porras, while in 1928 Porras himself requested US supervision; in each case such US assistance was refused, however. The election of 1932 was the first in which no party called for US intervention and was won by Harmodio Arias.

1.7.5: First Revision of Canal Treaty

Under an agreement signed on March 2, 1936, the US right of intervention to preserve order in Panama was revoked as being contrary to Roosevelt's "good neighbour" policy (see section 1.1.6). It was replaced by a declaration by both countries that they would co-operate for their mutual interests. The US annual rent for the canal was raised to $430,000 and a supplementary accord allowed Panama to build a highway from its territory to the city of Colón in the Canal Zone. The revised treaty came into effect when finally ratified by the US Senate in July 1939.

1.7.6: Political Developments, 1936–45—Controversy over US Military Bases

President Juan Demosthenes Arosemana, who had been elected to succeed Harmodio Arias in 1936, died in December 1938 and was replaced by the First Vice-President Augusto Boyd, who then completed the current term. The presidential election of June 1940 was won by Arnulfo Arias Madrid of the National Party (brother of Harmodio), after the opposition candidate, Ricardo Alfaro, withdrew from the contest. Arias pursued right-wing policies and introduced a new constitution (promulgated in 1941) extending the presidential term of office from four years to six and withdrawing Panamanian nationality from children of Asiatic and Negro parents "whose original language is not Spanish". Believed to have pro-Axis leanings (see also section 1.2, footnote 1), he was deposed in a bloodless coup in October 1941 and replaced by the pro-Allies Adolfo de la Guardia. On taking office the latter declared that the new government would collaborate fully in hemispheric defence and would respect Panama's contractual obligations with the United States.

In December 1944 a constitutional crisis erupted when de la Guardia refused to grant demands by the opposition parties (the Doctrinal Liberals, Reformists and Socialists) for a new constitution. Instead he suspended the current constitution, dissolved Congress and refused to resign at the end of his term, whereupon nearly 20 deputies fled to the Canal Zone and set up a rival "congress". The crisis was resolved in June 1945, however, when the Congress still in Panama City elected Enrique Jiménez to the presidency.

Panama concluded a defence agreement with the United States in May 1942, allowing the United States to hold military bases and airfields in Panamanian territory (outside the zone) on the condition that they withdrew from them after the war. This condition was not fulfilled, however, and by 1947 only 98 of the 134 bases had been evacuated. An agreement was initialled on Dec. 10, 1947, under which 14 bases would be leased to the United States for further periods of between five and 10 years, but the Panamanian Congress refused to ratify it after anti–US riots broke out in Panama City. The US State Department announced that although it held the 14 bases to be "essential" for the protection of the canal, it would accede to the Assembly's decision. Accordingly, all US personnel were withdrawn into the Canal Zone.

1.7.7: Disputed 1948 Presidential Election—Right-wing Coup and Counter-coup

The two leading contenders in the election of May 1948 were Arias Madrid (National Party) and Domingo Díaz Arosemana of the Liberal Party. When the votes were counted each side made allegations of fraud against the other and after clashes between Arias' supporters and the police, in which several died, a state of siege was declared on July 4. Arias claimed a majority and fled to the zone. The National Electoral Jury announced the final results on Aug. 7, according Diaz a majority of 2,364 votes, whereupon Diaz was sworn into office in October for a four-year term. Arias, meanwhile, had travelled to Costa Rica, but was arrested on arrival there in August because it had been reported in Panama that he intended to invade Panama with his supporters from Costa Rican territory.

President Diaz died in office in August 1949 and was replaced by First Vice-President Daniel Chanis, who was overthrown in November in a bloodless coup led by Lt.-Col. José Antonio Remón, the Chief of Police who installed Arias as President. (The previous day Chanis had demanded the resignation of Remón for failing to comply with a Supreme Court ruling relating to charges of corruption.) Although the US State Department initially announced that diplomatic relations had been severed, they were renewed a month later after assurances from Arias that the new government would fulfil Panama's international obligations.

In April 1950 Arias outlawed the Communist Party as "a negation of all democracy, contrary to Christian civilization and a menace to democratic regimes". In early May he claimed that "dissenters in league with international communism" were "imperilling the Republic, the canal and the security of the American continent" and announced that the 1946 constitution would be suspended in favour of the less liberal one of 1941. According to the Minister of Justice the 1946 constitution did not allow the government to "fulfil efficiently its international commitments and to contribute to the defence of the Panama Canal in the present world crisis"; moreover, he added, the 1941 constitution would be amended to suspend the right of habeas corpus "for a period of time indicated by circumstances".

A general strike was staged on May 9, 1950, in protest against the constitutional proposal, which was withdrawn the following day by Arias. He was subsequently impeached by the Assembly on charges of violating the constitution, imprisoned briefly and banned from public life. A provisional coalition government was formed under First Vice-President Alcibiades Arosemana pending fresh elections.

1.7.8: 1952 Election and Assassination of Remón

The presidential election held in May 1952 was won by Remón, who had resigned as Chief of Police in order to qualify as a candidate and who was supported by the five-party Patriotic Coalition (including the Authentic Revolutionary Party led by Alcibiades Arosemana). The other candidates were Roberto Chiari (whose father Rodolfo had been Liberal president in 1924–28) of the Civil Alliance (including the Liberal Party) and Pedro Morena of the small Conservative Party. As President, Remón introduced a number of economic, financial and agricultural reforms, and outlawed all forms of communism and fascism.

The government faced a crisis when Remón was assassinated on Jan. 2, 1955. First Vice-President José Ramón Guizado took over as President, but on Jan. 15 the Assembly received a letter from the self-confessed assassin, Rubén Miró, who implicated Guizado in the plot. Guizado was impeached and sentenced to seven years' imprisonment, but when his trial opened in October 1957 Miró retracted his confession and was acquitted. In consequence, Guizado was released.

The former Second Vice-President, Ricardo Arias Espinosa, held office as President until October 1956, when he was replaced by Ernesto de la Guardia of the National Patriotic Coalition (CPN), elected in May. In the concurrent legislative elections the CPN won 42 of the 53 seats in the Assembly.

1.7.9: Second Revision of Canal Treaty—Anti–US Riots

Remón's achievements in office included the negotiation of a further revision to the Canal Treaty to improve the terms for Panama, specifically those covering the US annual rent (which was still only $430,000 in 1953 even though the tolls on the canal for that year amounted to $52,000,000) and rates of pay for US and Panamanian employees in the zone. The new treaty, which was signed in Panama City on Jan. 25, 1955, contained the following main provisions: (i) the annual rent would be increased to $1,930,000 (whereas Panama had requested either $5,000,000 or a fixed percentage of toll receipts); (ii) the Panamanian government would be allowed to levy taxes on some 17,000 Panamanians working in the zone but living outside it; (iii) the United States would return to Panama land it no longer required, worth an estimated $20,000,000 to $30,000,000; (iv) the Canal Company (operating the canal on behalf of the US government) would abolish wage distinctions between US and Panamanian employees; (v) supplies mined, produced or manufactured in Panama and purchased in the zone would be exempted from the "Buy American" Act giving preference to US producers; and (vi) Panamanian ship dealers would have the right to supply everything except fuel to ships in transit through the canal. The revised treaty was ratified by Panama in March and by the United States in July.

In 1959 anti–US sentiments led to riots in the capital on Nov. 3, when demonstrators, who had tried to enter the zone and hoist the Panamanian flag, were driven back by US police using clubs, tear gas and fire-hoses, and then went to the US embassy in Panama City, tore down the US flag and replaced it with a Panamanian one. The US authorities protested against the damage to US property and claimed that the Panamanian police had failed to intervene. President de la Guardia deplored the violence and said that although the demands were justified they should be made through diplomatic channels. Talks with US representatives were held on Nov. 21–24, and it was understood that Panama accused the United States of failing to observe the terms of the revised 1955 treaty, notably by allowing foreign goods to be imported into the zone instead of giving preference to US and Panamanian goods.

President Eisenhower announced on April 19, 1960, that he had approved a nine-point programme to improve relations between the two countries with regard to the zone, incorporating (i) a 10 per cent rise in the wages of unskilled and semi-skilled workers; (ii) an extension of the apprentice scheme to allow Panamanians greater opportunities for promotion; (iii) the renovation of substandard housing for Panamanian workers in the zone; (iv) the construction of new housing for workers living outside the zone; (v) the installation by the Canal Company of a new water main for the suburbs of Panama City at a cost of $750,000; (vi) a substantial reduction in the rate charged by the company for water to Panama City and Colón; (vii) improved pension rights for Panamanian employees; (viii) a 10 per cent pay rise for teachers in Latin American schools in the zone; and (ix) a review of the list of jobs reserved for US citizens.

Later in the year the White House announced that the President had ordered that a Panamanian flag be flown next to the US flag on the Canal Company building as evidence of Panama's "titular sovereignty" over the zone. At the same time the Canal Company abolished the practice of having separate facilities for US and Panamanian employees in the zone.

1.7.10: Inauguration of President Chiari—Deterioration of Relations with USA

In his inaugural speech made on Oct. 1, 1960, President Chiari, (elected in May as the candidate of the National Opposition Union) thanked the United States for the recognition of Panama's titular sovereignty, but said that the United States had not adhered to the Canal Treaty and that this "injustice" had caused "the sometimes acute and sometimes becalmed but ever-present tension in the relations between the two countries". In September 1961 he wrote to President Kennedy calling for further revision of the treaty, and two months later the Assembly unanimously adopted a resolution demanding (i) the reaffirmation of Panamanian sovereignty in the zone, including Panamanian jurisdiction over the ports of Balboa and Cristóbal; (ii) the elimination of the clause in the Hay-Bunau-Varilla Treaty granting the United States the lease of the zone in perpetuity; and (iii) the limiting of the US lease to a definite term of years.

President Chiari went to Washington for talks in June 1962 and on Jan. 10, 1963, the two governments announced their joint decision that a Panamanian flag should be flown alongside every US flag in the zone and that Panamanian postage stamps should be used. Twelve months later, however, Panama broke diplomatic relations with the United States after widespread rioting provoked by local American resistance to the order concerning the flags. Relations were resumed on April 4, 1964, after the two governments had agreed to enter talks on "the prompt elimination of the causes of conflict".

1.7.11: 1964 and 1968 Presidential Elections—Coup by National Guard

The May 1964 presidential elections were won by the government-sponsored candidate, the Liberal Marco Aurelio Robles, who gained a narrow majority over Arias Madrid, now leading the Panamanian Party (PP). In October 1967 Robles announced that he had chosen David Samudio (Minister of the Economy) as official candidate for the May 1968 elections, causing a split in the ruling coalition. Several supporters left to form the National Union, which included the PP, whose leader, Arias Madrid, was selected as presidential candidate. In March the Assembly impeached Robles for violating the constitution by giving official support to a candidate, and appointed First Vice-President Max del Valle as President, even though Robles refused to recognize their decision. The 1968 election was contested acrimoniously before Arias Madrid was declared the winner on May 30.

Within a few days of his inauguration Arias was on Oct. 10, 1968, overthrown by the National Guard, under the command of Col. Omar Torrijos Herrera, who accused Arias of planning to establish a dictatorship and of wanting to turn the Guard into "a political instrument of persecution". (The National Guard was responsible for internal security since the army had been disbanded under the 1904 constitution.) A new Cabinet was sworn in on Oct. 13 under Col. José María Pinilla, but in 1969 Torrijos increased his hold over the executive, and political parties were dissolved. In October most of those detained during the coup were amnestied and Torrijos (now Brig.-Gen.) announced the adoption of a land-reform programme. In November the constitutional guarantees on freedom of expression, public assembly and speech suspended in October 1968 were restored.

In 1972 a new constitution was drafted, concentrating power in the hands of the Chief of Government, a position assumed by Torrijos, who acquired powers to dismiss members of the Cabinet and judiciary, nominate deputies to the new National Assembly of Community Representatives (comprising 505 non-party urban and rural officials), formulate government policy and control all government contracts. Meeting in September the Assembly acclaimed Gen. Torrijos as "the Supreme leader of the Panamanian Revolution".

Under Torrijos Panama achieved a considerable measure of political stability and adopted a more broadly left-wing foreign policy. Relations with Cuba, which had been broken in 1961, were resumed in 1974, relations with Guatemala were severed in 1977 in support for the proposed independence of Belize (but were restored in 1978) and in July 1979 Panama was one of the first countries to recognize the new Sandinista government in Nicaragua (see section 1.5.21). Many left-wing Latin American exiles lived in Panama at the personal expense of Gen. Torrijos, and some Sandinistas operated openly in Panama before the 1979 revolution, possibly even obtaining arms there.[1] (For Panamanian assistance to Costa Rica against Somoza in 1978, see section 3.4.3.) During the 1970s Panama became increasingly critical of US foreign policy in Latin America and in July 1978 the government issued a statement calling on the United States to relinquish its naval base at Guantánamo in Cuba, to lift its trade embargo on Cuba and allow Puerto Rico self-determination.

1.7.12: Appeal to UN Security Council—US–Panama Declaration of 1973–1975 Joint Declaration on Zone

At the request of the Panamanian government, supported by other Latin American countries, a special session of the UN Security Council was convened on March 15–21, to discuss "measures for the maintenance and strengthening of international peace and security in Latin America in conformity with the provisions and principles of the Charter". On the opening day

Torrijos said that Panama was reaching "the limit of its patience" on the question of the zone, asked why the United States should maintain a colony "in the heart of our country" and declared "every hour of isolation of Cuba is 60 minutes of shame". (For exclusion of Cuba from inter-American system, see section 5.3.2.)

A resolution drafted by Panama and Peru called on the Council (i) to note that Panama and the United States were willing to replace the Hay-Bunau-Varilla Treaty by a new and fair settlement guaranteeing "full respect for Panama's effective sovereignty over all its territory"; (ii) to ask both nations to keep negotiations in a friendly spirit; and (iii) to keep the matter under consideration. The resolution received 13 votes in favour, one abstention (United Kingdom) and was vetoed by the United States.

Talks began in November 1973 between the Panamanian Foreign Minister, Juan Antonio Tack, and a US team led by Ellsworth Bunker, and on Feb. 7, 1974, a US–Panama Declaration was issued laying down "points of departure" for future negotiations as follows: (i) the abrogation of the Hay-Bunau-Varilla Treaty and the conclusion of a new treaty; (ii) the elimination of the perpetuity clause in favour of a fixed termination date for the US lease; (iii) the prompt termination of US jurisdiction in accordance with the terms of the new treaty; (iv) the return of the zone to the jurisdiction of Panama, which would then grant the United States the right to use land, water and airspace as necessary for the operation, maintenance, protection and defence of the canal and of ships in transit; (v) recognition of the canal as Panama's "principal resource" and of Panama's right to a just and equitable share of the benefits of its operation; (vi) Panamanian participation in the administration of the canal, eventually assuming total responsibility for it; (vii) Panamanian involvement with the United States in the protection and defence of the canal; and (viii) joint agreement on provisions for new projects to enlarge canal capacity should the canal become inadequate for traffic.

In March 1975 Presidents Alfonso López Michelsen of Colombia, Oduber of Costa Rica and Carlos Andrés Pérez of Venezuela signed a joint declaration with Torrijos expressing "deep concern at the dilatory way in which negotiations between the United States and Panama for a new Canal Treaty have been developing since they began 11 years ago" and calling for "an urgent solution" to "a matter which Latin America considers to be of its own concern". Colombia formally renounced all rights in areas under the exclusive sovereignty of Panama, and Colombia and Costa Rica were promised tax-free passage through the canal. (According to Torrijos the two main difficulties encountered in the negotiations were the resistance of the zone inhabitants and disagreement over the use of the zone by the United States for training foreign troops—see section 5.2.7.)

The prospect of any early conclusion of negotiations appeared increasingly faint in 1975 in view of the opposition within the United States to relinquishing any rights in zone. In September 1975 Henry Kissinger (then US Secretary of State) said that the United States must retain the right to defend the canal "unilaterally" and "for an indefinite future", although he later changed the second phrase to "several decades". Torrijos received expressions of support from Castro during his visit to Havana in 1976, when the Cuban leader said that "time is on our side against the imperialists", adding: "The struggle of the Panamanian people is not very easy because Panama is small, but to the 1,200,000 Panamanians we can add 9,000,000 Cubans." By the beginning of 1976 negotiations had reached deadlock and were halted, and relations with the United States deteriorated further when in September the Panamanian authorities accused the United States of encouraging student riots over the high cost of living as part of a plan to destabilize the government. A formal note to this effect was sent to Washington on Sept. 17, 1976, by Foreign Minister Aquilino Boyd, but the US administration denied the allegation.

1.7.13: Resumption of Negotiations—Conclusion of New Treaties—US Amendments

Within weeks of his inauguration President Carter instigated the reopening of US–Panamanian negotiations in February 1977, but they collapsed in less than 10 days, apparently as when agreement was reached on a 25–year limit on the US lease the United States insisted on the right to defend the zone for 50 years afterwards. Prior to this the Presidents of Colombia, Mexico, Costa Rica, Guatemala, Honduras, Nicaragua and Venezuela had written to Carter calling the treaty negotiations "the most urgent issue that the new administration will face in the western hemisphere in 1977", and declaring that "negotiating a new canal treaty and recognizing legitimate Panamanian aspirations have become the crucial test of the degree of sincerity of the inter-American policy of the United States".

It was announced on Aug. 10, 1977, that agreement in principle had been reached on two treaties, one giving Panama full control of the canal and zone by the year 2000 and the other making the guarantee of the permanent neutrality of the canal the joint responsibility of Panama and the United States. The two treaties were signed by Carter and Torrijos in Washington on Sept. 7 and were approved in Panama by a national referendum on Oct. 23, with 65 per cent of the electorate voting in favour. The treaties were supported by the Liberal Party, the (Moscow-line communist) Panamanian People's Party (PPP), the Federation of Panamian Students and the Panamanian Association of Businessmen, and opposed by Arias Madrid (from exile in Miami), the Independent Lawyers' Movement (MAI) and left-wing student groups. During the campaign Torrijos had warned that the only alternative to a negotiated settlement would be a "war of liberation", and he was reported to have said later that although he was not happy with the terms of the treaty he signed it "to save the lives of 40,000 young Panamanians".[2]

In the United States, however, there was considerable doubt that the treaties would gain the required two-thirds majority in the Senate. In early October 1977 the Republican Party voted overwhelmingly against granting Panama eventual control of the canal, and to lead the party's campaign against the treaties it nominated a long-standing opponent of yielding any US rights in the zone—Ronald Reagan. The tension between the two countries had increased when it was reported in September that the CIA had bugged the private conversations of the Panamanian negotiating team, although an investigation into the allegation found no conclusive proof.

Clarification of defence matters arising from the treaties was reached at a meeting between Torrijos and Carter on Oct. 14, 1977, when they issued a statement declaring: "Each of the two countries shall . . . defend the canal against any threat to the regime of neutrality and consequently shall have the right to act against any aggression or threat directed against the canal or against the peaceful transit of vessels through the canal. This does not mean . . . a right of intervention of the United States in the internal affairs of Panama. Any US action will be directed at ensuring that the canal will remain open, secure and accessible, and it shall never be directed against the territorial integrity or political independence of Panama."

The US Senate approved the treaty on permanent neutrality on March 16, 1978, and the basic treaty on April 18 by 68 votes to 32, but added two addenda as follows:

"(1) If the canal is closed or its operations are interfered with, the United States and the Republic of Panama shall each independently have the right to take such steps as it deems necessary, . . . including the use of military force in Panama, to reopen the canal or restore the operations of the canal as the case may be.
"(2) Nothing in this treaty shall preclude Panama and the United States from making . . . any agreement or arrangement between the two countries to facilitate performance at any time after Dec. 31, 1999, of their responsibilities to maintain the regime of neutrality established in the treaty, including agreements or arrangements for the stationing of US forces or maintenance of its defence sites after that date in the Republic of Panama that Panama and the United States may deem necessary or appropriate."

The Panamanian government agreed to these addenda on April 25, but formal ratification was delayed by the US Senate for a year and the treaties did not come into effect until Oct. 1, 1979. The main provisions of the basic treaty were as follows: (i) Panama gained general territorial jurisdiction over the Canal Zone (which was abolished), although 40 per cent of the area would remain under effective US control until Dec. 31, 1999; (ii) Panama gained control of 11 of the 14 military bases in the zone, the railway linking Panama City and Colón, the ports of Cristóbal and Balboa and other installations; and (iii) the Canal Company was replaced by the Panama Canal Commission (PCC), consisting of nine members, five of whom would be US delegates (obliged to cast their votes as directed by the US Defence Secretary).

With regard to defence the Senate-House conference inserted a non-mandatory provision defining a security threat to the canal as "any circumstances in which foreign combat troops or military forces other than those of the United States . . . are located within the Republic of Panama".

1.7.14: Preparations for Return to Elected Government

Torrijos announced in April 1978 that political exiles would be allowed to return and that parties would shortly be legalized. Although parties were not officially recognized in the August 1978 elections to the National Assembly of Community Representatives, a majority of successful candidates could be identified as being pro-government. Arias Madrid's PP boycotted the campaign after an abortive attempt to form a united opposition front. After the elections Torrijos convened a commission to work on an electoral law and constitutional changes, and in September he announced that he would step down as Chief of Government when his six–year term expired in October but would remain Commander of the National Guard. The new National Assembly was inaugurated on Oct. 11 and by 452 votes to 13 Torrijos' nominee, Arístides Royo (a former minister of education and one of the treaty negotiators), was elected President with Ricardo de la Espriella as Vice-President.

The first three political parties to emerge (in the period March–June 1978) were the Democratic Revolutionary Party (PRD) led by Torrijos, the Liberal Party led by David Samudio and the pro-Torrijos Broad Popular Front (Frampo), which had evolved from the MAI. The commission formed in August recommended presidential elections by 1980, while Torrijos insisted on a delay until 1984. In 1979 ten smaller political parties and groups formed the United Opposition Front (Freno), demanding immediate elections, the direct election of representatives to a new legislative body and full freedom of expression. Elections to 19 seats in the National Legislative Council (an upper house in which the other 38 delegates were appointed from the Assembly) were held on Sept. 28, 1980. The PRD took 10 seats, the Liberal Party (now lead by Arnulfo Escalona Ríos after a faction of the party refused to take part) five, the Christian Democratic Party (PDC) two and independents (one of whom was a member of the PPP) two. The abstention rate was about 50 per cent, caused at least partly by the PP call for a boycott.

1.7.15: Foreign Policy under President Royo

In December 1979 Panama was drawn into closer alignment with the United States when the deposed Shah of Iran arrived in Panama at the invitation of President Royo "on humanitarian grounds" for an initial period of three months. The arrangement was apparently made by the White House Chief of Staff, Hamilton Jordan (a personal friend of Torrijos), and US Senator Frank Church described it as "the first great friendship dividend" of the Canal Treaty. When the new Iranian authorities announced in January 1980 their intention of requesting the Shah's extradition, the Panamanian government said that he was in the protection of the National Guard; however, on March 24—the day before the formal extradition request was presented to Panama—he left for Egypt. (He had in any case objected to his isolation on the island of Contadora and claimed that he was being overcharged for his stay.)

In a reversal of former foreign policy the government announced on March 1981 that it would reconsider its close relations with Cuba because of what it termed "Cuba's provocation in the armed struggle" in Latin America.

1.7.16: Death of Gen. Torrijos

Torrijos was killed in an aircrash in western Panama on July 31, 1981, along with six others in the aircraft. In his book *Getting to Know the General*, Graham Greene raises the question of the cause of the crash (the official investigation into which found no evidence of engine trouble) and examines the allegations of CIA involvement. He cites in particular a CIA report addressed to the US State Department dated June 11, 1980 (of which he received a copy), which expressed anxiety over links between Panama and the left-wing in El Salvador and described Torrijos as "volatile, unpredictable . . . a populist demagogue with a visceral anti-American bias".[3]

1.7.17: Resignation of Royo—Resignation of de la Espriella

After the death of Torrijos relations deteriorated between the presidency and the National Guard, of which Col. Florencio Flores Aguilar became Commander until March 1982, when he was replaced by Gen. Rubén Dario Paredes. There was strong disagreement between President Royo and Gen. Paredes over foreign policy and over US activities in Panama. Royo gave firm support to Argentina in the Falklands (Malvinas) conflict with Britain and repeatedly accused the United States of failing to fulfil the terms of the new treaties, whereas Paredes, an avowed anti-communist, favoured an increased US role in Panamanian affairs. Royo was obliged by Paredes to resign on July 30, 1982, and the following day a group of opposition parties issued a joint statement claiming that "the National Guard has deposed the President and imposed on his successor [Ricardo de la Espriella] a programme of measures which in many cases goes beyond the legal and institutional frameworks set up in this country by the National Guard itself". Paredes, who was officially due to retire in September 1982, agreed to requests from de la Espriella and the military command to remain in his post, but he eventually retired the following year in order to stand in the 1984 presidential election.

President de la Espriella resigned on Feb. 13, 1984, for personal reasons and was replaced by Vice-President Jorge Illueca. Illueca had come into conflict with the National Guard in 1983 when in a speech to the UN General Assembly on Nov. 11 he denied that Panama was participating in the activities of Condeca; two days later a National Guard spokesman said that the speech had not been authorized. In July 1984 Illueca accused the United States of "flagrant violation" of the canal treaties in an apparent reference to a recent decision by the PCC to extend privileges to US canal employees, costing Panama an estimated $4,000,000 a year; he also announced the closure of the US Army School of the Americas (see section 5.2.7).

1.7.18: Constitutional Amendments—1984 Presidential Election—Resignation of Ardito

In preparation for elections in 1984 a series of constitutional amendments were drafted in 1983, including a reduction of the presidential term of office from six years to five, a ban on serving members of the National Guard from taking part in the elections, and the introduction of a system of direct election of all members of the National Legislative Council after nomination by political parties. The amendments were approved in a referendum held on April 24, and during the campaign the only party opposed to them was the centrist Popular Action Party (Papo).

The presidential elections were held on May 6, 1984, and the PRD candidate, Nicolás Ardito Barletta, gained a majority of only 1,713 votes over the nearest contender, Arias Madrid, whose party was now called the Authentic Panamanian Party (PPA). Supporters of Arias made allegations of fraud, and some observers claimed that Arias should have gained a lead of some 2,600 votes. There were five other candidates, including Paredes for the National People's Party, but he polled only 15,976 votes.

The new President was sworn into office on Oct. 11, 1984, and said that his government would give priority to the economy, that relations with the

United States would be maintained at a "very constructive level of co-operation between equal associates in the operation, maintenance and defence of the Panama Canal", and that he took "at face value the military's commitment that they will withdraw from politics". In the concurrent elections to a 67–member Legislative Assembly to replace the National Assembly of Community Representatives, the National Democratic Union (Unade, a six–party grouping including the PRD, Frampo and the Liberal Party, renamed the National Liberal Party) gained 40 seats against 27 for the Opposition Democratic Alliance (ADO, consisting of four parties including the PPA and the PDC).

Ardito resigned on Sept. 27, 1985, and was replaced by First Vice-President Eric Arturo del Valle (PRD president), who promised to "return to *Torrijista* principles". Ardito had been criticized for his handling of the economy and claims continued to be made that his election had been rigged in order to keep Arias Madrid out of office. It was also believed that Gen. Manuel Antonio Noriega Morena (who had succeeded Paredes as head of the National Guard) had been instrumental in removing Ardito from office, in a reassertion of the Guard's control over political life.

Notes

1. Graham Greene, *Getting to Know the General—The Story of an Involvement*, London, Bodley Head, 1984, passim.
2. *Ibid.*, p. 122.
3. *Ibid.*, pp. 223–24.

SECTION TWO

ECONOMIC AND SOCIAL DIMENSIONS

2.1: THE REGIONAL ECONOMY

2.1.1: Introductory

The countries of Central America have high agricultural potential with naturally fertile soil and a generally temperate climate. However, centuries of uncontrolled forest exploitation and the persistent use of "slash-and-burn" methods had led to the erosion of much arable land. Lying on the San Andreas Fault Central America has frequently been hit by earthquakes, such as those in Nicaragua in 1972 (see section 1.5.8), Guatemala in 1976 (killing 24,103 people and leaving over a million homeless) and El Salvador in 1986, and also by hurricanes from the Caribbean (as in Honduras in 1974). When the Spanish arrived, a great variety of crops was grown and much of the economy operated on a barter system; as the Spanish had come looking chiefly for precious metals there was little immediate change to the agricultural pattern. In the late 18th century, however, increasing textile production in Europe using the new industrial techniques created a demand for indigo, which became the Central American region's first major export crop. By the end of the 19th century agriculture had become dominated by the production of coffee and bananas, which together accounted for 31.3 per cent of exports by value in 1913.

The region was severely hit by the Wall Street Crash of 1929, not only because of its increasing economic dependence on the United States but also because of its effect on the prices of basic commodities; the price of coffee per ton fell from $415.75 in 1928 to $5.97 in 1932, at a time when coffee accounted for 70–80 per cent of the region's total exports.

2.1.2: Mineral Wealth

Historically, the main mineral wealth in the region was Honduran silver and Nicaraguan gold, which together accounted for 9 per cent of the region's exports by value in 1938, gold being Nicaragua's leading export between 1938 and 1949. Honduras has continued to mine silver, gold, lead and zinc, and there are believed to be substantial deposits of iron ore, tin and antimony yet to be exploited. However, the Honduran mining sector has been severely hit in recent years, with gold production falling from 15 kg in 1980 to 4 kg in 1983, while a decline in world market prices for silver since 1980 has reduced its share of national export earnings to about 2.5 per cent in 1983, compared with 3 per cent for lead and zinc. In Nicaragua gold production has fluctuated, the export total of 1,719 kg in 1980 having fallen in subsequent years because of internal security problems in the north east of the country. Silver production has been less important, standing at an annual average of about 5 tonnes at the beginning of the 1980s; there are also known to be deposits of lead, tungsten, iron ore and zinc in Nicaragua.

Elsewhere there are much smaller quantities of silver in El Salvador and Costa Rica, and in the latter gold production stood at 800 kg in 1984, with nearly double this figure projected by the end of the decade as a result of new workings. It is also planned to resume work on Costa Rica's bauxite reserves, which had been suspended since the withdrawal of ALCOA in 1976 (after six years' prospecting and mining—see section 1.6.6). In Guatemala and Panama mining projects have concentrated on copper reserves, with other minerals left untapped because of the depressed state of the international metal markets in the early and mid–1980s.

To date only Guatemala has discovered substantial and commercially viable oil reserves (see section 2.2.1); accordingly, all Central American countries have devoted considerable resources to developing hydroelectric energy schemes.

2.1.3: Bananas

Central American banana production has traditionally been exploited by foreign fruit companies, notably the (US) United Fruit Company (UFCO), which were largely responsible for the building of much of the region's railway network (see early history of Honduras, section 1.3.3). The fruit companies exerted strong influence over national economies, gaining land at low cost (or even free of charge) and substantial privileges. For example, UFCO's contract in Guatemala allowed it unlimited use of the country's best land for 25–99 years, exemption from stamp, port and other taxes and from import duties and unlimited profit remittance (for relations between UFCO and Arbenz government, see section 1.2.3). By the end of the 1950s UFCO controlled 75 per cent of the world banana trade; however, after the loss of its holdings in Cuba as a result of the 1959 revolution it began to diversify its activities and to sell off some of its land to local growers as "associate producers". During the 1960s UFCO met competition from Standard Fruit and Del Monte (which entered the banana business in 1968); in the 1970s these three companies (UFCO becoming United Brands in 1970) controlled 70 per cent of the world banana trade at a value of some $2,600 million per year.

The producing countries attempted to assert some control over the trade by the formation in 1972 of The Union of Banana Exporting Countries (UPEB) by Guatemala, Honduras, Costa Rica and Panama, later joined by Nicaragua, Venezuela and the Dominican Republic (although the other main producer, Ecuador, remained outside). The aim was to co-ordinate export policies and to improve prices, which had varied little for over 20 years, with the producing countries still receiving only 11½ cents per 64 kg box in 1972. In 1974 UPEB tried to impose a tax on bananas of $1 per box (see also section 1.3.8), but only Panama was successful in levying the new amount; elsewhere the companies forced concessions, with Standard Fruit cutting back production in Honduras and Costa Rica and destroying 145,000 boxes of bananas rather than pay the tax.[1]

UPEB members found it still more difficult to resist pressure for concessions in the late 1970s because of a fall in the banana price; moreover, a surfeit of fruit in 1984, caused by recuperation in Ecuador, Guatemala and Honduras after climatic problems the previous year, reduced the US price by 14.2 per cent over 1983. As this fall in price coincided with a strong US dollar in 1983–84, the exporting countries suffered severe balance-of-trade problems, especially as the value of traditional imports rose by 6.1 per cent between 1983 and 1984.

Although in the late 1970s the fruit companies began withdrawing from the actual growing (selling off land in Costa Rica and Panama), they retained control of marketing (except in Nicaragua after the Sandinista revolution). Those that remained did so only after negotiating what they considered to be sufficient incentives or concesssions, while there was persistent pressure from the companies for reductions in the tax per box of bananas levied by the regional governments concerned.

The arrival of a new UPEB director, Abelardo Carles, in August 1984 led to the adoption of a new strategy, with members concentrating less on trying to get the maximum possible of the $1 tax and more on achieving stability in international prices. At a conference of the (UN) Food and Agriculture Organization (FAO) held in Rome in 1984, UPEB and Ecuador tried to secure an international accord on bananas, but were unable to do so because of opposition from the United States (the recipient of 80 per cent of UPEB exports).

In February 1985 Bandegua (a subsidiary of Del Monte) threatened to close operations in Guatemala unless the government agreed to make a $30,000,000 grant for imports and to cancel a debt of $9,700,000 contracted in 1983. Under pressure from the Tela Railroad Company (United Brands) and Standard Fruit the Honduran government announced in March 1985 planned legislation to fix a decreasing scale of export taxes, which was expected to result in a reduction of $3,750,000 per year to budget revenue in spite of an increased volume of banana exports.[1]

2.1.4: Coffee

The first country to concentrate on coffee production for export was Costa Rica from the 1830s. The economies of the two other major regional coffee producers, El Salvador and Nicaragua, were boosted by the completion of the Panama Railway in 1855, which shifted the trading centre from the Caribbean to the Pacific coast. In the second half of the 19th century coffee became the region's chief export under the Positivist governments, which encouraged foreign investment and so increased their economic dependence on foreign markets and capital. Boom conditions prevailed in the 1880s; harvests doubled, prices trebled, and local plantation owners made considerable fortunes.

A coffee agreement was concluded on Oct. 18, 1957, between Brazil, Colombia, Costa Rica, El Salvador, Guatemala, Mexico and Nicaragua (together producing some 80 per cent of world demand) to stabilize prices and control exports; it was superseded the following year by an agreement also including Honduras, Panama and six other Latin American countries. In the wake of the 1973 oil crisis Venezuela, in December 1974, announced the Declaration of Guayana, in which it undertook to raise between $60,000,000 and $80,000,000 over two years to finance a scheme of coffee stockpiling in Central America and to place $60,000,000 in the Central American Bank for Economic Integration (BCIE). Under this agreement the Central American countries would pay only half the current oil price and deposit the other half in their own central banks as an investment fund—under Venezuelan supervision—for local development loans.

By 1978 coffee, bananas and (from El Salvador) cotton accounted for 60 per cent of the exports of the region, which had also increased its production of beef, sugar, vegetables, fruit and light manufactures. There was also a boom in agribusiness concerns, which further increased dependency on foreign capital and especially the multinational companies; Costa Rica has the largest number of multinational concerns or subsidiaries of US origin, closely followed by Guatemala, where the main one is the Coca-Cola plant (see section 2.2.1) The predominance of agriculture within the economy, the system of land tenure (see section 2.3.1) and the limited nature of the industrial base (often controlled from abroad) combined to prevent the growth of any substantial urban middle class.

2.1.5: Trading and Economic Trends

During the 19th century the largest single foreign interest was Britain, but by 1900 the United States and Germany had supplanted it. In 1913 Britain accounted for 18 per cent of the region's trade, Germany for 21 per cent and the United States for 45 per cent; by 1938 these proportions had changed respectively to 7 per cent, 18 per cent and 56 per cent. In the early 1930s 20 per cent of the coffee harvest went to the United States and 75 per cent to Europe, but a decade later the US share had grown to 97 per cent, and US direct investment in the region rose from $121,000,000 in 1936 to $389,000,000 in 1959, concentrated mostly in Guatemala.[2] (For US economic aid, see sections 5.2.1–5.2.6.)

In the 1970s the Central American countries experienced economic growth rates averaging 6 per cent annually, but in 1980 the rate fell to 1 per cent (except in Nicaragua). Since then rates in the separate countries have fluctuated, except for a steady decline in Guatemala, and the cumulative changes in gross domestic product (GDP) for the period 1980–85 were declines of 6.0 per cent in Guatemala and 11.3 per cent in El Salvador, with rises of 4.7 per cent in Honduras, 10.2 per cent in Nicaragua and 1.3 per cent in Costa Rica. The world recession cut prices for basic commodities, while oil import bills continued to rise. The investment policies of the 1970s led to the amassing of large foreign debts, so that credit ratings deteriorated as interest rates increased. Moreover, economic problems encouraged capital flight and production has been hit by economic sabotage of crops, electricity supplies and general infrastructure, while the political and military situation has restricted growth in the tourist market. Between 1980 and 1985 foreign investment in the region fell by 27 per cent from $3,826 million to $2,810 million, fuelling a similar rate of decline in imports over the same period. The political violence has resulted in a loss of foreign confidence and in El Salvador the kidnappings of 1978–79 by the guerrillas (see section 3.3.3) caused many foreign businessmen to leave the country, including all but 200 of the 2,000-strong Japanese community.

Political instability and violence also resulted in a decline in inter-regional trade, which had reached a peak in 1980; by 1985 it had shrunk by 53 per cent, with the sharpest fall—25 per cent—registered in 1985. Despite the downturn in domestic economic growth, government expenditure increased sharply (except in Guatemala) to cope with higher national security costs in Honduras, El Salvador and Nicaragua, and with increased payments on social and economic benefits in Costa Rica. By 1986 a new threat had emerged to the national economies as ever increasing use of the region as a staging post for the transport of Colombian cocaine to the US market made possible the development of alternative unofficial economies, dealing in considerably larger sums than their official counterparts. In Costa Rica, for example, seizures of cocaine in the first six months of 1986 totalled 3,500 kg, compared with under 40 kg for the whole of 1985.

The economic expansion of the 1970s did not lead to a general improvement in living standards; it was estimated in 1972 that 57 per cent of the region's population had calorie and protein deficiency of up to 53 per cent, while 14 per cent had sufficient and 29 per cent had an excess, with the inequalities being especially marked in Guatemala, Honduras and El Salvador. According to an ECLA report in 1980 64 per cent of the region's population was living in poverty, and half of these in "extreme poverty" where death from malnutrition was not uncommon; the most acute situation was in Guatemala where 74 per cent lived in poverty, with GDP per head falling from $589 in 1980 to $498 in 1984. In El Salvador in the 1970s it was estimated that 60 per cent of the population lived below the survival line determined by the Ministry of Agriculture of an income of $533 per year for a family of six, to cover basic food requirements.

2.1.6: 1980 San José Agreement

In an initiative to help the Central American states to cope with the oil crisis and help their growing debt problems, an agreement was reached at a meeting in San José in August 1984 under which Mexico and Venezuela undertook to supply the total oil requirements (then of 160,000 bpd) of six Central American countries (Guatemala, Honduras, El Salvador, Nicaragua, Costa Rica and Panama) and of Barbados, the Dominican Republic and Jamaica. The recipients were to pay the current market price for the oil, but 30 per cent of the remittances was to be returned to them as a five-year loan, with a rider attached that if the loans were used for primary development (especially energy) projects, their term would be extended to 20 years and the rate of interest reduced from 4 per cent to 2 per cent. Although it was a joint initiative, the agreement was implemented in the form of separate contracts between either Mexico or Venezuela and the individual countries.

In August 1984 Mexico and Venezuela agreed to extend the agreement for five years, with a few minor amendments, including a clause stating that supplies would be suspended to any country in the region which initiated military action or intervention against another state in the region.

Notes

1. Pearce, *op, cit.*, pp. 97–98.
2. *Ibid*, p. 26.

2.2: ECONOMIC PERFORMANCE OF CENTRAL AMERICAN STATES

2.2.1: Guatemala

By 1985 Guatemala's GDP growth rate had fallen to minus 1.1 per cent and annual inflation had reached 95 per cent; by mid–1986 staple food prices had risen by 40–50 per cent since the beginning of the year. Public spending was subject to drastic cuts (except for the military allocation of the budget, which was expanded) and unemployment (or underemployment) affected about 45 per cent of the workforce. Capital flight, estimated at $500,000,000 between 1979 and 1982, continued to drain foreign exchange reserves and over the same period foreign investment had fallen by about three-quarters. President Ríos Montt's economic policies (including the highly unpopular introduction in August 1983 of VAT—see section 1.2.13) were designed to improve the balance-of-payments situation by taxing the wealthier, but alienated the business sector, which especially objected to his attempts to preserve the parity of the quetzal (the national currency) with the US dollar. In December 1982 he had been forced to accept the resignation of the president of the Central Bank, Jorge González del Valle, after only a few months because of his refusal to pursue the monetarist policies advocated by the private sector. A month later Ríos Montt accused the latter of lacking patriotism and of failing to pay even minimum wages to the workers on sugar and cotton plantations, adding that "in this country there are just two sectors—the exploited and the exploiters".

At the beginning of 1985 the Central Bank had forecast an encouraging year, but by mid-year the country faced severe economic depression. On July 24 the government deposited one-fifth of national gold reserves (worth $30,000,000) to pay for oil already purchased. President Mejía Victores had attempted to introduce economic austerity measures in April, but had been forced by the Co-ordinating Committee of Agricultural, Commercial, Industrial and Financial Association (CACIF) to revoke them and also to dismiss the ministers of finance and the economy. The government then invited CACIF, certain politicians and some members of the press to a debate on the national economic crisis. Some of the recommendations made by this conference became law in June 1985, when the government central budget was cut by 7 per cent, new taxes and stricter foreign exchange controls were introduced and the prices of selected basic items frozen. The economic crisis was made still more serious by an earthquake on Oct. 11, 1985, which was estimated to have made about 12,000 people homeless.

In 1986 the incoming civilian administration faced a number of severe economic problems, including an acute lack of foreign exchange (further demands on national gold reserves to pay for imported oil having reportedly been made in November 1985) with $550,000,000 of debt repayments due in the first six months of the year. In January 1986 the Mejía Victores government introduced a series of taxes and fiscal reforms, including taxes on luxury items and a 3.5 per cent levy on international transactions, but these measures appeared to be inadequate to cover the 33 per cent budget increase also approved. (Indirect taxes accounted for 85 per cent of revenue.)

On March 6, 1986, President Cerezo announced an Economic and Social Reform Plan, allocating $100,000,000 to developing basic services in rural areas and a further $100,000,000 to infrastructure projects, to be financed by aid received by a number of foreign countries, notably Spain, France, Venezuela, Peru, Argentina and Japan. In June he introduced currency and fiscal reforms, under which parity with the dollar was retained for debt repayments and a new rate established of $1.00 = 2.50 quetzals for exports and essential imports, and a new 30 per cent export levy imposed. These measures did not meet the high expectations of the unions for the new civilian government, and there was growing labour unrest at the government's failure to reduce inflation and unemployment.

Guatemala's foreign debt has grown rapidly in the 1980s, from $772,000,000 in 1980 to $1,994 million in 1983 and an estimated $2,100 million in 1985. The Public Finance Minister, Col. Leonardo Figueroa Villate, said on Sept. 3, 1984, that "Guatemala will be compelled to renegotiate its foreign debt in order to find economic breathing room", because of "no-one's having taken adequate measures at the appropriate moment". The budget deficit for 1984–85 was expected to be in excess of $500,000,000, compared with total revenue of about $1,300 million, and debt-service was expected to appropriate 40 per cent of export revenue in 1985.

The government had reached agreement with the IMF in November 1981 on a standby loan of SDR 19,100,000 (then about $21,000,000) and again in September 1983 for a standby loan of SDR 144,800,000 ($120,000,000), on approval of a government economic programme aimed at cutting the public-sector and current-account deficits. The agreement was suspended by the IMF at the beginning of November 1983 on the grounds that VAT had been cut to 7 per cent during the previous month, and this suspension also halted the disbursement of some $360,000,000 in credits due from other multilateral lending institutions. After a review of the case in mid–1984 the IMF decided to maintain its suspension of payments to Guatemala as the tax reforms of August 1983 had yielded only 40 per cent of the revenue anticipated, owing to evasion, corruption and the reduction in the rate of VAT, and also as President Mejía Victores had (despite an undertaking to the Fund) allowed two modifications to the reforms.

In the late 1970s exploitation began of Guatemala's considerable oil reserves in the north, near the Mexican border; and by the mid–1980s output from these fields met 35 per cent of domestic demand. In 1985 foreign oil still accounted for 21.3 per cent of total imports, but it was anticipated that this figure would fall to 18.0 per cent in 1986. Annual production had risen from 1,513,300 barrels in 1980 to 2,549,300 by 1983, but fell to 1,715,200 in 1984 and 935,900 in 1985 (because of the departure of the main foreign oil company—see below), and the 1986 total was forecast at 1,916,200 barrels.

In late 1983 a new law on oil exploration had been passed, designed to encourage foreign oil companies to initiate new projects in the northern jungle areas (on the Mexican border), by reducing the share of the amount payable to the government from 55 per cent of turnover to 30 per cent, adjustable upwards in line with the level of production. The new law elicited protests from the French oil company Elf Aquitaine (the only current foreign producer in Guatemala), which claimed that it was prejudicial to existing contracts, as previously the government's share had been payable from the date production started whereas under the new law companies would not be liable until they had first covered their financial outlay for exploration and development. After a legal wrangle and a decline in production Elf Aquitaine withdrew from the country in October 1984. Early in 1985 the foreign oil companies gained further concessions, effectively reducing the government's royalties on oil to 6 per cent, while the government agreed to keep the companies supplied with foreign currency for imports.

The largest of many foreign-owned or multinational concerns in Guatemala was Embotelladora Guatemalteca S.A. (EGSA), the Coca-Cola bottling plant. In 1976 a union (STEGAC) was formed at the plant, which began a four-year battle with the management to gain official recognition as the workers' representative body. During these four years many of the workers were kidnapped or assassinated by death squads, including union leaders Pedro Quevedo and Manuel López Balán, killed in December 1978 and April 1979 respectively. Against this background, the president of EGSA, John C. Trotter from Houston, was accused by a US congressman (Don Pease, Democrat) of "orchestrating . . . an unmercifully ruthless campaign of intimidation and terror" against his workforce. Under an agreement reached in July 1980 (concluded after an international boycott organized in the winter of 1978–79 by the Geneva-based International Union of Food and Allied Workers, IUF), the parent company recognized the union, removed Trotter and his management team and took direct control of the plant for five years.

Trouble flared again at the plant in February 1984 when the parent company closed EGSA and dismissed all 400 workers, claiming that the company had gone bankrupt. STEGAC occupied the plant, and in a repeat of events in 1976–80, the families of union members faced death squad reprisals as well as economic hardship. Agreement was reached in May 1984 through the head office in Atlanta, with management agreeing to sell the franchise and to guarantee respect for trade union rights; however, when the plant failed to open (apparently because no buyer for the franchise had been found) the IUF initiated another boycott of the company in October. The plant eventually re-opened on March 1, 1985, when the franchise had been bought by a group of Guatemalan investors. The name was changed to Embotelladora Central and the workforce reduced to 265, with a promise of 85 more jobs to come later; the union organization was retained.

2.2.2: Honduras

Its economy traditionally dependent chiefly on bananas, Honduras is the least industrially-developed member of CACM, despite efforts made to diversify and modernize the economy after the replacement of Carias in 1948.[1] Traditional rivalries with El Salvador were aggravated by the formation of the Market in 1960, after which El Salvador replaced the United States as the main supplier of manufactured goods to Honduras. The extent of Salvadorean investment in Honduras was such that El Salvador was referred to as the "imperialist" neighbour and alleged to be treating Honduras as its "economic colony". The hurricane of September 1974 wiped out three-quarters of the Honduran banana crop (which still accounted for half the national export revenue), total damage to the country being estimated at $500,000,000.

Coffee surpassed bananas as the country's leading export earner in 1978 (the two other main exports being meat and timber), but both commodity prices fell on the world market in the early 1980s, and severe flooding in May 1982 caused damage worth $500,000,000. In 1982–83 Honduras' quota under the International Coffee Agreement was cut by 16 per cent, but in February 1985 the quota system was lifted and a substantial increase in production together with a rise in world prices was expected to boost coffee export revenue from $178,000,000 in 1984 to over $300,000,000. However, a new threat to the crop developed because of the military activities of Nicaraguan contras, and in October 1985 coffee producers from El Paraíso department tried unsuccessfully to persuade the president to expel the contras. In 1982 it emerged that several state corporations, notably the National Investment Corporation (Conadi), had been inefficiently and even corruptly managed, and similar allegations against Conadi were levied in January 1986.

Although in the 1980s some 60 per cent of the workforce was still involved in subsistence agriculture, over 75 per cent of export income came from commercial agribusiness. This and other sectors have traditionally been extensively controlled by or dependent on US interests which in particular have dominated the financial sector. By the early 1970s nearly two-thirds of all banks in the country were under foreign ownership or control, notably in that the (US) First National City Bank held a majority share in the Banco de Honduras. In mid–1986 the government introduced a new economic package offering incentives to private-sector enterprises, with over $4,000,000 promised to agricultural concerns. The package also made concessions to current union demands with a housebuilding programme and an undertaking to create 4,000 new public-sector jobs. By the end of 1985 unemployment had reached 29 per cent, according to official statistics, with unemployment and underemployment together believed to affect over half the workforce.

The country's public-sector foreign debt rose from $276,000,000 in 1974 to $600,000,000 in 1978 and to $2,300 million by December 1985; between 1973 and 1985 the debt-service rose from under 4 per cent to 44 per cent of export income. In common with its neighbours Honduras suffered a massive flight of capital in the early 1980s, and in 1984 the balance of payments deficit reached $311,000,000. An economic austerity programme was agreed with the IMF in June 1981 in exchange for a standby loan of SDR 12,750,000 (then $14,660,000). However, the government failed to meet the fiscal targets and a new agreement was concluded in November 1982 for a SDR 76,500,000 standby ($81,100,000) loan as part of a programme "to reverse the fiscal deterioration of the previous two years by strengthening public savings through a combination of revenue and expenditure measures".

2.2.3: El Salvador

At the beginning of the 1960s only about 55 per cent of the Salvadorean economy was based on a developing capitalist system, with 35 per cent operating in a semi-feudal system based on the large estates (*latifundia*) and 10 per cent still working within the pre-colonial barter system. The "techno-cratic" policies of the 1950–56 Osorio government (see section 1.4.4) had made El Salvador the most industrially-developed country within CACM, but these changes affected a relatively small sector of the population; whereas the manufacturing sector expanded by 24 per cent in 1961–71 the size of its workforce grew by only 6 per cent. (By the 1980s the manufacturing sector accounted for 15 per cent of the GDP compared with 25 per cent for agriculture.) The boom attracted surplus rural labour to the urban areas, but many migrants remained unemployed; moreover, the growth of the shanty towns was accelerated by the flood of refugees caused by the 1969 "football war" with Honduras.

In the 1970s only about 35 per cent of the male workforce was in full employment throughout the year. An official commission reported in 1980 that 90 per cent of the economically active population received insufficient income to cover basic food needs, with this percentage rising to 96 per cent by 1983. The distribution of land was one of the prime causes for the extreme inequality of wealth; as Archbishop Chávez y González declared in 1975: "The best lands are dedicated to coffee, cotton and sugar cane for export, while only the worst land remains to provide Salvadoreans with their daily bread."

By the early 1980s the national economy was being seriously affected by the civil war and its consequences; GDP fell by 22 per cent between 1979 and 1983, largely as a result of the sabotage of crops and economic installations, the concentration of state resources on the military effort against the guerrillas and the flight of several thousand refugees. The country's principal economic product, coffee (accounting for 55 per cent of total export revenue in 1983) suffered a loss of nearly 40 per cent of output between 1980 and 1984, and cotton (successfully introduced in the 1950s to become the second main national commodity, accounting for 8 per cent of export revenue by 1983) was even more severely hit with both output and area planted falling by two-thirds between 1979 and 1985, although the loss of export revenue was to some extent offset by a simultaneous rise of 15 per cent in the world cotton price. Repeated attacks on hydroelectric and geothermal electricity generators led to their replacement by less vulnerable but more expensive oil-powered plants. FMLN sabotage of transport during 1985 resulted in losses of $21,000,000.

By 1984 the war effort was consuming about 40 per cent of the national budget, the public-sector foreign debt stood at $1,200 million and the budget deficit had reached $240,000,000. Although the year's statistics showed a rise in GDP of about 1.5 per cent, this was almost entirely due to the inflow of US aid to the government. The trade deficit expanded from $165,000,000 in 1984 to about $350,000,000 in 1985. Moreover, the drain on the budget for military purposes placed a severe constriction on expenditure on public services: many state employees remained unpaid in 1984–85 and by late 1985 some 2,000 schools had been closed either because of lack of funds or directly as a result of the civil disruption.

In an attempt to keep the annual inflation rate within 20 per cent (compared with about 60 per cent in 1985) and to reduce the budget deficit, which had now reached $300,000,000, Duarte introduced a series of economic measures on Jan. 2, 1986, including a devaluation of the currency. Previously the rate for selected import items had been $1.00 = 2.50 colones, with a parallel rate of $1.00 = 4.75 colones, and the new rate established was $1.00 = 5.00 colones. To offset the possible consequences of this measure the government also raised the rate of interest on private savings and recommended a pay rise of 5 per cent and up to 15 per cent for rural and urban workers respectively. In addition price controls were introduced for certain essential foodstuffs and controls imposed on rents, but the petrol price was increased by 60 per cent and so bus owners were allowed to increase public transport fares by up to 20 per cent. By the end of March, however, it was clear that the original inflation target would be unattainable.

The measures were criticized by coffee producers, who objected to the 15 per cent surcharge placed on production, and by labour leaders, who had become increasingly restive during 1985 over the government's failure to improve—or even halt a decline in—their members' standard of living. The government claimed that the unions' increased activity in 1985 was orchestrated from outside the country and organized by "subversives", i.e. the FMLN. In their own response to the government's measures the FMLN on Jan. 16 staged a sabotage attack on the national transport system which, according to Radio Venceremos, paralysed 95 per cent of services.

A severe earthquake hit the capital, San Salvador, on Oct. 10, damaging 90 per cent of buildings in the city centre, killing 1,000 people and leaving a further 200,000 (about one-fifth of the city's population) homeless.

2.2.4: Nicaragua

Nicaragua's main exports are coffee, cotton, sugar, meat (mostly beef) and seafood, with cotton booming in the 1950s because of the demand for textiles on the US market created by the Korean war. As in El Salvador the growth of the manufacturing sector, which by the 1970s accounted for over 20 per cent of GDP, did not compensate for the jobs lost in the agricultural sector, and by 1979 at least 28 per cent of the Managua workforce was unemployed. The two characteristics of the economy prior to the 1979 revolution were its close association with US interests since the US occupation of 1916–33 and its domination by the Somoza family.[2]

Within days of coming to power in June 1979 the Sandinista-led regime nationalized domestic banks and took over the mining, fishing and forestry sectors, declaring all unexploited mineral resources the exclusive patrimony of the state on Sept. 1. It was announced on Aug. 10 that the state would be the chief buyer for major export crops, and in the same month the government expropriated over 600,000 ha of cattle-grazing land owned by the Somoza family. The economy was not entirely nationalized (only 25 per cent of manufacturing and 19 per cent of agriculture coming under state management) and the private sector continued to own 60 per cent of the total.

The Planning Minister, Henry Ruiz, announced an economic austerity programme on Jan. 2, 1980 (Plan 80); it was originally intended as the forerunner of a medium-term plan for 1981–83 to diversify and restructure the economy, but in the event contra activities made such a plan impossible. The main aims were to cut public expenditure and oil imports, to boost exports, to implement a construction programme, to cut inflation from about 60 per cent to about 20 per cent, to create 95,000 jobs (112,300 were created during the year, mostly in services and commerce), to strengthen the agricultural co-operatives already established on state farming land (through the Agricultural Workers' Association—ATC) and to boost agricultural production and the consumption of basic foods. Boosted by the plan and general reconstruction after the revolution GDP grew by 7.3 per cent in 1981, but fell by 4.2 per cent in 1982 with the launch of contra activities, growing again by 4.9 per cent in 1983; the biggest growth areas over the three-year period were agriculture and central government. Thereafter rates became more modest, with a decline of 1.4 per cent in 1984, a rise of 2.6 per cent in 1985 and a nil growth rate anticipated for 1986.

In September 1981 the government introduced a state of "economic and social emergency", which carried severe penalties for striking, occupying land outside the agrarian reform programme and taking over factories and obstructing production; it cut public spending by reducing subsidies on food and transport, imposed heavy duties on imported luxury goods, and made it a criminal offence to publish false economic news, raise prices without official permission or "incite foreign governments to inflict damage on the national economy". This state of emergency was strongly opposed by the private sector, which also complained of a shortage of foreign exchange, a lack of raw materials and spare parts, low levels of labour productivity and what they considered to be an insecure investment climate. In 1982 and 1983 the economy also faced flooding in one part of the country and drought in another, continued low world prices for its staple products, contra sabotage and diversion of manpower and resources to the military effort.

The most serious sabotage was the FDN arson at the port of Corinto in October 1983 designed to stop the supply of oil from Mexico (totalling some 4,600,000 barrels a year, most of it docked at Corinto). It was reported in December that in the course of 1983 freight rates for oil shipments to Nicaragua had risen from $90,000 to $350,000 per 120,000-barrel load. Nicaragua had been receiving all its oil requirements from Mexico and Venezuela under the San José agreement; however, Venezuela suspended supplies in late 1983 because of an outstanding debt of $30,000,000, and in February 1985 Mexico (which was owed over $230,000,000) also suspended the agreement. In consequence, Nicaragua began to adopt a system of bartering commodities for oil with the Soviet Union and to encourage alternative energy projects. The loss of Mexican and Venezuelan oil was temporarily filled by Cuba, and in May 1985 the Soviet Union agreed to guarantee up to 90 per cent of the country's oil needs for the rest of the year. However, the Mexican suspension (which was believed to have been encouraged by the US administration) was revoked at the end of May when Mexico announced renewed oil supplies to Nicaragua.

The cost to the economy in 1984 of damaged installations and production losses was put at $225,000,000, or over half of the year's estimated export earnings; in addition, harvests were not gathered in northern areas of the country because of contra threats that any farmer reaping would be decapitated. In the face of these troubles the government licensed supermarkets to sell normally rationed goods freely at higher prices and granted a substantial rise to government employees to prevent disaffection among the middle classes. In order to finance such concessions a package of austerity measures was introduced in February 1985, ending state food subsidies (and immediately doubling the official price of basic foodstuffs), devaluing the córdoba by introducing a multiple exchange rate (favouring agricultural exports and discouraging non-essential imports), freezing state expenditure and raising taxation (especially for the commercial and service sectors) and interest rates. (The state subsidies had cost some $75,000,000 per year.)

Total economic damage to the country caused by the civil war and contra activity in the period 1978–84 was $1,452 million: infrastructure $180,300,000, production $504,900,000 and decapitalization $766,300,000. The 1984–85 coffee crop fell to about 85,000 tonnes as a result of contra activity, but government measures to protect the next year's crop, including arming the pickers and providing EPS patrols, deterred similar sabotage and the 1985–86 crop reached levels similar to previous years at about 100,000 tonnes. Production of beef fell by 24 per cent in 1985 because of what the agriculture minister, Wheelock, described as the "clandestine" slaughter of animals and sale of carcasses on the black market, along with the smuggling of livestock into Honduras and Costa Rica. Attacks by contra forces on state farms and co-operatives resulted in 1986 in the worst food shortages experienced in the country since 1979. These agricultural problems, including a 14 per cent fall in the 1985–86 cotton crop because of disease, were expected to result in a trade deficit of $400,000,000 in 1986 and to help foster an inflation rate as high as 500 per cent.

In January 1986 the government replaced the 1985 multiple exchange rate by a new official rate of $1.00 = 70 córdobas, except for payment on oil and debt contracted before February 1985, which would continue at the rate of $1.00 = 28 córdobas. The official free market or parallel rate was set at $1.00 = 750 córdobas, but by August a rate of $1.00 = 975 córdobas was being quoted on international markets.

Additional economic measures introduced on March 9 raised taxes on luxury items, increased a variety of food prices (including basic foodstuffs) by 150 per cent and petrol prices by 45 per cent (along with a freeze on bus fares in the capital), and decreed a 50 per cent across-the-board pay rise. In an apparent change of emphasis in economic policy an incentive scheme was established linking salary increases to production targets, and the salary increases compounded the effect of a January rise weighted in favour of higher salaries to redress the previous erosion of pay differentials.

At the beginning of January 1981 the United States suspended all aid to Nicaragua, and confirmed in April of that year that the aid had been terminated (see section 5.2.5). Nicaragua continued to receive aid from Western Europe (see section 5.4.4), Venezuela, Mexico and Brazil, while Libya announced (also in April 1981) a grant of $100,000,000 to create a mixed agricultural enterprise with Libyan technical advice, and offered to guarantee Nicaraguan oil supplies in any future emergency. The government aimed to reduce Nicaragua's traditional dependence on the United States by diversifying both its economic activity and its international markets, so that when the United States cut its Nicaraguan sugar quota by 90 per cent in 1983 alternative buyers were found in Algeria, Mexico and the Soviet Union. After his visit to Eastern Europe and the Soviet Union in April–May 1985, Ortega announced that he had secured commitments for aid worth $200,000,000 (see also section 5.3.5). In May 1985 the United States introduced a trade embargo against Nicaragua (see section 5.2.5), and although the US lead was not followed by other countries, the gesture being regarded as more of a political than a serious economic one, its chief impact in Nicaragua was a loss of spare parts. By mid-1986 the cost of the embargo to the country was estimated at $35,000,000 to the productive sector, $33,000,000 to the commercial and financial sector and $26,000,000 to the national infrastructure.

When the Sandinistas came to power Nicaragua's foreign debt stood at $1,600 million, which the new government said it would honour (except for the sum of $5,200,000 owed to Argentina and Israel for arms purchased by the Somoza government). After nine months of talks agreement was reached in September 1980 for rescheduling nearly half the foreign debt, with a 12-year repayment term and an initial five-year grace period (during which only interest at 7 per cent would be paid). With domestic economic difficulties and substantial capital flight (amounting to $112,900,000 in 1982), the foreign debt continued to grow, reaching about $2,800 million in December 1982 and about $4,500 million by the end of 1984. Of this $4,500 million, some $1,500 was owed to private international banks and $5,000,000 to Mexico (mostly for oil) and the rest to other governments and international financial organizations.

Debt service rose from an average of about $75,000,000 (or 17 per cent of export earnings) in the mid–1970s to $171,000,000 (34.2 per cent of exports) in 1981, falling to $89,000,000 (21.7 per cent) in 1983 after the conclusion of a rescheduling agreement covering the entire national short-term debt. In 1985 debt service to private international banks was expected to exceed $295,000,000, against national exports of only $400,000,000—about half the anticipated imports figure.

In May 1985 it was reported that the government was making particular efforts to establish good credit, paying off its debt of $7,500,000 to the IMF (in April) and keeping up to date with its payments to the IDB. Despite these efforts Nicaragua's application to the IDB for a loan of $58,000,000 in support of agricultural projects was repeatedly shelved because of intervention on the part of the US administration. In mid–June 1985 government representatives successfully negotiated a refinancing agreement for the year with 130 private banks (including about 70 US banks, in violation of the official economic embargo).

Despite Nicaragua's continuing economic problems, the Sandinista regime claimed to have made significant progress during its first six years in altering the structure of Nicaraguan society, particularly to the advantage of the poorer sections of society. It is conceded that many original targets have not been fully achieved, but the shortfalls in performance are attributed both to the scale of the tasks confronting the government and also to the effects of contra activities (including economic sabotage) and the consequent need to concentrate state resources on national defence. Nevertheless, a welfare state has been created and major progress has been made in improving educational, literacy, nutritional and health standards[3] as well as in redistributing land (see section 2.3.5).

Most of the social and economic reforms since 1979 have been implemented through, or with the assistance of, the Sandinista popular organizations, such as trade unions and community representative bodies called Sandinista Defence Committees (CDS), the latter being based on the *comunidades cristianas de bases* and on the groups which emerged in the *barrios* in the September 1978 insurrection. The reform programme has also relied substantially on foreign volunteers from a variety of countries, including Cuba, Western Europe and the United States.

2.2.5: Costa Rica

In the early 1980s Costa Rica faced the worst recession in its history, with GDP registering negative growth of 5 per cent in 1981 and 6 per cent in 1982. The colón, which had been pegged to the US currency at $1.00 = 8.57/8.60 colones, was allowed to float in December 1980. After a number of adjustments the rate had reached $1.00 = 45 colones by November 1984. When it was devalued to $1.00 = 48 colones, further mini-devaluations took the rate of $1.00 = 52.70 colones as of Nov. 6, 1985 (although under the country's parallel exchange rate system the official rate remained at $1.00 = 20 colones). Despite signs of an economic reactivation in early 1985, largely through non-traditional exports, the economy faced severe difficulties, arising chiefly from its debt crisis; by mid-year the rate of inflation had reached 80 per cent and unemployment 10 per cent, compared with 15 and 5 per cent respectively in 1984, sparking off an increase in civil unrest.

In July 1984 a strike broke out among 3,500 workers at the Cía. Bananera de Costa Rica (a United Brands subsidiary) base at Golfito on the southern Pacific coast, in pursuit of a demand for a 72 per cent wage rise. The Higher Labour Tribunal declared the strike illegal, but 11 members of the National Assembly (including seven PLN deputies) declared themselves in favour of the workers' action on the grounds that the fruit companies could afford the demands, having benefited from a recent cut in the banana tax and from repeated devaluations of the colón. In November 1984 United Brands announced that it would halt operations at Golfito and the Palmar Sur base because of the rising cost of production and transport and the recent labour problems, terminating its 100-year contract with the government, due to expire in 1988. Negotiations were started for the government's acquisition of the Pacific coast plantations, and in March 1985 an agreement was signed giving the government just over half of the 3,000 hectares of land in exchange for a payment of $1,245,000. Although United Brands had now withdrawn from banana production, it retained its control of the more lucrative marketing and transport operations (which were run entirely by the multinational fruit companies).

By the end of 1980 Costa Rica's public-sector foreign debt had reached $1,800 million and debt service amounted to a quarter of export earnings. In September 1981 the government announced an official moratorium on external debt payments and sought to reschedule its debt, then standing at $2,600 million, as it did not possess sufficient foreign reserves to meet the service payments. By the end of 1985 the debt had reached $4,250 million, and between 1980 and 1984 debt service had grown from 30 per cent of export revenue to 55 per cent.

In September 1981 the government had introduced a moratorium on the payment of part of the public-sector debt, and the suspensions declared in 1983 and 1984 took the total amount amortized to about $180,000,000. The public-sector foreign debt was estimated to have risen by $109,000,000 in the first six months of 1985, and debt service for the year was anticipated at $480,000,000 against exports of $1,000 million and imports of $1,150 million.

Negotiations with the IMF began at the beginning of 1981, precipitating a political crisis in the form of the resignation of the finance minister, Hernán Saenz Jiménez, in April 1981 when President Carazo refused to support the proposed austerity programme. Agreement was finally reached on an extended facility of SDR 276,750,000 ($329,000,000) in June, with Costa Rica undertaking to devalue the currency, impose restraints on public spending and wages, cut price controls and subsidies and introduce changes in the tax system. The agreement was suspended in October 1981 before any tranches were advanced as the introduction of economic measures including import controls in September had contravened the Fund's recommendations.

Agreement was reached on a standby loan of SDR 92,250,000 ($100,710,000) in December 1982 in conjunction with a programme in which the main aim (at IMF insistence) was to reduce the public-sector deficit from 11.5 per cent of GDP to 4.5 per cent in the course of 1983. A new letter of intent was sent to the IMF in March 1984, originally delayed by a congressional refusal to ratify the austerity proposals, as agreement of an economic programme with the IMF was necessary in order to conclude negotiations with creditors over the rescheduling of the total foreign debt.

A further IMF standby loan was agreed in March 1985, worth SDR 54,000,000 ($55,000,000), but disbursements were halted in September because of the government's failure to meet the Fund's schedule for reducing its debt-service arrears. This suspension also blocked payments of a loan of $75,000,000 concluded with creditor banks in March as part of a 10-year rescheduling package covering payments of $344,000,000 in 1985–86.

2.2.6: Panama

Although Panama's main traditional exports—bananas, sugar, shrimps and coffee—are typical of the region, its economy was drastically altered by the building of the canal and the operation of the offshore financial sector, which developed from the late 1960s. The canal made Panama one of the world's most important shipping centres, and although in recent years it has been unable to accommodate larger oil tankers the problem was eased with the completion of a transisthmian pipeline in October 1982. Petroleum products have become a leading export, but the national trade deficit has remained high, amounting to $942,000,000 in 1983. In the same year services accounted for 67.5 per cent of GDP: 7.1 per cent came from the canal and 15.8 per cent from the financial sector.

In two other respects, however, Panama's economy resembles those of its northern neighbours, with a rising rate of unemployment, estimated at over 20 per cent in 1983, and a growing debt burden. By early 1985 the total foreign debt had reached $3,700 million (representing about three-quarters of GDP), and the government introduced a package of austerity measures in March 1985 to prepare for the conclusion in July of a 21-month IMF standby agreement for SDR 90,000,000 ($92,700,000).

Notes

1. Lapper op. cit., chapter 3; for table of national economic indicators 1960–82, see James A. Morris, Honduras: Caudillo Politics and Military Rulers, Westview (Boulder, Colorado), 1983 p. 22.
2. Black, Triumph of the People, pp. 34–36.
3. For further details of social reforms, see Black, op. cit., and Dianna Melrose, Nicaragua: The Threat of a Good Example?, Oxfam Public Affairs Unit, 1985.

2.3: LAND REFORM

2.3.1: Introductory

The Spanish colonizers introduced a form of serfdom, known as the *encomienda*, which was officially outlawed in 1542 and replaced by the *repartimiento*, a system under which peasants worked on the settlers' land but were rarely paid in cash. As land became more prized in the late 19th century with the development of large coffee and banana plantations, and in the 1950s and 1960s with cotton growing and agribusiness, the problems of landlessness (or ownership of plots of land too small to support a household) and rural unemployment increased. The unequal distribution of land became such a prominent grievance that the call for agrarian reform became a powerful political rallying point, but one which provoked considerable opposition both from national large landowners and foreign vested interests. This point had been demonstrated in Cuba after the 1959 revolution, when the expropriation of land and the nationalization of sugar production caused the first major dissension in relations with the United States.

2.3.2: Guatemala

On June 17, 1952, the Arbenz government introduced legislation giving the state the power to confiscate uncultivated land on large estates, land on large estates where the rent was paid in kind or by labour service and the *"fincas nacionales"* (large estates previously owned by German nationals and taken over during the war); under the legislation, landowners were to be compensated in bonds at 3 per cent interest redeemable over a maximum period of 25 years. The legislation applied to estates of between 95 and 270 hectares, unless at least two-thirds of the land was cultivated, and of over 270 hectares, unless fully cultivated; it did not affect major export product plantations. The land was redistributed in smallholdings of up to 17 hectares, and beneficiaries were given plots for life without legal title, in order to prevent resale and speculation.[1]

The next phase of the reform began in February 1953 when the Guatemalan government informed the United Fruit Company (UFCO) that about 90,000 hectares of its land (out of a total of over 222,000 hectares) on the Pacific coast would be expropriated on the grounds that it was uncultivated. (It was estimated that some 85 per cent of UFCO's estates were uncultivated in order to control the banana market, although the company claimed that the real figure was about 20 per cent, and that the land was being held in reserve.) The government offered the sum of $627,572, based (as with other expropriations) on the declared tax value of the land by the owner; although UFCO had bought the land for just over $300,000 nearly 20 years before and had kept the declared taxable value low at about $4,000,000, it appealed—unsuccessfully—for compensation of $15,854,849. Two further expropriations in October 1953 and February 1954 took the total of land confiscated to 156,640 hectares.

Within 18 months of the Castillo Armas military coup in 1954 all but 0.5 per cent of the peasants who had been given plots of land under Arbenz lost them. In the 1970s 2 per cent of the population owned 53 per cent of cultivable land (compared with 70 per cent of cultivable land in the 1940s), and according to a USAID study completed in 1982 Guatemala had the most inequitable distribution of land in Latin America.

Although President Cerezo pledged that there would be no "agrarian reforms" nor land expropriations under his administration, he promised a plan of "rural development". In response to a protest demonstration staged in the capital on May 2, 1986, by about 11,000 landless peasants from Escuintla (who had moved there from Quiché to escape the fighting), he announced a scheme to found a land bank, which would offer easy credit terms for the purchase of land. The scheme, which would be formed with technical assistance from USAID, was expected to benefit 20,000 of the 420,000 landless peasants in the country. In the first week of September work began on a special land project near Tiquisate (on a former UFCO plantation) in which about 1800 hectares of land were distributed to some 2,000 families, to grow coffee, bananas and other fruit on a co-operative basis. The project was headed by Fr Andrés Girón, who had organized the May demonstration, and was funded by the government to the tune of $5,000,000.

2.3.3: Honduras

Launched in the same year (i.e. 1961) as the declaration of the Alliance for Progress and the formation of the National Agrarian Institute (INA), the land reform programme pursued in Honduras was far less radical than that attempted in Guatemala in the early 1950s. The impetus for change faded after the coup of 1963 and between 1962 and 1974 only 36,000 hectares of land were redistributed.[2]

The new military government under Col. Melgar Castro announced in April 1975 that it would give priority to implementing the land reform programme launched in January that year to distribute 526,000 hectares of land to 120,000 landless peasants over a period of five years, although this proposal excluded United Brands and Standard Fruit land. The demand for land reform aroused much popular support among the peasants, who began seizing land in May 1975 when negotiations on appropriation had failed. In June and July a total of 21 peasants were killed (and some mutilated) in Olancha province and four army officers and two landowners were subsequently charged with their murder.

In July 1975 an investigatory commission on land reform established by the government recommended the partial nationalization of the banana industry, proposing that the government acquire a 51 per cent share each in United Brands and Standard Fruit in their Honduran operations, and that legal action should be brought against United Brands for "moral damage" to the country. It added that as the United Brands railway and dock concessions had expired and the Standard Fruit railway was in a "dreadful condition" these assets should be taken over without compensation. Melgar Castro announced in August 1975 that with effect from Sept. 15 all special privileges for foreign banana companies would be cancelled so that "the Honduran people and the government will have direct influence" on economic decisions which previously "were taken in Boston, New York, San Francisco and Washington".

Land distribution reached its peak in 1973–75, with 116,804 hectares going to 17,680 families (out of a total of 226,455 hectares allocated to 36,472 families in the period 1962–80), but tailed off sharply after the replacement of the Melgar Castro government in 1978.

Early in April 1985 more than 60 peasant groups belonging to the National Peasants' Union (UNC) occupied 20,000 hectares in the first such land seizure for 10 years. The action was a protest over what they considered to be the government's failure to implement the agrarian reform law concerning idle land; the UNC secretary general, Marcial Caballero, claimed that "Out of 197 groups which have solicited land from INA, we can count on both hands the number of positive responses".

2.3.4: El Salvador

The pressure on land and the problem of landlessness has been greatest in El Salvador, where the proportion of the rural population without land rose from 12 per cent in 1961 to 29 per cent in 1971 and an estimated 65 per cent by 1980, evicted to make room for cotton and sugar cane. In 1881, during the coffee boom, the government had abolished all communal forms of land tenure, and in the course of the 20th century wage labour and rental have come to replace the earlier system of hiring small plots in exchange for working on the landowners' estates.[3]

In response to pressure from small peasant organizations the government adopted an agrarian reform law in 1975, establishing the Salvadorean Institute of Agrarian Transformation (ISTA) in June. However, the law immediately met with vociferous opposition from landowners and elements of the armed forces and there were reports of ill-treatment of peasants trying to gain land lawfully. In October 1975 the National Assembly approved legislation modifying the law (which had originally envisaged the distribution of 58,000 hectares to 12,000 families with compensation to the 250 landowners involved) to include some state-owned land in the scheme. In frustration many peasants resorted to land invasions with the sympathy—if not the support—of many rural priests, resulting in a campaign of terror against radical rural clergy (see section 2.4.5).

The junta announced a programme of land reform on Feb. 11, 1980, subsequently nationalizing 60 per cent of the country's farmland; it was intended that 1,250,000 people (80–90 per cent of the rural population) would benefit. Phase I of the programme provided for the takeover of 20 per cent of farmland on estates of over 500 hectares, which were turned into peasant co-operatives, with farmers compensated in government bonds and direct payments. The violence of 1975 reappeared, with ISTA reporting in January 1981 that at over 80 of the 330 co-operatives established so far peasants were paying protection money to local paramilitary groups and that over 200 peasant co-operative leaders and five ISTA employees had been killed since March 1980, apparently by the security forces or death squads.

Phase II covered over 23 per cent of farmland, or some 1,700 farms of between 100 and 500 hectares (where most of the coffee was grown), but was deferred in March 1981, leaving the bulk of productive agricultural land in the hands of relatively few. Phase III of the programme, introduced as Decree 207 and known as "land to the tiller", allowed tenant peasants to purchase plots of land of up to seven hectares. It was estimated that about 50,000 of the 150,000 potential beneficiaries had received provisional titles to land by the end of 1982, although in May 1982 Morales Erlich said that over 5,000 peasant families had been evicted since the March elections, while the peasant organizations put the number twice as high. The assembly voted on May 18, 1982, by 37 to 16 to suspend Phase III of the programme for one crop cycle as it deprived landowners of any incentive to plant cotton or sugar cane in anticipation of losing their land.

President Magaña later observed that Phase III was highly unlikely to work successfully, because it would make landowners extremely unwilling to rent out any land at all, pointing out that no new rental contracts were taken out in either 1980 or 1981.[4]

In March 1983 the Assembly voted a 10-month extension to the programme, with an amendment which cast doubt on the rights of beneficiaries by requiring them to produce proof of having rented the land, whereas in many cases only verbal contracts existed because of the high rate of rural illiteracy. The issue of land reform proved the most controversial item in the drafting of the new constitution, and was not finalized until Dec. 13, when the Assembly voted by 34 to 25 in favour of an Arena proposal which effectively halted the programme. The terms of Phase II were altered to cover estates of 245–500 (instead of 100–500 hectares) but there were relatively few estates within this revised category and in any case landowners were given three years in which to sell their excess land. Phase III was extended for a further six months, but was eventually revoked by the Assembly in June 1984.

2.3.5: Nicaragua

Although the question of land reform in Nicaragua[5] was a key issue of Sandinista policy, it was not until July 19, 1981, that an agrarian reform law was enacted. It contained two main provisions:—(i) the redistribution of idle estates of over 500 hectares in the Pacific zone and over 1,000 hectares elsewhere; and (ii) the seizure of land and enterprises abandoned for over six months, with immediate application to 14 companies whose owners lived abroad. The land of those involved in "counter-revolutionary activity" had been seized prior to this legislation, and between July 1979 and May 1982 a total of 700,000 hectares was confiscated. As in other countries, the reform was seen by more conservative elements as highly radical, and one of the concessions made in the December 1983 liberalization measures was an undertaking given by Jaime Wheelock—head of the National Agrarian Reform Institute (INRA) and Minister of Agriculture and Agrarian Reform — that private farmers would be given certificates guaranteeing that their property would not be expropriated.

Between October 1981 and August 1984 a total of 49,661 families received titles to land, free of charge but subject to a ban on sale in order to prevent renewed land concentration or fragmentation. In contrast to the Salvadorean programme, no limit was set on the size of private holdings as the main aim was to make the land as productive as possible; moreover, peasant farmers were encouraged to form co-operatives, which were given priority in the allocation of land and offered more favourable credit terms. By 1984 nearly 40 per cent of the total agricultural land was owned by co-operatives or agrarian reform enterprises and the proportion of farmers with land over 350 hectares fell from 41.2 per cent of total land ownership to 11.0 per cent.

In 1985 the redistribution was accelerated to give help in particular to families displaced by the war (especially those recently relocated from the north) and to meet the demands of peasants in densely-populated Masaya. The total amount of land redistributed in the course of the year increased to 450,700 hectares, to the benefit of 23,526 families, taking the total number of beneficiary families to about 93,500 and total area distributed to 1,851,900 hectares.

The acceleration did not receive full domestic support, especially when two-thirds of the cotton-growing estates in Masaya belonging to Cosep president Enrique Bolaños were expropriated (although they were being worked "correctly"). The government said that this instance was a special case to ease the pressing local need for land, and the regional delegate of the ministry of agriculture and agrarian reform, Miguel Gómez, pointed out that the Bolaños family was still the largest private landowner in the region. (The private sector favoured the relocation of landless peasants to new territories in less densely-populated areas.)

Notes

1. Schlesinger and Kinzer, *op. cit.*, p. 55, point out that the law was much more moderate than the Mexican land reform of a decade before, and under other circumstances would have qualified for US assistance under the Alliance for Progress.
2. For further details, see Lapper, *op. cit.*, pp. 63–67, and Morris, *op. cit.*, pp. 96–101.
3. For land reform in El Salvador, see Armstrong and Shenk, *op. cit.*, pp. 142–45, 155–57, and Raymond Bonner, *Weakness and Deceit: US Policy in El Salvador*, Hamish Hamilton, London, 1984, pp. 187–210, 317–19.
4. Didion, *op. cit.*, pp. 91–92.
5. See Black, *Triumph of the People*, pp. 250–52, 264–72.

2.4: CHURCH–STATE RELATIONS

2.4.1: Introductory on Liberation Theology

In the 19th century the power of the Roman Catholic Church in Central America varied with the political complexion of the government. Privileges withdrawn under Morazán were restored by Carrera (and religious orders disbanded in the liberal reforms were restored throughout the region between 1840 and 1845), to be lost again under the Positivists, when church lands were confiscated, religious orders were curbed and Protestant immigration was encouraged. In the 20th century the position was reversed again, most notably in Guatemala, where the Church had been disestablished in 1871 under President Barrios, but regained its status in the 1955 constitution.

Traditionally the Catholic Church had been a pillar of the political status quo (except the Jesuits, who had always shown a greater concern for social justice in Latin America), but there was a radical change in the 1960s. A conference of Latin American bishops met in Medellín (Colombia) in 1968 and issued a statement, in which they declared:

> The Christian . . . believes in the value of peace for the achievement of justice, he also believes that justice is a necessary condition for peace. And he is not unaware that in many places in Latin America there is a situation of injustice that must be recognized as institutionalized violence, because the existing structures violate the peoples' basic rights: a situation which calls for far-reaching, daring, urgent and profoundly innovating change.

Three years later a highly influential book appeared called *The Theology of Liberation—History, Politics and Salvation*, written by a Peruvian theologian, Gustavo Gutiérrez, who asserted that "the outlines of a theology of liberation that we possess today are simply an expression of the poor and oppressed people's right to think"; he added that "evangelizing means proclaiming the Lord with words of life and acts of solidarity from the world of the poor and their struggles".[1] This new emphasis on the poor led to the establishment in the mid–1960s of the *communidades cristianas de base* (Christian base communities) in many Latin American countries.[2] One of the best known was the Nicaraguan community on the archipelago of Solentiname led by Ernesto Cardenal, nearly all of whose members subsequently left to join the FSLN.[3]

The Latin American bishops met again in Puebla (Mexico) in 1979 and issued a document entitled "The Poor—The Church's First Priority", in which they stated:

> Ten years [after Medellín] . . . the situation has deteriorated. . . . There has been a growing accumulation of wealth in the hands of a minority often at the cost of the impoverishment of many. Not only do the poor lack material goods but, at the level of human dignity, they are not full participants in the social and political life of their countries. . . . This Conference of Latin American Bishops, reaffirming its commitment to the poor, condemns as contrary to the spirit of the gospel the extremes of poverty found in our continent. We are compelled to denounce the system which generates this poverty.

This identification with the poor by one of the most influential of national organizations (especially in rural areas and shanty towns) had an enormous impact on the development of mass popular organizations and, because of the Church's international voice, on the amount of information available abroad on events in the region. The two issues on which identification was strongest were land disputes and the campaign against human rights abuses, leading to many priests and lay workers themselves being classed as "subversives" by the authorities.

Although liberation theology led some priests to take up arms on behalf of guerrilla groups, not all Central American clergy became adherents. The divide usually emerged along hierarchical lines (less so in El Salvador) and became particularly evident in Nicaragua after the Sandinista revolution, especially when the Pope raised objections to the continuation in government office of four priests.

2.4.2: Pope John Paul's 1983 Visit

Pope John Paul II visited the region in March 1983, although at the last moment there were doubts about the inclusion of certain countries in his itinerary. Such doubts (in the event overcome) applied to (i) Nicaragua, because of the priests in government in defiance of his request; (ii) El Salvador, because he was thought to be at risk (particularly from the death squads after he announced his intention of praying at the tomb of Archbishop Romero); and (iii) Guatemala, because of the militant Protestantism of President Ríos Montt and the execution of six men in the first week of March in spite of a papal plea for mercy (see section 2.5.2).

In Costa Rica the Pope called for the establishment of social justice "without returning to methods of violence nor to systems of collectivism, which can turn out to be no less oppressive of man's dignity than a purely economic capitalism". He received a qualified welcome in Nicaragua, and while celebrating mass in Managua he was interrupted by shouts of "people's power" and "a Church on the side of the poor"; according to some reports these demonstrations had been organized by the government. In El Salvador he stated that priests were "called to make a preferential option for the poor" and spoke of the need for peace, "not an artificial peace which disguises the problems and ignores the corrupt mechanisms which must be reformed . . . [but] a peace for all, of all ages, conditions, groups, origins and political opinions". In Guatemala he said that the church, regardless of denomination, "continues to raise its voice to condemn injustice and to denounce abuses, especially against the poor and humble", and advised his congregation of Indian peasants to "organize associations for the defence of your rights", but warned them not to "confuse evangelization with subversion". In Honduras he appealed for the rejection of "everything that is against the gospel: hatred, violence, injustice, lack of work and the imposition of ideologies which suppress the dignity of men and women".[4]

Taking as the constant theme of his tour a warning against recourse to violence, Pope John Paul endorsed the Contadora line by saying that the tensions of the region originated in "old and unjust socio-economic structures" and that the social system "must be changed" (making no reference to the East–West conflict).

2.4.3: Protestantism and Sub-Christian Sects

Although the large majority of the region's population is Catholic, the Protestant churches have grown steadily since the late 19th century, principally on the basis of efforts by US missionaries and the Moravians on the Atlantic coast. More recently there has been a rapid growth of extreme fundamentalist Protestant sects, and by the 1980s it was estimated that about 20 per cent of the population in Guatemala and El Salvador had Protestant allegiance. Unlike the mainstream churches (which became involved in similar projects to those of the Catholic Church organizations and also came into conflict with the authorities), the militant sects, most of which are of US origin, have usually been so strongly anti-communist that they have received backing from military governments. By the same token, their millenarianism and emphasis on personal spirituality rather than on corporate Christian living have resulted in these sects taking little interest in social and political reform. (For controversy over the role of World Vision International in helping Salvadorean refugees in Honduras, see section 4.1.4.)

In recent years there has also been an increase in the activities of sub-Christian sects in Central America, particularly of the Unification Church (the "Moonies"), which has its largest followings in Panama and Honduras (see section 1.3.11) and whose US community was reported to be financing the Nicaraguan contras (see section 5.2.5).

2.4.4: Guatemala

In March 1968 Archbishop Mario Casariego appealed in a sermon for an end to violence in Guatemala.[5] Shortly afterwards he was abducted and held for several days by a right-wing paramilitary group, which had previously circulated leaflets accusing him and the other members of the hierarchy of pro-communist sympathies. In the 1970s the Catholic Church became increasingly outspoken against the excesses of the armed forces and on social and economic inequality. Both Catholic and Protestant priests were accused by President Laugerud of stirring up civil unrest in the town of Panzos (north-east of the capital) in May 1978 by inciting peasants to invade private estates. The commander of El Quiché military region, Col. Roberto Metta, commented in 1982: "We make no distinction between the Catholic Church and the communist subversives."[6]

In July 1980 the Catholic Church decided to suspend its pastoral activities in El Quiché department and to withdraw 50 priests and nuns working in the area after one priest had been kidnapped, three murdered and the bishop of El Quiché had only narrowly escaped a military ambush. He later travelled to Rome and on his return in November 1980 was refused re-entry to Guatemala. Some priests left the area and established a Guatemalan church in exile in Costa Rica, moving later to Managua. Between January 1980 and July 1981 at least 10 priests were killed by the armed forces or paramilitary groups, and in August 1981 the national episcopal conference said that the Church had become more than ever before the target of "unjust attacks and violent oppression", and that there was a deliberate campaign to discredit the Church and implicate it in guerrilla activities; in the same month the Minister of Education, Col. Clementino Castillo Coronado, warned that the government would be "implacable" with priests or nuns who abused their office to "indoctrinate schoolchildren".

Relations between the Catholic Church and the government deteriorated further after the Ríos Montt coup of March 1982, and did not substantially improve after the coup of August 1983, with Mejía Victores attacking the activities of lay and clerical Catholic members in a speech in November of that year. The report of the national episcopal conference in September 1984 traced the roots of violence in the country to "constant exploitation" imposed by unjust social and economic structures", and said that the current national situation was even worse than the devastation caused by the 1976 earthquake.

In May 1983 the Catholic bishops of Guatemala denounced "an aggressive escalation of Protestant sects" which, they feared, could lead to "a religious war with incalculable consequences". The spokesman for the archdiocese, Fr Juan José Córdoba, expressed the view in a newspaper interview that "this Protestant invasion is just part of a [US] State Department policy to crush Latin American hegemony" and pointed out that whereas the Catholic Church suffered from a lack of resources and manpower, large budgets had been available to build five Protestant radio stations, 102 colleges, 47 schools, five theological colleges and 60 bookshops.[7]

2.4.5: El Salvador

Within Central America the Salvadorean Church has been the most influenced by liberation theology. Moreover, its criticism of the government and the violence against many clergy (especially the murder of Archbishop Romero) have been major factors in undermining support for the government from abroad.[8] The national episcopal conference stated in July 1975: "It is no secret that there exists here a climate of violence, repression and lack of respect for fundamental human rights; without doubt the main reason for this violence and insanity is the injustice suffered by the great majority of the people."

In 1969 the National Guard surrounded the town of Suchitoto and demanded that the priest, Fr José Inocencio Alas, leave because of what they regarded as his subversive teaching; however, the local population refused to let him go. Three years later Alas was abducted and tortured, while another priest, Fr Nicolás Rodríguez, was arrested by the National Guard and his body found a few days later completely dismembered. Attacks against the clergy soared in 1977 after the introduction of the land reform programme of the previous year, when priests and layworkers in the *communidades de bases* (known as delegates of the Word) encouraged the peasants to join together in defence of their rights, and were accordingly denounced as communists by the landowning oligarchy.

The most famous of the priests killed in the ensuing violence was Fr Rutilio Grande, who had developed a reputation for his outspokenness while in training and retained this when he became priest in Aguilares. When asked about the new political awareness among his parishioners, he replied that "by virtue of their conversion and growing in faith they naturally are becoming agents of change—as the very gospel asked them to be". On March 12, 1977, a group of armed men, including policemen, ambushed Grande and his two fellow travellers and shot them all dead. The murder was reported to have had a profound effect on Mgr Romero (a personal friend of Grande), who as a moderate had been appointed archbishop in part to check the radical priests; in protest against the killings he temporarily left the country and the Church refused to take part in any official functions (including the inauguration of Gen. Romero in June).

After the kidnap and murder of Foreign Minister Mauricio Borgonovo in April–May 1977 (see section 4.2.4), a leaflet was circulated in the capital entitled "The Church and the Kidnappers"; in an apparent act of retaliation the UGB death squad (see section 3.2.3) killed a Jesuit priest, Fr Alfonso Navarro Oviedo. In the new few weeks a death-squad slogan "Be a patriot, kill a priest" became prominent, and in July 1977 the UGB issued a threat to the entire Jesuit community: "All Jesuits without exception must leave the country forever within 30 days. . . . If our order is not obeyed within the indicated time, the immediate and systematic execution of those Jesuits who remain in the country will proceed until we have finished with all of them." In August 1977 a delegate of the Word, Felipe de Jesús Chacón (father of Juan Chacón, subsequently killed in November 1980—see section 3.2.3), was arrested by the National Guard in Chalatenango, and his body was later found in a severely mutilated condition.

At the end of June 1978 Mgr Romero said that he was "deeply anxious at this climate of terror and insecurity forced upon the people of El Salvador, whose only crime is to express their dissatisfaction at the lack of work and of a small piece of land out of which to earn a living". In January 1979 he excommunicated members of the security forces responsible for the recent killing of Fr Octavio Ortiz and four young people in the capital, and said that he believed that Fr Ernesto Barrera Moto (officially reported to have been killed in a gunbattle in November) had been tortured by police and then shot; it subsequently emerged that Barrera, who had been working in the slum areas of the capital, had been a member of the FPL guerrilla group (see section 3.1.4). In late 1978 Mgr Romero had declared: "I oppose violence, and priests involved with guerrillas should leave the Church or leave the guerrillas. On the other hand, with all peaceful avenues closed off by the government, with such official obstinacy, with such misery in the country, I can understand that youths turn to violence in frustration. I do not sanction it, but I can understand it." (For assassination of Romero in March 1980, see section 1.4.12.)

The Jesuit University of Central America was closed in June 1980, and in January 1981 the Archbishop's office in San Salvador reported that troops had occupied the buildings, evicting staff students, as well as entering several churches and ransacking two Jesuit houses. Morales Erlich defended the action on Jan. 17 on the grounds that there had been reports of an imminent guerrilla takeover of the university. Later in January the national headquarters of the Catholic aid organization *Caritas* was raided and the director, Carmen González, and four other workers arrested on charges of smuggling arms and medication to the guerrillas.

Attacks on the Church continued in the early 1980s, because of its defence of human rights and its links with the popular organizations; there were also reports of actions against Protestant clergy. In October 1984 an Emmanuel Baptist pastor, Miguel Tomás Castro García, was arrested but later released and sent into exile after pressure from the US-based Christian Urgent Action

Network for El Salvador (CUANES); in November 1984 a Lutheran pastor, David Hernández Espino, a local organizer of a food distribution programme for the displaced was abducted and killed.

The Church's offer to act as a mediator between the government and the FMLN–FDR was taken up for the La Palma Talks in October 1984 (see section 6.4.5), but after the national episcopal conference blamed the guerrillas for the failure to resume talks in August 1985, the FMLN responded by alleging that "the biased conduct of the Church is yet another obstacle on the road to dialogue". (The previous month Rivera y Damas had been severely criticized by right-wing elements for being a guerrilla partisan in saying that in condemning guerrilla terrorism people should not forget the "terrorism of the armed forces".) The Church resumed its mediatory role in the abortive attempt to hold talks at Sesori in 1986 (see section 6.4.6).

2.4.6: Nicaragua

The Nicaraguan Catholic Church under Somoza was less imbued with liberation theology than its counterparts in Guatemala and El Salvador, but in the 1970s several Jesuits supported the activities of popular organizations. By 1977 even the hierarchy was becoming openly critical of the government and the armed forces, and in general the Church favoured the Sandinista revolution. (The Moravian Church on the Atlantic coast became an important channel of communication between the local population and the FSLN government, and with the exception of its treatment of the Miskitos, the government has generally enjoyed the support of the Protestant churches.)

Divisions began to emerge after about a year over the question of priestly involvement in government, focusing on a debate over whether or not there should be a church representative on the Council of State. The lower clergy were unanimously in favour of membership and one of them, Fr Félix Jiménez, said: "Our participation is a reflection of the class struggle which is taking place in our country, and logically within the Church itself as part of our society."[9] Although the government repeatedly stated its commitment to religious freedom, the bishops accused it of "manipulating" religious sentiments and of promoting "class hatred", which in turn led to several priests charging the bishops with defending "class privileges".

In October 1980 the national episcopal conference issued an order to all priests in senior government posts to resign them by the end of the year, the main people in question being d'Escoto, Ernesto Cardenal, Edgar Parrales and Fr Alvaro Argüello, the church representative on the Council of State. None of them complied with the order and the dispute was partially resolved in July 1981 when the conference agreed that the priests concerned should be allowed to retain their posts provided that they did not exercise their religious duties.

Church–state relations continued to be tense and in August 1982 there was national furore over an incident involving the church spokesman, Fr Bismarck Carballo, who was shown in a television news broadcast on Aug. 12, 1981, running naked down a city street from the house of a female parishioner; the authorities said that the film camera had been in the area for a demonstration and that Carballo had got into the picture by a sheer coincidence, whereas Carballo claimed that he had been forced by armed men to remove his clothes and run in front of the camera, as part of a deliberate campaign to discredit him. The MDN called a rally of students at Catholic schools and during a demonstration in Masaya on Aug. 16 two people were killed, 10 wounded and over 80 arrested; Borge asserted that the CIA had helped right-wing elements provoke a confrontation between the Church and the government. In an effort to reduce tensions the FSLN issued a communiqué reiterating its respect for religion and saying that the incidents of mid–August "did not constitute a confrontation between the revolution and religion"; however, the nine bishops said that the government's version of events was "presented in a partial and distorted way, without it being possible to use the same channels of communication to defend oneself".

The next major issue was the military service bill of August 1983 (see section 1.5.27), in response to which the Church called for anti-government protests and tried to organize a civil disobedience campaign in the form of strikes and sit-ins at schools and churches. On Oct. 31 two foreign priests at the Salesian college in Masaya were expelled from the country for allegedly having "taken advantage of their position as clergymen and educators to carry out various political actions which violated the law, including urging young people to disregard the law on military service". Talks were held in November 1983 to try to improve church–state relations, but Carballo reported afterwards that these had been "an exchange of views, nothing more", as the government had refused to meet the Church's demands for "freedom of expression for all the media" and recognition of "the church hierarchy as the legitimate voice of the faithful".

The entry into effect of a new code of canon law in November 1983 renewed the controversy over priests in government, since one article specifically prohibited priests from accepting "public posts that entail exercise of civil authority". In August 1984 the Vatican issued a formal warning that the four priests—i.e. d'Escoto, Cardenal, Fernando Cardenal (appointed minister of education in July)—and Parrales (ambassador to the OAS since 1982)—should resign by the end of the month, and they agreed to leave the government if they could remain in their posts until after the November elections. They were, however, reappointed in January 1985 and so were banned by the episcopal conference from exercising their priestly functions; in December 1984 Fernando Cardenal had been expelled from the Jesuit order for retaining his government office.

In April 1984 the nine bishops wrote a pastoral letter requesting the inclusion of the contras within a "national dialogue". However, the letter was criticized by the government, the Jesuit and Dominican orders and the chairman of the PSCN, Agustín Jarquín Anaya, for failing to condemn the actions of the contras or US involvement (despite the recent mining of Corinto and the reports of contra atrocities). The letter asserted:

> It is dishonest constantly to blame internal aggression and violence on foreign aggression. It is useless to blame the evils of the past for everything without recognizing the problems of the present. All Nicaraguans inside and outside the country must participate in this dialogue, regardless of ideology, class or party loyalties. Furthermore, we think that Nicaraguans who have taken up arms against the government must also participate in this dialogue. If not, there will be no possibility of a settlement, and our people, especially the poorest among them, will continue to suffer and die.

In June 1984 Archbishop Obando y Bravo led protests against the arrest of Fr Luis Amado Peña, who was charged with involvement in a plot to open an FDN internal front; he was later pardoned by the Council of State after its commission had found him guilty as charged. During a protest march in July by about 150 people, four foreign priests were detained and expelled (along with six others) for having "violated the laws of our country, engaged in intense political activities against the government of national reconstruction and participated in plans intended to provoke a confrontation between the Catholic Church and the Sandinista people's revolution". In June 1985 Obando y Bravo, returning from a visit to Rome (where he had been elevated to the rank of cardinal) provoked a controversy by stopping off in Miami to celebrate a mass for Nicaraguan exiles living there, which was attended by Calero and Pastora.

From late 1985 relations between Church and State deteriorated further, in particular with the indefinite closure of Radio Católica, the Church's radio station, on Jan. 1, 1986 (see also section 1.5.29). In a televised interview broadcast in late March 1986 d'Escoto claimed that Obando y Bravo was "on the side of the imperialist aggressor", and a few days later the national episcopal conference accused the pro-government "People's Church" of "manipulating the fundamental truths of our faith . . . in order to make it fit their own ideology and use it for their own ends". In late June and early July Carballo and another leading churchman, Mgr Pablo Antonio Vega Mantilla (Bishop of Juigalpa and vice-president of the national episcopal conference) were refused re-entry into Nicaragua because of their political support for US policy against Nicaragua.

There were signs of attempts to heal the breach in August 1986 when a new papal nuncio, Fr Paolo Giglio, arrived in Managua and on meeting President Ortega offered to do everything possible to "overcome current differences and difficulties" and declared that bishops—and the Church in general—should respect the laws of the land. In September preparations began to renew the dialogue between the Church and the government, the Church wanting agreement on a pre-determined agenda, including the matters of the continued closure of Radio Católica and the return of Carballo and Vega, along with about a dozen foreign priests expelled from the country over the previous two years.

By contrast, the General Assembly of CEPAD—the Evangelical Committee for Development, formed after the 1972 earthquake—sent a letter to "the Christian churches of the United States, the people of the United States, and all people of goodwill" in March 1982, declaring: "We have been saddened because of the moral and, possibly, the direct backing which the American government has given, and continues to provide, to groups who have the clearly expressed purpose of destroying our government and preventing it from carrying out its programmes, which benefit the great majority."

Notes

1. Gustavo Gutiérrez, *The Poor and the Church in Latin America*, CIIR, 1984 (pamphlet).
2. See *Central America Report*, Issue 12, March/April 1985, pp. 2–3.
3. See Black, *Triumph of the People*, pp. 102–03.
4. For Church in Honduras, see Morris, *op. cit.*, pp. 81–83.
5. See Black, *Garrison Guatemala*, pp. 101–04.

6. Quoted *ibid.*, p. 141.
7. *The Guardian*, Aug. 17, 1984.
8. In his novel *Un Día en la Vida* (UCA Editores, San Salvador, 1980) Manlio Argueta describes the impact on a small rural town of the change from the "old" to the "new" priests, pp. 20–36.
9. Quoted Black, *Triumph of the People*, p. 247.

2.5: ROLE OF THE ARMED FORCES

2.5.1: Introductory

Since independence the armed forces in Central America have wielded considerable political power, often being responsible for changes in government (by direct intervention or by allowing civilians to take office). During the Positivist era this power increased as the military undertook the construction and maintenance of roads and bridges throughout the region and were appointed to senior public posts. Given the relative weakness of central government the armed forces and the Roman Catholic Church were often the two strongest national institutions, and enrolment into the military offered one of the best chances for social advancement in a society with limited economic, political and professional openings.

In Guatemala, Honduras and El Salvador the senior commands have generally supported right-of-centre political parties (and have occasionally been challenged by reformist junior officers), while in Nicaragua under the Somoza family the National Guard was bound to a single party, the PLN; under the Sandinistas the EPS was linked to the FSLN (at least until the inauguration of the elected government in January 1985), but in a very different structure. Costa Rica is the exception in the region, having abolished its army in 1948; its Civil Guard (unlike the National Guard in Panama, where the army was disbanded in 1904) has had neither the constitutional nor the de facto authority to intervene in national political affairs.[1]

2.5.2: Guatemala

Since the overthrow of Arbenz (himself an army officer) in 1954, all national presidents until Carezo have been serving officers (except President Méndez 1966–70), sometimes taking power by force, sometimes by means of the ballot box. As the PDCG leader Danilo Barillas commented in 1975: "In Guatemala it is useless to think of governing, except as the result of a political decision by the army."[2]

The armed forces could also act independently of the judiciary, as in the case of the military tribunals set up by Ríos Montt under the July 1982 state of siege (see section 1.2.13); the operations of these secret courts aroused much domestic and international opposition to the government because of their power to impose the death sentence. The government announced on Sept. 16, 1982, that of the 40 people so far tried by the tribunals, 22 had been acquitted, eight had been released pending a verdict, six were awaiting verdicts and four had been convicted and sentenced to death; these last four, who belonged to the Guerrilla Army of the Poor (EGP), faced a firing squad the following day. In January 1983 a further 10 defendants, classed by the tribunals as "guerrillas", were sentenced to death, and although four sentences were overturned for "insufficient evidence" the other six were executed on March 3 despite international appeals for clemency. (One of them was a Honduran national, said to have arrived in Guatemala City only two weeks previously and to have been arrested after quarrelling with a policeman at a football match.)

Although many sectors in Guatemala became increasingly disaffected from the Ríos Montt administration, it was the loss of support within the armed forces which ensured his removal in August 1983. A senior officer, Brig-Gen. José Guillermo Echevarría Vielman, published an open letter on June 5, 1983, urging the President to announce a timetable for elections "to satisfy the popular will" and "end Guatemala's international isolation", and calling on "all the military occupying public posts to return to barracks". Three days later he was discharged from the army for violating army regulations, but the affair sparked off a wave of anti-government protest. Three weeks later the commander of the Quezaltenango garrison refused to obey presidential orders and his lead was followed by other army garrisons and air force bases, virtually ensuring success for Mejía Victores's coup of Aug. 8.

Mejía Victores was himself conscious of a threat from within the armed forces and in October 1983 initiated several changes in the high command among those who had originally supported him, including the removal of the Army Chief of Staff, Gen. Héctor López Fuentes. A new law passed on Dec. 7, 1983, defined the role of the army as "apolitical, essentially subordinate and non-deliberating" and required the retirement of all members who had served for 33 or more years or had reached retirement age. On Jan. 27, 1984, the government announced that those officers removed under this clause had tried to stage a coup, along with Gen. Araña Osorio (former President) and López Fuentes.

While the armed forces held power the allocation of the national budget to the defence sector increased sharply, rising from 10.3 per cent of the total in 1980 to 22.4 per cent by 1985, when exemption from a cut in government expenditure effective in June increased the allocation still further to 24 per cent.

2.5.3: Honduras

The Honduran army did not develop as an efficient professional organization until after the Second World War, when the United States offered training (from which over 1,000 Honduran soldiers had benefitted by 1969—see also section 5.2.7). The constitutions of 1957 and 1965 placed direct command in the hands of senior officers and the post of minister of defence carried purely administrative authority. (For the development of factions within the army after the football war of 1969 leading to a revolt by junior reformist officers, see sections 1.3.7–8.)

Although the election of President Suazo in 1981 was hailed (especially by the United States) as a return to civilian-controlled democracy, the army continued to wield political influence, particularly with the appointment of Gen. Alvarez as C.-in-C. in 1982 (see section 1.3.10). The eventual removal of Alvarez in March 1984 (see section 1.3.11) occurred not because of mounting political opposition to him but as a result of growing dislike of him and his personal power among fellow officers. It was reported in mid–1982 that up to 70 officers had been dismissed since Alvarez's appointment in a deliberate purge of liberal elements.

In late August 1982 Col. Leonidas Torres Arias, army intelligence chief since 1976, accused Alvarez of "trying to launch the Honduran people on a criminal and bloody campaign against the Nicaraguan revolution", of "turning Honduras into a theatre of operations for a foreign power", of having an "uncontrollable obsession to become the all-powerful man of the country" and of running his own personal death squad to eliminate "subversion and opposition". He further alleged that Alvarez had been involved in political intrigue with Suazo and Negroponte (the current US ambassador), undertaking to prevent a coup against the elected government in return for Suazo's support for his policies, with this agreement being favoured by the United States in the form of increased military and economic aid. There followed mutual accusations by Torres and Alvarez of corruption, repression and human rights abuses. Torres's appointment as defence attaché to Argentina (made in May 1982) was revoked in September by presidential decree, and he was then accused of treason and dishonourably discharged from the army.

After Alvarez's departure for Miami, López made moves to improve the army's image, taking measures against officers implicated in the two-year "dirty war", but reports of human rights abuses continued (see section 4.2.3). During 1984 certain sectors of the armed forces began to protest against the traditional Honduran adherence to US policy in Central America, while long-standing antagonism towards El Salvador contributed to the decision to close the US training base at Puerto Castilla (see section 1.3.14). After the constitutional crisis of April–May 1985 (see section 1.3.12) there were reported to be three distinct factions within the armed forces: the extreme right, favouring the policies of Alvarez, supporting the Suazo government and the President's re-election; the centrists behind López, who had advocated that Suazo's term be extended for two years; and the reformists (largely young and less influential officers), wanting changes in the high command and holding the Suazo government responsible for most of the country's current economic and political problems.

López announced his retirement on Jan. 30, 1986, more than a year before the official expiry of his term of office, and was replaced by the conservative Navy Commander Col. Humberto Regalado Hernández. Although López asserted that he had decided to leave for purely personal reasons it was widely speculated that his resignation had been the result of an internal struggle in the army command between the extremist and centrist factions, the former resenting López's independent status.

2.5.4: El Salvador

In many respects the history of the 1979 "revolution" against Gen. Romero was dominated by the struggle for political control between the young reformist officers and the hardliners, beginning with the split between Col. Majano and Col. Gutiérrez (see section 1.4.10).[3] The division became deeper and more evident after the May 1980 coup attempt, when Majano tried to initiate dialogue with left-wing elements. In August 1980 a number of military commanders urged that Majano be tried for "treason against the armed forces" and on Sept. 2 most of his strongest supporters were deprived of their commands under an order signed by Gutiérrez, Col. García and Col. Carranza, withour prior consultation with the other members of the junta. When Majano was ousted from the junta in December 1980 he said that the "October 15 Movement" had been betrayed because of "infiltration of the high command of the armed forces and the government by the extreme right".

As in Guatemala the army showed its independence of the civilian judiciary even over matters involving the civilian population; when a new code of military ethics was introduced by the junta in January 1981 García, as minister of defence, was made responsible for its supervision. (The code had been drafted in response to the growing number of reports of human rights abuses on the part of the armed forces and paramilitary groups.)

García himself became the object of criticism within the armed forces during 1982 among sections who held that his conduct of the war against the guerrillas lacked firmness and decision. The commander of the garrison at Sensuntepeque (Cabañas department), Lt.-Col. Sigifredo Ochoa Pérez, announced on Jan. 6, 1983, that he had refused García's order to leave his command for a diplomatic post in Uruguay and placed his troops on alert. Ochoa eventually agreed to resign his command on Jan. 10, but instead of going to Uruguay he became defence attaché in Washington (a much more senior post), further eroding García's control; he returned to a command post in Chalatenango department a year later. The air force commander, Col. Juan Rafael Bustillo, informed President Magaña on April 14 that he would cease to obey García's orders from the next day, forcing García's resignation on April 18; he was replaced by Gen. Carlos Eugenio Vides Casanova, director of the National Guard since 1979.

2.5.5: Nicaragua

In 1925 the Nicaraguan Congress approved a US proposal for the formation of an apolitical National Guard, which was then trained by US troops after their return to the country the next year (see section 1.5.4). By the time of their withdrawal in 1933 the new National Guard had come under the control of Gen. Somoza, and the Somoza family then held power for over four decades through the Guard and the PLN. The United States continued to assist with the training of the Guard, receiving final-year cadets from the Nicaraguan military academy at Fort Gullick in the Panama Canal Zone from 1944, setting up a scheme in Nicaragua under its Military Assistance Programme (MAP) in 1954 and from 1963 granting the Guard an annual sum of $1,600,000.[4]

The domination of the Guard by the Somoza family was enhanced by the creation in June 1978 of the Basic Infantry Training School (EEBI), under the command of Col. Anastasio Somoza Portocarrero (son of Gen. Anastasio Somoza Debayle). The EEBI was an elite force, whose members had special privileges, and it was feared even by the rest of the Guard; the success of Pastora's attack on the National Palace in August 1978 (see section 1.5.12) was due at least partly to the fact that the commando was disguised as an EEBI unit.

The link between the EPS (the People's Army formed by the Sandinistas —see section 1.5.20) and the FSLN government was acknowledged from its inception as a force specifically to defend the revolution. Luis Carrión declared: "The character of our popular army will come not from its operational structures but from its politicization and its objectives." The EPS was formed out of FSLN combatants (of which there were some 15,000 in July 1979, although only a third of these were regular fighters), including women (for whom new units were created), and those the government described as "soldiers and officers who have behaved with integrity and patriotism in the face of the dictatorship's corruption and repression, and those who have taken part in the struggle to overthrow the Somoza regime". The militia (MPS), was officially inaugurated in February 1980 with 1,200 members, but by July it had nearly 100,000 armed and trained men and women; a year later (with the launch of contra activities from Honduras) the total number had risen to 200,000.

Notes

1. See Bird, *op. cit.*, chapter 12, for debate on whether the Civil Guard is merely a police force or "an army in disguise".
2. Quoted in Black, *Garrison Guatemala*, p. 35.
3. For further details on the armed forces, see Bonner, *op. cit.*, chapter 4.
4. For further details of the development of the National Guard, see Black, *Triumph of the People*, chapter 4; for US military training, see pp. 47–48.

SECTION THREE

INTERNAL AND CROSS-BORDER CONFLICT

3:1 POLITICAL AND GUERRILLA MOVEMENTS

3.1.1: Introductory

The presence of disaffected groups within the Central American states struggling to overthrow the government (with or without foreign support) is not a new phenomenon in the region, but has been characteristic of them since independence. The Cuban revolution of 1959 and the more recent victories of the FSLN in Nicaragua and the NJM in Grenada in 1979 encouraged guerrilla groups and made it seem possible for a few thousand armed men and women to be successful. In addition to such military groups, a number of popular organizations have formed, sometimes as political wings of guerrilla groups, sometimes as trade union, human rights or community-based organizations, capable of mobilizing international support on economic, social or political issues. There are several of these groups in Guatemala and El Salvador, with a few much smaller ones in Honduras, while those that developed in Nicaragua in the 1970s have now become an integral part of the Sandinista administration, which is itself now opposed by foreign-backed guerrilla movements.

3.1.2: Guatemala

PGT—Guatemalan Labour Party. Communist party, renamed in 1962 from PCG after being outlawed in 1954 (see section 1.2.6), Cuban-line policy; involved in military action since 1961, although two dissident groups have criticized the main body of the party for not pursuing the path of armed struggle rigorously enough; guerrilla activities based on Guatemala City, Escuintla, Retalhuleu and Suchitepéquez.

MR–13—November 13 Revolutionary Movement. Formed in February 1962 by the officers involved in the abortive coup against Ydigoras of November 1960 (from which the group took its name), and led by Capt. Marco Antonio Yon Sosa and Capt. Luis Turcios Lima; started to launch a guerrilla front, but many members died in the first months.

FAR—Rebel Armed Forces. Formed in December 1962 by MR–13, PGT guerrillas and a student-based organization formed during the riots of April 1962 (see section 1.2.7); throughout the 1960s it remained a coalition of forces, with MR–13 continuing to be led by Yon Sosa, although weakened by his death in Mexico in 1970, while Turcios Lima led the Edgar Ibarra Guerrilla Front (FGEI); the FGEI became the strongest fighting force and under a new agreement between the component groups the FGEI provided the combatants and the FAR supplied organizational structures. Even at its peak in the first decade of existence the numerical strength of the FAR did not exceed about 500, and after the army's intensive counter-insurgency campaign of 1966–68 the organization took a decade to recover; since then its activities have extended from northern parts of the country and around Lake Izabál to the departments of El Petén and Chimaltenango.

ORPA—Revolutionary Organization of the People at Arms. Formed in 1971 by FAR dissidents who criticized the main organization for paying scarcely any attention to gaining Indian support; withdrew to the Sierra Madre in the north-western region of Ixcan, where 92 per cent of the population were Ixil Indians, and which they described as "the geographical, political and social region of Guatemala where the state apparatus and imperialist penetration were at their weakest"; launched efforts as military group in September 1979 based in the western and central departments of San Marcos, Totonicapán, Quezaltenango, Sololá and Escuintla, and around the capital; linked to the FDCR.

EGP—Guerrilla Army of the Poor. Formed in 1972 by FGEI survivors and Christian grassroots workers in the *communidades cristianas de bases* (see section 2.4.1); initially concentrated on building up support among sub-sistence farmers in the north west before launching its military actions in 1975 with the assassination of an Ixcan landowner (Luis Arenas Barrera), which provoked a massive army reprisal campaign; it gradually came to be the largest of the main guerrilla groups, operating mostly in the highland departments of Huehuetenango, El Quiché and Alta Verapaz, and in Escuintla and the capital. On Sept. 5, 1980, the press secretary at the ministry of the interior, Elias Barahona, announced at a press conference in Panama that he was a member of the EGP who had infiltrated the government the previous year and then returned to fight alongside other members.

FP–31—January 31 Popular Front. Formed in 1980, taking its name from the Spanish embassy siege (see section 3.3.2), an alliance of the Guatemalan Workers' Federation (FTG), Peasant Unity Committee (CUC), with some 6,000 members, the Revolutionary Workers' Nuclei (NOR) with 1,500 members, the Slum-dwellers' Committee (CDP) with 150 members, the Revolutionary Student Front (FERG) with 200 members, and the Vicente Menchú Revolutionary Christians with 4,000 members. (Vicente Menchú was one of the Indian peasants who died in the Spanish embassy siege.) FP–31 aimed to provide "a unitary structure to deepen the support, co-ordination and solidarity between the mass organizations and as a consequence raise [their] fighting potential"; linked to the EGP.

URNG—Guatemalan National Revolutionary Unity (also known as the Unitary Representation of the Guatemalan Opposition—RUOG). Formed Feb. 8, 1982, by PGT, FAR, ORPA and EGP, committed to ending government repression, cultural and racial discrimination and economic and political domination by the "repressive national and foreign powers which govern Guatemala", and to the establishment of a representative government pursuing a non-aligned foreign policy; by mid–1982 its fighting strength was estimated by Western sources at about 6,000; linked to the PSD.

MRP–Ixim—People's Revolutionary Movement. Formed in 1982 by ORPA dissidents opposed to the formation of the URNG; advocating Marxist–Leninist programme. ("Ixim" is an Indian word meaning "food".)

CGUP—Guatemalan Committee of Patriotic Unity. Formed Feb. 16, 1982, as a political counterpart of the URNG by the FDCR, FP–31, several members of the FUR, 26 prominent Guatemalan exiles (led by Luis Cardoza y

Aragón—a member of the Arbenz government), the FTG, the People's Co-
ordinating Commitee (CCP) and the Rutilio Grande Front (named after a
Salvadorean priest murdered in 1977—see section 2.4.5). The CGUP
supported the URNG basic programme and advocated popular revolutionary
war as the only path left open, rejecting elections as "electoral fraud,
corruption, persecution and assassination of democratic leaders and of
hundreds of party members have been the permanent practices of the regime". Its declared aim was to construct "a new society which responds to [the
Guatemalan people's] interests and aspirations, confronting the bloodiest
dictatorship that Latin America has known".[1]

3.1.3: Honduras

A number of very small armed groups emerged in 1978–79, as offshoots of
either the main Communist Party (PCH), formed in 1927 and outlawed in
1957, or the Marxist–Leninist splinter group (PCH–ML), formed in 1971, or
from radical student groups.[2]

FMLH—Morazanist Front for the Liberation of Honduras. Formed in
September 1979 and also known as the Francisco Morazán Front, pledged to
continue the "revolutionary struggle" after the 1980 elections, and committed
to the redistribution of land to the peasants.

MPLC—Cinchonero Popular Liberation Movement. Emerged in 1981 as the
Cinchonero Commando; derived from the PCH and became the armed wing
of the Revolutionary People's Union (URP); believed to have links with the
FMLN in El Salvador.

FRP—Lorenzo Zelaya Popular Revolutionary Forces. Originated in the
PCH–ML; emerged in 1981 as the Lorenzo Zelaya Popular Revolutionary
Commando, with the aim of pursuing the "armed struggle against Yankee
imperialism".

DNU—United National Directorate. The formation of the DNU was reported
in Managua on April 3, 1983, by the FMLH, the MPLC, the PCH, the
Froylan Turcios group (named after an early 20th–century left-wing writer),
the Central American Revolutionary Workers' Party of Honduras (PRTCH)
and the Revolutionary Unity Movement (MUR); its stated aim was to form
"a single popular army under one command . . . first to struggle for our own
liberation" by means of popular war, and "second to play an active part in the
event of the regionalization of the Central American crisis".

Popular Armed Forces (FAP). Emerged early in 1984, when it issued a threat
to "exterminate" all US military advisers and Salvadorean soldiers trained by
US forces in Honduras (i.e. at the Puerto Castilla base).

3.1.4: El Salvador

Guerrilla and mass organizations gained their most widespread support in El
Salvador, receiving the approval and active encouragement from several
sectors, notably the Church. In March 1980 Archbishop Romero stated:
"Given the present situation in the country, I believe more than ever in the

popular organizations. I believe in the necessity for the Salvadorean people to organize themselves because I believe they are the social forces which are going to advance, which are going to persevere, which are going to achieve a society with genuine social justice and freedom."

Feccas—Salvadorean Christian Peasant Federation. Formed in 1964 by the Christian Democrats to campaign for "fair salaries, the right to organize and the radical transformation of our society in order to construct a new society where there is no misery, hunger, repression nor exploitation of one group by another"; after leaving FAPU (see below) in 1975 Feccas joined with the Union of Rural Workers (UTC), and both organizations were declared illegal by the government because of their supposed "communist" links; the government accused Feccas/UTC of killing members of Orden and local peasants, but other sources reported that Feccas/UTC were victims of Orden; affiliated to the BRP (see below).

UCS—Salvadorean Communal Union. Formed in 1968 by the government and with the support of the American Institute for Free Labour Development (AIFLD) to counter the influence of "communist unions".

FPL–FM—Popular Liberation Forces–Farabundo Martí. Formed 1970 by the radical wing of the PCS led by Salvador Cayetano Carpio (opposed to PCS support for the war against Honduras—see section 1.3.7); favoured the prolonged popular war approach "until it achieves an ultimate popular revolution towards socialism", and sought to establish worker-peasant alliances to counter Orden, although there was more of a bias to military activity in the mid–1970s. Carpio commented in 1980: "If we had to begin with guerrilla warfare, it was a passing stage, part of an overall plan that conceived the people as mastering all means and forms of struggle. That conception took us far away from the idea that the guerrilla force on its own can make a revolution, that the guerrilla force isolated from the people replaces the people in their prime task of carrying out their own transformation." The FPL did not respond favourably to the new government of October 1979, calling it merely a regime of "new imperialists".

Divisions within the FPL came to a head in 1983 with the murder on April 6 of Ana Melida Montes ("Ana María", the second-in-command and a member of the FMLN high command) at her home in Managua; she was stabbed violently by another FPL member, Rogelio Bazzaglio Recino (of a hardline faction, opposed to integration into the FMLN) "for the good of the revolution". An FPL communiqué described his motive as being one of "resentment and alleged ideological and political differences with compañera Ana María". (Bazzaglio and the five others arrested in Nicaragua were kept in detention there, to be handed over for trial in El Salvador after the establishment of a popular government in the event of an FMLN–FDR victory.) Six days later Carpio ("Marcial") committed suicide at his home in Nicaragua because of what the FPL initially termed an "emotional crisis" over the death of Ana María; eight months later the FPL said that Carpio had ordered her murder as he had been "blinded by his political ambitions and fanatical sense of self-importance".[3]

The FPL issued a statement on Dec. 9, 1983, condemning a new splinter group called the Salvador Cayetano Carpio Labour Movement (formed in

November) on the grounds that it "maintained the sectarian anti-unitarian position of the past upheld by Marcial, denying the FMLN's role as vanguard of the revolution and proclaiming itself the sole representative of the working class, . . . [denied] the role that all democratic and progressive forces can play alongside the working classes, and was imbued with a deep anti-party concept".

ERP—People's Revolutionary Army. Founded in 1971 by dissident members of the PDC and left-wing politicans, becoming the most militant of the guerrilla groups and concentrating on attacking government and military installations; conflict broke out between opposing factions leading to the murder in 1975 of the group's most famous member, the celebrated national poet and historian Roque Dalton, by other members; in an effort to create a new, less militaristic image, the ERP formed a separate political party in 1976 called the Party of the Salvadorean Revolution (PRS); led by Joaquín Villalobos and linked to LP–28.

FAPU—United People's Action Front. Formed in 1974 by a number of organizations including Feccas, but disintegrated within a few months (see section 1.4.8); resumed protest activity in the late 1970s.

FARN—Armed Forces of National Resistance. Formed in 1975 after the division within the ERP caused by Dalton's murder, when those closer to the popular organizations left to form National Resistance (RN) and its armed wing FARN; financed by kidnappings which raised $40,000,000 by 1979; led by Fermán Cienfuegos.

BPR—Popular Revolutionary Bloc. Formed 1975 as a political wing for the FPL, from several groups including Feccas/UTC, the National Teachers' Federation (Andes), the Trade Union Co-ordinating Committee (CUS, combining many union federations), the Slum Dwellers' Union (UPT), the Revolutionary Forces (FUR–30, based at the University of Central America) and the Revolutionary Union of Students (UR–19); (Andes had some 30,000 members, or about a quarter of the nation's teaching staff, and between 1979 and early 1985, 326 of these members were assassinated;) the BPR announced on Oct. 29, 1979, that it would not accept the new "counter-revolutionary" government.

LP–28—Popular Leagues–February 28. Formed 1977 (see section 1.4.9); announced on Oct. 19, 1979, that it would suspend its violent activity but would continue to "organize the masses".

CRM—Revolutionary Co-ordinating Council of the Masses. Formed January 1980 by the BPR, LP–28, FAPU, UDN and MLP (formed in 1979—see section 1.4.11); a march staged on Jan. 22 to celebrate the new group was fired on by security force snipers, killing 22 people and wounding 135.

FDR—Democratic Revolutionary Front. Formed April 1980 (see section 1.4.13), and in May leading members travelled to Europe and the United States to gain support for their cause; the organization announced on Jan. 14, 1981, the formation of a seven-member diplomatic–political commission with a view to establishing a "democratic revolutionary government", comprising Ungo, Fabio Castillo (of the MLP), Ana Guadalupe Martínez of the ERP,

José Napoleón Rodríguez Ruiz of FAPU, Salvador Samayoa of the FPL, Mario Aguinada Carranza of the UDN and Rubén Zamora of the MPSC. In late November 1983 Zamora announced that the FDR would close its office in Managua and move to Mexico (where it had been allowed to operate since 1980) because of the "constantly growing danger" of a US invasion of Nicaragua (in the wake of the Grenada crisis; it was also reported that the Nicaraguan authorities had suggested the move).

FMLN—Farabundo Martí National Liberation Front. Formed October 1980 by the FPL, ERP, RN/FARN, PRS, PCS (led by Jorge Schafik Handal) and the Central American Revolutionary Party (PRTC, formed 1979 and linked to the MLP, led by Roberto Roca); all these except the PRTC had earlier united in the Unified Revolutionary Directorate (DRU) formed in May, with Carpio as overall leader; in November 1980 a joint politico-military direc-torate was formed with the FDR (i.e. the FMLN–FDR); FMLN fighting potential was placed at about 5,000 combatants with a further 5,000 organized in local militias, and in early 1981 Cienfuegos claimed that the FMLN–FDR had some 30,000 reservists engaged in political work; (in 1984 the FMLN confirmed reports that it had on occasion resorted to forcible recruitment to its ranks, but this practice was seemingly abandoned in 1985;) the deaths of the two FPL leaders in April 1983 resulted in a weakening of FPL influence within the FMLN in favour of the ERP.

By early 1985 there was evidence of a change in FMLN strategy, necess-itated by its losses during the army's offensives in 1984 and the increased air power of the armed forces (see section 2.5.4), away from large-scale military operations to moving in small groups, rebuilding political bases and stepping up urban sabotage; it was reported that within the FMLN the ERP favoured this concentration on urban welfare whereas the FPL wanted to ease up in the cities and keep its rural activities going.

In September 1985 the FMLN issued a document entitled "Strategic Appreciation of the Situation", which marked not only a change in strategy, but also in political philosophy, as it included the plan to form within the FMLN a single Marxist–Leninist political party—constituting the group's first description of itself as Marxist. This move further alienated members of the FDR, who had become increasingly uneasy over the rising number of civilian casualties at the FMLN's hands in 1985, resulting in the change of strategy. It was reported in January 1986 that some Social Democrats, chiefly the MPSC and some MRN members, were returning to El Salvador in order to assess the possibility of "political solutions", and were considering redefining their links to the guerrilla movement.

Clara Elizabeth Ramírez Brigade. Formed November 1983; an FPL faction which concentrated on urban guerrilla activities.

MUSYGES—Unitarian Movement of Salvadorean Trade Unions and Associations. Formed May 1, 1983 by the CUS along with five independent unions and two government-controlled unions. (The trade unions, which by the end of 1984 were estimated to represent about 55 per cent of the work-force, suffered particularly from right-wing violence and the CUS reported that in 1979–81, 5,123 of its members were assassinated, 1,875 had dis-appeared, 539 were imprisoned, and 793 wounded by troops firing on union demonstrations.) The MUSYGES declaration of May 1, 1983, listed the following demands: (i) an immediate general wage increase in line with inflation; (ii) government reduction and control of rents and prices of basic commodities; (iii) rejection of further taxation; (iv) a 50 per cent cut in public transport fares; (v) an end to the current wage freeze, to the legal ban on strikes by public sector employees and to restrictions on the freedoms of assembly, mobility and expression; (vi) an end to the militarization of public services and to the practice of incorporating public sector workers into the armed forces; (vii) an end to the state of siege; (viii) the return of the running, buildings and assets of the National University to its own authorities; and (ix) the introduction of a properly-administered national health service.

Salvadorean Suicide Commandos (CSS). Formed Oct. 18, 1984; threatened action against extreme right wing politicans, and specifically to kill those directly responsible for the death squads. (It was, however, suggested by some sources that this group might have been formed by right wing elements to confuse the issue and discredit the left wing.)

Roberto Sibrián Revolutionary People's Movement. Formed Oct. 29, 1984; a Marxist–Leninist military-political group which said it would participate in "the revolutionary struggle in El Salvador, advocating a strategy with a Central American perspective". (Although the group did not affiliate itself with any other organization, it was believed to be an FPL faction.)

3.1.5: Nicaragua

FSLN—Sandinista National Liberation Front. Formed in 1962 by Carlos Fonseca Amador, Tomas Borge and Silvio Mayorga; Fonseca and leading strategist Eduardo Contreras Escobar were killed in November 1976 in a gun-battle with the National Guard, and other serious losses caused the number of members to fall to 1,500 in 1978, rising to 5,000 by early 1979; contained three trends: two Marxist–Leninist groups, the Prolonged Popular War (GPP) and the Proletarian Tendancy (TP), and the *Terceristas*, the largest and most militant group favouring popular insurrection, led by Pastora and enjoying the support of business, professional and church sectors and of certain European social democratic parties within the Socialist International; the three trends had united by the end of 1978; gained military victory in 1979 and subsequently became a political party.[4]

ELN—National Liberation Army. Formed in 1979 in Honduras by former members of the Somozist National Guard, with an estimated strength of about 5,000, operates independently of other contra groups.

UDN/FARN—National Democratic Union/Nicaraguan Revolutionary Armed Forces. Formed 1979 in Honduras as a politico-military organization led by Fernando Chamorro Rapaccioli, claiming a membership of 2,000; a spokesman announced in March 1981 that a "freedom force" of 600 members was waiting near the Nicaraguan border for "thousands" of supporters in Guatemala and Miami to stage an invasion designed to ignite a popular insurrection with the help of the Honduran, Guatemalan and Salvadorean governments; in August Chamorro was sentenced to death in absentia by a court in Managua and his property confiscated for his subversive actions;

joined the FDN in November 1981 and then left to join Arde in September 1982, although Chamorro rejoined the FDN in 1983 (see below).

Misurasata. Indian organization set up to represent the Atlantic Coast Indians in their dealings with the central government (see section 4.3.3); initially led by Steadman Fagoth Müller. In mid–1982 it split into two factions: *Guerrilla Miskito*, led by Fagoth Müller, which stayed within the FDN (see below), and which was later renamed *Misura*; and Misurasata, led by Brooklyn Rivera, which joined Arde (see below). In 1984 Misurasata split again when in October Rivera entered into negotiations with the Sandinista government (see section 6.3.3), thereby breaking with Arde, while a minority broke with him to form a pro-Arde faction. It was reported in August 1985 that both Fagoth Müller and Rivera had been expelled from leadership of the Miskito groups, and at the end of that month a new Indian organization was formed, called *KISAN* (see section 4.3.3).

FDN—Nicaraguan Democratic Force. Formed in November 1981 to "liberate our people from Marxist totalitarianism" by the UDN/FARN, Misurasata and the "September 15 Legion" (formed in 1979 by members of Somoza's National Guard); although it claimed to be "somewhere in our fatherland" it was clearly based in Honduras, with representation in Tegucigalpa and Miami, and all seven members of the military command were former National Guards. The FDN issued a statement on April 13, 1982, giving its conditions for the cessation of its military actions: (i) the immediate expulsion of all "internationalists" (i.e. Cubans working in the country—see section 5.3.4); (ii) the introduction of a general amnesty; (iii) the holding of free elections to a national assembly within six months; (iv) "identification of all political parties separate from the armed forces"; (v) repatriation of all exiles with full guarantees; and (vi) a public condemnation by the government of Central American and international terrorist groups.

The defection of UDN/FARN and the split in Misurasata in mid–1982 strengthened the more right-wing factions of the FDN, although when Chamorro Rapaccioli rejoined it in March 1983 he soon became the recognized main political leader. The formation of an eight-member political leadership had previously been announced in October 1982, including Edgar Chamorro Coronel, Alfonso Callejas and Col. Enrique Bermúdez, and it was because of Bermúdez' past service in the National Guard that Arde originally refused to consider forming an alliance with the FDN, despite US encouragement. In February 1983 the PCD leader Adolfo Calero Portocarrero joined the FDN, having decided that "the armed road is the only way left open". In March the police took possession of the Milca Coca-Cola bottling plan where he was director, and a subsequent article in *Barricada* claimed that part of his firm's funds had been used to finance the counter-revolution. Calero was nominated president-in-exile in October, and was named C.-in-C. in December within a new civilian-military command, in which Bermúdez was military commander, Chamorro Coronel head of communications and Indalecio Rodríguez head of civil services. It was reported in February 1984 that Chamorro Coronel had declared that the FDN leadership would be purged of former National Guards in order to co-operate with "other combat groups" (i.e. the formation of UNIR a few months later—see below). The linking of all anti-FSLN groups was strongly promoted by the United States and the FDN was known to have substantial US connections, despite Bermúdez' assertion in 1982: "We would never accept the role of American mercenary. . . . It is not acceptable to us to carry out missions to interdict Cuban and Russian supply lines to El Salvador [the declared US reason for aiding the contras]. We are Nicaraguans and our objective is to overthrow the communists and install a democratic government in our country."

By May 1984 the FDN claimed to have over 10,000 fighting members already in Nicaragua, while other sources put their total strength at about 9,000; an article in the *International Herald Tribune* (April 4, 1984) reported that the CIA had told the US Congress that it was willing to raise the number of Nicaraguan guerrillas it supported from 15,000 to 18,000, and although this number included Arde members it was still in excess of all other estimates of guerrilla strength.

Arde—Democratic Revolutionary Alliance. Formed in September 1982 in Costa Rica by the Sandinista Revolutionary Front (FRS, recently founded by Pastora), the MDN (led by Alfonso Robelo), Misurasata and UDN/FARN, and was joined in September 1983 by the Christian Democratic Solidarity Front (FSDC), led by José Dávila Membereno. (After leaving Nicaragua Pastora had joined the Guatemalan group ORPA, but had broken with its leaders in March 1982 after refusing to participate in guerrilla fighting in Guatemala, and he then unsuccessfully sought for support for a new anti-FSLN group from Cuba and the Socialist International.) Pastora did not want to overthrow Sandinism but to "rechannel the revolution" and to prevent the Somozists regaining power. Even with the defection of UDN/FARN and Misurasata, Arde was always weaker than the FDN, and two years after its formation it still numbered around 3,000.

One source of this weakness was the disagreement between Pastora and Robelo over the questions of CIA funding and of alliance with the FDN, both of which were favoured by Robelo. Two months after Arde launched its first offensive in April 1983, Pastora announced a "strategic retreat" because of the lack of support from "democratic governments and parties"; Robelo had just travelled to Washington to seek $300,000 a month from the US administration, but had been refused on the grounds that such a grant would not be justifiable under the arms interdiction campaign. (The government in Managua described the announcement of the retreat as a "trick to win more money from the Reagan administration".) Pastora later stated that he had decided to withdraw the decision to retreat as he had begun "to receive the response to my demand for more arms and economic support", and although he denied it, the CIA was reported to have started giving economic assistance to Arde from June 1983. (While in Washington Robelo had also met with Calero and Thomas Enders, apparently to discuss plans for greater co-operation between Arde and the FDN, and although no formal arrangement was announced Arde reorganized its "southern front" in May to co-ordinate its actions better with those of the FDN in the north.) On Oct. 25, 1983, Pastora resigned, accusing Robelo of trying to kill him and of sending Arde recruits to Argentina for military training alongside FDN members, and declaring that he would continue to lead the FRS as a separate military-wing. Robelo denied these accusations and after a meeting with Dávila in Panama at the beginning of November the rift was healed.

M–3V—Third Way Movement. Formed October 1983 in San José (Costa Rica) by Abelardo Taboada, Luis Riva, Cdr Eduardo Sánchez and Cdr Sebastián González; according to González the new group aimed "to provide an option which would fill the void between the northern forces and Arde". Its fighting strength in late 1984 was estimated at 300.

UNIR—Nicaraguan Unity for Reconciliation. Formed Sept. 5, 1984, by the FDN, Misura and the component members of Arde except the FRS; in May the Arde directorate had voted by 24 to three in favour of unity with the FDN and so Pastora resigned, and on May 30 there was an assassination attempt against him when a bomb exploded at a press conference at La Penca (an Arde post one kilometre into Nicaraguan territory), and Pastora described the incident as a CIA-inspired "punishment for not yielding to it, for not joining forces loyal to Somoza". Preliminary agreement had been reached on July 24 when the FDN and Arde had announced that they would "fight together until the liberation of the country, oppressed by the totalitarian Marxist–Leninist regime and occupied by foreign forces [i.e. Cuban]", with the eventual aim of establishing "a temporary government of national conciliation with a priority mission to begin the democratic process". Pastora and Robelo agreed on Sept. 6 that Arde and the FRS would co-ordinate their military activities but would otherwise "act separately".

UNO—Nicaraguan Opposition Union. Formed June 12, 1985, to supersede UNIR, as "an umbrella group for all democratic forces seeking a new government in Nicaragua" and incorporating Cruz of the political opposition. Like UNIR, however, it failed to unite all contras as Robelo joined, but Pastora and Dávila refused to do so. In September the new Miskito organization *KISAN* (see section 4.3.3) became a member.

BOS—Southern Opposition Bloc. Formed Aug. 2, 1985, by Arde (without Robelo) and two other Costa Rican-based anti-Sandinista organisations, *Rescate* (Rescue) and *Conciliación Nacional*. BOS issued a statement giving the four conditions it required for unity with UNO: (i) agreement on a common political project; (ii) guarantee of equal rights for each party within a new alliance; (iii) "a change of attitude" on the part of those said to be discriminating against BOS members in giving aid (i.e. the United States); and (iv) effective unification of all contra activities.

   BOS and UNO signed a "unity document" on March 15, 1986, in attempt to co-ordinate their activities, but the move lacked force as of the main leaders of the two organizations, Cruz, Robelo and Calero, refused to sign the document, and Pastora disagreed with UNO leaders over whether it would allow UNO to play a part in the direction of Arde forces. When on May 9 six top Arde commanders announced their decision to form an alliance with the UDN/FARN—which was also joined by Dávila—Pastora gave himself up to Costa Rican authorities and found political asylum (see also section 3.4.3).

3.1.6: Costa Rica

A number of very small units have been formed, including:

Central American Revolutionary Commando. Appeared by the 1970s; in February 1981 members kidnapped a wealthy businessman, Patrocinio Arrieta, and demanded a $120,000 ransom, but police freed Arrieta two weeks later.

Carlos Argüero Echevarría Commando. Named after a Costa Rican who fought in Nicaragua alongside the FSLN; emerged in 1981 when it launched a bazooka attack on a car in San José and planted a bomb at the Honduran embassy; in response the government deported 36 Central American and Argentinian exiles and announced plans to restrict the entry of foreign exiles, claiming that foreign terrorists had directed the explosion.

In June 1981 three civil guards, one "suspected guerrilla" and a civilian died in a gunbattle in the capital, and another guerrilla suspect was shot dead in prison in July by a civil guard in an apparent act of retaliation.

Notes

1. For further details on Guatemalan guerrilla and opposition groups, see Black, *Garrison Guatemala*, Part II, especially pp. 113–16.
2. For labour-based popular organizations in Honduras, see Morris, *op. cit.*, pp. 78–81.
3. Bonner, *op. cit.*, pp. 97–98.
4. For growth of Sandino's army, see Black, *Triumph of the People*, Chapter 2; for development of FSLN, see Chapters 6–9.

3.2: PARAMILITARY GROUPS AND DEATH SQUADS

3.2.1: Introductory

A feature of the Central American conflict since the 1960s has been the emergence of unofficial paramilitary groups and "death squads" (particularly in Guatemala and El Salvador), believed—and somtimes proved—to consist of or be led by serving army personnel and police and to be responsible for the assassinations of left-wing politicians or sympathizers, community and union leaders and human rights workers.

3.2.2: Guatemala

The first right-wing death squads emerged in Guatemala in the 1960s, the most active being the White Hand, the Secret Anti-Communist Army (ESA) and the Squadron of Death (EM). The founder of the White Hand was reputed to be Col. Enrique Trinidad Oliva, who had fought alongside Castillo Armas in 1954, and whose assassination in May 1967 unleashed a futher wave of political violence.[1] (Another reputed White Hand leader, Brig.–Gen. Manuel Francisco Sosa Avila, who later became National Chief of Police, was killed in an ambush by an unidentified group in March 1985.) The ESA published a list of 38 names in October 1978, whom it had "tried and sentenced to death"; several of these were university staff and students, and within two days one of those named, Oliverio Castañeda (president of the University Students' Association), had been murdered.

In January 1980 the Jesuits in Guatemala issued a declaration in the Guatemalan press that there had been 3,252 murders by death squads in the first 10 months of 1979, carried out "with absolute impunity", with most of them directed against politicians, trade union leaders and staff and students at the University of San Carlos (USAC). Many members of the Roman Catholic Church also became targets for death squad activity (see section 2.4.2) and in February 1980 it was announced in Rome that all 52 of the Jesuit priests in Guatemala had received death threats. USAC continued to lose many members and reported at the end of 1982 that in recent months 16 staff and students had been kidnapped, including the university rector, and that on Sept. 29 the rector of one of the university campuses, Raúl Romero Rodríguez, had been shot dead by a group of armed men in front of his class (see also section 4.2.2).

Elias Barahona (an EGP member who infiltrated the government—see section 3.1.2) claimed in September 1980 that the ESA and the EM were directed by Lucas García (minister of the interior), Donaldo Alvarez Ruiz, and a number of senior military officers. An Amnesty International report of February 1981 asserted that there was a systematic programme of murder and torture commanded from within the presidential palace under the direct supervision of Lucas García, adding that there was no convincing evidence for the government's claim that the ESA and the EM existed as separate organizations.

The creation of the Civilian Armed Patrols (PAC) peasant militia began in November 1981 and the government claimed to have armed 25,000 civilians in patrols within six months. The numbers continued to increase to reach about 350,000 by early 1983 and reportedly 900,000 by early 1985, chiefly because refusal to join was believed to be punishable by death.[2] The establishment of the PACs aroused considerable controversy as they were said in some areas to operate more like private armies because of their association with certain local interests. At the end of January 1983 a peasant delegation from El Quiché protested to Mejía Victores (as the current minister of defence) over threats made against them by their local patrol operating an extortion racket for local business interests. The patrols were also unpopular even among the urban business groups as their funding was met in part by a special tax levied on chambers of industry, agriculture and commerce, and banking corporations, which was expected to raise $60,000 in a period of 13 months.

Following an escalation of death squad killings in the weeks after the return to civilian rule in January 1986, President Cerezo on Feb. 5 ordered a raid on the Technical Investigations Department (DIT), which had operated as a plain clothes police force and had been accused of many political assassinations and kidnappings. As a result of the raid 600 DIT agents were arrested and the DIT was abolished, to be replaced, according to the new interior minister, Juan José Rodil Peralta, by a "real criminal investigations police, which would dispel the fear and terror which people currently have of this corps and its members", and which was called the Criminal Investigations Unit (UIC).

3.2.3: El Salvador

The main right-wing groups active in El Salvador have been (i) Orden, which continued to operate its extensive national network despite being officially banned in 1979 and was blamed for the murder of five PDC mayors and eight other PDC workers between October 1979 and mid–1982; (ii) the White Warriors' Union (UGB), responsible for Mario Zamora's death in 1980 (see section 1.4.11); (iii) the Secret Anti-Communist Army (ESA), believed to be directed by Col. Reynaldo López Nuila, the deputy minister of defence; and (iv) the Maximiliano Hernández Martínez Anti-Communist Alliance (or Brigade), generally thought to be directed by d'Aubuisson and to have assassinated Archbishop Romero in March 1980 (see section 1.4.12). D'Aubuisson, Gen. Vides Casanova (who was also accused of complicity in Romero's death) and Capt. Eduardo Avila (see also section 4.2.4) had all trained within Orden apparently compiling lists of suspects which became the bases for death squad activity, under the orders of the organization's founder, Gen. Medrano (who was assassinated in March 1985 by unidentified assailants). D'Aubuisson was also reported to have had links with elements in the United States in the development of death squads and to have had contacts with the Republican Senator Jesse Helms concerning the formation of the political party Arena.[3]

The activities of Orden and its reputation for political violence made many people wary when it was announced in 1984 that a new civil defence force was to be created to defend villages (in particular the protected villages—see section 3.3.5) against guerrilla attacks. Col. Adolfo Blandón said that much of the $128,000,000 US military aid for 1985 would be used to train and equip these units, and by January 1985 it was reported that 49 of the country's 261 municipalities (mostly in San Vicente) had formed such groups, although some villages preferred to attempt to remain neutral.

The close links between the death squads and the armed forces were confirmed by incidents such as the abduction of five FDR leaders in November 1980 by the Maximiliano Hernández Martínez Brigade in full view of army units. The five—Enrique Alvarez, Manuel Franco (UDN), Enrique Barrera (MNR), Humberto Mendoza (MLP) and Juan Chacón (BPT)—were subsequently tortured and strangled.

In April 1981 Capt. Ricardo Alejandro Fiallos of the Salvadorean army told a US congressional committee: "It is a grievous error to believe that the forces of the extreme right, or the so-called 'death squads', operate independently of the security forces. The simple truth of the matter is that the death squads are made up of members of the security forces and acts of terrorism credited to these squads such as political assassinations, kidnappings and indiscriminate murder are, in fact, planned by high-ranking military officers and carried out by members of the security forces. I do not make this statement lightly, but with full knowledge of the role which the military high command and the directors of the security forces have played in the murders of countless numbers of innocent people in my country."[4]

The inability or unwillingness of the Salvadorean government to control the activities of the paramilitary units caused considerable frustration to US representatives. In mid–1983 ambassador Deane Hinton delivered a verbal attack on "the right-wing mafia" and his replacement, Thomas Pickering, said in December: "No-one can afford to continue in the self-deluding belief that nothing is known about the shadowy world of these individuals, and [that] therefore nothing can be done."

Within days of the second round of the 1984 presidential election Duarte announced that the army had formed a special commission to curb human rights violations by its members and specifically by the death squads, and that the army would be responsible for bringing offenders to account. The highest-ranking officer to be dismissed in the resulting purge was Col. Nicolás Carranza, the head of the treasury police (which had a particular reputation for politically-motivated brutality) and a close associate of d'Aubuisson. His replacement, Col. Golcher (formerly head of the pacification programme in San Vicente—see section 3.3.5) announced on June 12, 1984, that the treasury police's S–2 intelligence unit had been disbanded and its 100 members sent into combat, and said that in future the treasury police would be confined to pursuing financial offences such as smuggling and would not enter into politics. These measures by no means eradicated death squad activity, which increased again from late 1984.

The death squads were particularly active against "radical" priests and trade unionists. The UGB was apparently responsible for the murder of Fr Alidio Napoleón Macias at San Esteban Catarina on Aug. 4, 1979 (the sixth priest killed since Fr Rutilio Grande in March 1977—see section 2.4.5), and also for that of the secretary-general of the union Feccas in late September 1979. After the murder of Archbishop Romero in March 1980 and the increasing outspokenness of the church hierarchy on human rights abuses, the campaign against clergy was stepped up. On Oct. 31, 1983, the Maximiliano

Hernández Martínez Brigade described the weekly sermons of Archbishop Rivera y Damas and auxiliary bishop Gregorio Rosa Chávez (listing the disappeared or murdered of the previous week) as "disturbing", as they provided "false arguments" used abroad in "misinformation campaigns", and warned that unless the sermons were halted the two men would be "the objects of drastic penalties".

Some assassinations on the part of the right wing were carried out as reprisals against FMLN activities, although not always directly against FMLN members. After the "execution" by the FMLN of Arena deputy Rene Barrios Anaya on June 28, 1983 (allegedly for being a CIA agent), the ESA strangled two civilians in the capital the following week, leaving their bodies in a hotel car park with labels bearing the message: "For every good Salvadorean killed 10 terrorists will be executed", and warning that the ESA would kill "all communist bandits implicated directly or indirectly" with left-wing guerrillas who refused to "contribute to the peace so desired by the Salvadorean people". Five days after an FMLN attack on Tenancingo on Sept. 25, 1983, the ESA killed a man they claimed was a member of the ERP "as a warning and demonstration of the military steps that the ESA will take with traitors to the fatherland, whether these are communists or those who lend themselves to their manoeuvres". In response to the death of Col. Monterrosa in October 1984 (see section 3.3.5) the ESA murdered three boys, leaving their bodies with the letters ESA carved into their foreheads; one of the boys was the son of Alirio Montes, the official spokesman of the pro-government UCS, and a note was found near the body telling Montes to "stop working for the UCS". After Duarte opened negotiations with the FMLN–FDR at La Palma in October 1984 (see section 6.4.5) the ESA denounced him as a traitor and said that he would now be considered a "legitimate target". In November 1984 a new group emerged called the Domingo Monterrosa Commando (also known as the Patriotic Front), which threatened to "demolish all communist elements in the government" and in particular opposed the "traitors" and "Judases" who supported Duarte's peace initiative.

Although the UN Human Rights Commission reported in November 1984 that there had been a decline in crimes "attributable to the state apparatus and armed paramilitary organizations presumably tolerated by or connected with that apparatus", and commended the new government for its "greater prevention and control of the activities of death squads and specific state organs", the improvement proved only temporary. There was a marked rise in death squad activity from mid–1985, and on July 12 the ESA announced its intention to kill 11 people connected with the university, said to be linked with Marxist groups, and especially the Clara Elizabeth Ramírez Brigade, "until all the communists who are once again taking advantage of the university are eliminated".

Notes

1. For details of death squad activities, see Black, *Garrison Guatemala*, pp. 50–53.
2. *Sunday Times*, March 20, 1983, which also reported that soldiers had been dressing as guerrillas, carrying out indiscriminate killings and then returning to villages in their own uniforms to force the survivors to join the PACs.
3. *El Salvador News Bulletin*, No. 23, Spring 1984, p. 14.
4. Quoted Bonner, *op. cit.*, p. 327.

3.3: GUERRILLA WAR IN GUATEMALA, EL SALVADOR AND HONDURAS

3.3.1: Emergence of Guatemalan Guerrilla Campaign

Inspired by the example of Castro's forces in Cuba, anti-government insurgents in Guatemala began a campaign of kidnapping in the mid–1960s, partly to gain attention but chiefly to raise funds; from 1966 kidnappings became so common that they were scarcely mentioned in the press unless the victim was a well-known national figure. The war against the guerrillas was then led by Col. Araña Osorio, who gained the nickname "the Butcher of Zacapa" during the campaign of 1966–68 in which (according to a report by Amnesty International) at least 8,000 people lost their lives (although the guerrilla movements at that time were numbered only in hundreds—see section 3.1.2). Counter-insurgency programmes continued through the 1970s, with an increase in military activity under Gen. Lucas García, including the use of helicopter gunships and aerial bombardment to clear the population out of areas regarded as guerrilla strongholds.

In 1968 the guerrillas spread their activities into urban areas, with the announcement on Jan. 16 that the FAR had "executed" two US military attachés (Col. John D. Webber and Lt.–Cdr. Ernest A. Munro) on the grounds that Guatemalan paramilitary groups "created under American orders" had been "sowing death and terror". The FAR gained international attention when on March 31, 1970, they abducted the West German ambassador to Guatemala, Count Karl-Maria von Spreti, assassinating him when their demand for the release of 17 guerrillas in detention was not met.

The campaign of individual killings and kidnappings resumed in the late 1970s, with the assassinations of Rafael Arriaga Bosque (defence minister 1966–70) on Sept. 29, 1977, and of Jorge David García (a leading member of the MLN) on Dec. 27, and the kidnapping by the EGP on Dec. 31 of Roberto Herrera Ibarguen (foreign and interior minister 1970–74 and more recently President Laugerud's personal representative on the Council of State). Herrera Ibarguen was released on Jan. 30. 1978, after the government had agreed to the publication of a manifesto condemning his record as minister and to the release of Mario Alberto Domínguez of the EGP (who went into political asylum in Costa Rica); it was understood that a ransom might have been paid, although no sum was disclosed.

3.3.2: Guatemalan Conflict in the 1980s

With the emergence of the EGP and ORPA many rural areas were under virtual military occupation from the mid–1970s, and by the end of the decade there were frequent reports of disappearances and murders of the local population by the armed forces. In October 1979 a group of Indian peasants from El Quiché marched to Guatemala City to protest over these disappearances, returning to their homes after assurances were given that an investigation would be established. They marched again on the capital in

Janury 1980 with renewed protests after the bodies of several of the disappeared had been discovered, and 30 of them occupied the Spanish embassy on Jan. 31, taking the Spanish ambassador (Máximo Cajal y López) hostage. In spite of Cajal's stated wishes, the Guatemalan police stormed the embassy building and the peasants responded by throwing petrol bombs, starting a fire in which 39 people were killed, including all but one of the Indians; he was taken to hospital but then kidnapped, and his body was found shortly afterwards dumped on a university campus. (On Feb. 1 Spain broke off diplomatic relations with Guatemala in protest over the conduct of the police and their violation of the diplomatic mission.)

The Brazilian embassy in Guatemala City was seized on May 12, 1982, by several members of the FP–31, claiming to represent those "who have been persecuted and whose harvests and farms have been burned"; in particular, the insurgents protested against the killings carried out by security forces in rural areas, saying that the Ríos Montt coup had made no difference to the scale of rural terror. They took nearly a dozen hostages, including the Brazilian ambassador, and were granted a press conference in which they denounced the massacres before being flown to Mexico and releasing the hostages.

In the 1980s the practice of kidnapping prominent figures was used less for financial gain than for publicity for the cause. The following, having been kidnapped, were all released after the publication of manifestos: the son of the minister of the interior (Col. Ricardo Méndez Ruiz) and the nephew of Ríos Montt, kidnapped in June and October 1982 respectively; Judith Xiomara Suazo Córdova (the daughter of President Suazo of Honduras but of Guatemalan citizenship, working as a doctor at a hospital in the capital), seized in December by the MRP–Ixim; the director of the conservative newspaper *Prensa Libre*, abducted by the PGT in October 1983; and the sisters of both Ríos Montt and Mejía Victores, kidnapped by the FAR in June and September 1983 respectively and released in October.

By the beginning of the 1980s the guerrillas were concentrating less on individual targets, amid almost daily reports of assaults against military personnel or bases. In June 1981 the guerrillas (by now co-ordinating their actions to a certain extent), claimed that they had extended the "people's war" to 19 of the country's 22 departments; they were reported to be focusing their efforts in the Verapaz oil region near the Mexican border. The Guatemalan authorities alleged that Mexico was harbouring guerrillas in the refugee camps set up to cope with the exodus of rural inhabitants, but the Mexican government denied the allegation (see section 4.1.2).

There was a sharp increase in military activity in the period prior to the March 1982 elections, as the guerrillas (now united in the URNG) planted bombs in the capital and sabotaged national electricity installations, causing the army to intensify its presence in the capital and to launch offensives in Chimaltenango (December 1981), El Quiché (January 1982), Huehuetenango and Sololá. As with other regional guerrilla movements, economic sabotage became a common tactic, especially of vital communications networks. It was reported that in November 1981 the guerrillas felled hundreds of pine trees in a single night to block a stretch of the Pan-American Highway between the capital and Sololá.

After the March 1982 coup a month's amnesty was declared, taking effect from May 28, and extended to guerrillas and also to members of the security forces guilty of crimes in the "anti-subversion" campaigns, After the expiry of the amnesty and with the imposition of the state of siege in July 1982 (which lasted until March 1983), certain areas of the country in the departments of El Quiché, Huehuetenango, Quezaltenango, Chimaltenango and Totonicapán were declared zones of exception and operations were intensified; the armed forces claimed to have killed 184 guerrillas in the first fortnight of July. Commenting on the military strategy of clearing these zones, Ríos Montt told President Reagan at their meeting in the Honduran town of San Pedro Sula on Dec. 4, 1982 (see also sections 5.1.1 and 5.2.2): "We have no scorched-earth policy, we have a policy of scorched communists."

During 1982 a small proportion of the Guatemalan displaced were put into army camps under a programme titled "guns and beans" (*fusiles y frijoles*), which had originally been proposed by Lucas García but was not put into practice until after the March coup. In this project the peasants were offered food and medical assistance in return for enrolment into the PACs (see section 3.2.2). By early 1983 the army had begun designating "protected villages" as part of a major reconstruction of the social and economic fabric of the country (the "communitarianism" advocated by Ríos Montt—see section 1.2.12), in a project called "shelter, food and work" (*techo, tortilla y trabajo*). In addition, the government began an Aid Programme for Areas in Conflict (PAAC), modelled on the strategic villages built by the Israeli troops in the occupied territories of the West Bank and Gaza, under the command of Col. Eduardo Wohlers, who said that consideration was being given to the idea of using the Israeli kibbutz system in the Indian highlands. (According to Cuban radio, Israeli officials had started helping with the construction of protected villages in 1982.)

The "shelter, food and work" programme was replaced in 1984 by a straight "food for work" scheme, with wages paid in food rations. The new model villages were located in areas known as "poles of development", concentrated in predominantly Indian communities in the departments of El Quiché, Alta Verapaz and Huehuetenango; by early 1985 there were 74 model villages in six development poles, housing 48,000 refugees (or up to 100,000 according to military sources). The villages were, however, more than simple "safe" areas, and were described by an army spokesman as "re-education centres for those peasants who have been infiltrated by the country's insurgents".[1]

There was renewed fighting in mid–1983 in Alta Verapaz, Chimaltenango and Huehuetenango and in early 1984 in Alta Verapaz, El Petén and El Quiché, with FAR units attacking army positions in La Libertad (El Petén) and EGP members staging a raid on Xabal (El Quiché) in February. ORPA launched offensives in Suchitepéquez in March, in El Petén in May 1984 and in San Marcos in August. In March 1984 the army said that it was deploying 2,000 specialized troops in Suchitepéquez, while in August it announced a three-week offensive in San Marcos involving 8,000 soldiers. ORPA claimed to have inflicted 122 casualties on the army after the first 10 days of fighting in August, and the guerrillas maintained the military initiative when in October 1984 they resumed activity in Izábal after a two-year lull.

It was reported at the end of February 1985 that the URNG had announced its intention "to accelerate the development of the revolutionary war", and from February there were almost daily accounts of incidents between army and guerrilla units, chiefly in El Quiché, San Marcos, El Petén and Alta

Verapaz. The guerrillas broadened the scope of their attacks in April and May 1985 with direct assaults on military posts in San Marcos, where a state of emergency was declared by security forces in several areas on May 28.

Early in March 1986 the national press published a document, supposedly issued by the URNG, declaring its willingness to disarm as a gesture of goodwill in the interests of the people and in view of the promises made by the new government; however, the URNG said that the document was false and denied that the guerrillas had any intention of declaring a unilateral truce.

3.3.3: Salvadorean Guerrilla Activities in the 1970s

The first Salvadorean insurgent group to come to prominence was the ERP, which seized a central radio station on Aug. 6, 1975, in order to broadcast its manifesto. In September 1975 it murdered five policemen and opposition deputy Rafael Carranza, while in November it seized a further eight radio stations to broadcast a call for the overthrow of President Molina. The FPL kidnapped a wealthy industrialist in December 1975 and held him for two weeks, and in April 1977 abducted the foreign minister, Mauricio Borgonovo Pohl, demanding the release of 37 named political prisoners; the authorities claimed that only three of those on the list were in prison (and did not release them) and in May Borgonovo's body was found at Santa Tecla. Roberto Poma, who was seized by the ERP in January 1977, also died while in the hands of the kidnappers; the ERP had successfully demanded a ransom of $1,000,000 for his release and then disclosed that he had died of a gunshot wound received during the kidnap. By 1978 the guerrillas had selected certain foreigners as likely targets, and in November of that year FARN kidnapped two British executives of the Bank of London and South America, calling for the release of five political prisoners (including Lil Milagro Ramírez—see also section 4.2.4), which the government refused; also demanded was the payment of a ransom, the size of which was not disclosed but was believed to be about £4,000,000. In the following months kidnapped employees of the Philips electronics firm and of a Japanese textile company were also released after payment of substantial ransoms; on the other hand, the body of Ernesto Liebes (a member of the "14 families" who was acting as Israeli honorary consul), who had been kidnapped in January 1979, was found in March, after the ultimatum had been allowed to expire. The South African ambassador, Archibald Dunn, was kidnapped on Nov. 28, 1979, by the FPL, which announced the following October that he had been killed as their demands had not been met.

A wave of peasant unrest erupted in late March 1978 in the central departments after Feccas/UTC members had called for wage rises, a reduction of land rents and an end to the use of force against rural workers by the security forces and Orden. The government claimed that Feccas/UTC had deliberately inspired the unrest with the support of the church, but Archbishop Romero denied the charge, saying that members of Orden had tortured and killed Feccas members before the armed forces had moved in and arrested peasant leaders.

From 1977 the popular organizations began to draw attention to their claims by occupying important buildings, such as the ministry of labour taken over by the BPR in November in their campaign for wage rises; they eventually agreed to leave after mediation by the ICRC. In April 1978 about 150 members of Feccas/UTC (apparently directed by the BPR) peacefully entered the Venezuelan, Swiss and Costa Rican embassies, calling on embassy officials to "intercede with the government of El Salvador to stop the repression of the people and immediately withdraw the army, the police and the paramilitary groups from the occupied zone and allow the peasants who were forced to flee to return to their homes" (see also section 4.2.4); again the siege was ended after Church and ICRC mediation.

In January 1979 some 60 members of FAPU occupied the Mexican embassy and the local OAS offices, taking 150 people hostage, and demanded the release of all Salvadorean political prisoners; however, after Mexican mediation they agreed to free the hostages and to accept asylum in Mexico. The BPR were more successful in their occupation of the Costa Rican and French embassies in May 1979, after which the government released two of the five prisoners they specified (BPR secretary-general Facundo Guardado and José Richard Mena), claiming that the other three were not in their custody. Also in May 1979, the BPR began a sit-in at the metropolitan Cathedral (which ended on June 1 when 25 of those involved were flown to Panama and subsequently given asylum in Cuba) and occupied the Venezuelan embassy. All the hostages from the embassy managed to escape and so the security forces laid siege to the BPR members inside; when a demonstration was staged outside the building demanding the resumption of food supplies to the nine BPR members inside, the security forces opened fire, killing 14 and wounding 20 more.

The popular organizations intensified their protests in the latter part of 1979, with FAPU and LP–28 organizing anti-government rallies and another occupation of the Cathedral (and of 13 other churches) to demonstrate against the recent arrest of a number of students. A crowd of about 12,000 people (including BPR, FAPU and LP–28 members) marched through San Salvador on Oct. 4 in protest against the killing by the security forces of four peasant leaders arrested on September 29, including the UTC secretary-general, Apolinario Serrano.

The popular organizations did not lessen their activities after the October 1979 coup, since they held that the change of government had made little difference to the reality of life in the country. The BPR occupied two government ministries on Oct. 24, 1979, taking some 300 hostages to demand the release of all political prisoners, a 100 per cent wage increase for the less well-paid, the dissolution of the security forces, cuts in food prices and the payment of compensation to the families of the victims of political violence. The government made some attempt to meet the demands by issuing a decree on Nov. 7 cutting certain food prices, but the nominal disbanding of Orden remained a dead letter (see section 1.4.10).

3.3.4: Onset of Civil War in El Salvador

Although the civil war commenced in earnest with the FMLN offensive of January 1981, the guerrillas had launched military operations in May 1980, attacking National Guard and Orden members and posts in the departments of Chalatenango, Morazán, San Miguel, Cuscatlán, Cabañas, San Vicente,

Sonsonate, Santa Ana and La Unión (having briefly claimed Chalatenango as "free territory" in April) and then temporarily holding the town of San Miguel in July 1980. In October 1980 the army deployed about 5,000 troops, along with helicopter gunships, to turn back an ERP offensive in Morazán and La Unión. (Until mid–1981 the guerrillas faced a relatively cumbersome and inefficient army, which had not yet received any major allocations of US financial and technical aid—see section 5.2.4.)

The FMLN "final offensive" of January 1981 was largely repulsed by the armed forces, but the guerrillas continued to hold areas in the departments of Morazán, Chalatenango, Cabañas and San Vicente, and by May were using these bases to launch sporadic attacks on the capital. At the beginning of July 1981 Havana Radio claimed that the FMLN had inflicted about 900 casualties on the army during the previous month, mostly in Chalatenango and around the area of the Chichontepec volcano in San Vicente (a strategic communications station, which became the scene of repeated armed engagements); the army, on the other hand, claimed that 14 soldiers and 225 guerrillas had been killed in the first week of June. In mid–August the FMLN intensified its economic sabotage programme, damaging over a quarter of the national electricity network and cutting off supplies of water and electricity for several days. By the end of the year the guerrillas were holding bases in Morazán, Chalatenango, San Vicente and Usulután and there was heavy fighting in Cabañas in November.

The FMLN maintained these positions during 1982, and by the end of November 1982 held 19 settlements along the Honduran border, which the army took for 10 days and then abandoned again to the guerrillas; this pattern of occupation and withdrawal became very common and by the end of the year several villages were left in ruins and the population had fled. The casualty figures were frequently difficult to establish as the figures given by the armed forces for guerrilla deaths included a substantial proportion of civilians: for example, in late August 1982 the army conducted a sweep through San Vicente, during which troops attacked Amatitlán on the Pan-American Highway, claiming to have killed 250 "terrorists", whereas refugees from the fighting in the area reported that the army had killed over 300 unarmed civilians, claiming that they were guerrilla sympathizers.

Radio Venceremos announced on Jan. 9, 1983, that the FMLN had launched its "January Revolutionary Heroes" campaign. In the next few days guerrilla forces took 12 towns in Morazán (including the departmental capital San Francisco Gotera), and repulsed an army counter-offensive by blowing up a road bridge over the Torola River, cutting off the army's supply route. (The town of Meanguera was recaptured twice by the guerrillas after being taken and retaken by the army.) The town of Berlín in Usulután (an important centre for the production of coffee, sugar and cotton, with a population of 35,000) fell to the FMLN on Jan. 31, although they were forced to withdraw on Feb. 2 by a military counter-attack, which involved aerial bombardment and displaced a quarter of the population. According to the archbishop's office in San Salvador, most of the 258 people who died in the last week of January 1983 were victims of the air force's "indiscriminate bombing" of Berlín.

In February 1983 there was renewed fighting at the Guazapa volcano, where the FMLN based some of its forces (and which the army had claimed to have captured at least 13 times since January 1981). Over the next few months FMLN activity was concentrated on single assaults, the main guerrilla claims being (i) an ambush on the Ramón Belloso battalion on March 30 in which 67 soldiers and 17 members of the National Guard were killed; (ii) an attack on the town of Cinquera (17 km from Cerrón Grande) on May 8, in which over 60 soldiers were killed and 19 taken prisoner; and (iii) the capture on May 31 of a military communications centre on the Cacahuatique volcano (near San Francisco Gotera). The Cacahuatique centre had been guarded by 75 soldiers and was retaken by 7,000 troops on June 3, 1983.

In an effort to disperse troops deployed on the military pacification programme "Operation Wellbeing", the FMLN launched a new offensive in September 1983, mounting scattered attacks in the east of the country and claiming at the end of the month to have captured 21 towns and to have inflicted 670 casualties. Under the "Yankees Get out of Grenada" campaign (referring to the US intervention in that island) launched on Oct. 30, the FMLN took and held briefly the town of San Vicente on Nov. 2, but in November and December 1983 the army launched a large-scale counter offensive to protect the coffee harvests in Usulután and San Vicente.

After the presidential elections of 1984, the FMLN began a new series of attacks on May 8, seizing a bridge in Usulután, ambushing an army patrol (65 km west of San Salvador) and blowing up two electricity pylons near the town of Nejapa (16 km north of San Salvador). During a sweep of Morazán in June the army took Perquín, which a few months previously had contained about 1,000 inhabitants but which air force bombing, forcible recruitment by the guerrillas or simple flight had reduced to only four families. On June 28, 1984, a group of 1,500 FMLN fighters attacked the Cerrón Grande hydroelectric station (which was permanently guarded by 400 troops and produced 70 per cent of the country's electricity) and claimed to have killed 76 soldiers (for a loss of only 15 of their own forces) and to have inflicted $3,500,000 worth of damage to the plant. At the end of July the state railway corporation Fenadesal closed all railway lines in the country because of the FMLN's continuing sabotage, which was intensified in the weeks prior to the March 1985 legislative and municipal elections with attacks on the capital and on local town halls (where the electoral registers were kept).

Although the FMLN claimed to have killed 5,286 soldiers, taken 283 prisoner and captured 1,047 arms during 1984, it appeared that it had been substantially weakened and was regrouping in early 1985. According to Villalobos, however, the guerrillas recognized that the war could become one of attrition and were preparing for another five years of war.

In a dramatic action on Sept. 10, 1984, the FMLN kidnapped Inés Guadalupe Duarte Durán, the president's daughter, holding her until Oct. 24, when she and at least 23 abducted mayors and municipal officials were set free in exchange for the release of 22 political prisoners and the promise of safe passage abroad for 96 wounded guerrillas seeking medical treatment. The president was heavily censured by senior army commanders for the virtual cessation of military operations in Chalatenango during the negotiations, accusing him of endangering national security. (Although the FMLN gave an undertaking during the talks to refrain from further kidnapping, the group revoked this decision on Feb. 22, 1986, because of the recent unexplained disappearances of several left-wing civilians and labour union activists.)

The FMLN resumed its military offensive in October 1985 with an attack on the La Unión barracks, and over the following months concentrated on assaults on army targets (including a major one on the San Miguel barracks on June 19, 1986) and economic sabotage. As in 1984–85, the coffee, cotton and sugar harvests in the eastern region of the country were prime targets, both in the gathering and the transportation; according to official estimates, sabotage to the transport network during 1985 totalled $21,000,000 in cost of repairs. Villalobos stated on July 5, 1986, that this strategy was designed to "carry the war to the entire country within one year", to stretch the army, to wreck the economy and to destabilize the government.

Within months of its 1981 major offensive the FMLN had begun a policy of establishing "zones of control" or "liberated zones", and by 1984 areas claimed to be under guerrilla control covered over 20 per cent of the country and contained some 250,000 people. The human rights worker Marianella García Villas said in early 1983 that life in the zones "represents the new El Salvador; it is a just and egalitarian society . . . where religion plays an important role". Within these zones people elected their own governing bodies and implemented programmes for farming, education, health care and military training, and were organized in groups of between 15 and 30 families, meeting in a base assembly. The short-term aims of the zones were war production, the distribution of goods and services and meeting the people's primary needs, and the medium-term objective was to achieve collectivized production and self-sufficiency. The programme was very similar to the reforms carried out by the FSLN in Nicaragua and included the commissioning of literacy brigades and political education.[2]

3.3.5: Salvadorean Government's Military Response

Although the Salvadorean army emerged from the 1969 football war with fewer losses and higher morale than its Honduran counterpart, it was placed under severe pressure by the post–1981 FMLN military initiative. A statement issued by the US Defence Department on Feb. 20, 1981, compared the Salvadorean army with a "19th–century constabulary" with "no hope" of defeating the guerrillas, following which the US administration (now under President Reagan) began to concentrate on efforts to strengthen the Salvadorean armed forces in order to prevent an FMLN victory on the pattern of the Sandinistas in Nicaragua. (For US policy, see section 5.1.2; for US military aid, see section 5.2.4.)

The army launched a broad offensive on July 8, 1981, deploying the US-trained Atlacatl battalion, and after intensive bombardment in the border region around Chalatenango on July 10–14 about 2,000 Salvadoreans fled to Honduras as refugees. The armed forces also appeared to have increased their range of weaponry and a report released on Aug. 11 by the Commission for the Defence of Human Rights in Central America (Codehuca—based in Costa Rica) claimed that the army had used "toxic gases, white phosphorus and bacteriological weapons" causing the deaths of "thousands of children and elderly people"; the army denied the claim, however, and denounced the commission as "a group of militant leftists". The president of the independent El Salvador human rights commission, Marianella García Villas, was killed in 1983 while investigating "the alleged use of napalm and chemical weapons by the armed forces" (see section 4.2.4), and on Oct. 1, 1984, a US plastic surgeon announced after a fact-finding visit to the country that he had found conclusive evidence of the use of napalm. The church-based Legal Aid group (*Socorro Jurídico*) and the ICRC also reported the use of chemical weapons causing "haemorrhagic diarrhoea, dehydration and disintegration of muscles and tissues".

The army's next major offensive was in the department of Morazán in mid–December 1981 with the apparent objective of halting the transmissions of the FMLN Radio Venceremos broadcasts; it was temporarily successful, but the broadcasts recommenced after the army withdrew. The government claimed that during the offensive 175 guerrillas and 12 soldiers died, but reports from the local population put civilian casualties at 733 (estimated by Radio Venceremos at 1,000). Gen. García conceded on Feb. 17, 1982, that the areas had been the target of "aerial bombardment" with "a lot of people" killed, but "not in the way nor quantity alleged by the subversives".

The air force suffered a severe blow when in January 1982 a group of about 100 guerrillas attacked the Ilopango airbase near San Salvador, claiming to have destroyed half the national military aircraft (i.e. 28 aircraft and helicopters), although a military spokesman said that only six aircraft and six helicopters had been hit. The attack boosted still further the US commitment to the armed forces, and six Huey UH–1H helicopters arrived in the first week of February, followed by six A–37 Dragonfly bombers and four O–2 reconnaissance aircraft in June; a further four Huey helicopters were sent in August, since of the 10 aircraft delivered in June seven had been damaged and three grounded for technical reasons.

By 1983 the army's strength (including paramilitary forces) was in excess of 30,000, rising to 42,000 by early 1985; morale remained low, however. Soldiers taken prisoner by the FMLN were generally reported to be well treated (as deliberate policy to encourage soldiers to surrender rather than risk being killed) and in some cases soldiers released by the FMLN (through the mediation of the ICRC) were judged to have such a demoralizing effect on their colleagues that they were discharged. The army, by contrast, very rarely took prisoners among their insurgent opponents.

The bombardment of the town of Berlín on Feb. 1, 1983, marked the beginning of a redoubled air campaign against the guerrillas, with 227 bombing operations recorded in 1983, mostly in the departments of Usulután, Cuscatlán, Chalatenango, Morazán and San Vicente; there followed 338 operations in 1984, when the departments of San Salvador and Santa Ana were also hit. The FMLN had first accused the United States of conducting air reconnaissance flights over Salvadorean territory in 1982; by 1984 the United States had conceded that such flights were made in an attempt "to control the illegal arms trade", while in March 1984 US officials confirmed that US military intelligence units based at the Palmerola air base (Honduras) had been "carrying out observation missions over El Salvador since the beginning of the year". (For further details of US miltiary activity in Honduras, see section 5.2.3.)

In spite of increasing US training and military aid, in the reported view of many US military training officials the Salvadorean forces remained inefficient, inexperienced and inflexible in their strategy; by early 1983 many members of the Atlacatl and Ramón Belloso battalions had been replaced by soldiers not trained in the United States. Whereas the US trainers wanted the Salvadorean troops to operate in small fast-moving units, they perisisted in large-scale sweeps of the countryside to try to dislodge the guerrillas. The army launched an "intensive anti-guerrilla search and destroy operation" on Dec. 21, 1983, recapturing towns in Morazán and San Vicente held by the FMLN for over a year, but then withdrew leaving the guerrillas to retake the towns (a frequent pattern).

In the weeks prior to the 1984 presidential elections the army embarked on an offensive designed to prevent the guerrillas from committing any acts of sabotage and disrupting the balloting; the offensive was only partially suc-cessful, however, as on the eve of polling day (for the first round) the FMLN managed to bomb the country's main electricity plant and black out the capital. After the opening of the La Palma talks in October 1984 (see section 6.4.5) the army sought to step up its sweep operations in Chalatenango and Morazán and the guerrillas also maintained their military activities, since both sides wished to demonstrate that they were entering the negotiations from a position of strength.

The army leadership suffered a reverse in October 1984 when four senior officers and 10 others travelling together in a helicopter died in an aircrash; an army spokesman originally said that the crash had been caused by a mechanical failure but later confirmed the FMLN's claim that a bomb had exploded on board. The most important of the officers was Col. Domingo Monterrosa (see also section 3.2.3), a former commander of the Atlacatl battalion and the top military commander for the eastern sector of the country (the main theatre of war), whose competence as a military comman-der was widely acknowledged.

The armed forces were strengthened by the arrival in early 1985 of the first of three new C–47 gunships from the United States. The aircraft (which cost $1,500,000 each, had rapid-fire machine-guns capable of firing 1,500 rounds a minute and had much greater manoeuvrability than previously-used models) were put into action in San Vicente. By August 1985 the Salvadorean air force had doubled in size over the previous year, with the new US supplies enabling it to take the initiative against the guerrillas. According to María Julia Hernández of *Socorro Jurídico*, "what the death squads did on the ground the air force now does from the air", by using its helicopters to track down and eliminate those considered to be guerrilla sympathizers.

Relying on its new military equipment from the United States, the army launched two major offensives in early 1986, in both cases using preparatory bombing of the area under attack before the infantry moved in. In Operation Carlos, started in the first week of February, the army gained temporary control of the towns of Torola, Jocaítique, Meanguera, Arambala and Joateca, but failed to sustain this effort (for reasons which were not entirely clear) and the operation was called off at the end of the month. More successful was Operation Phoenix, which by March had concluded the army's six-year siege of the guerrilla stronghold on the Guazapa volcano. In the course of this manoeuvre 1,045 civilians were captured, many of whom subsequently disappeared. Further offensives in March 1986 were con-centrated on Chalatenango, and aimed to cut links between the FMLN strongholds in the north and the east of the country.

At the instigation of the US military trainers, the army had in August 1983 adopted the National Campaign Plan, under which combat operations were to be supplemented by redevelopment plans, the training of civil defence groups, the restoration of local economic installations and the protection of agricultural production. The first step of this plan had been launched in June under the name "Operation Wellbeing", concentrated on the department of San Vicente, and by mid-September a substantial area had been cleared by troops commanded by Col. Rinaldo Golcher, who promised that his men would stay as long as necessary; in fact, fewer than 100 families chose to return to the region, and again the troops withdrew, allowing the FMLN to resume its positions. The FMLN regarded this kind of operation as no less military than the army sweeps and issued a communiqué on June 22 saying that all commercial vehicles belonging to "the oligarchy or multinationals", or carrying fuel and construction equipment to repair roads and bridges, would be targets of "constant sabotage"; it warned drivers not to offer lifts to military personnel to "avoid confusion and future confrontations which involve many civilians". Several attacks on working parties in San Vicente were staged in July and August 1983.

Duarte supported the pacification programme, which by 1984 aimed to settle displaced peasants on abandoned farms with grants to establish small-scale manufacturing concerns; however, the plan met with limited success because of the continued fighting and inadequate funding, many farms being abandoned. Early in 1984 the US-based Americas Watch Committee reported that settlers were being used as "pawns" in a military operation (since there was no sign of war abating in the area) and called on the US authorities to withdraw funds from what it termed this "ill-conceived" project. At the end of 1984 the US Agency for International Development (USAID) announced a budget of $800,000,000 for "Plan Mil", designed to settle 500,000 refugees in 1,000 villages over a four-year period using the slogan *techo, tortilla y trabajo* adopted in Guatemala the previous year. An article in *The Guardian* of Aug. 24, 1984, studied the Achichilco co-operative in San Vicente, where only about one-tenth of almost 150 hectares of cultivable land were being used for sugar cane, while the residents predicted that if the co-operative were to become economically viable then the guerrillas would become interested and fighting would resume there.

In early 1985 the Salvadorean foreign ministry announced that 200 displaced famiies would be resettled in Argentina under its "Family and Migration" plan, under which the cost of purchasing land for the refugees and providing them with technical assistance would be met by international organizations. Sources in the interior ministry reported in July that a total of 412,000 people (over 8 per cent of the population) had been displaced by war since 1981, and the government justified its relocation policy on the grounds that it had been undertaken to ensure the safety of many civilians.

In April 1986 Gen. Blandón described the displacement of large sections of the population as an "integral part of military plans for 1986", and said: "We want to know their names, where they are going to live, what they plan to do for a living, in order to have control of the population . . . for their own safety more than anything else." In the same month it was reported that a group of displaced persons taking refuge in another village in Chalatenango had been tortured and killed by an army battalion, and the other villagers had been given 48 hours to leave. Three months later, on July 27, Gen. Blandón announced a further phase of the plan to resettle the displaced in areas under army control called "United for Reconstruction", and the US embassy in El Salvador declared that $18,000,000 in US aid would be advanced to the plan.

3.3.6: Honduran Involvement in Salvadorean Civil War

Although the hostilities of the football war had ceased in 1969, the two countries were still officially at war a decade later when, after the fall of Somoza in Nicaragua and the increasing activity of the left-wing guerrillas in El Salvador, the United States began to work at improving Honduran–Salvadorean relations. Since the adoption of a ceasefire (see section 1.3.7), Honduras had insisted that before any settlement could be reached the border must be finalized, but this demand was dropped in April 1980, after the US Congress had approved an aid package for Honduras and talks had been held in Miami. In the next month the Salvadorean and Honduran armies began a series of joint manoeuvres, the first of which involved a "sandwich operation" at the Sumpul River (where it forms the border), during which hundreds of Salvadoreans trying to reach Honduras were prevented from crossing the river by Honduran troops, and were forced back to the pursuing Salvadorean soldiers.[3] The improved co-operation between the two armies, which had been deeply antagonistic towards each other, also extended to Salvadorean refugees already in Honduras (see section 4.1.4) and to left-wing organizations in both countries. (For US interest in the conclusion of the peace treaty to implement its own policy in Central America, see also section 1.1.18.)

In 1981 several members of Honduran opposition parties and peasant organizations reported having been kidnapped by Honduran security forces, tortured and interrogated on their alleged connection with the supply of arms to the FMLN. Other left-wing leaders received death threats from paramilitary organizations said to have links with other Central American countries. The Honduran left-wing Cinchonero Commando on March 27, 1981, hijacked a Boeing 737 belonging to the Honduran airline SAHSA en route from Tegucigalpa to New Orleans, with 81 passengers on board. At the demand of the hijackers, who diverted the aircraft to Nicaragua, 13 Salvadorean and two Honduran political prisoners were released and flown to Panama.

The FMLN radio station, Radio Venceremos, reported in June 1982 that between 2,000 and 3,000 Honduran troops had been involved in combat operations against the FMLN in Morazán department alongside units of the Salvadorean army. The Honduran authorities denied this claim, although it acknowledged that a number of soldiers had been posted to guard the Salvadorean border and in mid–July the government admitted that its forces had clashed with FMLN units in the *bolsones territoriales*. The FMLN continued to accuse the Honduran army of aggression and said in July that it now considered itself to be at war with Honduras. (Nine Honduran soldiers and a civil guard were killed on July 16 in a clash between two Honduran patrols on the border, which the military officials blamed on bad weather and lack of co-ordination; the incident suggested that the army was at least ready to engage in armed conflict on the border.)

Gen. Alvarez attributed to the FMLN the five explosions at suburban power plants on July 4, which blacked out Tegucigalpa for several days, affected water supplies and caused the deaths of 16 people, although responsibility was claimed by the Froylan Turcios group. Alvarez said that Honduras now faced "not a war with a physical frontier, but a war in which the front is our liberty, our democracy, our Christian faith and our social harmony".

As a result of these explosions the military presence in Tegucigalpa was increased and President Suazo announced on July 9 that civilians would be expected "to co-operate with the authorities and the armed forces in preventing unscrupulous people from achieving their goal of dragging Honduras into the turmoil of violence and anarchy now flooding Latin America". It was reported at the end of the month that the government had ordered all departmental governors to establish civil defence committees "of people who have proven democratic ideas and who are free of sectarian discrimination" to combat "terrorist and subversive actions" and the "campaign of misinformation" launched by "a neighbouring country [i.e. Nicaragua] with the complicity of unpatriotic Hondurans".

In September 1982 the Cinchoneros stormed the Chamber of Commerce building in San Pedro Sula to demand the release of about 70 Honduran and six Salvadorean political prisoners. One of the Salvadoreans was a leading member of the ERP guerrilla movement, Alejandro Montenegro, reportedly arrested by Honduran security forces in Tegucigalpa the day before the storming, but shortly afterwards said to be in the custody of the Salvadorean authorities. Early in 1983 Montenegro gave a television interview in Bogotá (Colombia) denouncing the ERP and was expelled from the FMLN, but the FMLN radio station announced on March 12 that Montenegro had only agreed to take part in this "publicity show" after being subjected to torture.

Relations between the Honduran and Salvadorean armies cooled after the dismissal of Alvarez in March 1984, when the Honduran army suspended the training of Savadorean soldiers at Puerto Castilla and attempted to assert a measure of independence from US policy (see also sections 1.3.7 and 5.2.7). Although Gen. Blandón stated in early 1985 that there had been high level contact between the two armies to co-ordinate their actions along the border, talks held on July 10–11 over the border dispute foundered when President Duarte accused Honduran troops of making incursions into Morazán department, and Paz Bárnica (the Honduran foreign minister) levelled counter-charges against Salvadorean units for entering Honduran territory. Honduran radio reported on April 3, 1986, that FMLN guerrillas had briefly entered Lempira a few days earlier in what was described as part of a "general operation against Honduran territory" by the FMLN and Nicaraguan armed forces.

3.3.7: Honduras: Guerrilla Activities in the 1980s

The Honduran armed forces had been severely weakened by the 1969 football war, but by 1982 their numerical strength had been increased to about 30,000, and the air force had come to be regarded as one of the most powerful in the region because of recent imports of military supplies from the United States. By comparison the guerrilla groups were extremely small and concentrated on staging localized protests in support of their demands for the release of political prisoners and the expulsion of foreign military advisers from Honduras.

The Cinchonero Commando claimed responsibility for a bomb explosion at the Constituent Assembly building in Tegucigalpa on Sept. 23, 1981, as part of a protest against the joint military manoeuvres with US military forces starting on Oct. 7, and on the same day the Lorenzo Zelaya Commando shot and wounded two US military advisers in the capital. Three bombs planted by the FRP exploded on Aug. 4, 1982, at the offices in Tegucigalpa of the Salvadorean airline TACA, the US airline Air Florida and the Pan American Life Insurance building. The FRP detonated bombs at the Argentine and Chilean embassies in Tegucigalpa in April 1982, and in late August 1983 the MPLC caused explosions in San Pedro Sula, La Ceiba and La Lima in a further anti-US protest, as long-term joint manoeuvres had started earlier in the month (see section 5.2.3).

The FRP hijacked a plane on a flight from La Ceiba to San Pedro Sula on April 28, 1982, demanding payment of $1,000,000 and the release of 52 political prisoners (subsequently reduced to $100,000 and 32 prisoners), but the hijack ended on May 1 when 10 hostages escaped while the FRP members were asleep and the only concession they gained was a safe passage to Cuba. An MPLC unit attacked the chamber of commerce building in San Pedro Sula in September demanding the release of Salvadorean and Honduran detainees in Honduran prisons (see also section 3.3.6), the expulsion of all Argentine and Israeli military advisers, repeal of the April 1982 anti-terrorist law (see section 1.3.10), Honduras' withdrawal from the CDC (see section 1.1.14), the expulsion of Nicaraguan contras, an end to the "intervention of the [Honduran] army against the Salvadorean people" (see section 3.3.6), the reallocation of foreign military aid to workers and peasants in the form of economic assistance, and an end to "the repression of the Honduran people". The Honduran authorities made no response to this list of demands, but the MPLC members were granted a safe passage to Cuba a few days later.

There were also several incidents involving people not aligned to—or not attributed to—any particular organization. A gunbattle in the capital on Nov. 27, 1981, left one policeman and a "suspected guerrilla" dead, with two more suspects wounded and seven taken into detention, and a few days later police announced that they had discovered an arsenal and a "people's prison" at a guerrilla base in San Pedro Sula. The August 1982 bombings by the FRP provoked a large-scale security operation by the armed forces and paramilitary groups, and it was reported on Aug. 31 that Cobra units (specially-created counter-insurgency squads) had discovered a large arms cache and a store of munitions and explosives again at San Pedro Sula. In the course of this operation the PCH leader, Rigoberto Padilla Rush, was among those detained by the security forces, although the party denied any involvement in the bombings.

In August 1983 Gen. Alvarez claimed that 3,000 Hondurans were being trained in guerrilla subversion and destabilization, mostly in Cuba and the Soviet Union, and that recently some 200 of them had crossed into Honduras from Nicaragua. In September it was reported that a unit of the regular Honduran army had easily defeated a force of 96 guerrillas in the eastern province of Olancho, killing its leader, José María Reyes Mata, on Sept. 18.

Meanwhile there was growing civilian unrest, sparked off in particular by the kidnap on March 18, 1983, of Rolando Vindel, the head of the union at the national electricity company; in the resultant strike 300 workers were detained by security forces, leading in turn to a demonstration on March 22 by the progressive United Federation of Honduran Workers (FUTH). The dismissal of Alvarez in March 1984 encouraged broader opposition to government policies, and popular rallies were held protesting against government policy (especially on economic matters), asserting Honduran neutrality in the Central American conflict, calling for the withdrawal of all US troops from the country and demanding an end to human rights abuses.

Notes

1. For a description of the model villages and poles of development, see *Central American Report*, issue 29, July/August 1986, pp. 6–9.
2. For further details of liberated zones, see Armstrong and Shenk, *op. cit.*, pp. 203–06; and El Salvador News Bulletin, no. 24, autumn 1984, pp. 8–9.
3. Armstrong and Shenk, *op. cit.*, pp. 217–19.

3.4: NICARAGUA, ITS NEIGHBOURS AND THE CONTRAS

3.4.1: Historical Background

Despite their close historical links, relations between the Central American states have often been strained by shifting alliances arising from economic and territorial problems (as in the football war), political alignments (as in the liberal struggles of the late 19th century) or personal animosity between rulers (as in the conflicts with Zelaya at the beginning of the 20th century). A long-standing territorial dispute between Honduras and Nicaragua caused direct military confrontation in 1957, when in February Honduras claimed sovereignty over an area of disputed territory on the Mosquito Coast. The area, which Honduras designated the province of Gracias a Dios, had been awarded to Honduras under a ruling made in 1906 by Alfonso XIII of Spain, who had been asked to arbitrate. A group of about 50 Nicaraguan soldiers crossed the Coco River on April 18 and occupied the town of Morocón, holding it until May 7 when they were driven back by Honduran ground and air forces. The dispute was then referred to the OAS, with the two countries agreeing in principle to withdraw troops and establish a buffer zone patrolled by neutral observers, and was finally settled in 1960.

Another recurrent tension in regional relations has been the problem of political dissidents from one country taking refuge in another, especially in the case of relations between Costa Rica and Nicaragua. This tension has been aggravated further by the personal animosity between the Somoza family and President Figueres of Costa Rica and the marked contrast between the political complexions of the two national governments (both before and since the 1979 revolution in Nicaragua).

The Costa Rican government claimed on Dec. 11, 1948 that supporters of former President Calderón, in league with Nicaraguan National Guardsmen, had attempted to invade Costa Rica, and placed the country on a war footing. (Calderón had fled to Nicaragua after the 1948 civil war in Costa Rica, see section 1.6.4.) Costa Rica appealed to the OAS and a commission of investigation was sent to report on the situation, which concluded that the invasion had been led by Costa Rican exiles and refuted the government's claim that the Nicaraguan government had been responsible. The OAS commission did, however, criticize Nicaragua for failing to stop the expedition organizing and crossing the border.

In 1955 Costa Rican exiles again grouped in Nicaragua in an attempt to overthrow Figueres, and on Jan. 11 they advanced and took the town of Villa Quesada (48 km north of San José) and other small towns near the border. Costa Rica immediately broke off diplomatic relations with Nicaragua and a state of emergency was declared. At the request of the Costa Rican government the OAS Council convened an emergency session and the fact-finding team which arrived in San José on Jan. 13 concurred with Costa Rican claims that insurgents were being backed by the Nicaraguan government. As Costa Rica had no army the Council called on OAS members to consider the

Costa Rican request for armed assistance, and US aircraft arrived on Jan. 16. A ceasefire plan drawn up by the OAS, providing for a demilitarized zone on both sides of the border, was accepted by both parties on Jan. 20 and they signed a treaty of friendship on Jan. 10, 1956.

The problem of foreign dissidents had also caused a rift between Nicaragua and El Salvador when in 1956 Nicaragua alleged that Nicaraguan exiles based in El Salvador had been involved in a conspiracy surrounding the assassination of Somoza, as the assassin, Rigoberto López Pérez, had recently returned from El Salvador (see section 1.5.6). The Salvadorean government refused the Nicaraguan demand for the extradition of certain exiles to face charges of complicity in the plot as being contrary to its constitution. The differences between the two countries were finally settled in January 1957 through the mediation efforts of the secretary general of Odeca.

Regional relations were strained still futher in the wake of the Cuban revolution of January 1959, and the first Central American state to complain of Cuban intervention was Panama. In April Panama requested OAS assistance in repelling "foreign invaders" as it had no army of its own, and the OAS told its members to use all means at their disposal "to prevent rebel bands leaving their territory for Panama". The 86 "invaders" were a group of Cubans, disowned by Castro as "irresponsible", and two Cuban officers travelled to Nombre de Dios (where they had landed) in an attempt to persuade them to give up their effort, and eventually they surrendered on May 1. At the request of the Panamanian government the OAS on May 2 authorized the dispatch of an international naval patrol to intercept and board any vessels heading for Panama with further invasion forces, but these boats (from the United States and Colombia) were called off on May 4. The 86 Cubans were flown back to Havana on June 29 at the request of the Cuban government.

Early in June 1959 a group of some 80 Nicaraguan exiles living in Costa Rica staged an unsuccessful invasion attempt of their own country, which was defeated by the National Guard within a few days. The OAS commission of inquiry, sent at the request of Nicaragua, laid the primary responsibility for the invasion with Cuba, and on June 13 Luis Somoza accused Castro of having conspired with Pedro Joaquín Chamorro (a leader of the political opposition). Cuba denied the OAS charge and said the plan was entirely the work of Nicaraguan exiles. The Costa Rican Government was not implicated in the attempt and President Echandí said on June 2 that his country was strictly neutral and would take action to prevent further abuses of asylum by Nicaraguan exiles.

Cuba was again seen as responsible for disturbance in the region when abortive uprisings occurred in Nicaragua on Nov. 9–10, 1959, and Guatemala on Nov. 13, although it strongly denied the charges. (In the case of Nicaragua the insurgents, numbering up to 300, were exiles based in Costa Rica, while in Guatemala they were dissidents working in their own country.) Col. Ydigoras of Guatemala said that his government was determined to "remove all Marxist–Castroite contamination from the army and the nation", while the Costa Rican authorities said that Cuban aircraft had been sighted and that the guerrilla forces, which had clashed with the Civil Guard on Nov. 12, included Cubans.

The presence of a "communist threat" in the Caribbean Basin had first brought the United States into regional relations in defence of states friendly to it in 1954, when the CIA reportedly used Nicaraguan and Honduran territory and co-operation against Guatemala (see section 1.2.5). In the case of the 1959 troubles President Eisenhower said on Nov. 17 that he had ordered US naval units to prevent any invasion of Guatemala or Nicaragua by "communist-directed elements". The Cuban government, denying in-volvement, protested to the UN on Nov. 18 that the activities of the US naval patrols constituted "a flagrant violation of the principle of non-intervention and an act of aggression"; the patrols were eventually called off on Dec. 7.

Two decades later the 1979 revolution in Nicaragua (and to a lesser extent the revolution in Grenada) caused similar alarm to the United States and the right-wing dictatorships in Central America, which had US military backing. The election of Reagan in 1980 enhanced US treatment of the region as a front line of the "cold war", and US policy became a crucial factor in determining relations between the states.

3.4.2: Nicaragua and Honduras

Although relations between the two countries had been uneasy in the last years of Somoza rule, especially when in 1977 Somoza accused Honduras of giving asylum to Sandinista guerrillas, the rift between them began to appear within months of the July 1979 revolution, when former National Guardsmen fled across the northern border into Honduras. Not only did these guardsmen set up armed resistance to the FSLN, it was claimed that the Honduran army gave them assistance such as covering fire for those crossing the border on military campaigns. The rift was aggravated by the presence of Nicaraguan refugees in Honduras (see section 4.1.3) and by Honduras' close political and military ties with the United States.

By the end of 1979 there were reports of incursions into Nicaraguan territory by anti-Sandinista forces and also of violations of Nicaraguan airspace by Honduran aircraft. The Nicaraguan ambassador to Honduras, Ricardo Wheelock Román, was recalled to Managua on Oct. 7 in protest over these aerial incidents, over threats of violence made against him and the embassy in Tegucigalpa, and over the reported detention of three Nicaraguan ships by the Honduran authorities. Borge warned Honduras on Nov. 12 that anti-aircraft weapons had been installed along the mutual border, and in December a young EPS soldier was shot dead by Honduran troops on the Honduran side of the border. The Nicaraguan request for an explanation of this event went unheeded and a few days later Honduran troops were re-ported to have attempted to attack the northern town of Somoto. Military leaders from both countries met for talks, as a result of which army units on both sides of the border were apparently withdrawn.

This border harrassment continued in 1980 and Nicaragua began protesting over Honduran tolerance of—and US support for—the contras. Initially the Honduran army made some attempt to claim neutrality and it was confirmed in February 1980 that the army had captured 270 former guardsmen in training camps near the border with Nicaragua, waiting for arms supplies in order to resume military activities. The guerrillas were believed to have set up a camp at Cape Gracias a Dios on the Mosquito Coast, where the Honduran army had military bases.

The border was closed briefly in November 1980 and troops reinforced on both sides. Honduras lodged a protest with Nicaragua on Nov. 11 over the violation of its airspace in the Choluteca region and claimed that its towns of Tempisque and Orlica had been bombarded, but Nicaragua denied both claims and said that one of its helicopters had been blown over the border by adverse winds and then captured by Honduran soldiers. At the same time Nicaragua announced that it had repulsed an attack by 50 armed contras crossing from Honduras and put the number of such incursions into Nicaragua over the past year at 60, also alleging that Honduran aircraft had violated Nicaraguan airspace on at least 25 occasions.

By April 1981 the two countries appeared to be on the brink of war, with troops on both sides of the border placed on alert on April 28 and the border closed again after Honduras claimed that EPS units had mounted an assault on a Honduran border post. Armed clashes broke out on May 3 and May 5, while on May 7 the Nicaraguan defence ministry issued a list of 120 "aggressions" against Nicaragua in recent weeks, accompanied by a complaint that no response had been received to five official notes of protest sent to Honduras. Gen. Paz García and Daniel Ortega met at the border post of El Guasale on May 13, when they released a joint declaration agreeing that their countries' national media should moderate their tone in reporting border incidents and that disputes should be resolved by dialogue. It was also reported that Nicaragua had demanded that the Honduran authorities stop the activities of the anti-Sandinista radio stations broadcasting within their territory.

This agreement did not succeed in defusing tension and after a meeting between Gen. Paz García, Gen. Lucas García of Guatemala and President Duarte of El Salvador on Aug. 12–13 it was reported that Honduras intended to establish a naval base on the island of Ampala in the Gulf of Fonseca (the island was completely militarized by Janaury 1982). Nicaraguan and Honduran patrol boats clashed in the Gulf of Fonseca on Aug. 13, and the Nicaraguan defence ministry said that Salvadorean vessels were also involved.

The Nicaraguan government ordered a general military and civil mobilization from Oct. 6 in anticipation of the joint US–Honduras naval manoeuvres in the Caribbean beginning on Oct. 7 (see section 5.2.3), and protested to the UN that these manoeuvres were "a rehearsal of aggression against the Nicaraguan people".

The first major armed encounter between EPS units and the contras in Honduras (grouped since August 1981 into the FDN—see sections 1.5.26 and 3.1.5) occurred on March 18, 1982, in the Atlantic Zone, and according to official figures 11 guerrillas and three EPS members were killed. In the following weeks there were further sporadic FDN attacks at various points along the border, and on July 24 FDN forces hit the frontier village of San Francisco del Norte (in Chinandega), killing one local official and 14 militiamen. D'Escoto accused the Honduran army of supporting the contras in this aggression and called Gen. Alvarez "the main tool of the USA" in provoking war in Central America.

The Nicaraguan government announced on Nov. 4 that the five northern departments of Chinandega, Madriz, Nueva Segovia, Jinotega and Zelaya would be designated a military emergency zone for the duration of the state of emergency (introduced on March 15; although it was lifted on Oct. 20, 1984, for the rest of the country it remained in force for the "war zones" in the northern and southern border regions—see also section 1.5.28).

The Honduran Foreign Minister, Edgardo Paz Bárnica, said during a visit to Managua on Nov. 12: "We are sure that a war between Honduras and Nicaragua will not occur. Honduras will not lift a finger which could be interpreted as an act of aggression, nor will it authorize an invasion of Nicaragua from Honduran territory." A few days later the Honduran army again cleared some of the FDN camps away from the border, but it subsequently appeared that these had been moved elsewhere rather than dismantled.

In December the FDN intensified its attacks on economic installations and export crops, and on Dec. 27 Humberto Ortega said that in the past 12 months there had been a total of 70 incursions from Honduras for propaganda and intelligence purposes and a further 166 ambushes on EPS patrols.

Early in 1983 the contras attempted to push deeper into Nicaragua in the hope of establishing a bridgehead. A force of about 2,000 FDN members, operating in small units, crossed the border on Feb. 15 and entered the departments of Jinotega, Nueva Segovia, Zelaya and Matagalpa, and on March 18 some 500 attacked the town of Esquipulas (south of Matagalpa), in what was reported to be the heaviest fighting since 1979. Humberto Ortega said on March 21 that the contra offensive had been halted and that "the danger now is not the penetration of Nicaraguan territory by genocidal guardsmen who are now being defeated, but in the threat of war with Honduras". By March 27 the contras had clearly been forced to withdraw.

In August the FDN advanced on Jinotega, blowing up a bridge outside the town, but were driven back by EPS units. By the end of the month there were estimated to be 2,000 guerrillas operating in northern Nicaragua and the incidence of sabotage increased; the most serious damage occurred on Oct. 10 when the fuel storage facilities at the port of Corinto were set on fire, and only three days previously the FDN had announced that it had mined the port. In December FDN forces again entered Nicaragua and tried to secure towns in the north in the hope of instigating an anti-Sandinista uprising, but after a month's fighting they were forced to withdraw and regroup. The next major offensive began on April 13, 1984, when 5,000 contras crossed the border (with 3,000 reinforcements waiting inside Honduran territory), and in May the FDN leadership claimed to have over 10,000 soldiers fighting within Nicaragua. The offensive appeared to weaken from June and border incidents between FDN and EPS units became less frequent after September, although at the beginning of May 1985 EPS units crossed into Honduras in "hot pursuit" of contras, and Honduran troops were mobilized along the border (see section 3.4.4). In a conciliatory move the same month the Honduran army removed the large FDN base at Las Vegas, six km from the border, which had been the object of Nicaraguan forays.

By 1984 it was widely held that the contras were not strong enough to defeat the Sandinistas militarily without substantially increased foreign assistance, which was expected to come from the United States. During the April offensive the Nicaraguan Chief of Staff, Cdr Joaquín Cuadra, claimed that the FDN now had the use of C–47 and DC–3 aircraft operating from CIA bases in southern Honduras at Las Vegas, Banco Grande and El Aguacate.

On May 8, 1984, a Honduran military helicopter was shot down over Nicaraguan territory, and although Paz Bárnica claimed that the helicopter had accidentally strayed over the border because of bad weather, the Nicaraguan authorities claimed it was engaged on an espionage mission as it had taken off from Tiger Island (El Tigre, a radar base in the Gulf of Fonseca, manned by about 200 US marines). On the following day the Honduran ambassador in Managua was recalled, and two days later the government in Tegucigalpa declared the Nicaraguan ambassador persona non grata, giving him 48 hours to leave the country.

Considerable controversy was aroused over apparent links between the FDN and the Honduran army by the publication of an article in the Oct. 31, 1985, edition of the Honduran newspaper *El Tiempo*. The article reported the presence of an FDN training site, known as the Fifth School Supply Centre, within 500 metres of the army's Francisco Morazán Military Training School (situated about 10 km outside Tegucigalpa). Gen. López asserted, however, that the country would never permit FDN forces to make use of Honduran military installations.

The Nicaraguans had become increasingly apprehensive about US involvement with the contras after the start of the joint US–Honduras Big Pine II military exercises in August 1983, which included naval manoeuvres in the Caribbean and Pacific. The exercises were followed almost immediately by others, ensuring a virtually continuous US presence in the region based on Honduras (see section 5.2.3). The deployment of US warships off the Pacific coast aroused suspicion that the United States might be implicated in the mining of the Pacific ports of Corinto and Puerto Sandino in March 1984, when five vessels at these two ports were struck by mines, including a Soviet oil tanker. The US administration did not officially admit that it had ordered the mining of the ports, but faced strong criticism within Congress and it was reported in April that the FDN had decided to suspend its mining campaign because of its detrimental effect on securing funds from the US Congress. (For further details of reaction to mining of ports, debates within Congress over US policy and US military aid to the contras, see sections 5.1.3 and 5.2.5.)

In response to US allegations that Nicaragua was adopting an aggressive stance towards its neighbours, and particularly to Honduras, d'Escoto declared in November 1984: "Not only would Nicaragua not threaten another country on principle, but obviously it is in no condition to do so. . . . We know quite well that if we were to take this type of action and transform ourselves into aggressors of another country we would be serving the pretext that Mr Reagan has always been looking for on a silver platter."

3.4.3: Nicaragua and Costa Rica

Although relations between Nicaragua and Costa Rica had been poor since the Costa Rican civil war of 1948 (see section 3.4.1) there was a sharp deterioration in the last two years of Somoza's rule. On Oct. 14, 1977, Nicaraguan military aircraft strafed three boats on the Costa Rican side of the Frio River (which forms part of the border), one of which was carrying the Costa Rican minister of public security, Mario Charpentier Gamboa. President Oduber accepted the Nicaraguan government's contention that the boats had been mistaken for Sandinista vessels and ordered the Costa Rican civil guard units to avoid confrontation with the Nicaraguan National Guard.

The Costa Rican government accused Nicaragua on Sept. 12, 1978, of having bombarded and entered Costa Rican territory in "hot pursuit" operations against the FSLN, while the Nicaraguan government countered that guerrilla attacks had been launched from Costa Rica. Two days later Venezuela and Panama each sent four military aircraft to Costa Rica, and Venezuelan and Panamanian volunteers began to gather in Costa Rica to form a volunteer force to support the FSLN. Somoza then recalled the Nicaraguan ambassadors in San José, Caracas and Panama City, and on Nov. 21 Costa Rica severed diplomatic relations with Nicaragua and called for its expulsion from the OAS after clashes between the Nicaraguan National Guard and the Costa Rican Civil Guard, in which two civil guardsmen were killed. At a press conference given on Dec. 27 Somoza warned that if Costa Rica continued to allow the FSLN to use its territory to launch attacks against Nicaragua, the National Guard would be ordered to invade. It was reported in March 1979 that President Carazo had ordered a clean-up operation along the Costa Rican side of the border to flush out elements of both the FSLN and the National Guard, but after further border incursions Somoza again threatened invasion on June 2.

Initially relations with the Sandinista government were friendly, Costa Rica being the first country to recognize the new regime, and although cross-border incidents began when opponents of the Sandinistas moved south, the fact that Costa Rica had no army (only a 6,000–strong Civil Guard) meant that there was little possibility of the two countries going to war.

In February 1982 both countries agreed to form joint border patrols and in June a bilateral commission was established "to analyse and solve any border problem which might arise in the future". It was reported in May that the Costa Rican government had asked Pastora to leave the country after 11 EPS soldiers had deserted and crossed into Costa Rica to join him, and in October two more Arde members (Fernando Chamorro Rapaccioli and Juan José Zavala) were arrested in Costa Rica and charged with possession of firearms, Chamorro being expelled a month later for "compromising the country's neutrality". In January 1983 the Civil Guard located and dismantled several Nicaraguan guerrilla camps on the border and in June Pastora was declared persona non grata as a result of the start of Arde's military activities in April. Arde, which was smaller than the Honduran-based FDN and more prone to divisions within its leadership, became a greater threat to Nicaragua from 1984 when it tried to form an alliance with the FDN (see section 3.1.5).

When Arde temporarily seized the Nicaraguan town of San Juan del Norte in the offensive of April 1984, the Nicaraguan government sent a formal protest to San José demanding "immediate urgent measures" to disarm Arde forces in Costa Rica. In response Costa Rican security forces raided the Arde headquarters in San José on April 24, closed down its radio communciations centre and took 12 of the group's representatives into custody.

After a clash on May 4, 1984, at Peñas Blancas (a border town on the shore of Lake Nicaragua) a "commission of supervision and prevention" was set up to defuse tension between the two countries at the instigation of the Contadora Group. The commission, which incorporated members from Costa Rica and Nicaragua as well as from the Contadora member countries, began work on May 26. (According to the Costa Rican version of the May 4 incident Nicaraguan forces had attacked a border guard post with machinegun and mortar fire, whereas the Nicaraguan government claimed that the incident had been staged by the Civil Guard with the complicity of Arde.)

Further measures against Arde were taken after the assassination attempt against Pastora in San José on May 31 (see section 3.1.5), after which the Minister of Public Security, Solano, announced that the government would tolerate Arde's political but not its military activities. Moreover in late June Solano ordered security forces to shoot down an unidentified aircraft flying over the northern border region, believed to belong to the guerrillas. (For subsequent dismissal of Solano, see section 1.6.11.)

Despite these measures of co-operation, however, relations between the two countries had begun to deteriorate in 1981. During the 1982 presidential campaign in Costa Rica Monge expressed regret over what he saw as the Sandinistas' increasing association with Cuba and the Soviet Union, and said that Costa Rica wanted "peace on our borders and normal diplomatic relations in spite of our ideological differences". In his speech to the 13th General Assembly of the OAS in November 1983 he said that his country would undertake "not to initiate any war and to stop our national territory from being used by those participating in war".

By 1984 the Costa Rican government was adopting an increasingly right-wing stance as a result of US pressure in its economic crisis (see section 1.6.11). The United States indicated its desire to involve Costa Rica in its regional military policy when it announced (i) in 1983 that it was sending military engineers to the country; (ii) in 1984 that joint manoeuvres would be held (although Costa Rica denied that any such measures would take place); and (iii) in May 1985 that military advisers would be sent to Costa Rica to train the security forces (see section 5.2.6).

Tension had increased further in June 1984 when a Costa Rican Civil Guard patrol was ambushed (and two guards killed) on the Nicaraguan border, in what Monge described as a "premeditated attack" by the EPS; Ortega claimed that the ambush had been part of a "campaign of tension" organized by the United States, and other reports suggested that Arde could have been responsible. On June 2 Monge downgraded diplomatic relations with Nicaragua "to the most minimal level", and the Nicaraguan government responded by proposing the creation of an internationally supervised demilitarized zone "with the support of the Contadora Group and with the collaboration of France". Relations were eventually normalized on Feb. 13, 1986, when President Ortega issued a statement accepting Nicaraguan responsibility for the deaths of the two Costa Rican guards.

The Costa-Rican president-elect, Arias Sánchez, expressed the hope (in February 1986) that this improvement might advance peace efforts in the region, and later in the month on Feb. 24, the Costa Rican and Nicaraguan deputy foreign ministers met for talks (under the auspices of the Contadora Group) and agreed to the establishment of "a permanent force of inspection and vigilance" to patrol the border. This initiative collapsed when on March 12 the Costa Rican representative walked out of another round of talks in protest against the use of the term "a demilitarized corridor from the Pacific to the Caribbean, under the administrative control of an international commission"; he claimed that the word "demilitarized" could not be used as Costa Rica possessed no army.

With regard to Costa Rican tolerance of contra leaders known to be on its soil, Chamorro Rapaccioli was deported from the country on April 25, having arrived only two days earlier, and the same day another contra leader was detained in connection with drug offences (see section 3.4.4). After dissociating himself from Arde in May, Pastora was granted political asylum in Costa Rica on June 3 (see section 3.1.5), in return for which he had given an undertaking to abide by the country's laws and to refrain from taking any part in the armed struggle to overthrow the Sandinista government.

3.4.4: Contra Activities, 1983–86

(For launching of FDN and Arde offensives from Honduras and Costa Rica respectively, see sections 3.4.2 and 3.4.3.)

By mid–1983 the FDN and Arde had established a pattern of raids into Nicaraguan territory, such as the FDN assault on Puerto Cabezas on May 8 and the Arde attack on military and administrative targets at El Corral (near Lake Nicaragua) a week later. The two groups launched a major concerted military effort in September, when on Sept. 8 two Arde light aircraft attacked Managua airport (one of them crashing, killing the two Miskito pilots on board), and the following day the FDN conducted an air raid on Corinto in US-made T–38 jets, hitting oil tankers and causing minor damage to the main oil pipeline. (Pastora claimed that the two Arde aircraft "took off from, and the surviving plane returned to, airstrips we have built in the liberated territory of Nicaragua", which he said extended for 4,200 sq km around San Juan del Sur, but this was a greatly exaggerated estimate. The FDN had attempted to gain territory in the north of the country in an offensive in Jinotega during August—see also section 3.4.2—but after an unsuccessful attack on the town of San Rafael del Norte had continued with minor military engagements and sabotage attacks.) FDN units destroyed the border post at El Espino on Sept. 26 and then tried to take the town of Ocotal (north of Estelí), claiming that "the war in the mountains has ended—we have launched an urban war", and two days later Arde destroyed the main southern border post at Peñas Blancas.

The joint offensive of December 1983 (see section 3.4.2) had largely collapsed by the end of January 1984, and at the end of the month Edgar Chamorro Coronel conceded that the forces were "not able to liberate land nor control territory", with the guerrillas blaming the failure of the offensive on inadequate supplies from the CIA. These supplies apparently resumed a couple of months later (at the time of the mining of the port of Corinto—see sections 3.4.2 and 5.2.5) and in April 5,000 FDN members crossed the border into Nicaragua (claiming to have a further 3,000 fighters in reserve in Honduras) and Arde took the town of San Juan del Norte, holding it for four days before EPS units recaptured it. Nicaraguan military intelligence reported that there were 6,000 FDN fighters in Jinotega department alone, and the EPS northern regional commander, Cdr Manuel Salvatierra, said that there had been 156 clashes between his forces and the FDN in March–June and that the FDN was "trying to influence the peasants and create a social base for themselves"; he gauged that the guerrillas had gained some success with local farmers (in contrast to workers on co-operatives and state farms) partly because of the lack of FSLN "mass organizations" in the area and partly because of abuses by certain government and army personnel.

In June 1984, however, the contras were weakened by the resignation of Pastora and the withholding of CIA support (see sections 3.4.2 and 5.2.5), and the EPS launched its largest offensive to date in the south of the country, regaining control over large sections on the northern bank of the San Juan River, and Arde leaders admitted that they had lost seven bases in Nicaraguan territory and that 300 guerrillas had deserted. Officials in Costa Rica subsequently reported that about 1,000 contras had fled southwards over the border for refuge. The EPS also prohibited the flight of civilian aircraft over Nicaraguan territory with effect from June 18 out of anxiety over the new US–Honduran military exercises, codenamed Big Pine III. Rivera attributed the decrease in CIA assistance to US policy aimed at encouraging the contras to unite, saying on June 19: "For two months we have received no munitions, boots or food. The Reagan administration, which has great influence in this area, is manipulating the situation to force us to agree to an alliance."

The number of armed clashes abated in September and October 1984, although the contras continued a campaign of abductions (seizing 82 people between early July and the first week of September), and on Oct. 12 carried out their first sabotage attack in the capital when they set fire to a government warehouse. Fighting was renewed in February 1985 and the contras (in an apparent attempt to enhance their image in the United States as a credible force) announced their intention to establish a provisional government on Nicaraguan soil by the end of the year. It was reported in March that the Nicaraguan authorities had started relocating many inhabitants from the north of the country to create a free-fire zone (although the move was denounced by President Reagan as "Stalin's tactic" against those who "do not support their tyrannical regime"). In April and May the EPS again went on the offensive, crossing the Honduran border in pursuit of contras who, according to US intelligence reports, had virtually run out of ammunition until fresh supplies arrived from the United States after April 21. (US intelligence sources also claimed that 40,000 regular EPS members were currently deployed in the northern combat zone.)

The contras had aimed their attacks particularly at Sandinista officials, including health promoters, teachers and members of the literacy brigades (see section 1.5.23), and in 1983 and 1984 they killed over 7,000 Nicaraguan civilians. In February 1985 reports began to emerge of atrocities on the part of the contras, including that of the abduction and rape of two West German women working in the village of Dominico (Jinotega) on a housing project for peasants made homeless by the war. The US-based Central American Health Rights Network announced in March that the contras had started a new campaign to terrorize the local population, in which doctors and nurses were particular targets, and it was also reported that they had been especially brutal to captured Sandinista militiamen, on occasion torturing and burning them to death.

In May 1985 the EPS launched "Operation Sovereignty", to regain control of the northern bank of the San Juan river, and by the beginning of August had largely achieved this aim, pushing Arde southwards or cutting off its lines of supply into Nicaragua. Meanwhile in July the FDN launched a new offensive in Jinotega, taking the town of Trínidad (120 km north of Managua) on Aug. 2, and holding it for four hours, before withdrawing under aerial fire; the authorities claimed to have killed 129 contras, including eight leaders, and captured another 41. Two more major attacks occurred the following week in the departments of Estelí and Chontales, during which about 95 EPS and militia members were reported to have been killed.

In response to contra attacks on EPS units in October and November 1985 the government announced on Dec. 12 that it would call up 30,000 people for reserve military service. By the end of the year the continuous EPS offensive had driven contras fighting in border areas back into either Honduras or Costa Rica, making the first use of air-mobile operations with Soviet MI–24 assault and MI–8 transport helicopters. In contrast to the increased capability of the EPS, the contras suffered severe training, logistics and supply problems, and by the end of March 1986 it was estimated that at least three-quarters of the 2,000 contras operating in central Nicaragua had been forced to retreat. (The EPS offensive did arouse some anti-government sentiment within the country as it involved the relocation of a further 100,000 peasants out of the areas under fire.)

Humberto Ortega stated on Dec. 30, 1985 that during that year the contras had suffered 5,649 casualties, including 4,608 dead and 500 taken prisoner, compared with death tolls of 1,143 for the EPS and 281 for the civilian population. President Ortega announced on Feb. 21, 1986, that the total estimated number of casualties since 1981 had reached 23,822, of which 13,900 had died.

There continued to be substantial allegations made against several contra elements, not only for human rights abuses but also for arms offences, trafficking in Colombian cocaine (bound for the US market) and embezzlement of US aid. US officials originally denied the claims, particularly in connection with drug offences, but on April 16 the US administration said that it now had reason to consider that some contras "may have engaged in such activity", but asserted that these members would not have been acting on orders from contra leaders. A few days later, on April 25, it was reported from San José that the Costa Rican authorities were holding Chamorro Rapaccioli and three others on possible narcotics charges (see section 3.3.3).

Contra attacks on rural aid projects involved them in particular in actions against foreign nationals; for example in May 1986 eight West Germans working at a refugee camp for displaced peasants were kidnapped by the FDN and held until June. Between February and August 1986 aid workers from Spain, Belgium, Switzerland and West Germany were killed in contra raids, and so in August President Ortega ordered the withdrawal of all foreign development workers from the war zone areas.

SECTION FOUR

REFUGEES, HUMAN RIGHTS AND THE INDIAN QUESTION

4.1: THE REFUGEE QUESTION

4.1.1: Introductory

As a result of the fighting and military operations by guerrillas and government forces, many thousands of people in Guatemala, El Salvador and Nicaragua have been displaced from their homes in recent years. While many left their country, mostly for Mexico or Honduras, in El Salvador and Guatemala many more were resettled in special communities by the armed forces as part of a "strategic village" campaign (see sections 3.3.2 and 3.3.5). This section deals mainly with the plight of refugees outside their native land.

4.1.2: Guatemalan Refugees

The rising tide of violence in Guatemala, and particularly in the countryside, gradually forced many people from their homes from mid–1981. By early 1983 it was estimated that some 500,000 people had been displaced (about 6 per cent of the population), of which some 100,000 had travelled north to Chiapas state in Mexico, while a smaller number had fled south to Honduras.

Once in Chiapas, however, the refugees were still not entirely safe from attacks from the Guatemalan armed forces, which claimed that the camps harboured guerrillas. Between the end of 1981 and mid–1984 the camps recorded 69 incursions by Guatemalan soldiers, during which 21 refugees were killed and 20 more were kidnapped, while seven Mexican peasants helping the refugees were also killed. In October 1982 the Mexican authorities began moving the camps away from the border areas to Campeche, but the refugees resisted this move and claimed that the Mexican and UNHCR officials were putting pressure on them to move by measures such as withholding food. The refugees said that they did not want to be uprooted again, especially as they had begun to establish their own livelihoods through crop-cultivation and handicrafts such as weaving, and maintained that Campeche was far less suitable to their needs.

An armed group entered Mexico from Guatemala on April 30, 1984, attacking a camp and killing six refugees. The Guatemalan government denied that the group consisted of Guatemalan troops and refused to set up an investigation into the incident; accordingly, the Mexican government decided to move more refugees further into Mexican territory. The UNHCR, which had a 1984 budget for work with Guatemalan refugees of $7,000,000 for food, medicine and shelter, gave additional financial assistance to the relocation. The Guatemalan government claimed that in consequence of the move about 8,000 refugees had chosen to return to Guatemala, but Mexican officials put the number at only 400. The relocation of the refugees began in mid-June 1984, and by mid-October some 17,000 refugees in Chiapas (out of the official total of 46,000) had been moved to Campeche or Quintana Róo. The US-based Americas Watch Committee accused the Mexican security forces of "gross abuses" in the course of the relocation operation, including arrests, burning refugee camps and withholding food and services.

4.1.3: Nicaraguan Refugees

According to figures released by the UNHCR, over 110,000 Nicaraguans fled the country between September 1978 and July 1979, mostly to either Costa Rica or Honduras, while in Nicaragua there were about 600,000 internal refugees out of a population of only 2,500,000. An estimated 30,000 of the internal refugees were cared for at ICRC centres in Managua.

Many of those who fled the country returned after the fall of Somoza, but when fighting began in the north of the country as a result of raids by the contras, more people fled to Honduras, and the number of Nicaraguan refugees in Honduran camps reached 7,500 by July 1980. After this initial influx the numbers grew relatively slowly to reach about 10,000 by early 1982; many of these refugees were Miskito Indians from the Caribbean coast, whose way of life had been disrupted by the new Sandinista government and a substantial proportion of them joined the FDN (see section 3.1.5).

In a letter to the UNHCR dated July 30, 1982, Paz Bárnica requested help with the resettlement of 30,000 refugees in third countries on the grounds that "despite the continued determination of my government to maintain neutrality, the presence of refugees and especially people who pretend to be refugees, guided by preconceived aims, raises problems both of an international and domestic nature which, as time goes by, become increasingly serious". Although most of the refugees in Honduras came from El Salvador, this statement was apparently made in reference to Nicaraguans in view of the poor relations between the two countries. No progress was made with the request as no other country was willing to take the refugees.

After Arde began its operations some Nicaraguans fled south, although the numbers were not as high as initially expected. US relief agencies in particular had forecast a large influx of refugees to Costa Rica after April 1983, and camps were set up along the border to cater for up to 100,000 displaced persons, but it was reported at the beginning of July that they were still almost empty.

After the US congress had halted aid to the contras in June 1984 (see section 5.2.5), a number of US-funded projects for Nicaraguan refugees were launched as a means of continuing aid to the FDN and Arde disguised as "humanitarian aid". One such organization was the Friends of the Americas relief organization formed in late 1984, which co-operated with USAID on refugee programmes on the border (despite UNHCR policy to avoid operations within 50 km of the border). In October 1984 the sum of $7,500,000 was allocated to USAID for work among Miskito refugees in the border area, and it was reported that nearly a quarter of the Miskito refugees in the border region left their camps to join the new projects.[1]

The number of Nicaraguan refugees in Honduras had risen after the passage of the military service bill in August 1983 (see section 1.5.27) as a number of young men, mostly students, fled north to evade conscription. The number increased when recruiting was accelerated in early 1985, so that by mid–1985 there were nearly 19,000 officially registered refugees in three camps and many thousands more reportedly unregistered. According to some Costa Rican officials several groups of refugees had refused to participate in work programmes run by international relief organizations and had escaped from the camps to become wandering criminals.

4.1.4: Salvadorean Refugees

The Honduran authorities announced in July 1980 that 4,500 Salvadoreans had sought refuge in Honduras so far that year (a number which by early 1982 had grown to 25,000). According to UNHCR figures in late 1981, there were 70,000 Salvadorean refugees in Mexico, 40,000 in Guatemala, 35,000 in Honduras, 10,000 in Nicaragua, 10,000 in Costa Rica, 7,000 in Belize and 1,500 in Panama. By 1984 it was estimated that up to 1,000,000 Salvadoreans were displaced, although only a quarter of these were officially registered as such. Like the Guatemalan refugees in Mexico, the Salvadoreans in Honduras were not entirely safe from their own armed forces once over the border, as the army claimed that the camps harboured guerrillas.

The US ambassador to Honduras was reported in the Salvadorean press in June 1981 as having alleged that half of the international aid sent to Salvadorean refugees in Honduras was being diverted to the FMLN, although he later conceded that only "circumstantial evidence" existed for this allegation and amended his statement to say that "small quantities" of aid were reaching the guerrillas. The original charge was denied by the director of the Honduran office of the UNHCR, Charles-Henri Bazoche, who said that there were "tight controls" over the allocation of funds.

The UNHCR faced further criticism, from a different quarter, when in August 1980 it designated the Evangelical Committee for Development and National Emergency (CEDEN) as the co-ordinating agency for relief work in Honduras—CEDEN being an essentially Protestant body but incorporating Roman Catholic and other relief organizations. The following year a dispute arose over the role of the California-based World Vision International, which was accused by other relief organizations of having handed over some refugees to Salvadorean soldiers, of having links with the CIA and of concentrating more on efforts to convert the refugees to Protestantism than on meeting their immediate physical needs. In January 1982 World Vision gained control of the CEDEN executive council, which then voted to sever all links with the World Council of Churches (WCC) and to receive assistance only from USAID and World Vision. Many CEDEN officials left to form a new organization supported by the WCC and the more moderate US and European Protestant churches. The intervention of Gen. Alvarez in March 1982 ensured that the Honduran government confirmed CEDEN as the responsible organization and so in April the UNHCR decided to assume direct control of the relief operation itself.

In early 1981 Bazoche lodged a protest with the Honduran government that its army had behaved brutally towards the Salvadorean refugees, claiming that three of the refugees had been killed by Salvadorean troops in March after being handed over by the Honduran army. He also stated that the Honduran army had made raids on the camps, and had turned back refugees at the border. It was reported that on March 16 the Salvadorean air force had bombed 8,000 refugees trying to cross the Lempa river, while their escape route was blocked by Honduran soldiers, and that about 200 refugees —mostly women and children—had been killed in the operation. Honduras was also said to be allowing regular Salvadorean air force raids over its territory and to have permitted members of Orden (which continued to operate despite its official disbanding in 1979) to search the camps. In

November 1981 1,000 Salvadorean troops entered Honduras to comb the camps, and at one of the largest, La Virtud, 20 refugees were rounded up and taken away.[2] In December two members of the Roman Catholic relief organization Caritas were killed by Salvadorean soldiers while working at La Virtud. (For increased co-operation between Honduran and Salvadorean armed forces, see also section 3.3.6.)

In February 1984 the bodies of 14 Salvadoreans were found some 25 km from the Mesa Grande camp, and although the Honduran army denied any involvement it appeared that the Salvadoreans had been shot, while escaping, by Honduran troops patrolling the area. It was reported that between January and July 1984 at least 20 refugees were killed by Honduran troops; on June 2 a Spanish doctor and two Salvadoreans were killed by Honduran troops, in what the military command said was an exchange of fire, but it was later discovered that all three had been shot in the back.

Despite these reports, Salvadoreans continued to cross the border and after the military offensive in Chalatenango in September 1984 a further 700 sought refuge in Honduras. There was renewed trouble when on Aug. 27, 1985, several hundred Honduran troops, claiming they were searching for FMLN guerrillas, entered the Colomoncagua camp. They reportedly opened fire on the refugees, killing two and wounding 50 others, before taking 10 prisoners. The incident was strongly condemned by Honduran church and human rights officials.

The UNHCR had decided in 1981 to move the refugee camps away from the border because of the dangers faced by Salvadoreans there. A delegation from the British Council of Churches, led by Lord Avebury, toured the camps in Feburary 1982, reporting that the refugees were in "extreme peril" from Salvadorean death squads and submitting evidence of torture, rape, kidnapping and murder of refugees in the camps. The decision to move the camps some 50 km eastwards was accelerated by the start early in 1982 of a joint Salvadorean–Honduran military operation to clear the border, but was criticized by the church and relief agencies and by the refugees themselves on the grounds that it would make it yet more hazardous for Salvadoreans wishing to flee their country.

In 1983 the head of the Honduran National Commission for Refugees, Col. Turcios, told the refugees that "you are an obstacle to our military plans . . . and you will be moved, like it or not". The refugees continued to oppose the relocation and complained that the UNHCR had withdrawn food supplies in order to pressurize them to leave. In 1984 the Honduran authorities began to suggest that some 18,000 refugees still in camps near the border should be repatriated, in a move to help force a settlement of the unresolved border dispute with El Salvador, although officials were said to have promised that there would be no forcible repatriation.

Many Salvadorean political exiles chose to go to Nicaragua, and in 1981 projects for Salvadorean refugees were begun, such as the Luciano Vilches co-operative on the outskirts of Managua, funded by the UNHCR and the Salvadorean Students' Union (AGEUS). By 1984 the co-operative had 117 inhabitants (mostly Salvadorean women and children, and also including a few Nicaraguan citizens) and had started to raise crops and livestock.

The vast majority of Salvadoreans who left their homeland chose to go north, via Mexico, to the United States. In mid–1982 the US Immigration and

Naturalization Service estimated that up to 500,000 Salvadoreans had entered the United States, most of them illegally in that US government policy categorized them as economic refugees and regarded them as ineligible for political asylum (especially as the United States gave full support to the Salvadorean government). The State Department reviewed its policy in 1981, announced in May of that year that it would continue to oppose the granting of even temporary legal status. In 1983 the Immigration Service stated that 5,566 Salvadoreans had been deported, 1,067 had been denied asylum and only 74 had been allowed to stay. It was reported in the press in 1983 that some US church leaders had decided to defy the official ruling and to give secret assistance to Salvadoreans leaving their country out of fear for their lives.

By early 1985 the US cities of Cambridge (Massachusetts), Berkeley (California), St Paul (Minnesota) and Madison (Wisconsin) had declared themselves to be sanctuaries for Central American refugees, in defiance of the administration. They called on the government to abide by the 1980 Refugee Act offering asylum to people with a "well-founded fear of persecution", and refused to co-operate with immigration officials tracking down illegal immigrants from El Salvador and Guatemala. Over 200 churches (mostly in the south-west) openly declared their support for the sanctuary policy and a number of church officials and members were charged with harbouring aliens.

Notes

1. *Sunday Times*, 14 April 1985.
2. Armstrong and Shenk, *op. cit.*, p. 217.

4.2: HUMAN RIGHTS

4.2.1: Introductory

Since the mid–1960s there has been an increasing volume of reports of persistent and systematic violation of human rights in Central America, most notably concerning Guatemala, El Salvador and (until the 1979 revolution) Nicaragua. In December 1981 the Inter-American Human Rights Commission (of the OAS) reported that the disappearance of detainees was declining throughout most of Latin America, except in Guatemala and Honduras (and Argentina). The Commission singled out Guatemala and El Salvador as countries where summary executions of political opponents were "directly committed by security forces, which act with impunity outside the law, as well as by paramilitary groups which operate with the acquiescence or tacit consent of the government" (see also sections 3.2.2 and 3.2.3).

Guatemala and El Salvador have remained the two countries with the worst human rights records in the region, with Amnesty International (AI) describing Guatemala as the worst human rights violator in the world in 1983, and from Honduras there have been several reports of abuses under Gen. Alvarez' "dirty war". (According to figures published by the Central American Human Rights Commission—Codehuca—in 1985 the 38,000 recorded disappearances in Guatemala since 1978 constituted 42 per cent of the total for Latin America in that period.) The situation in Nicaragua has improved considerably since 1979; although there were some abuses in the first months of FSLN victory, and subsequently some harassment of political opponents, the only recent atrocities have been perpetrated by the contras (see section 3.4.4).

There has been strong international criticism of human rights violations in Central America. For example, on Dec. 15, 1980, the UN General Assembly passed a resolution by 70 votes to 12 (including Guatemala, El Salvador and Costa Rica) with 55 abstentions expressing "deep concern at the grave violations of human rights and fundamental freedoms in El Salvador" and especially the murder of Archbishop Romero and five FDR leaders. The UN Human Rights Commission adopted a resolution on March 8, 1983, by 23 votes to six denouncing "violations of human rights of the most serious nature" in El Salvador, and urging the suspension of foreign aid; the United States, which voted against the resolution, described it as unbalanced in that it "heaps blame on one side and ignores the other". As US involvement in the region increased (particularly its support for the Salvadorean government), so the issue of human rights became one of the central points of disagreement, especially in debates in the US Congress over the continuation of military assistance to the Salvadorean and Guatemalan armed forces.

4.2.2: Guatemala

Violence against detainees, guerrilla suspects and rural villagers began with the counter-insurgency campaign launched in 1966 under Col. Araña. In December 1976 AI stated that over the past 10 years over 20,000 people had

died or disappeared for political reasons at the hands of regular or paramilitary forces, that torture was frequently used and that "extrajudicial detentions and executions" occurred daily; the report concluded that "extensive
official and semi-official violence has not proved effective in curbing violent
opposition, and indeed has induced further violence".

The rate of killings, which had been decreasing from about 1972, rose again
from 1978, to 2,000 between June 1978 and December 1979 and 3,000 in the
first 10 months of 1980 (according to AI estimates), in addition to which
hundreds more disappeared. AI also documented eyewitness accounts of
torture and executions, carried out as part of a "pattern of selective and
considered official action" based on denunciation. Most of the dead had been
associated with religious, community or labour organizations or had had some
contact with political organizations. USAC, described by the Guatemalan
authorities as a "centre of subversion" because of its operation as an advice
centre on labour and civil rights, lost many members (see also section 3.2.2),
and 21 leaders of the National Workers' Central and 24 other trade unionists
were arrested in June and August 1980 respectively. In July 1980 the independent human rights commission dissolved itself, on the grounds that it
would be "suicide" to continue to operate within the country (claiming that
the death toll had reached 15–20 people per day). In October the commission's head, Irma Flaquer, was kidnapped and her son murdered; she was
found in August 1982 alive but clinically insane in an underground cell at the
house of the former interior minister, Donaldo Alvarez Ruiz. (The commission later resumed its work from a headquarters in Mexico.)

With the escalation of the guerrilla campaign and the army counter-
offensive, the emphasis in human rights reports shifted after 1981 to rural
massacres. For example, in January 1982 some 50 villagers from San
Francisco el Tablón (San Marcos department) were abducted, and a few days
later the bodies of 38 of them were found with marks of torture and bullet
wounds; in March 1982 about 200 villagers from near Zacualpa (El Quiché
department) were found with their throats cut. In July 1982 a group of about
500 soldiers on patrol in the mountains was reported to have entered the
village of San Francisco, where they hacked the women and children to death
with machetes before shooting the men, and also the village of Petenac,
where they shot the men and burnt the women and children alive.[1] (The brunt
of these massacres and other rural violence was borne by the Indian peasants
—see section 4.3.2.)

The government claimed that the massacres were committed by the
guerrillas, although it was widely held that the armed forces were responsible,
and there was some confusion with reports of soldiers disguised as guerrillas
and guerrillas disguised as soldiers (carrying out punitive raids in order to turn
communities against the regular army). In October 1982 several thousand
Cakichiquele Indians in the town of San Martín Jilotepeque (near
Chimaltenango) said that they had been threatened with death by soldiers
unless they declared that a previous massacre in the area had been
perpetrated by guerrillas. According to a British newspaper report of March
1983, soldiers often entered a village, seized a local inhabitant, hooded him
and then forced him to identify guerrilla suspects in the community, who were
then beheaded and their heads sent to the local army commander.[2]

The US State Department said in February 1982 that political killings in

Guatemala had reached a rate of 250–300 a month in 1981 (compared with 70–100 a month in 1980), while local church sources put the number at over 900 a month. Although the US administration claimed that the human rights situation had improved under Ríos Montt, such improvement applied only to urban areas, and violence continued unabated in rural areas. According to AI and UN reports, 2,500 people died betwen the March 1982 coup and the end of June (i.e. before the imposition of the state of siege), mostly at the hands of the armed forces. The Latin American organization *Justicia y Paz* (Justice and Peace) estimated the total number of killings between March and the end of September 1982 at 9,000 (out of 100,000 since 1954). In addition, it was reported that the armed forces tortured and mutilated detainees, and even, in some cases, practised cannibalism. (In 1984 an Indian peasant told AI workers that "his uncle had had his fingers, then his hand, then his arm cut off in stages by the army", his story being verified by a local nun.[3])

Foreign workers were also subjected to military violence. In February 1983 four USAID officials were detained by security forces at a roadblock in Huehuetenango and later found dead; the army claimed that they had been shot while trying to escape.[4] The US ambassador, Frederic Chapin, asked to see Ríos Montt, but was told that the general was too busy, and so he was briefly recalled to Washington in a gesture of protest.

In October 1983 the Inter-American Human Rights Commission reported: "Recent information indicating that the violence in rural areas continues, the exodus of the rural population goes on . . . and the violence in urban centres is tending to increase, with signs of the reappearance of death squads. . . . While the commission has no doubt that the guerrillas have committed grave and shameful deeds in these areas of conflict, it also considers the Guatemalan army directly responsible for the violations of the right to life that have occurred in these zones." The US embassy in Guatemala City stated that political violence had claimed the lives of 220 people in October 1983, compared with 163 in September and 98 in August, and at the end of January 1984 the US-based Americas Watch Committee said that killings and kidnappings had increased since the August 1983 coup. (The total number of disappeared since the 1960s was estimated by early 1984 at about 35,000.)

There was a marked increase in political killings after the July 1984 elections, with the total deaths for the year set at up to 3,000. Particular assassinations included those of the vice-president of the PID, Ramiro Quijada Fernández, in September; the sole FUN deputy, Santo Hernández, in October (see also section 1.2.15), probably by left-wing elements; and two USAC teachers and a US peace corps volunteer, also in October. The USAC Higher Council called for an immediate investigation into the killing of its staff, but the government said that those responsible were "communist and subversive" groups at the university wanting to impede the return to constitutionality and harm Guatemala's international reputation.

In March 1985 the British peer Lord Colville of Culross completed a report on Guatemala commissioned by the UN in which he commended the establishment and operation of the model villages and generally detailed an improvement in human rights. (He had visited the country in August 1984 and again in January 1985.) His claims were immediately contradicted by Archbishop Peñados of Guatemala, and the UN Human Rights Commission voted by 28 to three to ignore the report, passing a new resolution on March

14 denouncing human rights abuses in Guatemala (by 32 votes to none with 10 abstentions, including the United States). Lord Colville was criticized in particular because he had conducted his investigation accompanied by two Guatemalan military intelligence officers. In contrast, a report by the UK Parliamentary Human Rights Group (PHRG), headed by Lord Avebury and researched in October 1984, saw no improvement in the situation in Guatemala.[5]

During 1984 disappearances averaged 60 a month and deaths from political violence averaged nearly 50 a month; in 1985 deaths rose to 80 in January and disappearances to 75 in September. The economic crisis of 1985 (see section 2.2.1) led to further civil unrest, and in early September at least 10 people died and over 1,000 were arrested after protests calling for wage increases. At the same time troops again entered USAC buildings, destroying documents and confiscating files, while army units using tanks and helicopters began patrolling the streets of the capital.

A new human rights organization, called the Mutual Support Group (*Grupo Apoyo Mutuo*—GAM), was formed on June 5, 1984, by six women with the aim of helping relatives of the disappeared. By October 1984 some 250 families had joined and a march was staged in the capital by over 1,000 people—the first public demonstration since 1980; by April 1985 the number of member families had risen to 620. In March 1985 Mejía Victores described the group as "subversive", claiming that it was supported by left-wing guerrillas, and within days death threats arrived at the homes of the group's leaders. On March 31 the body of one of the leaders, Héctor Gómez Calito, was found with his tongue and teeth wrenched out. A few days later the group's vice-president and one of the founders Rosario Godoy de Cuevas (whose husband had disappeared in May 1984), was found severely beaten and asphyxiated, along with the bodies of her younger brother and her two-year old son. She was succeeded as the leader of GAM by Nineth Montenegro de García and GAM continued its activities despite harassment. In June 1985 it rejected the findings of a government special commission into 700 cases of kidnappings and disappearance, and in an unprecedented step for Guatemala the group on Aug. 9 presented 862 writs of habeas corpus to the courts (including 702 to the Supreme Court).

It was anticipated that the human rights situation would improve with the inauguration of the Cerezo government in January 1986, and also that moves might be made to bring to account those responsible for human rights violations in recent years. Accordingly, a few hours before Cerezo took office on Jan. 14, the outgoing military government declared "a general amnesty for all persons responsible for . . . or connected with political and common crimes between March 23, 1982 [the date of the Ríos Montt coup], and Jan. 14, 1986", which effectively precluded the possibility of any officers being charged on these grounds. Figures released by the Americas Watch Committee in July 1986 recorded 277 assassinations in the three months April to June, and a total of 120 disappearances in the first six months of the year.

4.2.3: Honduras

Reports of human rights violations in Honduras were first made in the last period of military rule (which ended in 1981). In late 1979 the national episcopal conference excommunicated the members of the junta on human rights grounds, while in May 1980 AI expressed concern over a number of political prisoners, including nine members of the Socialist Party (Paso—a member of the FPH). These complaints accelerated following the appointment of Gen. Alvarez as C.-in-C. of the armed forces, especially after the discovery in early February 1982 of an unmarked grave containing the bodies of 15 men who had been shot.

In September 1982 the PDC accused the government of planning a systematic extermination of opposition leaders (several of whom had already disappeared). In the following month the episcopal conference spoke of "disenchantment in many sectors of the people" at the behaviour of the authorities since the 1981 elections, and warned that "terrorism, dis- appearances, the mysterious discovery of bodies, assaults, thefts, kidnappings [and] individual and collective insecurity all appear to have grown over the past two years". It was widely held that the security forces had compiled a list of about 4,000 names, including some foreigners, who were banned for political reasons from either entering or leaving the country, in which context the president of the independent human rights commission (Codeh), Ramón Custodio López, said in October: "Now we have a sort of religious war to save democracy, in which clandestine imprisonments, disappearances and torture are tolerated." By the beginning of June 1983, 11 trade unionists and left-wing politicans had been killed and another four had disappeared (all of them linked with the National Autonomous University), and according to local human rights groups a total of 42 people had disappeared since Suazo took office in January 1982.

Up to 30,000 people took part in a demonstration held on April 5, 1984, to protest against corruption in the senior military command, and to demand an end to repression, greater justice and the opening of an investigation into the fate of 103 people who had disappeared since January 1982. The bodies of 40 of the disappeared had been discovered in unmarked graves over the past two years, and on May 13, 1984, more corpses were found at two new graves (one in Paraíso department and the other at Limón), apparently having been buried by paramilitary forces between April 15 and 20. Also in May, Custodio López claimed that despite his departure from Honduras for Miami in March, Alvarez continued to direct the death squads, which had killed at least 88 people since January 1982.

Gen. López Reyes (Alvarez's successor) made an effort to improve the reputation of the armed forces, and in August, 1984 sent four officers into exile, including Maj. Alexander Fernández Santos (head of special in- telligence since January 1982) and Capt. Alonso Candes Núñez (also in military intelligence); both were believed to be members of paramilitary groups operating in Alvarez's "dirty war" against the guerrillas. López Reyes also established a commission in June 1984 to investigate the disappearance of 112 people between 1981 and the end of March 1984; although its findings were never published, Codeh and the Committee of Relations of the Dis- appeared (Cofadeh) claimed to have evidence implicating the regular armed forces in these cases. Despite hopes that the situation would improve after Alvarez's departure, Codeh reported that in the first 10 months of 1984 there had been 29 cases of torture (27 since March), 36 political assassinations (15 since March) and 28 disappearances (23 since March), adding that 80 political prisoners were still held and 32 people had "disappeared" temporarily.

One of the people detained by the security forces was Inés Consuelo Murillo, abducted on March 13, 1983, and held without trial for 80 days. During that time she was handcuffed, blindfolded, repeatedly beaten, sexually abused, given electric shocks and shown a picture of herself which had been distributed to security police, calling her a "suspicious foreigner". She was eventually released as a result of pressure from abroad as her mother was a German national.[6]

It was reported in 1985 that during the US–Honduran Cabañas exercises (see section 5.2.3) troops of both nationalities had illegally detained 20 people in the Atlantic coast villages of Jocón, San Lorenzo, Las Lagunas and Olanchito, and a nurse working in the area claimed that she had been physically assaulted by US military personnel. Codeh's 1985 annual report (which appeared early in 1986) stated that six Hondurans who disappeared in 1985 were still missing, and in March 1986 the National Assembly gave its approval to the release of 31 political prisoners, detained illegally by the security forces and denied their legal rights.

4.2.4: El Salvador

In January 1978 an investigatory team from the Inter-American Human Rights Commission visited El Salvador at the invitation of President Molina; it was able not only to inverview families of the disappeared and some former detainees but also to see one of the National Guard secret prisons. At this centre they found torture equipment (including metal bedsprings used for administering electric shocks) and a series of cells, one of which was only a metre high, a metre wide and a metre deep.[7] Their report, which was issued 12 months later, spoke of "secret death places where people whose capture has been denied by the government have been deprived of their freedom in extremely cruel and inhumane conditions"; it urged that a further enquiry be undertaken into the cases of the "dead, detained, tortured and disappeared".

After the October 1979 revolution Archbishop Romero handed the junta a list of 176 people who had disappeared in recent years, and the junta announced on Oct. 18 that Majano (one of its members) had personally supervised the release of 74 of them and that no others were to be found. It was believed that the others, who included Lil Milagro Ramírez (a member of the national leadership of RN, who had disappeared in November 1976, whose name had been observed in the cell found by the OAS team, and who had last been seen just before the coup having suffered starvation, rape, beating and a violent abortion), had been killed by the armed forces to prevent the details of their captivity being publicized. In response to a demand from the Mothers of the Disappeared (see below), Mayorga said: "I'm overwhelmed by the problem. I have no idea where your children are. I pray they are still alive. I just don't know."[8]

Although many hoped that the revolution would bring an end to the violence, there was in fact an increase in political killings in early 1980. *Socorro Jurídico* (Legal Aid)—founded in 1975 by a group of Catholic lawyers to represent the poor in court and recognized as the official human rights body of the Archbishop's office in June 1977—reported that the number of "progressive persons and people from popular sectors" killed by the army, security forces or death squads between October 1979 and April

1980 was about 480, rising to nearly 1,200 by May. The Jesuit University of Central America declared in July 1980 that "the security forces and other organizations, operating under the state of siege, have violently entered schools, national teaching institutes and private colleges, capturing and murdering students, searching the buildings and destroying installations", adding that in the first six months of the year 72 teachers had been killed because "they have become agents of the truth about what is going on in the country". (The *Socorro Jurídico* offices were raided on July 3 by troops who removed signed depositions on human rights abuses and documents on the murder of Archbishop Romero.)

According to church figures 9,000 people died in 1980, many of whom were peasants killed during army operations in outlying areas; according to a document published by the Honduran Church in June, 600 Salvadoreans had been killed (and some tortured) by the armed forces and Orden in Chalatenango in May while trying to escape to Honduras across the Sumpul River (see also section 4.1.4).

After the launch of FMLN military operations in January 1981, the reports of army massacres among the rural population (especially on the Honduran border) increased; many more poeple disappeared under a decree of December 1980, which allowed anyone suspected of crimes against the state to be held incommunicado for up to 180 days and sentenced to four months' corrective detention even if no proof of guilt had been established. At the beginning of April 1981 the army published a list of 138 "traitors to the country", which Duarte claimed was merely a "working paper" which gave people the chance to know that they were under suspicion and clear their names, but was described by the church as a hit list; the list included priests, university staff and former members of the government. Foreign-based relief organizations were also considered subversive by elements of the security forces; in March 1980 the Central American field staff of Oxfam said that in the past year over 300 people working on its aid projects in the country had been killed and that all nine of the projects had been destroyed or suspended; in June a Red Cross worker, Carlos Mandredi Hernández, was found murdered.

Estimates of the death toll for 1981 varied considerably: the independent human rights commission gave 16,276, *Socorro Jurídico* 13,353 and the US embassy 6,116; *Socorro Jurídico* added that 20 per cent of the killings had been committed by left-wing guerrillas, 60 per cent by the armed forces and the remainder by paramilitary forces and death squads. Church sources put the number of dead in 1982 at over 5,000, one official, Mgr Ricardo Urioste, observing that "so many people have now been killed that there are fewer candidates". (The president of the independent human rights commission, Marianella García Villas, was killed in March 1983 after being arrested in La Bermuda—Cuscatlán department—while investigating reports of the use of napalm by the armed forces—see also section 3.3.5; the army claimed that she had been killed in combat, but she was reported to have been arrested the day before she died and her body bore the marks of torture.)

By 1983 there was rising concern among US officials that extrajudicial killings were committed with impunity, ambassador Deane Hinton having pointed out in November 1982 that there had been fewer than 200 convictions for the cases of 30,000 "murdered—not killed in battle" since 1979. In

February 1983, 18 peasant farmers were assassinated apparently as a result of a land dispute arising from the land reform programme (see section 2.3.4), and the local military army commander, Col. Elmer González Araujo, said that the names of eight of the peasants (from Las Hojas co-operative) had been on a list of subversives. A judicial investigation was set up, but the appointed judge resigned and was not replaced.

Socorro Jurídico reported that 4,800 people died in military operations during 1983, that 3,658 more were selectively assassinated by the armed forces, 1,596 by the paramilitary death squads and 68 by the guerrillas; it also maintained that 938 were imprisoned by security forces for political reasons, that 526 had disappeared and that 43 had been kidnapped by the guerrillas.[9] The office added that there had been a marked increase in death-squad activity in the second half of the year, with a greater general level of violence than in 1982. There were also a number of reports of massacres by the army in 1983. In late August church sources confirmed that in July units of the Atlacatl battalion had killed 68 civilians during an offensive in Cabañas department.

During 1984 a total of 3,418 civilians died in the fighting (according to Mgr Rosa Chávez), a further 2,506 were assassinated, 2,000 new refugees fled to Honduras, and there were 121 documented cases of torture in military prisons in the four months from June to September 1984, by early 1985 the death toll over the past five years had exceeded 50,000. On Jan. 6, 1985, Rivera y Damas stated that "an atmosphere of threats and political killings has returned", citing as an example the murder that day of Pedro Rene Yánez, the head of a special investigatory commission on human rights, by a local Arena party member. (Yánez had recently accused Arena leaders of illegal business practices.)

The Committee of Mothers of the Disappeared (*CoMadres*) continued to campaign on behalf of the disappeared, habitually dressing in black clothing, white headscarves and dark glasses, and staged the first political demonstration to be held in the country for four years on Nov. 5, 1984. It was attended by 3,000 people and although no-one was arrested at the time (possibly because the American television organization CBS was filming it) the security forces tracked down and detained several of the participants over the next few days. The Americas Watch committee reported in mid–1985 that the number of murders attributable to death squads was higher in the first six months of 1985—at about 60—than in the same period of 1984.

Human rights first emerged as a major point of issue between the US administration and the Salvadorean government with the rape and murder in the first week of December 1980 of four US missionaries: Sister Dorothy Kazel, Sister Ita Ford, Sister Maura Clarke and Jean Donovan (see also section 1.4.13). On the basis of the work of an investigatory commission the US State Department published a report on Dec. 23, saying that it was "very probable" that local Salvadorean authorities had tried to cover up the crimes. Six national guardsmen were arrested in connection with the murders in April 1981 and proceedings against them opened in February 1982, during which the judge ruled that there was sufficient evidence to hold five of them on charges of "aggravated homicide". Their trial opened in November 1982, but the following March the case was adjourned on the grounds that insufficient evidence had been presented on the charges of rape and robbery (although evidence on the count of murder was adequate).

After strong pressure from US officials the trial was resumed in May 1984, and the five were convicted and sentenced to terms of up to 100 years' imprisonment (reduced to 30 under the new constitution). During the trial the guardsman who had originally confessed to the crimes attempted to retract his confession, claiming that it had been extracted under torture and that US officials had threatened the defendants and offered them bribes to confess. Also in May the US State Department said that there had definitely been an attempt by senior officers to conceal evidence of the crimes, maintaining that Gen. Vides Casanova was quite possibly "aware of, and for a time acquiesced in, a cover-up".

The other major source of contention was the murder on Jan. 3, 1981, of the president of ISTA, José Rodolfo Viera (who had denounced corruption in the army in a recent television broadcast), and of his two US assistants, Michael Hammer and Mark Pearlman in the coffee shop of the Sheraton Hotel in San Salvador. (Viera was also a leading member of the pro-government and US-supported UCS; Hammer and Pearlman were AIFLD officials and possibly also CIA agents.)[10] In September 1982 two national guardsmen were indicted for these murders; they confessed and said that they had been acting on the orders of Lt. Rodolfo López Sibrián (a former security aide to d'Aubuisson) and Capt. Eduardo Avila (a member of Orden—see section 3.2.3). The judge ordered the detention of these two officers, but ruled in October 1982 that there was insufficient evidence to hold López Sibrián; moreover, although Avila was arrested in December, it was only for a minor infringement of military regulations and he was released in January 1983. He was called to give evidence at the trial of the guardsmen, but under Salvadorean law their testimony against him was inadmissable because they had confessed to the murders. In April 1983 the prosecutors were given a year to produce any new evidence against López Sibrián, and when they failed to do so he was cleared by an appeals court in May 1984. (In January 1985 he was dismissed from the army by Duarte, and on March 31, 1986, he was one of 20 people arrested by police investigating a series of kidnaps of wealthy businessmen by a group connected with the armed forces and Arena.)

Although the progress made in prosecuting those responsible for these crimes was relatively moderate, and made only after persistent US pressure, there was a marked difference between these cases and domestic crimes. As Rivera y Damas remarked in April 1983: "Curiously, in the cases of North American citizens elements belonging to the security forces have been detained, while in the cases of hundreds of assassinated Salvadoreans very rarely has justice been done."

One example of the pressure brought to bear by the US administration was the visit of Vice-President George Bush to El Salvador in December 1983, when he warned that the United States would withdraw its support for the government unless action were taken against the death squads. A few days later a group of 31 senior officers issued a statement denouncing the death squads and calling for civilian help in identifying and capturing those involved in them. Bush also presented a list of demands to the government, including the names of 25 people who should be sent into exile, but in January 1984 Magaña said that the government had no authority to order them abroad as they preferred to stay in the country and risk facing possible investigation.

(During his visit Bush was also careful to underline the basis of US support for the government, declaring: "El Salvador and the United States share many common values; both of our societies are determined to resist communist aggression.")

It was hoped in some quarters that the inauguration of the Duarte government in June 1984 would lead to an improvement in the human rights situation, especially when in August a presidential commission was established to investigate political killings. This commission may have helped to instigate a move reported on Aug. 21, 1985, in which a court ordered the reopening of the case relating to the murder of Archbishop Romero, and to the conviction on Feb. 13, 1986, of the two national guardsmen (José Dimas Valle Acevedo and Santiago Gómez González—both now demobilized) who had confessed to the murders of Viera, Hammer and Pearlman. The commission did not, however, achieve any direct results, and was disbanded in November 1985.

In Resolution 40/139, passed on Dec. 13, 1985, on the basis of a specially-compiled UN report, the UN General Assembly condemned the continuation of grave human rights violations in El Salvador, and asserted that, despite the Salvadorean government's promotion of respect for civil rights, the situation had not substantially altered. In particular, the report censored the army's use of indiscriminate aerial bombardment, the prevention of the supply of food and medical services to the civilian population by humanitarian organizations and the army's practice of burning crops and houses in an attempt to erode support for the FMLN. According to *Socorro Jurídico*, the number of politically-motivated deaths rose from 402 in 1984 to 1,655 in 1985, and arbitrary arrests and disappearances rose from 402 to 777. Early in 1986 the Ministry of Justice disclosed that there were currently 4,373 prisoners being held, only 407 of whom had been tried and convicted.

In May and June 1986 several members of *CoMadres* were abducted by security forces, including one of the group's leaders, Laura Pinto, who was seized on May 9 and held for two days, only to be seized again on May 29. On the first occasion she reported having been tortured, raped, beaten and stabbed, and others also reported being tortured. This spate of arrests was apparently connected with an allegation made by a member of the independent human rights commission, that humanitarian organizations had been infiltrated by the FMLN. (Several of those detained reported being photographed signing depositions which they had not been allowed to read.) In its May 1986 report on the country the Americas Watch Committee claimed that "torture remains a serious problem in El Salvador" and "consists increasingly of physical abuse which does not leave physical marks".

4.2.5: Nicaragua

The Inter-American Human Rights Commission published a report on Nicaragua in November 1978. One of its most critical assessments to date, the report detailed the extensive use of torture, obstruction of the work of the ICRC, "summary and mass executions" and "generalized repression against all young men between the ages of 14 and 21". Two months previously the Nicaraguan alternate representative at the UN, Enrique Paguaga, had resigned his post and denounced the Nicaraguan government for its "genocide".

In the first weeks after the July 1979 revolution there were reports of some collective executions in the southern and eastern parts of the country made by the independent human rights commision (which said, however, that it was not accusing the government of human rights violations); in November 1979 the new leadership admitted that there had been many abuses of power, including torture and murder, since July. The Inter-American Human Rights Commission issued a report in August 1981 which stated that although there continued to be unjustifiable limitations on political, judicial and press rights, the extreme abuses of human rights in Nicaragua had been virtually eliminated. Subsequently the main allegations have been US protests over the relocation of the Miskito population (see section 4.3.3), although the government was strongly criticized in Nicaragua and abroad for breaches of civil liberty after the reintroduction of the state of emergency in October 1985 (see section 1.5.29).

An AI report published on Feb. 12, 1986, detailed persistent abuses by the US-backed contra forces, specifically torture, mutilation and execution of prisoners; it also criticized the Nicaraguan government for its imposition of repeated short prison sentences on its political opponents. (The report noted some abuses on the part of some officials in rural areas, but added that in most cases those responsible had been tried and sentenced.) The National Assembly voted on June 3, 1986, to grant pardons to 108 political prisoners, currently held in connection with offences ranging from acts deemed to threaten national security to murder; this was in response to a request from the National Commission for the Promotion and Protection of Human Rights for the exoneration of some 300 prisoners. The US government, however, continued to accuse the Sandinistas of severe abuses, and in June 1986 the Americas Watch Committee said that while all parties in the Nicaraguan conflict were to blame for its recent deterioration, the US government was culpable of "providing false information" on contra abuses (by under-playing them) and also of making unsubstantiated allegations of human rights offences by the Nicaraguan authorities.

Notes

1. For details of main reported massacres 1975–82, see Pearce, *op. cit.*, pp. 196–98 and 275; for massacres in August–October 1983, see *Amnesty*, No. 8, April/May 1984, p. 5.
2. *Sunday Times*, March 20, 1983.
3. *Amnesty*, No. 13, February/March 1985, p. 14.
4. For disappearance of other USAID members in Guatemala, see *Amnesty*, No. 8, April/May 1984, p. 4.
5. Entitled "Bitter and Cruel" and published with the support of War on Want, the report is available from PHRG, c/o CAHRC, 20 Compton Terrace, London, N1 2UN.
6. *Central America Report*, Issue 19, November/December 1984, p. 8.
7. Armstrong and Shenk, *op. cit.*, pp. 106–07.
8. *Ibid.*, pp. 124–25.
9. For calendar of assassinations, disappearances and detentions in June–October 1983, see *Amnesty*, No. 7, February/March 1984, p. 24.
10. *Ibid.*; see also Michael J. Sussman, *AIFLD: US Trojan Horse in Latin America and the Caribbean*, Special Report published July 1983 by EPICA, 1470 Irving St, N.W. Washington, DC 20010 (in English and Spanish); including a special section on El Salvador.

4.3: THE INDIAN QUESTION

4.3.1: Historical Background

The Spanish conquest had a devastating effect on the civilization of the Central American region, not only because of the number of Indians who died (largely through European diseases to which they had no immunity), but also because of the racist attitudes of the colonists. In order to be allowed to go to the New World Spaniards had to present a certificate of their "cleanness of blood", and throughout Latin America upward social mobility became related to "bleaching out" of the family line, i.e. avoiding inter-marriage with those of Indian stock. Moreover, the mixed-blood Ladinos, who became numerically dominant during the colonial period, also regarded themselves as superior to the pure Indians, being generally more aggressive and outwardly-oriented.[1]

By the 16th century the only Central American Indians with a high degree of "political" organization were those of what subsequently became Guatemala, where to this day the 21 Maya-descended groups have retained the strongest cultural identity of any Indian group in the region, with their own languages and in certain areas their traditional religious practices and annual calendars. (The main linguistic groups are the Chui, Kanjobal, Jacalteca, Ixil, Kekchi, Aguacateca, Uspanteca, Pokomchi, Mam, Quiché, Cakchiquel, Tzutuhil and Pokomán.[2]) The next largest Indian group is that of El Salvador, but those who managed to survive *La Matanza* of 1932 (during which President Martínez is said to have ordered his troops to kill any peasant seen dressed in Indian costume) have tended to abandon their distinctive cultural traits, and have gained no separate official recognition.

In Honduras, Nicaragua, Costa Rica, Panama and Belize the Indian population (including those of mixed Afro-Caribbean descent down the Caribbean coast, who were largely ignored by the Spanish) is comparatively small and concentrated in isolated communities. In Costa Rica and Panama special government provision has recognized Indian rights to land, and Indian organizations have themselves petitioned for greater guarantees,[3] while in Belize the number of indigenous Indians has been swelled by an influx of Guatemalan and Salvadorean Indians. The predominant black Carib (Garifuna) group is the Miskitos, who from the 17th century had more contacts with the British than either the Spanish or latterly the Central Americans, and who, because of the influence of German missionaries, became Moravian Protestants by religion. As a recent commentator has observed, it was "probably only an accident of history that 'Mosquitia' did not become, like Belize, a separate and predominantly Anglo–Caribbean state in the region".[4] (Mosquitia was cut into two parts by the resolution of the border dispute between Honduras and Nicaragua in 1960, which set the frontier along the River Coco—see section 3.4.1.)

By the 1980s official figures for the Indian population in the region were: Guatemala 2,700,000 (38 per cent of the total), although unofficial statistics gave the total as at least 3,600,000 (comprising 50 per cent of the total); Belize 15,000 (10 per cent); Honduras 250,000 (7 per cent); El Salvador 960,000 (20 per cent); Nicaragua 135,000 (5 per cent); Costa Rica 20,000 (0.1 per cent); and Panama 100,000 (5 per cent).[5]

This section deals in some detail with the Indians in Guatemala as well as with the Miskitos in Nicaragua, who after centuries of indifference from the authorities in the west of the country came into conflict with the government after the 1979 revolution.

4.3.2: Guatemala

In a report published in September 1979 the International Commission of Jurists (ICJ) stated that the Guatemalan government was currently waging a "campaign of systematic oppression" in which the Indians were the main victims; according to the report, they had been subjected to "inhumane methods of conscription", thrown off their land, placed at the mercy of money-lenders and many "eventually physically eliminated" with the help of military police. In October 1984 the World Council of Indigenous Peoples accused the Mejía Victores government of pursuing a "policy of systematic extermination" of the Indian population. Moreover, the Indians suffered from discrimination in the allocation of services, notably health: "Life expectancy among Indians is 16 years lower than that of Ladinos—45 years compared to 61.4. Indigenous infant mortality might be as high as 100 per 1,000 live births. . . . Doctors working with Indians claim that virtually all are malnourished, anaemic and suffering from parasites."[6]

Indians have borne the brunt of army counter-insurgency operations, because for the most part these have been directed towards crushing the guerrillas' rural bases (centred on the poorest peasants, i.e. the Indians—see section 3.3.2). Thousands of Indians died in massacres carried out by the army and security forces in the early 1980s, and many more have fled to refugee camps in Mexico. For example, in June 1980 about 100 Indian peasants disappeared from the Tiquisate sugar plantations and 12 months later all but six of the 42 inhabitants of the village of San Mateo Ixatán (Huehuetenango deparment) were killed by armed men in what was believed to be a punitive raid following EGP recruitment in the area.

The guerrillas have appreciated the importance of support among the Indian population; as FAR leader César Montes commented in 1967: "We know that it is the Indians, half the population, who will determine the outcome of the revolution in this country . . ., but there are four centuries of justified Indian distrust of Ladinos."[7] During the late 1970s Indians in rural areas and urban slums began to organize, joining the CUC (part of FP–31—see section 3.1.2) and the National Committee of Trade Union Unity (CNUS) and staging strikes and demonstrations in pursuit of improved working conditions. At the same time the army, which had previously been 95 per cent conscripted from the Indian population, began to find difficulty recruiting the Indians and started to take Ladinos, reinforcing the racial aspects of the war.[8] Conscription had been used as a means to erode Indian culture, just as the "model villages" (see section 3.3.2) were later used to try to replace ethnic by national identity: "Although some Indian boys do return to their communities after service, recruitment has to be generally considered the most brutal form of ladinoization in Guatemala as well as yet another infraction of Indian rights. After being kidnapped in a local *cupo* (grab), indigenous conscripts are brutalized until capable of administering the same treatment themselves."[9]

In its sweeps on Indian villages the army reportedly made deliberate attempts to eradicate Indian culture by burning the villagers' maize (which not only provided their staple diet but also had a religious significance) and destroying the looms used for making traditional Indian clothes, making many Indians afraid to wear these clothes in case there were identified as "subversives".

4.3.3: Nicaragua

In 1964 the British relief organization Oxfam began work among Miskitos displaced by the 1960 border resolution, reporting that the incidence of tuberculosis was four times the national average and that 80 per cent of the population suffered from internal parasites and malaria. The area had also become an economic backwater because of the banana plagues of the 1930s, depletion of forest by the 1950s, exhaustion of mineral resources and over-fishing. (The Atlantic coast region covers 56 per cent of national territory but contains only 9 per cent of the population.) According to the newspaper *Barricada* (June 12, 1985) the Atlantic coast community comprised 120,000 *mestizos* (i.e. mixed blood), 70,000 Miskitos, 25,000 creoles or negro creoles, 15,000 Sumos, 1,200 Black Caribs and 800 Ramas.

The Miskitos were mostly untouched by the Somoza regime and so did not participate in the revolution against him: "To the Miskitos, the difference between the FSLN [as a guerrilla group] and Somoza's Guard was hazy. Both wore olive green uniforms and carried guns; neither could communicate with the sparse local population."[10] They subsequently resented the efforts of the Sandinista government to intervene in their lives, as although this intervention offered improved infrastructure and novelties such as electricity it also meant the imposition of Spanish culture, most obviously in the literacy campaign (see section 1.5.23), which was conducted entirely in Spanish. (The Miskitos spoke an English-based language.) In an attempt to improve relations and to provide a forum for dialogue, an organization was set up called Misurasata (*Miskito, Sumo, Rama, Sandinista, Asla Takanka*—Miskito, Sumo, Rama, Sandinista, All Together—see also section 3.1.5.)

By the end of 1980 there were anti-government riots in the region and demands for the recognition of the separate identity of the Zelaya region. The ministry of education initiated a literacy project in the local languages to be celebrated by a festival held on Feb. 28, 1981, but cancelled the festival when it was discovered that Misurasata planned to use the occasion to stage a protest calling for the demarcation of an Indian area, administered by a special local council and having extra seats on the Council of State, and possibly even representation on the junta. Three Miskitos died in clashes with security forces at Prinzapolca on Feb. 21, and three Misurasata leaders (including Fagoth Müller) were detained and accused of having been security agents for Somoza; Fagoth Müller was released provisionally several weeks later and fled to Honduras in May to join the contras (see section 3.1.5). During 1981 about 2,500 other Miskitos fled to the Mosquitia region of Honduras (Cape Gracias a Dios), and by August 1982 the total number of Miskitos in Honduras had risen to 20,000 (see also section 4.1.3).

In January 1982 the Sandinista government ordered the evacuation of between 8,500 and 10,000 people living on the banks of the Coco river "in order to protect them from the armed aggressions of contra groups operating with impunity from Honduran territory" (with reference to a contra assault on Puerto Cabezas), and accused some of the Miskitos of having encouraged some of these "aggressions". During the evacuation to camps further south, some Miskitos fled to Honduras, making substantial allegations of human rights violations by the government. (These claims were taken up by the US administration and on March 1 Jeane Kirkpatrick, then US ambassador at the United Nations, asserted that the abuses were "more massive than any other human rights violation that I am aware of in Central America today".) The Sandinista government in fact conceded that it had made some misjudgments in its dealings with the Miskitos, and Oxfam commented that "whilst criticism must be made of the handling of the situation, Oxfam feels that genuine efforts were made to help the 8,000 or more Miskitos who were resettled", pointing to government attempts to provide housing, agricultural and public health services at Tasba Pri.[11] The evacuation caused further controversy when in December 1982 a helicopter crashed while carrying mainly Miskito villagers from San Andrés Bocay, Anaca, Yakalpanani and Walaskitan (in Jinotega department) to camps near Managua, killing nine adults and all but three of the 78 children on board; the Nicaraguan authorities blamed the contras for shooting down the helicopter.

It was reported in Managua in December 1983 that the Bishop of Bluefields, Mgr Salvador Schlaeffer, had been kidnapped by a group of contras and taken to Honduras with a group of Miskitos (and possibly killed); it was later discovered that he had been at the Franca Zirpe camp in Zelaya Norte and had voluntarily accompanied over 1,000 Miskitos fleeing to Honduras on a march organized by Misurasata. Schlaeffer used the publicity given to the incident in the capital to make a plea for greater respect for the Indian communities from the Nicaraguan government.

In a report issued on June 7, 1984, the Inter-American Human Rights Commission said that the Nicaraguan government's treatment of the Miskito population had made "significant advances", although some abuses persisted, such as forced relocation, arbitrary detention and a few cases of torture or killing in reprisal for the killing of EPS members by the contras. A report by the Spanish Human Rights Association published in September 1984 also expressed dissatisfaction over the treatment of the Miskitos, while noting that Nicaragua had greater respect for human rights than many other countries in Central America.

A government initiative to improve relations with the Miskito population led to the formation on July 24, 1984, of the Misatán movement at a meeting in Puerto Cabezas attended by delegates from 63 communities. The prime objective of the new organization (which demanded the recognition of Miskito as the second national language) was to replace Misurasata as the official channel of communication between the Indians and the government.

In 1985 there was a rift in the Miskito community, caused largely by Rivera's negotiations with the Sandinista government (see sections 3.1.5 and 6.3.3), and in August Rivera was expelled from the official tribal community. (Fagoth Müller was also expelled because he had kidnapped 12 Misura members and accused them of treason.) Rivera and Fagoth Müller were therefore excluded from a meeting on Aug. 31–Sept. 3, 1985, designed to unite Misurasata and Misura in a new organization, KISAN (the Nicaraguan Communities Union), which was led by Diego Wykliffe. (KISAN subsequently joined the contra umbrella organization UNO[12]—see section 3.1.5—but later suffered a split similar to that in Misurasata—see below.) In March and April 1986 there was a large-scale migration of Miskitos from northern Nicaragua across the border into Honduras; the government initially gave the figure of 2,500, all of whom had, it claimed, been abducted by KISAN, but the figure was later revised to 9,000. The military commander of Zelaya Norte said that some Miskitos had moved voluntarily, although KISAN had certainly brought pressure to bear on them. (The Americas Watch Committee asserted that the exodus had been orchestrated by US authorities to invoke a public condemnation of the Nicaraguan government and so increase support for the current request to Congress for further financial aid to the contras—see section 5.2.5.)

The Nicaraguan government had made a conciliatory gesture towards the Miskitos by its announcement in May 1985 that legislation would be presented to the National Assembly in October to provide for Atlantic Coast autonomy. According to Borge, this autonomy would "give equality of rights to each ethnic group, so that they elect their own authorities, have access to land and natural resources, conduct education in their own language and exercise their religious convictions". In addition, the government said that the Miskitos displaced in 1982 would be allowed to return to their homelands from July 1986, although because of transport difficulties this process was expected to take up to two years.

In March 1986 Misatán reached an agreement with certain factions of KISAN (i.e. those willing to negotiate with the government), which led to the establishment of the Atlantic Coast Commission for Justice, Peace and Unity. This commission would be able to convene community meetings and join peace talks with the government, and members agreed on April 14 to the following principles: (i) economic, political, social and cultural equality for coastal residents; (ii) genuine national unity based on respect for the intrinsic rights of each distinct social group; (iii) preservation of cultural identity and development of a new self-image of a people free from domination; and (iv) a global view of the problems affecting the Atlantic Coast, and determination to resolve the conflict.

Notes

1. Woodward, *op. cit.*, pp. 23–24.
2. See *Central America's Indians*, Minority Rights Group, Report No. 62, 1984, p. 10, for linguistic map.
3. *Ibid.*, pp. 6–7.
4. *Ibid.*, p. 6.
5. *Ibid.*, p. 4.
6. *Ibid.*, p. 12.
7. Quoted in Black, *Garrison Guatemala*, p. 77.
8. Pearce, *op. cit.*, p. 192.
9. *Central America's Indians*, p. 13.
10. Black, *Triumph of the People*, p. 78.
11. Melrose, *op. cit.*, pp. 29–31.
12. *The Times*, Oct. 28, 1986, carried a photograph of KISAN's military leader, Adán Artola, displaying an arsenal apparently purchased with supposedly non-lethal US aid.

SECTION FIVE

FOREIGN INVOLVEMENT IN CENTRAL AMERICA

5.1: US POLICY

5.1.1: Introductory

The scale of US military and economic interest in Central America (often referred to as the United States' "own backyard") has made US policy in the region an important factor in the political development of the separate countries. The fears expressed, and action taken, by successive US administrations over communist—and specifically Cuban—influence in the Caribbean Basin have evoked repeated comparisons to US policy in Vietnam. In direct contrast to the stance taken by the Contadora Group (see section 6.5.1), the Central American Church and many other regional and international bodies, the United States has continued to give priority to its perceived security interests over supporting political and social reform in the region. As Kirkpatrick said in 1980: "If we are confronted with the choice between offering assistance to a moderately repressive autocratic government which is also friendly to the United States, and permitting it to be overrun by a Cuban-trained, Cuban-armed, Cuban-sponsored insurgency, we would assist the moderate autocracy."

In July 1958 Milton Eisenhower (brother of the President, and president of the Johns Hopkins University) travelled to all six Central American countries, and submitted a report urging: (i) "the imperative need for loans —not grants—in every country visited"; (ii) an adequate US response "to the appeal of the Latin American nations for more stable relationships between raw commodity prices and the prices of manufactured products"; and (iii) "the urgent and immediate need to bring about throughout the hemisphere a clear, accurate understanding of US policies, purposes, programmes and capabilities". It was not, however, until after the Castro revolution that Kennedy's Alliance for Progress was launched (see section 1.1.11), seeking to introduce moderate reforms with the basic aim of preventing a spread of Cuban influence, just as Reagan's Caribbean Basin Initiative (CBI—see section 5.2.9) of two decades later sought to limit the influence of the Nicaraguan and Grenadan revolutions.

This policy of encouraging reform met with only limited success. After a tour of Mexico and Central America in 1969, Nelson E. Rockefeller (governor of New York) said in a report issued in November of that year that the United States had allowed its "special relationship" with those countries to "deteriorate badly". He concluded that the Latin American nations were a "tempting target for communist subversion" and that it was "evident that such subversion is a reality today with alarming potential". Little notice was taken, however, and in May 1977 Zbigniew Brzezinski (presidential assistant for national security affairs) warned that "American longer range interests would be harmed by continuing indifference to the mounting desire in Central America for greater social justice and national dignity, as our indifference will only make it easier for Castro's Cuba to exploit that desire".

The persistent concern of successive US administrations that social revolution in one Central American state would trigger a chain reaction in the region, even including Mexico (the "domino theory"), came to the forefront of US policy after the Nicaraguan revolution of 1979, which altered the balance in the region. Certain Washington circles took the view that President Carter had allowed the FSLN to gain power by maintaining traditional US support for Somoza for too long and by vacillating, and that the same thing must not be allowed to happen elsewhere, and particularly in El Salvador. The election of Reagan was followed by an upsurge of US confidence in the administration's foreign policy and in its ability to achieve results. There were rumours of an imminent direct US military intervention in the region, although in a television interview given in March 1981 Reagan said in reply to a question that he saw no "parallels at all" between US policy towards El Salvador and the first phase of US military aid to South Vietnam, and "no likelihood" of US forces being sent to El Salvador.

By mid-1981 it became clear that the war against the FMLN had not been won (and had in fact only just started), whereafter the emphasis of US policy shifted from concentration on El Salvador to seeking to undermine the Sandinistas in Nicaragua by supporting the contras. Stopping short of a full intervention in the region, the US began a series of joint military manoeuvres with Honduras (and some Salvadorean troops—see section 5.2.3) which ensured their continuous presence near both the Salvadorean and Nicaraguan borders. (As early as November 1981 Edwin Meese, presidential counsellor, stated that there would be no deployment of US "military ground forces" against Nicaragua but refused to rule out the prospect of a naval blockade of the country.)

When Reagan visited Costa Rica and Honduras in December 1982 (as part of a tour which also included Brazil and Colombia), he announced that his aim was to strengthen the "three principles" of democracy, the inter-American system and regional development; however, the visit was viewed in certain quarters as an effort to boost arm sales and military links with Latin America and to isolate Nicaragua diplomatically. Reagan denied this latter charge, saying "we do not seek to isolate [Nicaragua] . . ., it is isolating itself by acting in this fashion" and adding that he found it "totally unacceptable that Nicaragua forms a base for sending arms into neighbouring countries". (In the course of this visit Reagan also met the Salvadorean and Guatemalan presidents, and initiated the resumption of US military aid to Guatemala —see section 5.2.2.)

The thrust of the domino theory was that unrest in Central America could pose a direct threat to the United Stateas, as expressed by Reagan in a speech made in March 1983: "Central America is simply too close, and the strategic stakes too high, for us to ignore the danger of governments seizing power there with ideological ties to the Soviet Union. . . . [If the FMLN were to win,] El Salvador would join Cuba and Nicaragua as a base for spreading fresh violence to Guatemala, Honduras [and] even Costa Rica. . . . The killing will increase and so too will the threat to Panama, the Canal and ultimately Mexico." A month later he expanded this point in his address to the joint congressional session, saying: "Central America's problems do directly affect the security and well-being of our own people", particularly as "two-thirds of all our foreign trade and petroleum pass through the Panama Canal and the Caribbean." On the same occasion he indicated that US ability to exert a measure of control on events in Central America was also an important element in its whole foreign policy: "If Central America were to fall, what would the consequences be for our position in Asia and Europe, and for alliances such as NATO? If the United States cannot respond to a threat near to our own borders, why should Europeans or Asians believe we are seriously concerned about threats to them?"

5.1.2: Policy on El Salvador

The Sandinista victory in Nicaragua gave encouragement to the popular organizations in El Salvador, and by September 1979 a new slogan had been coined, declaring: "*Si Nicaragua venció, El Salvador vencerá*" (If Nicaragua has triumphed, then El Salvador will triumph). The October 1979 coup and the installation of a more reformist regime did not satisfy the aspirations of the left-wing forces, especially since it was welcomed by the US administration, which recognized the new government on Oct. 23 and, in the words of US ambassador Frank Devine, viewed the new junta as "a much more acceptable international symbol for us" and as offering "some hope of easing the country's problems".[1]

By mid-1980, however, there were doubts among US officials about the viability of the junta as a reforming government in control of the extreme right, especially in view of Archbishop Romero's assassination. In December 1980 Devine's successor, Robert White, protested that his authority to carry out the policy of the outgoing Carter administration had been weakened by a report prepared by a transition team, describing him as a "reformer" and likely to be removed. He added that "a lot of pressure" was being brought to bear on the junta to move to the right politically and that the transition team's report would "strike a heavy blow at the Christian Democrats and moderate military officers seeking a constitutional centrist solution".

In January 1981 White again protested over the resumption of "lethal" military assistance to the Salvadorean government (see section 5.2.4), which had given him no reason to believe that it was conducting "a serious investigation" into the death of the four missionaries the previous month (see section 4.2.4); a few days later he was recalled to Washington. Speaking to the House of Representatives appropriations sub-committee in February, he said that he considered social reform and "political reconciliation" to be the only way to defeat the guerrillas and that the new military equipment from United States would simply allow the armed forces to "assassinate and kill in a totally uncontrolled way".

El Salvador was one of the major concerns of the Reagan administration during its first months, and in February 1981 Lawrence Eagleburger (assistant secretary of state for European affairs) travelled to West Germany, Belgium, France, Britain and the Netherlands to seek European support for the administration's policy. He based his arguments on documents allegedly captured from guerrilla groups and the PCS in November 1980 and January 1981, which he said showed that over the past year "the insurgency in El Salvador has been progressively transformed into a textbook case of indirect armed aggression by communist power through Cuba". (Later the accuracy of this "evidence" was questioned—see section 5.3.4.) Eagleburger also said he had "documentary evidence" of Nicaraguan co-operation with Cuba in the shipment of arms to El Salvador.

That support for the Salvadorean government remained a cornerstone of

US policy in the region was made clear by Thomas Enders, who said in early 1981 that the United States "is not going to allow a military triumph of the [Salvadorean] guerrillas" and had "the means and the desire to do so, irrespective of the political cost".[2] The complementary assertion came to be that the FMLN had no popular base within El Salvador but was entirely inspired by the Sandinistas, as William Casey, director of the CIA, claimed in March 1982: "This whole El Salvador insurgency is run out of Managua by professionals experienced in directing guerrilla wars."

The US Defence Department disclosed on Feb. 24, 1982, that for the past two months the navy had stationed a destroyer equipped with electronic surveillance devices in international waters off the Pacific coast of Nicaragua and El Salvador to monitor alleged arms shipments across the Gulf of Fonseca. In March Haig told the House of Representatives appropriations sub-committee that a "Nicaraguan military man" had been captured in Salvadorean territory helping to direct guerrilla operations; this evidence could not be used, however, as the man later sought asylum in the Mexican embassy in San Salvador, which subsequently reported that he was simply a student on his way home from holiday when arrested by the Salvadorean authorities. The same month another Nicaraguan detained in El Salvador, where he was reported to have admitted to being sent to train guerrillas, was flown to Washington to give his testimony to a press conference, but he unexpectedly told the reporters instead that he had no knowledge of any such involvement and that his earlier statement had been made under coercion by the Salvadorean authorities.

The announcement of three new appointments within the US administration in March 1983 indicated the adoption of a more hardline approach in the region: Enders was replaced as assistant secretary of state for inter-American affairs by Langhorne Anthony Motley; Richard B. Stone was appointed to the new post of US special envoy to Central America, despite opposition arising from the fact that he had been a paid official of the Guatemalan government in 1981–82, charged with trying to gain US aid for Guatemala; and Deane Hinton, who had succeeded White as US ambassador in San Salvador, was in turn replaced by Thomas Pickering. Like White, Hinton had become critical of US policy in El Salvador and of the Salvadorean government; in a speech to the Salvadorean Chamber of Commerce in October 1982 he had said that "neither internal confidence nor external support can long survive here in the absence of an effective system of criminal justice", threatened that US aid could be withdrawn if the situation did not improve, and warned that "the gorillas of this mafia, every bit as much as the guerrillas in Morazán and Chalatenango, are destroying El Salvador". (He was reported to have been censured by his government for this speech.) Stone resigned in February 1984 because of a personality clash with Motley, and was replaced by Harry W. Shlaudeman (executive director of the Kissinger Commission—see 5.1.4), who was in turn replaced by Philip Habib in March 1986.

Although Stone met Zamora of the FDR for talks in July 1983 (see section 6.4.3), the main focus of US policy in 1983 and 1984 was not negotiations with the political opposition and guerrillas, but the promotion of elections, and thereafter solid support for the Duarte government.

5.1.3: Relations with Nicaragua

Relations between the Sandinista government and the United States, strained but not critical in the first 18 months after the 1979 revolution, deteriorated sharply with the inauguration of Reagan in January 1981 and the imposition of the first US economic sanctions against Nicaragua (see section 5.2.5). On the Nicaraguan side, the major cause of antagonism was US support for the contras, fuelled by the long-standing anti-American sentiment of Sandino's followers—a legacy of the US military intervention of 1912–33 (see section 1.5.4) and of the subsequent US support for the Somozas.

When a report appeared in the *New York Times* on March 17, 1981, that former National Guards were undergoing training in Miami, the Nicaraguan government sent a protest note to Washington requesting that it be halted; however, the US administration responded that the groups were on private property and could not therefore be removed. After the suspension of US aid at the beginning of April 1981, the FSLN directorate said that the US arms interdiction campaign was an "infamous pretext to cover up the aggressive and ultra-reactionary foreign policy being applied by the United States throughout the region", especially as the US government had introduced "fabulous quantities of weapons, resources and military personnel" into the Caribbean.

US policy on Nicaragua aroused far more domestic concern than the administration's support for the Salvadorean government. In November 1981 the House of Representatives foreign affairs sub-committee asked for an assurance that the United States was not participating "and will not participate in, nor encourage in any way, direct or indirect efforts to over-throw or destabilize the current regime in Nicaragua". Secretary of State Haig replied: "No, I would not give you such an assurance", adding that his reply "must not be interpreted by mischievous inquisitors as articulation of our policy one way or the other".

Increasingly the United States stopped calling merely for the cessation of Nicaraguan arms supplies to the FMLN and instead for a change in the policies of the government; Reagan began to refer to the contras as "freedom fighters", comparing them with America's founding fathers, and said that relations could be healed if the Sandinistas would "say uncle" (i.e. say "sorry"). Enders claimed in April 1983 that "the Sandinistas have made clear their contempt for general dialogue", had "abandoned the democratic and peaceful goals" of July 1979 and had become "the armed vanguard of an isthmus-wide movement". On April 27 Reagan acknowledged that his administration was supporting the contras, stating in a speech to a joint sitting of both Houses of Congress (usually reserved for discussion of national emergencies): "The government of Nicaragua has treated us as an enemy, it has rejected our peace efforts. . . . We do not seek its overthrow. Our interest is to ensure that it does not infect its neighbours through the export of subversion and violence. . . . We should not—and will not—protect the Nicaraguan government from the anger of its own people."

Early in 1985 Reagan described Nicaragua as "the transcendent moral issue of our time". Even after the installation of an elected government in January he called for the removal of the regime "in the sense of its present structure, in which it is a communist totalitarian state . . . not chosen by the people".

Appearing before the House of Representatives foreign affairs sub-committee in February during its deliberations on US support for the contras, Secretary of State George Shultz said: "I see no reason why we should slam the door on people just because they have been taken behind the Iron Curtain. While we are promoting democractic reform throughout Central America, the Soviet Union and Cuba are abetting the establishment of a communist dictatorship in Nicaragua."

The possibility of direct US military involvement was brought closer when on June 27, 1985, the House of Representatives voted by 312 to 111 in favour of an amendment to the defence authorization bill, allowing the administration to send US troops to Nicaragua without prior congressional approval in the event of one of the following scenarios: (i) if US citizens, possessions or allies were in "clear and present danger of attack" from Nicaragua; (ii) if US citizens or allies were hijacked, kidnapped or otherwise terrorized by Nicaragua; or (iii) if Nicaragua were to acquire Soviet jet fighter aircraft or nuclear weapons.

5.1.4: The Kissinger Commission

It was announced on July 18, 1983, that a "National Commission on Future Policies towards Central America" had been created under the chairmanship of Dr Henry Kissinger (Secretary of State 1973–77), to act in an advisory capacity to the president. The choice of Kissinger was criticized by politicians of all complexions because of his former association with US policy over Vietnam, to which he responded a week later; "I think it is imperative that we avoid the bitter debates which characterized the Vietnam period, and also . . . the same kind of uncertainty about objectives and what was attainable." During its six months of work the commission made two fact-finding tours to Central America, including a visit to Mexico. Kissinger was strongly criticized over his decision to meet Robelo (of Arde) in October 1983 despite an earlier undertaking that he would meet only government leaders and not "people engaged in guerrilla warfare".

The commission presented its report in January 1984, noting that its members had not been in full agreement but broadly supporting the administration's policies. Its basic premises were: (i) "Central America . . . critically involves our own security interests"; (ii) "neither the military nor the political nor the economic nor the social aspects of the crisis can be considered independently of the others; (iii) "the roots of the crisis are both indigenous and foreign"; and (iv) the United States should seek to meet the economic and social needs of the people of Central America because of both "conscience and calculations of our own national interest". US interests were defined as follows: (i) "to improve the living conditions of the people of Central America"; (ii) "to advance the cause of democracy"; (iii) "to strengthen the hemispheric system"; (iv) "to promote peaceful change in Central America while resisting the violation of democracy by force and terrorism"; (v) "to prevent hostile forces from seizing and expanding control in a strategically vital area"; and (vi) "to bar the Soviet Union from consolidating either directly or indirectly or through Cuba a hostile foothold on the American continents". On this last point the commission concluded:

The United States cannot eliminate all Soviet political involvement and influence within Central America and the Caribbean, but we must curb Soviet military activity in the hemisphere, and we can reduce Soviet opportunities and increase the incentives for others to abstain from forging ties with Moscow that damage US and regional interests.

The principal recommendations made by the commission were: (i) that Costa Rica, El Salvador, Guatemala, Honduras and Nicaragua should conclude a "framework for regional security", based on "respect for the sovereignty, independence and integrity of all Central American countries"; (ii) that the United States should encourage the Contadora process (see section 6.5.4 for US approach to Contadora); and (iii) that there should be a major increase in US economic and military assistance, specifically $8,000 million over a five-year period from 1985 (representing a doubling of the 1983 level of total aid to the region), with Congress appropriating funds on a five-year basis. The report noted that military aid had so far been insufficient to enable the Salvadorean army to defeat the FMLN, but said that military aid to El Salvador should be conditional on "demonstrated progress" towards the establishment of a democratic system and on the "termination of the activities of the so-called death squads". The current role of the United States in the region was not mentioned, except as a provider of technical help or acting as an observer.

A few days after the publication of the report Reagan announced that a five-year programme on Central America had been drafted, based on the commission's work, including an economic incentive plan designed to achieve an annual growth rate (in real terms) of 3.5 per cent in per capita income to create new jobs, to boost exports, provide trade credits and provide a system of balance-of-payments assistance to stabilize the economies of oil-importing countries.

Notes

1. Quoted by Armstrong and Shenk, *op. cit.*, p. 119.
2. Quoted by Pearce, *op. cit.*, p. 250.

5.2: US ECONOMIC AND MILITARY AID

5.2.1: Introductory

The United States has been by far the largest supplier of economic and military assistance to the Central American governments (with the exception of Nicaragua since the 1979 revolution). The first country to receive substantial quantities of aid was Guatemala after the overthrow of the Arbenz regime in 1954; between 1954 and 1959 the staff of the US aid mission in Guatemala City grew from 28 to 165. The major part of funds allocated to the region under the Alliance for Progress were distributed through USAID, and between 1946 and 1976 Guatemala received $74,600,000 under the US Military Assistance programme (MAP), Honduras $21,600,000, El Salvador $16,300,000, Nicaragua $29,100,000 and Costa Rica $1,900,000;[1] the scope of MAP had been considerably extended in 1963 to include training in counter-insurgency.

Military training came to be an important part of military aid, and between 1950 and 1976, 3,213 Guatemalan soldiers, 2,888 Hondurans, 1,925 Salvadoreans, 5,167 Nicaraguans and 696 Costa Ricans were trained at US military bases in either the United States or Panama.[2] As the then US Secretary of Defence, Robert McNamara, stated in 1964: "The essential role of the Latin American military as a stabilizing force outweighs any risks involved in providing military assistance for internal security purposes."[3] (The School of the Americas in Panama came to be nicknamed the "school of coups" because of the subsequent military-political activities of its students, and was reputed to give political as well as military instruction.[4])

By the 1970s there was rising opposition within the US Congress to the continuation of MAP allocations to Central America in view of the increasing reports of human rights abuses in the region. The Harkin Amendment to the 1975 Foreign Assistance Act gave Congress the power to limit economic assistance to any government responsible for gross violations of human rights, unless it could be demonstrated that such funds would "directly benefit the needy people"; after it was passed MAP grants were gradually phased out. (In some cases the decline in MAP grants was matched by a rise in US military sales, which were less open to congressional control.)

In 1976 the first congressional hearings were held on human rights in Guatemala, El Salvador and Nicaragua. The following year (after Carter's inauguration) the US State Department issued a report on Guatemala, criticizing its human rights performance, with the result that in March 1977 the Guatemalan government cancelled in advance further US military supplies. After similar US criticism of El Salvador, President Molina announced (also in March 1977) that his government would accept no more military aid or training from the United States "for the sake of national dignity". After a congressional hearing on human rights in Nicaragua in July 1977, the State Department announced that military credits for Nicaragua would be withheld for the rest of the year, and in October the US government

(The table does not include certain allocations such as trade credits or USAID grants.)

$ million

	1980	1981	1982	1983	1984	1985*
Guatemala†						
Military aid	—	—	—	—	—	0.3
Economic support funds	—	—	10.1	—	—	12.5
Economic aid	11.1	16.6	13.8	17.6	33.3	61.3
Belize						
Military aid	—	—	0.03	0.07	0.6	0.6
Economic support funds	—	—	—	10.0	10.0	4.0
Economic aid	—	—	—	6.7	4.0	6.0
Honduras						
Military aid	4.0	8.9	31.3	37.3	77.5	62.5
Economic support funds	—	—	36.8	56.0	112.5	75.0
Economic aid	51.0	33.9	41.2	45.2	96.5	63.9
El Salvador						
Military aid	6.0	33.5	82.0	81.3	196.5	128.2
Economic support funds	9.1	44.9	115.0	140.0	210.5	195.0
Economic aid	48.7	68.7	67.2	91.1	120.7	131.1
Costa Rica						
Military aid	—	0.03	2.1	2.6	9.2	9.2
Economic support funds	—	—	90.0	157.0	130.0	160.0
Economic aid	14.0	13.3	30.6	55.4	47.9	48.0
Panama						
Military aid	0.3	0.4	5.4	5.5	15.9	20.0
Economic support funds	—	—	—	—	30.0	20.0
Economic aid	2.0	10.6	13.0	7.2	15.9	20.3
TOTAL	146.2	232.8	538.5	712.9	1,110.6	1,017.9

* Figures as initially approved by Congress; the final totals were expected to be higher.
† According to figures released by the US embassy in Guatemala total economic aid to Guatemala was $38,100,000 in 1984, $65,100,000 in 1985 and provisionally $70,000,000 in 1986; the provisional figure for military aid in 1986 was $10,300,000.

decided to withhold economic aid of $12,000,000 pending an improvement in human rights. The Foreign Assistance and Related Programmes Appropriations Act of 1978 prohibited military sales to Guatemala and El Salvador, although in May 1978 the $12,000,000 frozen economic aid to Nicaragua was released after a campaign by a pro-Nicaragua lobby in Congress led by Charles Wilson (Democrat, Texas).

The table on p. 239[5] gives details of US aid to Central America in fiscal years 1980–85 (except Nicaragua, which received some US financing in 1980 under an agreement signed with Carter—see section 5.2.5).

5.2.2: Aid to Guatemala

Although US economic aid to Guatemala continued after 1977, full military aid was not resumed until 1985. A month after the Ríos Montt coup in March 1982, a White House spokesman said that the resumption of military aid to Guatemala was being "very seriously considered". It was reported that the US administration planned to approve the sale to Guatemala of $4,000,000 worth of spare parts for Huey helicopters and to restore a grant of $50,000 in military training funds for the current fiscal year. (The previous year the administration had sold jeeps and tanks to the Lucas García government for reasons of "regional security".)

In the course of Reagan's visit to Central America in December 1982 (see section 5.1.1), he met Ríos Montt but to avoid the controversy of going to Guatemala the meeting took place in the Honduran town of San Pedro Sula, near the Guatemalan border. (President Monge of Costa Rica had objected to the proposal that Ríos Montt should go to San José.) Reagan subsequently described Ríos Montt, as "a man of great personal integrity, committed to restoring democracy", and said that he favoured the resumption of military supplies to Guatemala as he believed the country to be facing "a brutal challenge from guerrillas armed and supported by others outside Guatemala". However, his decision to meet the Guatemalan President was strongly criticized in Congress in view of the fact that the Ríos Montt regime had seized power in a coup and had imposed a state of siege, and because of the country's record on human rights. In January 1983 the White House announced that arms sales would be renewed to the value of $6,300,000 (chiefly in helicopter spare parts) "in the light of human rights improvements that have taken place in Guatemala since the Ríos Montt government came to power" (see section 4.2.2).

In November 1983 the United States temporarily suspended all aid to Guatemala by refusing to advance $35,000,000 credit from USAID after two USAID workers (Felipe Ralac Xiloj and Julieta Sánchez Castillo) were found dead near the Mexican border. Also frozen was the 1984 budgeted aid to Guatemala, consisting of $10,250,000 in military assistance, $13,000,000 economic development assistance and $40,000,000 in economic grants. Two months later, however, the sale of a further $2,000,000 worth of spare helicopter parts was approved, and in August the administration said that military aid to Guatemala in 1985 would be $300,000. The sum of $10,300,000 was proposed for fiscal 1986, along with $25,000,000 in economic support funds, $33,000,000 in security assistance and $19,000,000 in development assistance, largely to the "food for peace" programme (see section 3.3.2). The proposed military aid allocation included military training, the first received by Guatemalan troops since 1977.

Economic aid increased markedly after the installation of a civilian government in January 1986. In the first week of July 1986 the director of the USAID office in Guatemala, Charles Costello, announced that the Agency had already agreed to aid totalling $100,000,000, in support of the government's Programme of Economic and Social Reordering. This total had been established under a number of agreements, including $47,350,000 in balance-of-payments assistance, covering both development projects and food imports, and $23,925,000 as a soft loan, repayable over 25 years at a rate of interest under 4 per cent.

5.2.3: Aid to Honduras

To demonstrate its support for the transition to democratic government in Honduras in 1980–82, the United States substantially increased its aid: economic assistance was doubled in 1980 to around $50,000,000 and military aid was increased to enable Honduras to act as a "buffer state" in the region. Total economic aid exceeded $100,000,000 in fiscal 1983 and $200,000,000 in 1984 (see table in section 5.2.1). An economic stabilization package was agreed in March 1985, the second phase of which (over $65,000,000) was not released until an agreement had been signed with the incoming Azcona government in January 1986, detailing the government's plans to improve the balance-of-payments situation and reduce the budget deficit.

Military aid rose to $31,300,000 in 1982 (compared with $32,500,000 for the entire period 1946–81), of which $21,000,000 was advanced after President Suazo's visit to Washington in July 1982 (for the improvement and extension of airstrips to accommodate US military transport and jet fighter aircraft). The proposed sum for fiscal 1986 was $88,000,000. There was some confusion when on March 25, 1986, it was announced in Washington that Honduras would receive a further $20,000,000 in emergency military aid in view of what the US authorities alleged to be a Nicaraguan invasion. (There was no corroborative evidence of military action against Honduras, and the Nicaraguan government said that its forces had simply been pursuing contra forces in a "legitimate war zone".) It appeared that this offer had been entirely a US initiative as a Honduras government spokesman said in April that while the government had asked for US aid transport it "did not request military aid". (Much of the military equipment used by the Honduran armed forces was technically "on loan" from the United States and so did not feature in the official US military aid allocations.)

A more indirect form of US military aid—though perhaps a more effective and permanent form—was the series of joint military manoeuvres held in Honduran territory and waters. The first major ones were the "Big Pine" exercises, staged on Feb. 1–7, 1983, involving some 4,000 Honduran troops and 1,600 US support personnel mobilized to counter a hypothetical attack on Honduras by an opponent codenamed "Red Army". In July 1983 it was announced that Big Pine II would open in August and last for six months to show US support for its allies and to put pressure on Cuba and Nicaragua (in the case of the latter by "practising" a naval blockade). These manoeuvres involved 16,000 naval personnel over their duration on three groups of vessels: the aircraft carrier *Coral Sea* along with five ships in the Atlantic and the carriers *Ranger* (with seven ships) and *New Jersey* (with six ships) in the Pacific. An advance team arrived in Honduras on Aug. 8 to prepare for the land exercises deploying 5,600 US troops and 6,000 Honduran soldiers. Shultz said on Aug. 4 that the US forces in Honduras were not seeking a confrontation with Nicaragua and that if attacked "our forces will defend themselves, but they will withdraw; we have no intent to engage anyone actively".

The US Defence Department announced in January 1984 that after Big Pine II some 700–800 US troops would remain in Honduras, pending further exercises. (There were currently about 2,000 combat troops, 44 military trainers, seven military staff at the embassy, 60 air force members at the radar unit near Tegucigalpa and 116 instructors at Puerto Castilla.) The Grenadier joint manoeuvres in Honduras lasted from April until June 1984, concentrating on counter-insurgency training, and also in April there was a two-week Caribbean exercise involving 30,000 troops from all branches of the US armed forces.

In November 1984, during the Nicaraguan MiGs crisis (see section 5.3.5), the Defence Department said that US naval exercises would continue in Caribbean and Pacific waters, including the Gulf of Fonseca, but denied that this action was a prelude to an invasion of Nicaragua. The Department said that it believed that Nicaragua "might be planning a military offensive against neighbouring El Salvador or Honduras", but acknowledged that it had "no hard evidence" for the claim. (There were seven separate military and naval exercises in and off Honduras in November 1984, three of which began the day after the US allegation of the arrival of MiG aircraft in Nicaragua.)

In May 1984 the Defence Department submitted a report to Congress recommending that the Big Pine series of manoeuvres be extended until 1988, and the same month an agreement was signed with the Honduran government allowing joint exercises to continue until 1990. Big Pine III ran from February to April 1985 (overlapping briefly with "Universal Trek" in April), and in response the Nicaraguan army mobilized its Soviet-made T55 tanks and heavy artillery along the common border. In June 1985 the "Cabañas" exercises began, lasting until September, and in January 1986 a series of manoeuvres called "Blazing Trail" opened. The two major components of these were the exercises "General Terencio Sierra" (January–May), which involved some major road construction, and Cabañas 86 (March–June), during which troops built another airstrip capable of handling C–130 transport aircraft, and were deployed in a border area used by Miskito guerrillas for launch attacks against Nicaragua.

(Similar manoeuvres, codenamed "Blazing Trail" and "Kindle Liberty", were held in Panama in January–May 1986, involving some 10,000 US troops based in Panama and Puerto Rico; it was suggested in some quarters that they compromised Panama's neutral role in the Contadora process.)

US forces used the six airstrips for making reconnaissance flights over El Salvador and Nicaragua. By 1986 the US military regional headquarters in Honduras, known as Joint Task Force Bravo, had 1,000 troops permanently stationed at the Palmerola air base, with a further 500 on the Caribbean and Pacific coasts.

5.2.4: Aid to El Salvador

Between 1946 and 1975 direct US economic aid to El Salvador totalled $157,700,000 and between 1946 and 1979 direct military aid was $16,700,000.[6]

Within a few days of the October 1979 coup the United States expressed its readiness to supply assistance to combat extremist violence (although the junta had not as yet requested either financial or military aid). In November of that year Archbishop Romero responded by urging the US authorities to make any aid conditional on a purge of the Salvadorean security forces. In February 1980 the US administration announced that it was preparing an emergency aid package of $49,800,000 to cover basic social and economic needs and to help stabilize the government; soon afterwards it was reported that a military package of about $7,000,000 worth of equipment and the dispatch of US military trainers was also under consideration.

In response to this report Archbishop Romero wrote to President Carter on Feb. 17, 1980, expressing particular anxiety over the offer of military trainers, saying in part:

> If this information is true, the contribution of your administration, instead of favouring greater justice and peace in El Salvador will almost certainly intensify the injustice and repression of the common people who are organized to struggle for respect for their most basic human rights. Unfortunately the present government junta, and especially the armed forces and security forces, have not demonstrated any ability to solve structurally or in political practice our serious national problems. In general, they have only resorted to repressive violence and this has resulted in a much greater toll of dead and wounded than in previous military regimes whose systematic violation of human rights was denounced by the Inter-American Human Rights Commission.[7]

The US State Department said on Feb. 23 that it had conveyed to Salvadorean military leaders, businessmen and landowners that the United States (i) was supporting the government because of its declared commitment to reforms and human rights; (ii) opposed any attempt to change the government; and (iii) would cut off aid and oppose any government which did not include civilians or committed abuses of human rights.

After the murder of the four US missionaries in December 1980, new economic aid of $20,000,000 and military aid of $5,000,000 was withheld in protest, although the economic aid was later restored (see section 1.4.13). In January 1981 Carter said that the $5,000,000 of "non-lethal" military aid would be made available, and on Jan. 17 the delivery of "lethal" aid of $5,400,000 was authorized under the presidential contingency fund for military emergencies (in view of the FMLN offensive). This resumption in lethal aid (the first since 1977) was justified by the administration on the grounds that "the guerrillas have received a substantial supply of arms from abroad" (i.e. allegedly Nicaragua and Cuba—see also section 5.3.4), in which context ambassador White claimed that a group of about 100 guerrillas had landed in El Salvador from Nicaragua on Jan. 13. At the beginning of March 1981 the Reagan administration announced an extra $25,000,000 in military aid to El Salvador, including helicopters, M–16 rifles, mortars, machine guns and radar and communications equipment. Total military aid in fiscal 1981 amounted to $35,500,000 and total economic aid was over $120,000,000, half being allocated at the beginning of the year and the rest raised in March 1981.

When the allocations for fiscal 1982 were brought before the US Congress, they faced initial opposition from the Democrat-controlled House of Representatives, especially as the $115,000,000 economic support finance included $25,000,000 for the purchase of weapons and supplies and $1,000,000 for military training. After a long debate the foreign committees of both houses approved the aid on two conditions: a six-monthly certification on human rights and progress by the Salvadorean government on economic and political reforms (including land distribution) and the government's willingness to negotiate a peaceful settlement with the left-wing opposition.

Reagan granted such certifications in January and July 1982 and January and July 1983, each time citing what he regarded as the Salvadorean government's "concerted and significant efforts to comply with internationally recognized human rights"; he faced increasing opposition in Congress, however, after visits by congressional delegations to El Salvador to investigate the human rights situation. At the beginning of January 1983 a medical delegation returned home and reported "unmistakable physical evidence of torture, starvation and malnutrition" and a "complete breakdown in medical care", much of which was directly attributable to the armed forces. When a few days later the administration requested $60,000,000 in military aid Congress voted only the $26,300,000 originally proposed, although Enders had claimed that the Salvadorean armed forces would run out of arms within 30 days without this extra finance. In March 1983 Reagan said that the administration might seek $110,000,000, with most of the extra $50,000,000 being used for training Salvadorean troops in the United States; in May Congress finally agreed to one-half of the $60,000,000 and two-thirds of the $50,000,000.

In November 1983 Reagan vetoed a congressional bill approving $64,800,000 in military aid to El Salvador and the continuation of the certification procedure, with 10 per cent of the money being withheld until substantial progress had been made in the land reform programme (at that time being debated in the Salvadorean Assembly in the context of the new constitution —see section 2.3.4) and a further 30 per cent being suspended pending the conclusion of the trial for the murder of the four missionaries (see section 4.2.4). The White House spokesman, Larry Speakes, said that while "the administration is firmly committed to protecting human rights, economic and political reform, holding elections and progress in prosecuting the cases of murdered American citizens", it held that the certification procedure "would not serve to support these endeavours" and would rather "distort our efforts". In January 1984 the State Department sent a report to Congress stating that significant progress had been made on the land reform programme and that the only hindrance to its implementation was a lack of finance.

In February 1984 the administration proposed a further $312,000,000 in military aid for fiscal 1984–85, in addition to the $64,800,000 already approved, in line with the recommendation of the Kissinger Commission of $400,000,000 for the two years. Even though the administration agreed to tie this aid to human rights progress, Congress opposed it; while it was still under discussion in March the administration requested an emergency allocation of $93,000,000, only $32,000,000 of which was approved ($20,000,000 for ammunition and the balance for medical supplies).

Two weeks after his election in May 1984, President Duarte travelled to Washington to request military aid (but not US troops), hoping for a more favourable reaction from Congress now that the country had an elected government. The day after he left, the House of Representatives voted by 241 votes to 177 to approve a special grant of $61,750,000 in emergency military and medical aid; moreover, after the conviction in El Salvador of the five guardsmen charged with the murder of the missionaries, the House freed $19,400,000 of aid frozen pending a satisfactory outcome of the trial. The two houses disagreed again in July 1984 over a supplemental appropriations request, eventually settling on a compromise of $120,000,000 in economic aid and $70,000,000 in military aid. (The emergency $61,750,000 had first been debated in the Senate, which had said it should be forfeit in the event of a coup either before or after the election.)

A report released in February 1985 by the bipartisan Congressional Arms Control and Disarmament Caucus claimed that the administration had deceived Congress on the US military role in El Salvador and that most of the US economic assistance had been put to military uses; it concluded: "If US aid is composed in the future as it is at present, the next five years will be as violent and unproductive for El Salvador as the last five years."

In February 1985 the Reagan administration presented to Congress a request for $483,000,000 in aid for El Salvador in fiscal 1986, including $132,000,000 in military aid; nevertheless, in April the House of Representatives foreign affairs subcommittee approved only $378,000,000 (including $113,000,000 in military aid). In addition, the subcommittee attached a series of conditions to the disbursement of this sum: (i) that no funds be channelled to the contras; (ii) that no US land or air forces be used in combat in El Salvador "unless Congress declares war"; (iii) that the Salvadorean government continue talks with the FMLN–FDR, implement the promised reforms, increase its control of the armed forces and take action against the death squads; and (iv) that the US president be required to resume the certification process. By mid–1986, however, it appeared that total aid had reached the level initially requested.

5.2.5: Nicaragua—US Sanctions and Aid to Contras

Between 1968 and 1978 Nicaragua received nearly $20,000,000 from the United States in military aid. In August 1979 (i.e. after the overthrow of Somoza) a US State Department spokesman said that the United States would explore the possibility of selling arms to Nicaragua; however, after a few months of sending some economic aid to the Sandinista government, the United States subsequently directed all its financial assistance to the contras.

In the first three months of the new government the United States sent $8,000,000 in emergency aid and approved a further $8,800,000, and in October 1979 the two governments signed a $75,000,000 aid package, originally requested by Carter in November 1979 but held up by Republican opposition within Congress. Reagan had incorporated opposition to the Nicaraguan aid package in his electoral platform, and when he took office in January 1981 the package (of which $60,000,000 had been disbursed) was suspended, along with a wheat sale worth $9,600,000 and "food for peace" aid. The suspension was made pending the investigation of the reports that

Nicaragua was supplying arms to the FMLN in El Salvador, and on April 1, 1981, the State Department confirmed the suspension of all economic aid. The Nicaraguan representative at the UN, Alejandro Bandano, described the action as "the most recent manifestation of the aggressive policy of de-tabilization" by "certain sectors of the US government" against Nicaragua. (Later in April the Soviet Union and Bulgaria announced donations of 20,000 and 10,000 tonnes of wheat respectively to Nicaragua, while the Cuban government announced that it would grant $64,000,000 in aid in 1981.)

Although it was reported by early 1982 that the Reagan administration was giving financial assistance to the contras, it was not until the end of that year that the matter came into congressional debates on foreign spending with the passage in December of the Boland Amendment. Drafted by Edward Boland (Democrat, Massachusetts), the amendment to the 1983 defence appropriations bill prohibited the government from supplying "military equipment, military training or advice, or other support for military activities to any group or individual not part of the country's armed forces, for the purpose of overthrowing the government of Nicaragua or provoking a military exchange between Nicaragua and Honduras". It was passed unani-mously by the House of Representatives on Dec. 8 and incorporated into the emergency military spending bill signed by the President on Dec. 21. Early the next year, however, Boland visited Central America, and on his return at the beginning of April 1983 he said that the administration was violating the ban by classifying all US activities in Central America as being part of its overall arms interdiction campaign. (Assistance was initially given to the FDN on the grounds that it could assist in the campaign but was refused to Arde—see sections 3.1.5 and 3.4.4). The amendment, which specifically prevented intelligence agencies from aiding the contras out of contingency funds, was due to expire in September 1985 (see below).

Early in 1983 the administration requested congressional approval for $50,000,000 to fund contra activities in Nicaragua under the intelligence authorization bill, thus instigating a battle between the two houses. The proposal was defeated in the House of Representatives in July by 225 votes to 195, but the (Republican-controlled) Senate ignored the vote and returned the bill to the House, where it was defeated by the same margin in October. On the second occasion the House agreed to the required sum for "overt" activities (i.e. those which genuinely constituted part of the arms interdiction campaign), while the Senate approved "covert" aid, but reduced the amount to $19,000,000. A compromise was reached in November by which both houses agreed to $24,000,000 for covert aid (under the military appropriations bill for fiscal 1984), with a rider that the CIA must return to Congress after six months for any additional funding. Fred Iklé, Under-Secretary of Defence for Policy, remarked in September in a speech to Congress: "As long as Congress keeps crippling the President's military assistance programme, we will have a policy always shy of success. . . . The policy . . . has not been given a chance to work. . . . [If Congress were to continue in this way], the only way to protect the democracies might be for the United States to place forward-deployed forces in these countries, as in Korea and West Germany."

It was reported in the US press in October 1983 that the CIA had in-stigated—and helped to fund—the recent increase in contra attacks on economic installations on the basis that continuous harassment might force the Sandinistas to abandon their support for the FMLN, and that the success of incidents such as the arson attack on Corinto (see section 3.4.4) would persuade Congress to approve funding requests for covert activities. The mining of Corinto in March 1984 (see section 3.4.4) was generally regarded as another such CIA-inspired attack in view of the presence of US warships in the area (see section 5.2.3). A UN Security Council resolution condemning the mining and calling on other countries "to refrain from carrying out, supporting or promoting any type of military action against any state of the region, as well as any action which hinders the peace objectives of the Contadora Group" was on April 4, 1984, vetoed by the United States (in a vote in which 13 other members voted in favour and the United Kingdom abstained). Five days later the Nicaraguan government filed a suit against the United States with the International Court of Justice (ICJ) at The Hague calling for "a declaration in depth on the violations and aggressions of the United States"; however, the United States had pre-empted this move by announcing in advance "a temporary and limited modification" of its acceptance of the Court's jurisdiction in any dispute related to Central America for a period of two years. (For ICJ ruling in favour of Nicaragua in 1986, see below.)

Senator Edward Kennedy (Democrat) then sponsored a non-binding resolution "that no funds heretofore appropriated in any act of Congress shall be obligated or expended for the purpose of planning, executing or supporting the mining of the ports or territorial waters of Nicaragua", which was passed in the Senate on April 10, 1984, by 84 votes to 12. A similar non-binding resolution was passed in the House of Representatives on April 12 by 281 to 111. It was reported on April 16 that the FDN had decided to suspend its mining operation because it was feared that opposition in Congress could threaten future US aid, in particular a request for $21,000,000 currently under consideration. In March the administration had tried to speed approval of this request by attaching it as an amendment to a bill providing $150,000,000 to drought victims in Africa already passed by the House of Representatives; however, the amendment was rejected by the House in May and the following month the Senate withdrew the support it had originally voted.

The administration did not officially admit responsibility for the mining, but Kenneth Dam, Deputy Secretary of State, said on April 11 that if the United States had been involved in such an operation it would be justified as an act of "collective self-defence". A few days later Jeane Kirkpatrick said she thought the action "legal because Nicaragua is engaged in a process of armed aggression against her neighbours". The contra leader Calero denied that the United States had been in any way involved, but the Nicaraguan Chief of Staff, Cdr Joaquín Cuadra, maintained that the sudden escalation in contra activity, especially the April offensive, was due to a "voluminous and immense arms supply" from the CIA.

In October 1984 both houses of Congress gave their approval to a request for $28,000,000 in funds to the contras, but froze the allocation until the end of February 1985. The publication in January 1985 of a report from the Senate intelligence committee on the role of the CIA (see section 5.2.8), and the allegations of contra atrocities (see section 3.4.4), made it still more difficult for the administration to gain congressional support; even before it came before the houses in April, the administration's request for $14,000,000 was expected to fail. Anticipating rejection of the request in its original form, Reagan proposed at the beginning of April that the aid should be linked to peace talks between the Sandinista government and the contras, undertaking that the aid would not be used for two months if the Nicaraguan government agreed to hold church-mediated peace talks within that period. He also attempted to explain the administration's concern by describing the contras as individuals "fleeing from people who are burning down their villages, forcing them into concentration camps, and forcing their children into military service". In a further compromise it was announced on April 18, 1985, that the aid would be entirely humanitarian aid to the contras.

Also in April, 1985, prior to the vote, a White House report entitled "US Support for the Democratic Resistance Movement in Nicaragua" was leaked to the press; it said that the United States hoped to raise the number of contras in Honduras to 20,000–25,000, along with 5,000 in Costa Rica (see section 3.1.5 for controversy over contra numbers) on the grounds that "the containment approach is obviously deficient in that it does not contemplate changes in Sandinista behaviour".

Although the Senate approved the $14,000,000 by 53 votes to 46, the House of Representatives voted against it on April 23, 1985, by 248 to 180, even with a guarantee that it would be used "only for food, medicine, clothing and other assistance for survival and well-being and not for arms, ammunition and weapons of war"; the next day the House rejected even the sending of aid to Nicaraguan refugees. Reagan expressed his disappointment in Congress shortly afterwards, saying: "We have got to get to where we can run a foreign policy without a committee of 535 telling us what we can do." He added: "It was a dark day for freedom when, after the Soviet Union spent $500,000,000 to impose communism in Nicaragua, the United States could not support a meagre $14,000,000 for the freedom fighters in Nicaragua."

The final breakthrough for the administration came in June 1985, when Reagan dropped his insistence that the funds to the contras should be channelled through the CIA, conceding that instead they could be used by the State Department and USAID. On June 12 the House of Representatives voted (by 232 to 196) not to extend the current ban on military aid to the contras (i.e. the Boland amendment, due to expire at the end of September), and approved humanitarian aid (by 284 to 184) of $27,000,000 to be released in the next nine months, adding a rider that it was not to be interfered with by either the CIA or the Defence Department. The previous week the Senate had approved $38,000,000 non-military aid for a two-year period and authorized the CIA to distribute the money. After debate by a House-Senate conference the sum was set at $25,000,000 and the ban on CIA involvement retained.

Particularly in the light of President Ortega's visit to Moscow in April 1985 (see section 5.3.5), the US administration began to consider direct economic pressure on the Nicaraguan government. At the economic summit of major developed countries held in Bonn Reagan announced on May 1 that the United States would impose a trade embargo on Nicaragua; in addition all port access for Nicaraguan aircraft and ships in the United States was terminated and the 1958 treaty of friendship between the two countries was abrogated. The embargo was expected to have its most severe impact on the supply of spare parts to Nicaragua, although these were still available through other trading partners such as Canada. In 1984 Nicaragua had imported $111,500,000 worth of US products (about 20 per cent of its total intake), consisting mostly of pesticides, fertilizers, feed, agricultural machinery and spare parts; it had exported $57,000,000 by value to the United States, mostly in bananas, beef, shellfish and coffee. US firms were not forced to break existing contracts and the embargo was not joined by the United States' allies, thus limiting its effect.

In August 1985 Paz Bárnica (the Honduran foreign minister) announced that his government would not permit the US embassy in Tegucigalpa to administer US aid to the contras; accordingly, in October the first consignment of uniforms, boots and medical supplies sent under the $27,000,000 package was impounded at Tegucigalpa airport. There was, however, some doubt over the government's intention to uphold this prohibition, since although Honduran officials reported that the consignment had been returned to the United States contra leaders claimed two weeks later that it had reached them. The government subsequently reaffirmed its ban on these shipments, but it was believed that during his trip to Washington in January President-elect Azcona had agreed to their recommencement.

In December 1985 Reagan began campaigning for further aid to the contras, and on Feb. 25, 1986, he submitted a formal request to Congress to allow $100,000,000 of the existing defence budget to be allocated to the contras; $30,000,000 would be non-military aid and the remainder would be covert military assistance. Although the Senate agreed to the request by 53 votes to 47 on March 27, the House of Representatives had, a week earlier, rejected it by 222 votes to 210; accordingly, negotiations opened to reach a compromise. (Before the vote Reagan had proposed a plan similar to that advanced the previous year, whereby all the covert military aid and $5,000,000 of the non-military aid would be withheld pending an effort by Philip Habib to bring about a negotiated settlement.) The House of Representatives again rejected the bill on April 16, and a new version was agreed under which the $100,000,000 (to be paid in three installments up to April 1987) was incorporated into a bill providing $300,000,000 in economic aid for Guatemala, Honduras, El Salvador and Costa Rica. The other conditions were that military equipment could not be delivered before Sept. 1, 1986, US personnel would not be allowed to train or assist the contras within 20 miles of the Nicaraguan border, and that a process should be established "to monitor both the probity of the contra leadership and the prospects for peace".

In this modified form the bill was approved by the House of Representatives on June 21, 1986, by 221 votes to 209, and by the Senate on Aug. 13 by the same margin as in March. President Ortega described passage of the bill as a "declaration of war by the United States against Nicaragua", and the foreign ministers of the Contadora Group expressed their opposition to this or any other form of interference in the affairs of Central American states. The Nicaraguan government also convened an emergency session of the UN Security Council on July 1, at which only two of the 15 members (El Salvador and the United States) defended the measure.

Another expression of international criticism of US aid to the contras came on June 27, 1986, when the ICJ found in favour of Nicaragua, ruling that the United States was "under an obligation to make reparations" to Nicaragua for damages caused by the illegal intervention, and that it should "cease and refrain" in this action immediately. The ruling was 12 to three (the judges from Japan, the United Kingdom and the United States) to the effect that the United States had violated international law by (i) "training, arming, equipping, financing and supplying" the contras; (ii) mining the ports of Corinto, El Bluff and Sandino in 1984; (iii) attacking these harbours and neighbouring oil storage facilities in 1983 and 1984; and (iv) directing intelligence flights over Nicaragua.

The Court also (i) rejected the US argument that it had acted in the "collective self-defence" of Costa Rica, Honduras and El Salvador; (ii) ruled against the US trade embargo of 1985; (iii) stated that the CIA manual of 1984 (see section 5.2.8) "encouraged . . . acts contrary to general principles of humanitarian law"; and (iv) decided that there was insufficient evidence of Nicaraguan arms supply to the FMLN to indicate that Nicaragua was playing a major part in the Salvadorean civil war. It did not, however, rule on Nicaragua's claim for $370,000,000 in damages, leaving the sum to be settled in negotiations between the two countries.

In addition to the official US economic assistance to the contras, there were also a number of private US organizations and individuals raising money and even becoming involved in the fighting. During an air raid on Santa Clara (northern Segovia) in September 1984, two crewmen of the helicopter were identified as US citizens; both belonged to a volunteer group called Civilian Military Assistance, formed by Vietnam veterans in Alabama, and basing its actions on the premise that "communists should be stopped at all costs". (The *Washington Post*, Sept. 5, 1984, reported that the helicopter had been provided by the CIA.) According to a report in *The Times* (Sept. 9), the US magazine *Soldier of Fortune* had sent six groups of former soldiers to El Salvador since February 1983 to help train the Salvadorean army with the co-operation (but not the direct involvement) of US embassy and military staff.

In late 1984 Calero announced that the FDN had stockpiled ammunition and military supplies in anticipation of a shortage of US government-approved finance, and had privately raised funds since March 1984 at an average of $1,500,000 per month, "much of it donated by private Americans and corporations, including some large, well-known companies". A US State Department spokesman said that the administration had not "discouraged legal private US contributions" to the contras, some of which were reported to have come from the Moonies, although under the front of another name.[8]

5.2.6: Aid to Costa Rica

In the period between 1980 and 1984 US aid to Costa Rica increased by a factor of 13, reflecting both the country's economic crisis and its perceived strategic importance to US policy in Central America. The major increase in economic aid began in 1982 (see table in section 5.2.1), and during Reagan's visit to the country in his tour of December 1982 (see section 5.1.1) he met President Monge and agreed an aid package totalling $70,000,000.

The US administration announced in May 1984 that Costa Rica (which has no regular army, but some 8,000 paramilitary civil guards) had requested security assistance (of nearly $10,000,000, compared with $2,600,000 in 1983); in this context the US ambassador in San José, Curtin Winsor, said that "if Costa Rica were to need something extraordinary in the event of an invasion, the United States will be ready to co-operate". An assertion made by the US administration that the first US–Costa Rican joint manoeuvres would begin in July 1984 was denied by the Monge government. (Earlier, in November 1983, the administration had announced a proposal to send about 1,000 US military engineers to Costa Rica to help with infrastructural projects in the north of the country—i.e. near the Nicaraguan border; however, the plan was cancelled in January 1984 after Iklé had described them as "the first such joint exercises with Costa Rica".)

It was reported in October 1984 that recent incursions by Nicaraguan military units into Costa Rican territory had prompted Monge to ask for emergency military aid. At the end of the year it was reported that Costa Rica had received 80 jeeps, 25 patrol launchers, two helicopters and a consignment of two-way radio sets for use by the civil guard. This aid was not entirely popular within Costa Rica and when in February 1985 Winsor said that he had recently visited Gen. Paul Gorman (head of the US forces in Panama) to discuss the possibility of having US companies set up weapon-assembly plants in Costa Rica there was an outcry. Soon afterwards Winsor returned to Washington and it was reported that the Costa Rican government had asked for his tour of duty to be shortened.

In the first week of May 1985 about 20 US military advisers arrived in Costa Rica to train the civil guard and establish a 750–strong anti-terrorist battalion to operate along the Nicaraguan border. Under the $18,500,000 military aid allocation to Costa Rica in 1984 and 1985 the country received equipment such as helicopters, light aircraft and patrol boats and also its first consignment of "lethal" aid from the United States.

In February and March 1986 a group of 180 US army engineers arrived in Costa Rica for "Operation Peace Bridge 1986", a civil construction project on the Pacific Coast. Although the Costa Rican foreign minister, Carlos José Gutiérrez, said the engineers were unarmed, it was reported in the press that some of the 60 men who arrived on Feb. 24 had light weapons, and that over a third of the second batch, arriving on March 4, were "military support personnel".

5.2.7: US Military Presence in Central America

Although US troops have not been officially involved in internal fighting in either El Salvador or Nicaragua, they have nevertheless maintained and increased their presence in the region, not only by means of joint military exercises with Honduras (see section 5.2.3), but also in special training programmes. Moreover, even before the setting up of such special projects, the United States had about 10,000 troops permanently stationed at its 14 military bases in Panama, collectively forming its Southern Command (known as Southcom).

The largest US military presence in Central America (outside Panama) has been established in Honduras, where the first group of military personnel arrived in October 1980; the arrival in August 1981 of another 21 trainers (including a number from the US army's Special Forces, known as "Green Berets") took the total to about 50. Some operated in La Virtud province (on the border with El Salvador) and the rest in Cape Gracias a Dios (near the

Nicaraguan border). From April 1982 the Argentinian advisers in Honduras (see section 5.4.3) were replaced by US staff in the wake of the Falklands/ Malvinas conflict; the number had risen to nearly 100 by March 1983, and according to the State Department the presence was necessary to enable Honduras to "withstand pressures from Cuban-backed Nicaragua".

In March 1983 the US Defence Department announced that Honduras would be provided with radar stations to track small aircraft suspected of carrying arms from Nicaragua to the FMLN, to be staffed by about 50 US air force personnel and installed near Tegucigalpa at a cost of $5,000,000. In April it was added that AWACS (airborne warning and control systems) would be sent to Honduras to continue the monitoring which had been conducted for the past two months from the Tinker air force base in Oklahoma, and in the course of the year US troops began operating from the Palmerola airbase near Comayagua. By the end of 1984 the United States had built or improved eight airfields (to allow them to receive US military aircraft), four military camps and two radar stations in Honduras.

In July 1983 the United States opened a training centre at Puerto Castilla on the Atlantic coast of Honduras, at a cost of about $250,000 and an annual budget of $7,000,000. There was considerable opposition within Honduras to this project, and even after the first 120 US staff arrived in the country in mid-June the government insisted that "the project is being negotiated" and had not yet been fully approved. The main objection was that the centre was controlled and run entirely by the US armed forces, primarily for the training of Salvadorean troops; by October 1984 a total of 5,000 Salvadoreans and 3,000 Hondurans had completed training courses.

In July 1984 the Honduran army delayed the arrival of a new batch of Salvadorean soldiers (see also section 1.3.14), with the result that in October the US administration warned that it would withhold the sum of $18,500,000 due to Honduras for a permanent training facility unless the training of Salvadorean troops were allowed to continue. (Prior to the establishment of the centre at Puerto Castilla, Salvadorean troops had been sent to Fort Bragg in North Carolina and Fort Benning in Georgia, where the Atlacatl and Ramón Belloso battalions were formed.)

The presence of US troops in El Salvador itself has been far more contentious. The first proposal to send US trainers to El Salvador was made in 1979 (when it was fiercely contested by Archbishop Romero in his letter to Carter—see section 5.2.4). By January 1981 there were reported to be 19 military trainers, 14 helicopter technicians and a five-man command advisory group (in addition to several regular military attachés), with a further 20 trainers sent in March, 15 of whom were Green Berets. The US administration subsequently informally agreed with Congress a limit of 55 trainers in the country; Reagan's request for $110,000,000 in aid in March 1983 (see section 5.2.4) was in part designed to enable the United States to increase its help for the Salvadorean armed forces by training more at Fort Bragg, without exceeding the limit of trainers actually in the country.

The US administration drew a distinction between the term "advisers" (used in Vietnam) and "trainers", in that the latter were permitted to go only to military bases and not to accompany troops in combat; as Thomas Enders remarked in March 1983: "We do not have military advisers now, people who go out in combat, and we are not going to have military advisers in the future.

We have trainers." However, this distinction was not universally regarded as quite so clear in practice.[9]

Radio Venceremos claimed in January 1982 that two US military trainers had taken part in a recent attack on the Chichontepec volcano. Although the US embassy in San Salvador reiterated the official prohibition on US military personnel from "entering the combat zone", some credence was lent to the report by a film shot in February showing five US soldiers carrying M–16 rifles and other combat equipment and supervising the construction of a new bridge near the town of San Miguel. (The previous October there had been allegations of US troops in US helicopters opening fire on villagers near the Golden Bridge over the Lempa river, and in April 1982 two trainers were said to have witnessed the torture of two young Salvadoreans by Salvadorean soldiers in January 1981.) Moreover in February 1983 three Green Berets were found to have been involved in the fighting at Berlín (see section 3.3.5), as a result of which they were suspended from duty for acting without authorization. In July 1984 a former member of the treasury police claimed that some trainers had given instruction in "total warfare" and methods of torture. A year later it was disclosed that in June 1985 a US army helicopter had flown into a battle zone in Morazán to retrieve a Salvadorean military helicopter (the first recorded use of a US-piloted aircraft in a recovery mission). It was reported in February 1986 that under a $4,800,000 programme US advisers had been training Salvadorean police units in anti-terrorist techniques, despite the ban placed on such training by the US government in 1975 because of suspicions that Salvadorean security forces tortured prisoners.

At the end of February 1984 there were 97 US military personnel in El Salvador (excluding the Marine guards at the US embassy and military medical staff), 71 of whom were assigned to the official military group (with the status of 16 redefined so as not to exceed the 55 limit) and the rest at the defence attaché's office, involved in intelligence gathering for the United States. Gen. Paul Gorman (commander of Southcom) unsuccessfully proposed in August 1984 that the number of military trainers be raised from 55 to 125, arguing to a congressional hearing that such an increase would make it possible for the war against the guerrillas to be won within two years. The proposal was also opposed by Col. Blandón, who said that he favoured a reduction in the number since "many do not do anything". Later in the year, however, it was reported that extra US trainers based in Honduras were commuting to El Salvador on a daily basis to evade the 55 limit.

The presence of the US military personnel caused considerable controversy, President Duarte having warned in 1981: "Washington should not send too many military advisers here, otherwise this will soon be seen as America's war".[10]

In May 1983 the FPL killed a US naval officer in San Salvador, Lt.–Cdr Albert A. Schaufelberger, in what they described as a "patriotic operation" and "a warning to those who bring us war to preserve injustice"; the group added that "if Mr Reagan insists in sending his Marines to our homeland, we want him to know that many of them will return to their country as Albert Schaufelberger will return". With the increase in urban armed activity by the FMLN in 1985, US military personnel again became targets, and in mid–June 1985 a guerrilla commando group carried out a raid on a cafe in the capital,

killing four off-duty Marines as well as two US businessmen and seven
Salvadorean citizens. Radio Venceremos warned that "if they [the US forces]
come here for war, they will leave in boxes".

5.2.8: CIA Activities

Originally all US assistance to the Nicaraguan contras was directed through
the CIA, which was reported to have begun covert operations by early 1982
(according to the *Washington Post*, Feb. 14, 1982), with a budget of
$19,000,000, to create a force operating out of commando camps along the
Nicaraguan-Honduran border. Later in the year reports emerged of CIA
activity in Honduras and El Salvador directed against the Sandinista government, and by the end of the year senior US officials had conceded that
CIA activities had begun as early as November 1981 with presidential
approval. In January 1983 it was disclosed that in a secret testimony to the
congressional intelligence committees CIA Director William Casey had confirmed that the agency had backed contra sabotage attacks in Nicaragua,
ostensibly to cut the lines of arms supply to El Salvador.

The magazine *Newsweek* reported in April 1983 that the government had
spent $30,000,000 in CIA operations to arm and train the contras,
$11,000,000 of which had come from a "secret fund". Other press reports
suggested that there were currently about 20 CIA agents in Central America,
controlled from Southcom (Panama). At the beginning of June 1983 three US
diplomats were accused of conspiracy to murder FSLN leaders, having been
recruited by the CIA to poison d'Escoto. It was reported in Washington in
July 1983 that President Reagan had authorized an increase in CIA covert
operations in Central America including plans to sabotage Cuban military
installations in Nicaragua, although no such proposal had been placed before
the house intelligence committees.

In a letter to the Senate select committee on intelligence in April 1984, the
CIA confirmed that CIA agents had directed its operations in 1983 from a
"mother ship" and that the raid on Puerto Sandino in September 1983 had
been carried out by "unilaterally-controlled Latino assets" (understood to
mean agents solely controlled by the CIA). Later the same month Casey
apologized to the committee for failing to provide adequate information on
the CIA role and agreed to give prior notice of "any significant anticipated
intelligence activity". It was reported in May 1984 that the US administration
had secretly sent military equipment to El Salvador through the CIA in
addition to $32,000,000 in emergency aid (see section 5.2.4); this equipment,
it was reported, had been purchased from the defence department at specially
reduced prices (by being declared surplus) so that the amount recorded in
government accounts was well below the true cost. Four CIA agents died in a
light aircraft crash in El Salvador in October 1984.

Although the $24,000,000 covert aid to the contras for fiscal 1984 was
reportedly exhausted by June 1984, the CIA announced in May that it
planned to keep its agents in Nicaragua operational until the arrival of funds
for fiscal 1985. In the event the CIA was barred by Congress from distributing
the aid in 1985, resuming its official role in 1986 (see section 5.2.5).

Early in October 1984 it was discovered that the CIA had issued a manual
entitled *Psychological Operations in Guerrilla Warfare* for the use of the

contras, provoking an uproar in Congress in that the manual endorsed the "selective use of violence" and included advice to "neutralize" certain public officials "such as court judges, police and state security officials", adding: "If possible, professional criminals should be hired to carry out specific, selective jobs". The manual also advised the contras to use religious language by describing themselves as "Christian guerrillas" and using slogans such as "With God and patriotism we will overcome communism." A classified US Defence Intelligence Agency report leaked in the same month revealed that contras had carried out a number of such political assassinations since 1982. President Reagan ordered an investigation into the "possibility of improper conduct" by the CIA, and the agency ordered the "full recall" of the manual which it said was now "inoperative and should be ignored". (A few months earlier, in July, another CIA manual, the *Freedom Fighters' Manual,* had come to light; it offered advice on 38 ways to sabotage the "essential economic infrastructure that any government needs to function, . . . without having to use tools and with minimal risk for the combatant".

Further controversy developed over the agency's role when at the beginning of July 1985 two mercenaries (Peter Glibbery from Britain and Steven Carr from the United States who had been imprisoned in Costa Rica after being caught in a secret contra camp near the Nicaraguan border) claimed that they had been engaged by the CIA to direct sabotage operations and even to manufacture a border incident which "would be a great news story and give an excuse for an American intervention". In August 1985 the White House announced that members of the National Security Council had been "receiving information" and "fostering contacts" with the contras since the suspension of congressional aid in 1984 (see section 5.2.5).

There was renewed controversy over the role of unofficial US aid to the contras when on Oct. 5, 1986, a US citizen, Eugene Hasenfus, was shot down over Nicaragua and taken prisoner by the EPS. The other three occupants of the C–123, which had been carrying ammunition and jungle boots, died in the incident, which occurred when the aircraft was flying in Nicaraguan airspace about 20 miles north of the Costa Rican border. Hasenfus, a former marine now working for an air freight company, was said by Nicaraguan officials to be a CIA agent. In a televised press conference from captivity in Managua given on Oct. 9, Hasenfus said that he had been working with CIA employees on regular flights from Ilopango air base in El Salvador and Aguacate in Honduras, the operation of these regular flights by at least 19 aircraft being confirmed by (unnamed) contra officials. His trial in Managua opened on Oct. 20. He was convicted under the law on the maintenance of order and public security and given the maximum sentence allowed, i.e. 30 years' imprisonment. In December he was pardoned by President Ortega and returned to the United States.

5.2.9: The Caribbean Basin Initiative

The concept of a Caribbean Basin Initiative (CBI) as a large-scale aid project in the form of investment, trade arrangements and financial measures (such as tax incentives) was developed in 1981 as basically a US programme, although it was subsequently joined by Canada, Venezuela and Mexico. (Mexico joined the CBI on the condition that the plan had no military aspect, that its aim was to help the people of the region and not to combat perceived Soviet or communist influence in the area, and that no country in the region should be excluded automatically nor in principle from receiving development assistance.) Representatives of the six Central American governments met in Tegucigalpa in August 1981 to formulate a common position on aid, and set the immediate needs of their countries at $1,000 million, and for the period up to 1990 at $20,000 million. They recommended that three-quarters of this amount should be spent on regional co-operation and integration programmes, especially for energy, and the rest on national projects. At a meeting in San José in September 1981 they requested that the aid be "distributed equally without ideological discrimination".

The details of the CBI were announced by Reagan in a speech on Feb. 24, 1982, including the following passages:

> The events of the last several years dramatize two different futures which are possible for the Caribbean area: either the establishment or restoration of moderate constitutional governments with economic growth and improved living standards, or further expansion of political violence from the extreme left and the extreme right resulting in the imposition of dictatorships and inevitably more economic decline and human suffering. . . . It is an integrated programme that helps our neighbours help themselves, under which creativity and private entrepreneurship and self-help can flourish. . . . We seek to exclude no one. Some, however, have turned from their American neighbours and their heritage. Let them return to the traditions and common values of this hemisphere and we will all welcome them. The choice is theirs.

The distribution of loans and grants to the region under the CBI was as follows (1980 and 1981 are actual, 1982 original and 1983 projected allocations):

	1980	1981	1982	1983
	$ million			
Development assistance	225.0	168.4	211.1	217.6
Direct economic support	15.2	143.4	490.0	326.0
Food aid	83.7	108.7	123.1	120.9
Military assistance	13.8	50.5	172.1	106.2
Total	337.7	471.0	996.3	770.7

Of $350,000,000 in emergency economic assistance, $128,000,000 went to El Salvador, $70,000,000 to Costa Rica and $35,000,000 to Honduras.

President Duarte of El Salvador hailed the CBI as "a plan without precedent", which would "avoid a new colonization based on Cuban-style slavery". President de la Espriella of Panama called it a "good step towards the solution" of the region's problems, adding that there should be no "political price" attached to the aid, and the Mexican Foreign Minister Jorge Castañeda, said that "programmes for economic development of the CBI, no matter how ambitious or generous, cannot succeed in the midst of political confrontation or military threats". The CBI provoked some US criticism from those opposed to extra foreign aid at a time of cuts in domestic spending, those who saw the trade and other concessions as a threat to their own economic interests and those who opposed its political overtones. The most vehement criticism came from (i) Cuba, which called it "a mixture of lies, cynicism and threats", (ii) Nicaragua, which described it as "total political blackmail", and (iii) Grenada, where Maurice Bishop described it as "the biggest confidence game of the century". When President Reagan travelled to the Caribbean in April to meet Caribbean leaders and discuss the CBI, Grenada was excluded from the consultations. The President commented: "I think all of us are concerned with the overturn of party democracy in Grenada—that country now bears the Soviet and Cuban trademark, which means it will attempt to spread the virus of Marxism among its neighbours."

The CBI entered into US law on Aug. 5, 1983, as the Caribbean Basin Economy Recovery Act, after a substantial delay because of lobbying by special interest groups who feared the possible adverse effect on US jobs or who wanted more stringent protectionist measures against all imports. Although the measure passed fairly swiftly through the House of Representatives, it gained approval in the Senate only when incorporated as a rider to the repeal of certain tax legislation (contrary to presidential wishes). The Act, which Reagan said was designed "to bring the power of private enterprise—America's most potent weapon—to help Latin America and the Caribbean", established eight criteria by which the President could designate countries as beneficiaries, namely that the country in question (i) expressly requested aid; (ii) was not communist; (iii) met certain regulations on the expropriation or nationalization of US property; (iv) co-operated effectively with the US authorities in keeping narcotics out of the United States; (v) recognized arbitral awards to US citizens; (vi) did not afford preferential treatment to imports from any other developed country to the detriment of the United States; (vii) did not contravene US copyright of US material; (viii) had an extradition treaty with the United States. (The President was, however, entitled to waive any of these criteria for national economic or security reasons.)

In addition the President was required to take into account in making his assessment the country's (i) economic situation; (ii) willingness to provide equitable and reasonable access to its markets and basic commodity resources; (iii) adherence to the accepted rules of international trade; (iv) use of export subsidies or the imposition of export performance requirements; (v) trade policies towards other CBI beneficiaries; (vi) adoption of economic self-help measures; (vii) provision for its workforce of reasonable work-place conditions and accordance of the right to organize and bargain collectively; (viii) protection of the intellectual property rights of foreign nationals, including patents and trademarks, and (ix) readiness to co-operate with the United States in effecting statutory conditions.

Notes

1. Pearce, *op. cit.*, p. 54.
2. *Ibid.*, p. 55.
3. Quoted *ibid.*, p. 56.
4. *Ibid.*, pp. 58–59.
5. Source: *Infopress Centroamericana*, No. 627, Feb 7, 1985, p. 5.

6. See Armstrong and Shenk, *op. cit.*, pp. 260–61 for detailed table of US economic and military aid 1946–82.
7. See Pearce, *op. cit.*, for full text of letter.
8. "Newsnight", BBC, April 12, 1985.
9. See Bonner, *op. cit.*, pp. 237–77.
10. Quoted in Pearce, *op. cit.*, p. 241.
11. *Latinamerica Press*, Vol. 17, No. 4, Feb. 7, 1985.

5.3: CUBAN AND SOVIET INFLUENCE

5.3.1: Introductory

The extent of Cuban and Soviet influence in the Central American and Caribbean region has become a matter of some debate, particularly as the claims made by the US administration of "communist infiltration" have largely formed the basis for its policy there.[1] A prime objective of that policy has been the prevention of strong links being established between any state in the region and the Soviet Union. Against this background, US attempts (unsuccessful) to overturn the Cuban revolution and the (successful) US-led military intervention in Grenada have been crucial in fostering Nicaraguan fears of direct US military action against the Sandinista revolution.

In addition to its direct action in the Dominican Republic (in 1965) and Grenada (in 1983), the United States was accused in 1976 by the Guyanese government of attempting to destabilize Guyana and Jamaica because of the leftist orientation of those countries' elected governments. It has also been alleged that the CIA was instrumental in the replacement of Michael Manley by Edward Seaga in Jamaica in 1980. (Jamaica and Guyana, along with Nicaragua and Grenada, have been particular recipients of Cuban technical assistance, mainly from medical, construction and teaching staff.)

5.3.2: Impact of the Cuban Revolution of 1959

Cuba had not yet gained its independence from Spain when it first fell under US influence, US troops having occupied the island in 1898–1902. The constitution of the new republic (promulgated in 1901) incorporated the Platt Amendment, according the United States the right to intervene in Cuban affairs and to establish military bases on the island, including the naval base of Guantánamo. The United States exercised this right of intervention by sending troops to the island in 1906–09, 1912 and 1917–23.

By the 1950s there was growing opposition to the government of Fulgencio Batista (in power since the 1933 coup), who strengthened links with the United States and waged an internal security campaign in which thousands were detained, tortured and killed. Fidel Castro made his first armed attack on the government in 1953, but it was only during 1956 that his forces were strong enough to pose a real threat, eventually forcing Batista to flee the country on Jan. 1, 1957.

As in the case of Guatemala a few years earlier, Cuban relations with the United States deteriorated sharply with the introduction in June 1957 of a land-reform programme which seriously affected the interests of several US concerns (jointly owners of about 20 per cent of the expropriated land). Moreover, the nationalization in 1960 of the sugar industry (which accounted for 80 per cent of exports) further jeopardized US financial interests. The US government responded by cutting Cuba's sugar quota for the second half of the year from 3,119,655 to 39,752 tons. This action led in turn to closer economic links between Cuba and the communist countries (especially the Soviet Union).

Nikita Khrushchev, the Soviet leader, stated his government's full support for Cuba on July 9, 1957, and in reply President Eisenhower said that the United States would "never permit the establishment of a regime dominated by international communism in the western hemisphere". Three days later Khrushchev denounced the Monroe Doctrine (see section 1.1.6) and on July 14 the US State Department issued a communiqué reaffirming the doctrine's principles, declaring it to be as valid now as when first proclaimed in 1823, with its "purpose of preventing any extension to this hemisphere of a despotic political system contrary to the independent status of the American states".

US–Cuban relations reached a nadir in early 1961 when on April 17 a group of Cuban exiles from Miami landed in the Bahia de Cochinos (Bay of Pigs) in an abortive military operation. Within three days they had been routed by the Cuban army and 1,241 were taken prisoner. The landing had been intended to trigger off a national uprising against Castro and had relied on the premise of large-scale defection by the Cuban militias. It was known that the invasion had been planned in the United States, under guidance from the CIA, and that the project had been approved by Eisenhower in March 1960,[2] (although it occurred under the presidency of John F. Kennedy).

The incident provoked a swift exchange of words between the Soviet and US governments. Khrushchev, speaking on April 18, 1961, pledged that his country would give "all necessary assistance in beating back the armed attack on Cuba", and President Kennedy immediately replied that "the United States intends no military intervention in Cuba" while at the same time reiterating the Monroe Doctrine. Four days later Khrushchev said that, although the Soviet Union had no intention of establishing bases on Cuba, it could "not concede to the United States any right to control the destinies of other countries, the countries of Latin America included".

The following year tension between the United States and the Soviet Union escalated into a major crisis with an announcement from Moscow on Sept. 3, 1962, that the Soviet government had agreed to send Cuba an unspecified quantity of arms to counter "threats from imperialist quarters". Kennedy sent a message to the US Congress on Sept. 7 requesting "standby" authority to call up 150,000 reservists, this measure being described by the Soviet news agency Tass on Sept. 11 as preparation for "an act of aggression".

In a television broadcast of Oct. 22, 1962, Kennedy stated that the US authorities now possessed unmistakable evidence of the installation in Cuba of medium-range and intermediate-range ballistic missiles capable of sending warheads to Central America and the United States, adding that longer range missiles were in preparation. The next day the US administration imposed "a short quarantine on all offensive military equipment under shipment to Cuba" (to come into effect on Oct. 24), under which the United States could turn back ships of any nation carrying arms to Cuba. The Soviet Union said that the arms were solely for "defensive purposes" and accused the United States of "taking a step towards unleashing a thermo-nuclear war". An OAS meeting on Oct. 23 approved a resolution for "the immediate dismantling and withdrawal from Cuba of all missiles and other weapons with offensive capability", and adjured all OAS members to do everything in their power, "including the use of armed force", to stop Soviet arms reaching Cuba. All six Central American states gave their support to the United States in the crisis, with Honduras pledging an infantry battalion and an air squadron, while

Costa Rica offered a base for operations against Cuba. In the event, the Soviet Union drew back from this particular brink, recalling its vessels en route for Cuba before they encountered the US blockade.

The issue of Cuba and the Inter-American System had dominated the Punta del Este conference of the OAS in January 1962, when the six Central American states had strongly urged that collective action be taken against Cuba, which was finally excluded from the OAS on Feb. 14, 1962. A decade later, however, attitudes towards Cuba modified, and the question of the continued exclusion of the country was among the chief topics of the 4th regular session of the OAS held in Atlanta (Georgia) in April 1974. A year earlier Castro had attempted to use the difference of opinion among the member states when on May 1 he proposed the formation of a new regional organization excluding the United States, on the grounds that "US and Latin American interests are in total contradiction". He said that Cuba was ready to co-operate with any Latin American country with an "independent foreign policy", regardless of its political system, but that negotiations with the United States would be impossible as long as the economic blockade (imposed in 1964) lasted.

At the 15th consultative assembly of the OAS held in Quito (Ecuador) in 1974, a proposal was made to lift diplomatic and economic sanctions against Cuba, but it gained only 12 votes (including those of Honduras, El Salvador, Costa Rica and Panama), two short of the necessary 14 (Guatemala and Nicaragua abstained). The next year, however, a "freedom of action" resolution was passed at the OAS conference in San José (Costa Rica), held on July 16–26, 1975, allowing members "freedom to normalize or conduct, in accordance with national policy and interests, relations with the Republic of Cuba at the level and in the form that each state deems advisable". The resolution affected only bilateral relations (and among the Central American states was favoured in particular by Panama), but did not constitute an end to Cuba's exclusion nor to the 1964 economic sanctions.

5.3.3: The Grenadan Crisis of 1983

In March 1979 the conservative government of Sir Eric Gairy was overthrown in a coup led by the New Jewel Movement (NJM), which had originally been a left-wing nationalist movement but had developed a more pronounced Marxist-Leninist stance from 1976 under the influence of Bernard Coard. The new People's Revolutionary Government (PRG) was led by Maurice Bishop (a personal friend of Castro) who, in an address to a May Day rally in Havana in 1980 declared: "Fidel has taught us not only how to fight, but also how to work, how to build socialism, and how to lead our country in a spirit of humility, sincerity, commitment and firm revolutionary leadership."[3]

Grenada's relations with other Caribbean countries gradually deteriorated, as the governments most sympathetic to the PRG suffered electoral defeats in Dominica in July 1980, in Jamaica in October 1980 and in St Lucia in May 1982, while relations with Guyana cooled after June 1980. The PRG's failure to hold elections as originally promised (on the grounds that the PRG must first be given a chance to consolidate its reforms, like the Sandinista government in Nicaragua) was severely criticized at the Caricom conference held in Jamaica in November 1982, as was the continued detention without trial of a number of opponents of the new government. In response to these criticisms Bishop reiterated his government's commitment to the electoral process, within a framework of "participatory democracy", and 29 detainees held since 1979 were released. By 1983, however, the greatest foreign policy issue for Grenada was the deterioration of relations with the United States, especially after Grenada was excluded from the Caribbean Basin Initiative (see section 5.2.9).

By mid-1983 a rift had appeared within the central committee of the NJM, with Bishop and other leading PRG members favouring the adoption of an electoral timetable and attempting to improve relations with the United States, while NJM hardliners led by Coard advocated more rigorous state control of the economy and closer alignment with the Soviet Union. Eventually Bishop and other leading moderates were ousted from the party, and on Oct. 19 they were shot by army units at Fort Rupert (probably by firing squad on the orders of the new Revolutionary Military Council, led by Coard). The new regime gained little support either within Grenada or abroad, and the Cuban government (the PRG's closest ally) issued a statement on Oct. 20 denouncing the Council and in particular the murder of Bishop.

The US military operation, codenamed "Urgent Fury", began on Oct. 25, 1983, when 1,900 US troops landed on the island, followed by 392 soldiers and police from Jamaica, Barbados, Dominica, Antigua, St Lucia and St Vincent and the Grenadines; by Oct. 27 armed opposition from the Grenadan army and some Cuban construction workers had largely ceased. In official statements the US authorities overestimated the strength of the Cubans on the island, claiming originally that they totalled 1,500, although conceding on Oct. 29 that the real figure was similar to that given by the Cuban government, i.e. 784. Nevertheless, in statements on the operation, President Reagan claimed that Grenada had been "a Soviet-Cuban colony being readied for use as a major bastion to export terror", and indicated the importance of the US "success" in Grenada within US foreign policy: "The events in Grenada and Lebanon [i.e. the killing of over 200 US soldiers in Beirut on Oct. 23], though oceans apart, are closely related. Not only has Moscow assisted and encouraged violence in both countries, but it provides direct support through a network of surrogates and terrorists. We got there just in time."

The fullest expression of the official US position on the military intervention was made on Nov. 4, 1983, by Kenneth Dam, deputy secretary of state. He gave the administration's two basic objectives as being "to protect the lives of US citizens and to help Grenada re-establish order, . . . contributing also to the maintenance of regional peace and stability". The US citizens in question were 603 medical students at college in St George's, and in connection with them Dam asserted: "Inaction would have made a hostage situation more likely. . . . I don't think I need remind you that today is the fourth anniversary of the seizure of the US embassy in Tehran."

There was substantial controversy over the timing and the origin of the US decision to intervene, it being unclear whether the (British) Governor, Sir Paul Scoon, had invited assistance from the Organization of East Caribbean States (OECS) before any troops had arrived. (As Grenada still belonged to the OECS there had been doubt over whether a decision on the country's future could be taken by the Organization without consultation with the country's government; even more questionable was whether it had been appropriate to invite the United States to intervene in a country which belonged to the Commonwealth.)

Apart from being a cause of severe embarrassment to the British government the intervention aroused international reaction overwhelmingly hostile to the United States, and at the UN a draft resolution was presented to the Security Council by Guyana on Oct. 28, declaring the military intervention illegal. After intense debate 11 countries voted in favour while Britain, Togo and Zaire abstained, but the resolution was vetoed by the United States. A proposal submitted by Nicaragua and Zimbabwe to the General Assembly on Nov. 2, deploring the military intervention and calling for the withdrawal of all foreign troops from the island, was passed without debate by 108 votes to nine (the United States, Israel, El Salvador and the six OECS members, excluding Grenada), with 27 abstentions.

5.3.4: Cuban Relations with Nicaragua

In February 1980 the Sandinista government signed an agreement under which Cuba undertook to provide $50,000,000 in aid to Nicaragua over the rest of the year; the following month about 1,200 Cuban volunteers joined the Nicaraguan literacy campaign as *brigadistas*. A further 1,000 Cuban doctors, nurses and technicians also volunteered for service in Nicaragua, and at the end of September 1980 violent disturbances broke out in the Atlantic coast town of Bluefields in protest against the presence of Cuban teachers and doctors in the area, which turned into general demonstrations against communism. (Cubans were by no means the sole nor the majority of the foreign presence, constituting only about 15 per cent of foreign medical staff in the country in 1984.)[4]

Early in 1983 the CIA estimated the number of Cuban advisers in Central America (i.e. based in Nicaragua) at 8,000, claiming that 2,000 of these acted in a military capacity; Cuban and Nicaraguan officials put the total figure at 4,000. Enders claimed that there were also "50 Soviets, 35 East Germans [and] 50 PLO and Libyan personnel" working on "security missions" in Nicaragua, and a White Paper issued in May 1983 by the US State and Defence Departments alleged that these Cuban military personnel had trained left-wing guerrillas and conducted covert activities in Central America in collusion with Nicaragua.

In the wake of the US invervention in Grenada in October 1983 the Nicaraguan authorities took steps to reduce their links with Cuba and about 1,200 Cubans left the country, and by early 1985 the number of Cubans in Nicaragua (according to Ortega) had fallen to about 2,000, of whom less than half were military advisers. In February of that year Castro offered to pull these military advisers out of Nicaragua as part of a comprehensive settlement within the Contadora framework. In this context, Ortega announced on Feb. 28 that 100 Cuban military personnel would be asked to leave, and that the government had imposed an indefinite moratorium on the purchase of new weapons systems (including advanced fighter aircraft) as an unconditional gesture towards peace talks (i.e. the current Contadora negotiations—see section 6.5.3).

Earlier, in July 1983, Castro had expressed his government's readiness to agree to any comprehensive regional settlement on arms and advisers drafted by the Contadora Group: "If there were to be an agreement among all the parties involved about withdrawing all the advisers, we would be willing to support such a settlement, [and] if an agreement were reached on the basis of cessation of sending weapons to any state of Central America, we would be willing to abide by it."

It was reported in March 1986 that Cuban–Nicaraguan relations had been strained by the presence of a team of Libyan advisers in Managua and a secret Libyan grant to the Sandinista government worth $400,000,000; Castro was said to have expressed the view that Libyan contacts—and especially a Libyan presence—would be unnecessarily provocative to the United States.

5.3.5: Nicaraguan Links with the Soviet Union

Since its first months in power, the Sandinista government has maintained links with the Soviet Union, which have developed apace alongside the gradual deterioration of relations with the United States. In March and April 1980 Moisés Hassán Morales (a junta member) and three cabinet ministers travelled to the Soviet Union and Eastern Europe to reach trading agreements and prepare for the establishment of relations between the FSLN and the Soviet Communist Party (CPSU); subsequently, Soviet-bloc countries provided 32 per cent of all foreign aid to Nicaragua until 1982, rising to 41.4 per cent in 1983. (For replacement of US aid and trading links by other countries, including the Soviet Union, after the suspension of US aid in 1981, see sections 2.2.4 and 5.2.5.)

In June 1981 the *Washington Post* (June 2) reported that several Soviet T–55 tanks had recently been shipped to Nicaragua on Cuban vessels as part of a plan to equip the Sandinista armed forces with Soviet armoury, eventually including MiG aircraft. The junta described the report as "totally unfounded", although the Nicaraguan armed forces certainly obtained T–55 tanks in subsequent years.

During 1983 several Soviet spokesmen indicated that the Soviet Union might consider installing intermediate-range missiles at an unspecified location in Central America if the United States proceeded with its deployment of Pershing II and cruise missiles in Western Europe later in the year. In April Viktor Isakov of the Soviet diplomatic staff in Washington said in an interview on US television that the Soviet Union was disposed to install intermediate-range missiles in Central America, while a senior member of the CPSU, Vadim Zagladin, said in a broadcast on Hungarian television that the presence of further US missiles in Europe would force the Soviet Union to attain the capacity to strike US targets "within three to five minutes". A few days later Reagan responded by saying that if Soviet missiles were to be installed in Central America, the United States would impose a blockade similar to that of 1962 during the Cuban missiles crisis (see section 5.3.2).

In July 1983 the US Defence Department reported that a dozen Soviet-bloc ships were currently heading for Nicaraguan ports, and that nine loads of military cargo had already arrived since the beginning of the year, compared with five shipments in the whole of 1982. The first of these ships, the *Alexander Ulyanov*, docked at Corinto in August, with (according to the

Nicaraguan authorities) 1,342 tonnes of goods, including "spare parts, tractors, medicine and other items"; d'Escoto did not deny that the shipment included some military supplies, saying: "What would anyone do in our situation? There is a war on against our country. We do not manufacture arms, so obviously we are trying to obtain as much as we can to exercise our legitimate right of national self-determination."

After the mining of Corinto in March 1984 the Nicaraguan government said it would seek to buy minesweepers and military equipment from abroad. On March 28 a delegation led by Humberto Ortega (defence minister) left for the Soviet Union and North Korea. In June another government delegation led by Daniel Ortega visited the Soviet Union and other East European countries, and during a meeting with the then Soviet leader, Konstantin Chernenko, Ortega thanked the Soviet Union for its "political and economic support for Nicaragua"; both leaders expressed their satisfaction with the "successful development of Nicaraguan–Soviet relations in various fields". At the end of April 1985 President Ortega embarked on another East European tour, which he said was for the purpose of seeking aid "for the life of the Nicaraguan people" rather than military support, and in particular to counter the effect of the embargo that Reagan was expected to announce shortly (and did so on May 1—see section 5.2.5). An agreement was signed on the establishment of joint economic, scientific and technical programmes, and the Soviet leader, Mikhail Gorbachev, said that the Soviet Union would help Nicaragua in "resolving urgent problems of economic development and political and diplomatic support in its efforts to uphold its sovereignty". (For agreement on Soviet and East European financial assistance during this trip, see section 2.2.4.)

In November 1984 the US Defence Department claimed that there was a current flow of Soviet arms into Nicaragua "similar to Soviet behaviour in the weeks and months before the 1962 Cuban incident", alleging that the cargo of the Soviet ship *Bakuriani*, which had docked at Corinto, contained MiG–21 advanced warplanes. A spokesman for the State Department said: "We do not think the presence of high-speed aircraft delivered to a regime of that character to be in the interest of the United States or other countries in the area." (The administration had earlier warned that it "would not tolerate the introduction of MiGs into Nicaragua".)

The Nicaraguan foreign ministry and the Soviet Union denied that MiGs had been delivered, but amid fears that the US statements might be a prelude to an invasion the Nicaraguan authorities placed troops on "maximum alert" and called on the country's civilian population to mount a 24–hour guard duty. No evidence was presented for the US claim, and it was reported by dockers unloading the *Bakuriani* that the hold contained only ammunition in "a few boxes no more than three metres long".

5.3.6: US Allegations of Cuban and Soviet Military Activity

The US administration issued a White Paper on Feb. 23, 1981, purporting to show "incontrovertible evidence" (based on 19 "captured documents") that "Arab radicals", Vietnam, Ethiopia, Cuba and Nicaragua were involved in the shipment of arms to the FMLN in El Salvador. FDR leaders in Mexico City immediately challenged the claims of the Paper, pointing out that three of the FDR's five component groups were "strongly anti-Soviet", while the group's official spokesman, Héctor Oquelí, said on a visit to London that the main suppliers of arms to the FMLN were neither Cuba nor the Soviet Union, but Algeria, Libya, the PLO, Iraq and the US black market. Moreover, in early June the *Wall Street Journal* published an article claiming that the White Paper "contains factual errors, misleading statements and unresolved ambiguities that raise questions about the administration's interpretation of participation by communist countries in the Salvadorean civil war"[5]; the newspaper reported, moreover, that several of the documents said to have been written by guerrilla leaders had not been, and that some details and statistics had been "extrapolated" from other "still-secret sources" rather than based on the documents at all. Jon Glassman, the State Department official with the main responsibility for the paper's contents, conceded that parts of it could be "misleading" and "over-embellished"[6]; the State Department itself admitted on June 18 that the paper contained some errors, but maintained that "the few points of mis-stated detail or ambiguous formulations do not in any way change the conclusions of the report."

In December 1981 the State Department was reported to have sent a confidential report to some 50 allied and friendly governments giving details of alleged Cuban "covert activities" in Latin America and the Caribbean, claiming that Cuba's immediate goals were "to exploit and control the revolution in Nicaragua and to induce the violent overthrow of the governments of El Salvador and Guatemala".[7]

In August 1981 Secretary of State Haig claimed that Cuban activity in El Salvador had recently escalated, and would be matched by increased US military aid to the Salvadorean government; in September of that year the State Department alleged that Cuban advisers had joined in fighting with the FMLN. The government in Havana quickly responded by "categorically" denying that there had ever been a "single military or civilian adviser from Cuba alongside the revolutionary forces fighting in El Salvador", adding that the arms Cuba received from the Soviet Union were for national defence against US aggression and "not a single one of them has left Cuba for Latin America".

According to a report in the *New York Times* (datelined Sept. 25, 1982), the FMLN had no shortage of weapons, being equipped with US-made M–16 rifles, Soviet and East German demolition equipment, US 81mm mortars, Soviet and Chinese rocket-propelled grenades and M–60 and 30mm anti-aircraft guns. (The flow of arms from Nicaragua had been negligible since mid–1981.) The guerrillas and the Salvadorean armed forces both claimed to have captured considerable stocks of weapons from each other, although these claims were often hard to substantiate; for example, in December 1982 the Salvadorean ministry of defence announced the capture of 420 M–60 machine guns, 16,000 cartridges and 60 Chinese RPG–2 rocket-propelled grenade launchers, but failed to exhibit the haul saying that it had been ruined by sea water and so jettisoned into the ocean before journalists could see it. The FMLN was also reported to obtain US arms directly, purchased from sympathetic members of the Salvadorean armed forces.[8]

In September 1982 Wayne Smith (formerly head of the US interests section at the Swiss embassy in Havana) said that the evidence for the flow of arms from Cuba through Nicaragua to the FMLN had "never been solid", and that

CUBAN AND SOVIET INFLUENCE

although some supplies had been sent "the quantities are almost certainly far less than alleged; if the guerrillas had received all the arms reported by US intelligence, the Salvadorean army would be outgunned 20 to one".

In April 1985 two leading FMLN guerrillas (Napoleón Romero and Nidia Díaz) were captured by Salvadorean armed forces, along with some documents (which were declared by the US embassy to be authentic) indicating that the FMLN had received some form of training in Cuba, the Soviet Union, Bulgaria, East Germany and Vietnam.

Notes

1. See *The Soviet–Cuban Connection in Central America and the Caribbean*, Department of State and Department of Defence, March 1985, Washington, extracts of which are given in Appendix 2.
2. Pearce, *op. cit.*, p. 33. Wyden, *op. cit.*, gives detailed account of CIA operations. Black, *Triumph of the People*, p. 49, states that the Somoza government collaborated with the CIA in the Bay of Pigs operation by allowing the exiles to launch bombing raids from a Nicaraguan airbase and to use Puerto Cabezas as a departure point for the flotilla of landing craft.
3. Quoted in Hugh O'Shaughnessy, *Grenada: Revolution, Invasion and Aftermath*, Hamish Hamilton with *The Observer*, London, 1984, p. 105.
4. *Central America Report*, November/December 1984, issue 19, p. 6.
5. Quoted in Armstrong and Shenk, *op. cit.*, p. 194.
6. *Ibid.*, see also Pearce, *op. cit.*, pp. 242–43, and Bonner *op. cit.*, pp. 256–60.
7. *Washington Post*, Dec. 2, 1981.
8. Bonner, *op. cit.*, p. 267.

5.4: OTHER FOREIGN AID AND INVOLVEMENT

5.4.1: General

Although foreign aid and involvement in Central America has come largely from the United States (with substantial roles also being played by Cuba and the Soviet Union), several other countries have given direct economic or military assistance or have supplied arms. The variety of donors has been especially apparent in the case of Nicaragua, where bilateral aid in the period July 1979–March 1984 (comprising 75 per cent of total foreign aid) was composed as follows: Latin America 41 per cent, socialist countries 33 per cent, Western Europe 14 per cent, Africa and Asia 7.5 per cent and United States 4.5 per cent; the West European proportion of aid reached 25 per cent in 1983.[1]

5.4.2: Latin America

Prior to the overthrow of Somoza in Nicaragua in 1979 the FSLN was believed to have received considerable assistance from Panama (see section 1.7.11), Venezuela and Costa Rica. In May 1981 a three-member Costa Rican parliamentary commission investigating claims of involvement by the government in arms trafficking to left-wing guerrillas said that Costa Rica had received arms from Cuba since 1979, which had been sent first to the FSLN and later to the FMLN. The arms mentioned in the report came not only from Cuba but also from Venezuela, Panama and Western Europe, and in March 1981 five Costa Rican pilots had admitted to having flown in arms from Cuba to the Salvadorean guerrillas at least until January. (No further allegations of arms from Costa Rica to the FMLN were made after the installation of the more right-wing government of Monge in 1982.)

In February 1981 Gen. Vernon Walters travelled to Argentina and Chile and presented the US administration's "evidence" of arms trafficking to the FMLN (i.e. the White Paper—see section 5.3.6) to the two governments in an effort to encourage them to support the Salvadorean armed forces. In June Argentina signed an agreement with the Salvadorean government to provide $15,000,000 in economic and technical assistance, and although the Salvadorean foreign minister, Fidel Chávez Mena, asserted that the agreement covered neither military aid nor training it was reported a few weeks later that there were a number of Argentinian military advisers in El Salvador. In September President Galtieri confirmed that Argentina had, in response to Gen. Walter's request, agreed to send troops to fight with the Salvadorean army in an inter-American peace-keeping force if Duarte asked for one.

It was thought that Argentinian officers were acting as counter-insurgency advisers to the Salvadorean and Honduran authorities (especially as Alvarez was known to praise Argentinian counter-insurgency methods), and also as advisers to the Nicaraguan contra FDN based in southern Honduras, although many of these were replaced by US advisers after the outbreak of the Falklands/Malvinas conflict in April 1982 (see section 5.2.3). US intelligence sources claimed in mid–1982 that there were still 50 Argentinian military advisers in Honduras, along with a number of Chileans and Israelis; it was reported that in August 1982 Alvarez had been close to war with Nicaragua on the advice of the Argentinians for the purpose of "testing US commitment", but had been restrained from engaging in war by US officials.

Chile denied any involvement in Central America, and the new civilian government in Argentina (installed in December 1983) said in January 1984 that there were now "no members of the Argentine forces at the official level in this area", although there might be "Argentinians in Central America who were supporters of the former military regime but who have nothing to do with the present Argentinian government".

5.4.3: Israel and Other Countries

In the early 1970s Israel launched an arms sales drive, reaching the status of the fifth largest arms exporter in the world by the 1980s; Latin America became its best customer. In 1975 Israel concluded a deal to re-equip the Salvadorean air force with jet aircraft, and between 1972 and 1979 El Salvador received 81 per cent of its military supplies from Israel. As tighter controls were imposed by the Carter administration on the export of the US equipment, so Israel filled the gap, providing the Somoza government with 98 per cent of its arms imports and about $80,000,000 worth of military aid to Guatemala in 1977–82 (i.e. during the US ban—see section 5.2.2). Under Lucas García, Israeli advisers installed computers and supervised intelligence-gathering operations at the Regional Telecommunications Centre (from which the security force G–2 operated—see also section 4.2.2), and plans were announced for the building of factories in Guatemala to produce ammunition for Galil assault rifles and even Kfir jet aircraft. (The arms supplies to Nicaragua were terminated in July 1979, when the Israeli government annulled all arms contracts and ordered two shipments in transit to turn back.) In the same way Israel was reported to have agreed in July 1983 to a request by the US administration to send captured PLO weapons to the contras in Honduras in order to avoid the current congressional ban.[2]

It was reported in late 1982 that Costa Rica had decided to strengthen its ties with Israel after the visit of the foreign minister, Yitzak Shamir, to San José in October. The following year Israeli troops were reported to have provided training for security and intelligence units of the Costa Rican civil guard, although the Costa Rican government denied reports that the Israelis had also given the guard 1,500 assault rifles. Further security assistance was made available to the guard in 1983–84, apparently as part of an agreement by which Costa Rica moved its embassy from Tel Aviv to Jerusalem. El Salvador made the same decision in March 1984 and as a result the members of the Islamic Conference Organization broke relations with both countries. In January 1985 the *New York Times* reported that Israel, Honduras and El Salvador had replaced the United States as the main arms supplier to the contras, and in particular that Israel was sending them Soviet arms and ammunition captured in Lebanon.

Military assistance for the armed forces in Central America (except

Nicaragua) and the contras was also reported to have come from Taiwan, South Africa and South Korea, while the Nicaraguan armed forces and the Salvadorean guerrillas received arms from Libya and the PLO. In April 1983 four Libyan aircraft were detained by the Brazilian authorities during a refuelling stop in Recife, on the grounds that they had allegedly contravened international law on the declaration of cargo. The three Ilyushins and one C–130 Hercules, which were said by the Libyans to be carrying medical supplies, were forced to return home without their cargo, which US intelligence sources said consisted of weapons and explosives of Czech or Soviet manufacture bound for Nicaragua and ultimately the FMLN.

5.4.4: Western Europe

The main West European supplier of arms to Central America has been France, which concluded an agreement with Nicaragua in January 1982 worth nearly $16,000,000 and began arms deliveries in July in spite of expressed US disapproval. As far as economic aid to Nicaragua was concerned, the Netherlands overtook the United States as the largest single donor in 1981, with substantial contributions also from France, Sweden and West Germany; at a meeting in Madrid in July 1983 between the Spanish Prime Minister, Felipe González, and d'Escoto, agreement was reached on a loan from the Spanish government totalling $41,300,000 for the purchase of equipment, food and raw materials. By contrast, Britain has been the only European country to give less aid to Nicaragua in the early 1980s than in the 1970s, with the annual average figure falling from nearly £300,000 in 1974–78 to under £80,000 in 1980–83. British aid to Central America in 1983 amounted to £6,670,000 to Honduras, £6,098,000 to Belize, £1,800,000 to Costa Rica and £64,000 to Nicaragua, and the following year the British government resumed bilateral aid to El Salvador, with an immediate grant of £100,000 for "urgently needed civilian supplies", even though, as the foreign office noted, El Salvador was already the "sixth largest recipient of US bilateral aid in the world".

(In November 1984 the British government disclosed that it had agreed to accept "one or two" Salvadorean officers for military training at the army staff college at Camberley; in February 1985 Col. Blandón announced that a similar offer had been made tentatively by the Belgian government.)

On the other hand, the allocation of the European Community's 1983 aid budget for the region gave 33.9 per cent to Nicaragua, 32.2 per cent to Honduras, 5.4 per cent to El Salvador, 3.8 per cent to Guatemala and 1.7 per cent to Costa Rica (with the remaining 23 per cent going to Mexico, Panama, the Caribbean and regional programmes). Although the Community's aid to the region has grown in recent years, the increased value has been more than offset by the sharp drop in prices paid by European consumers for coffee, sugar and cotton, especially in the 1978–82 slump combined with the rising cost of European manufactured goods; for example, the cost to Nicaragua of importing chemical products, machinery and other goods from Europe more than trebled in 1979–83.[3]

Talks on European aid for Central America were held in San José in September 1984, involving the foreign ministers of the five Central American states, of the 10 members of the European Community and of the Contadora members (with observers from Spain and Portugal). The conference expres-

sed its support for the Contadora efforts and favoured a regional approach in
the allocation of aid. During the conference it was disclosed that two weeks
previously US Secretary of State Shultz had written to the European ministers
to the effect that while the United States welcomed further aid to Central
America, "we strongly urge that such region-to-region assistance does not
need to increase economic aid or any political support for the Sandinistas",
and had advocated that new agreements on aid should be bilateral. After the
meeting the European Commission announced an increase in its aid to the
region of $15,000,000 (in addition to the existing budget of $30,000,000).[4] In
May 1985 the Commission said that it would double its aid to the region in the
form of trade concessions, development finance and food aid to over
$300,000,000 over the next five years.

Notes

1. Melrose, *op. cit.*, p. 43.
2. *El Salvador News Bulletin*, No. 21, Autumn 1983, p. 10.
3. Melrose, *op. cit.*, chapter 5.
4. *Ibid.*, p. 51.

SECTION SIX

CENTRAL AMERICAN PEACE INITIATIVES

6.1: INTERNATIONAL DECLARATIONS AND INITIATIVES

6.1.1: Introductory

There have been a variety of bilateral and multilateral peace initiatives relating to the Central American region since 1981, of which the main ones have been (i) negotiations between the Nicaraguan government and the United States, and more recently with Miskito leaders; (ii) talks between the Duarte government and the FMLN–FDR; and (iii) the Contadora process. Although each initiative has raised hopes of viable solutions being found, as yet all such efforts have fallen far short of achieving a final settlement and have revealed the fundamental differences existing between the parties.

By 1984 President Belisario Betancur of Colombia had become a leading figure in the peace process, especially since the signing in August 1984 of a ceasefire between the government and guerrillas in Colombia was seen as a potential model for the negotiations between the Nicaraguan government and the contras (see section 6.3.3) and for the La Palma talks in El Salvador (see section 6.4.5). In addition to arranging talks between a US representative and the El Salvador guerrillas (see section 6.4.3), Betancur also sought to use his good relations with the Sandinistas to promote an accommodation with the United States, declaring in an interview with *The Guardian* (July 27, 1984): "I tell the Sandinistas: it all depends on you. The USSR won't fight for you. If the United States invades, it might do something somewhere else in the world, but not in Central America. Cuba won't help you. Look at Grenada."

6.1.2: UN Resolutions

In December 1981 the UN General Assembly passed a resolution (36/155) by 69 votes to 22, with five abstentions, calling on all states "to abstain from interfering in the internal situation in El Salvador and to suspend all supplies of arms and any type of military support so as to allow the political forces to restore peace and security"; those voting against the resolution included Guatemala, Honduras, El Salvador, Costa Rica and the United States. Another resolution (37/185) passed 12 months later reiterated this call, appealed to the government and the other political forces in the country to work together towards a comprehensive negotiated political solution and expressed the Assembly's "deep concern at the continued and unbridled violations of human rights and the resultant suffering of the Salvadorean people".

During the same 1982 session a resolution (37/184) was passed on Guatemala, expressing deep concern over the reports of widespread repression, killing and massive displacement of the rural and indigenous population, and appealing to (i) the Guatemalan government to allow international humanitarian organizations to help the displaced; and (ii) all concerned parties in the country to seek an end to the political violence. Both the 1982 resolutions were passed with 79 votes in favour, with Guatemala, Honduras, El Salvador and the United States voting against.

In a speech to the UN Security Council in March 1982, Daniel Ortega stated Nicaragua's position and demands in the region. A resolution was drafted which called on members to "refrain from direct, indirect, overt or covert use of force against any country of Central America and the Caribbean"; there were 12 votes in favour and two abstentions (the United Kingdom and Zaïre), with the United States exercising its veto. Nicaragua was elected to the Security Council in October as one of the five non-permanent members (to serve for two years from January 1983), despite intensive lobbying by the US delegation on behalf of the Dominican Republic (the other contender for the Latin American seat). Nicaragua called an emergency meeting of the Council in March 1983 to complain of the recent invasion by the contras, and another in May, when d'Escoto asserted: "Declaring that the United States is waging a war against Nicaragua cannot be taken as a figure of speech, much less as provocative rhetoric." After several days of debate unanimous agreement was reached on a resolution urging the Contadora Group "to spare no effort to find solutions to the problems of the region, and to keep the Security Council informed of the results of these efforts", and urging the interested parties "to co-operate fully with the Contadora Group through a frank and constructive dialogue".

6.1.3: The Socialist International

In April 1981 a special representative of the Socialist International (SI), Hans-Jürgen Wischnewski (of the West German Social Democratic Party) visited Central America, and in meetings with Salvadorean, Costa Rican, Panamanian and Cuban leaders proposed outside meditation in the conflict in El Salvador. The proposal was rejected by the Salvadorean high command, apparently because of the SI's consistent expressions of support for the FDR (within which the MNR is a member party of the SI). In May another SI leader, Edward Broadbent of the Canadian New Democratic Party, travelled to Mexico City for talks with FDR leaders and then to meet government representatives in El Salvador, Costa Rica, Nicaragua, Cuba, Venezuela and the United States; however, his proposal for SI mediation was rejected by Duarte as "an act of intervention". On his return to Canada in June, Broadbent appealed to the United States to support a proposal for negotiations to establish a moderate centre-left government and to send no more arms or advisers to the Salvadorean armed forces.

6.1.4: The OAS

In the first six months of 1981 the Salvadorean authorities appeared to believe that a military victory against the FMLN was possible and were therefore not inclined towards opening negotiations; apparently for this reason the government in March rejected a proposal made by President Carazo Odio of Costa Rica for OAS mediation. The Organization's 11th general assembly, held in St Lucia in December 1981, was dominated by Haig's efforts to convince the members of the need for action against what he portrayed as the increasing influence of Cuba and Nicaragua as "sources of subversion" in the region. The US Secretary of State declared that the United States was ready to provide military and economic aid and to join other countries to do "whatever is prudent and necessary to prevent any country in Central America from becoming the platform of terror and war in the region". At the conclusion of the assembly a resolution sponsored by El Salvador, Honduras and Costa Rica, supporting the Salvadorean government in its planned elections for March 1982, rejecting violence and terrorism, reaffirming the principle of non-intervention and expressing the hope that "all Salvadoreans may achieve a climate of peace and hope through a genuinely democratic process", was passed by 22 votes to three (Nicaragua, Mexico and Grenada), with four abstentions.

6.1.5: The Non-Aligned Movement

In its first reference to the situations in El Salvador and Guatemala, the Non-Aligned Movement's co-ordinating bureau adopted a resolution in June 1982 warning that the "imperialist intervention" of the United States posed a threat to regional peace, and proposed an extraordinary meeting of the bureau in Managua in January 1983, specifically to discuss Latin America and the Caribbean. The final communiqué (i) asserted that the United States was using Israel as a cover for its intervention in Latin America (see also section 5.4.3), "leading to an escalation in tension"; (ii) maintained that the Honduran-based contras "formed part of a deliberate plan to harass and destabilize Nicaragua", calling on the United States to adopt a positive attitude in favour of peace and dialogue with Nicaragua; and (iii) declared that the situation in El Salvador continued to deteriorate "due to the continuation of imperialist intervention and repression".

The statement issued at the Movement's seventh summit conference held in New Delhi (India) in March 1983 contained a substantial passage on Latin America and the Caribbean, based on the January discussions. It specifically (i) condemned "the new and increasing threats and acts of intimidation and the growing seriousness and increased number of acts of aggression against Nicaragua"; (ii) called on the US and Honduran governments "to adopt a constructive position in favour of peace and dialogue"; (iii) commended the positive response made by Nicaragua to "the peace initiatives presented by Mexico, France, Venezuela, Colombia and Panama"; (iv) noted with concern the tensions in Guatemala and the "repressive and expansionist policy" of the government there, reinforced by "the use of its special military ties with the Zionist regime of Israel and with imperialism"; (v) said that the conflict in El Salvador was caused by "unsolved social and economic problems and continuing repression and imperialist intervention"; (vi) called for an immediate cessation of intervention and rejected attempts to prevent or obstruct negotiations with the participation of all representative political forces; and (vii) condemned "the covert and overt actions and the political and economic pressures being exerted by imperialist forces against Grenada".

6.1.6: Spain

In December 1982 President de la Espriella of Panama suggested that the recently-elected Spanish Prime Minister, Felipe González, could be involved in the peace process as "we regard him as a man who can negotiate among all the parties in the conflict". González expressed his willingness to act as a mediator if asked by the parties concerned; however, although his nomination was supported by Costa Rica, Mexico and Cuba, this initiative faded in February 1983, when the US administration rejected one of his main proposals (namely an immediate improvement of US–Cuban relations), claiming that Cuba was not acting "responsibly" in international affairs.

6.2: REGIONAL EFFORTS

6.2.1: Mexico, Venezuela and Panama

In March 1981 the Mexican and Venezuelan governments initiated moves towards a negotiated political settlement in El Salvador, and Presidents López Portillo and Herrera Campíns met for preliminary talks in Mexico City at the beginning of April. The Venezuelan government (of the Christian Social Party) at that time supported the Salvadorean junta because it contained Christian Democrats, while Mexico was less favourable to it, issuing a joint declaration with France in August, recognizing the FMLN–FDR as a representative political force. This declaration was rejected by Argentina, Bolivia, Chile, Colombia, the Dominican Republic, Guatemala, Honduras, Paraguay and Venezuela in September as a "tacit invitation to other foreign countries to make statements in support of the subversive elements which are part of the crisis", and as an "attempt to change the democratic destiny of the Salvadorean people".

In February 1982 López Portillo tried to launch negotiations between the United States, Nicaragua and Cuba. The three points of the president's plan were (i) a negotiated settlement in El Salvador with Mexican mediation; (ii) a non-aggression pact between the United States and Nicaragua; and (iii) talks between the United States and Cuba. The non-aggression pact proposal stipulated that the United States should renounce the threat—or use—of force against Nicaragua, that the contra groups operating on the Honduran border should be dissolved, that the training of Nicaraguan exiles in the United States and Honduras with direct or indirect US support should be stopped; in return Nicaragua, would be required to reverse its major arms build-up and acquisition of Soviet aircraft, reduce the size of its army and conclude non-aggression pacts with its neighbours.

Two days previously the Nicaraguan government had offered to conclude non-aggression pacts and form joint border patrols with Costa Rica and Honduras and to hold negotiations with the United States, and shortly after the announcement of the plan the FMLN–FDR accepted the offer of Mexican mediation and reiterated its willingness to enter peace talks without preconditions to reach a negotiated political solution. The immediate response from the US administration was to reject the possibility of talks with Nicaragua and Cuba so long as these two countries allegedly sent arms to the FMLN (although the supplies had only been significant in the first months of 1981—see section 5.3.6). On the same day (Feb. 23) the House of Representatives adopted a resolution by 396 votes to three urging Reagan to press for "unconditional discussions among the major political factions in El Salvador in order to guarantee a safe and stable environment for free and open democratic elections". At the beginning of March over 400 members of Congress signed a letter calling on the president to change his policy and support negotiations between the Salvadorean government and the FMLN – FDR with Mexican mediation.

It was announced in September 1982 that Herrera Campíns and López Portillo had sent joint letters to Presidents Reagan, Suazo Córdova and Daniel

Ortega calling for "the exploration of ways that remain open to halt the current worrying escalation, the increase of tensions and the dangerous expectations as to the outcome of the crisis", and offering their good offices for any ensuing talks. (The notable change in the Venezuelan position had come about largely as a result of its objection to US support for the United Kingdom in the Falklands/Malvinas conflict.)

In March (1982) the Honduran foreign minister, Paz Bárnica, had announced his own proposal for regional peace, calling for (i) general disarmament; (ii) a reduction of foreign military and other involvement; (iii) an end to arms trafficking in the region; (iv) international supervision of agreements reached; (v) the institution of permanent dialogue between the states; and (vi) mutual respect for established frontiers. At the beginning of August the Nicaraguan government accepted this proposal as a basis for negotiation, but no date was set for talks. One of the major difficulties in reaching a settlement between the two countries was that Nicaragua favoured a bilateral settlement, while Honduras, in line with US policy, wanted all disputes negotiated within a regional formula.

In June 1982 Panama made a peace proposal based on the initiatives to date, including a system of non-aggression pacts between Nicaragua and the United States and between Nicaragua and Honduras, El Salvador and Costa Rica, a negotiated solution to the war in El Salvador, the opening of a process of détente between the United States and Cuba, and guarantees of territorial sovereignty for all Central American states to prevent hostile groups using neighbouring countries for sanctuary. The proposal was supported by the Colombian, Costa Rican, Honduran, Nicaraguan and Venezuelan governments, but no progress was made with it.

6.2.2: The CDC

The foreign ministers of the CDC (Guatemala, Honduras, El Salvador and Costa Rica—see section 1.1.14) met in San Salvador on July 7, 1982, to formalize a new political-military pact. In a communiqué issued after the meeting they (i) expressed their concern over the rise in "terrorism" and "subversion" in the region; (ii) supported Honduran proposals (i.e. Paz Bárnica's initiative) for disarmament, dialogue and the introduction of an international force; and (iii) informed the Nicaraguan government of their anxiety over what they termed Nicaragua's "disproportionate arms build-up" and its attitudes and actions which, they claimed, were "threatening regional peace and stability".

6.2.3: The Forum for Peace and Democracy

The Forum for Peace and Democracy was established at a meeting in San José in October 1982 of the foreign ministers of Colombia, Belize, Jamaica, Panama, Honduras, the Dominican Republic, Costa Rica and El Salvador; Nicaragua was excluded from the meeting, but from the United States Enders was present as an observer. The Declaration of San José issued at this meeting criticized "the disastrous nearsightedness of totalitarian forces of all trends, especially the Marxist-Leninist trend", and advocated a "verifiable and reciprocal" regional agreement banning arms trafficking, "subversion" and the presence of foreign military advisers in the region. The US State Department announced its support for this approach, saying that the Mexican-Venezuelan proposal was less preferable as it addressed "only one aspect of the regional problem", while the Forum stressed "national reconciliation" in each country.

In April 1983 Monge said that he believed that the Forum had failed to achieve regional peace because of its exclusion of Nicaragua and Cuba. In the same month the Costa Rican government issued a declaration upholding the principles of national self-determination, non-intervention, the peaceful solution of armed conflicts, dialogue and accord between governments of varying political orientations, the protection of human rights and the irrevocable right to asylum.

6.3: NICARAGUAN PEACE PROPOSALS

6.3.1: Proposals Involving the United States, 1981–83

The first high-level contact between the US and Nicaraguan governments since Reagan's inauguration in January 1981 occurred in August 1981 with the visit of Enders to Nicaragua, when he proposed a deal under which the two countries would conclude a non-aggression pact and, if Nicaragua would make certain changes in its political orientation and policy, the US administration would exert control over Nicaraguan exile groups in Florida. Enders stressed, however, that any improvement in relations between the United States and Nicaragua was entirely conditional on changes in Sandinista policies.

In November 1981 Haig travelled to Mexico City for talks with the Mexican government on Nicaragua, saying that he refused to rule out the possibility that the United States might use military force to halt the spread of "communist" influence in Nicaragua (while López Portillo declared that the use of US force in the region would be "a gigantic historical error"). Haig spoke of Nicaragua's "drift towards totalitarianism" and its "high influx of sophisticated armaments" from the Soviet bloc, but in response the Mexican foreign minister, Jorge Castañeda, said that Nicaragua must not be "cornered". The Mexican side also declared that, although it was willing to be a "communicator" between the United States and Nicaragua, it would not intercede "unilaterally" with Nicaragua on behalf of the United States.

Early in 1983 the Nicaraguan government offered to enter tripartite talks with the United States and Honduras under the auspices of the UN Secretary-General, Javier Pérez de Cuellar. However, US policy remained in favour of multilateral negotiations so that US relations with Nicaragua might be set in the context of its arms interdiction campaign. As Kirkpatrick stated in April: "The problems are complex, inter-related and multilateral in nature [and] do not lend themselves to simple solutions on the basis of bilateral talks", adding that she considered the OAS rather than the UN to be the correct forum for such negotiations. Shortly afterwards, the Honduran government also rejected the Nicaraguan offer. At the beginning of May Arce Castaño claimed that the United States had entered a new period of "cold war" and that the alleged US violations of Nicaraguan airspace (which he called "spy flights") were "preparations of American military aggression against Nicaragua". When Richard Stone met Daniel Ortega and d'Escoto in June the two sides merely restated their previous positions.

Ortega announced a new initiative on July 19, 1983, based on the multilateral approach of the Contadora Group "so that there will be an end to the excuses, and so that those who say they are interested in peace will take specific steps to develop the process which could lay the basis for it". The main points of his proposal were: (i) the "immediate signing of a non-aggression pact between Nicaragua and Honduras"; (ii) "a complete stop to arms supplies by any country to the forces in conflict in El Salvador so that the Salvadorean people can solve their problems without foreign interference"; (iii) "a complete stop to all military support in terms of weapons, training and the use of territories to launch attacks or any other type of aggression by forces which oppose any of the Central American governments"; (iv) "commitments which guarantee full respect for the self-determination of Central American peoples and non-interference in the domestic affairs of each country"; (v) "a halt to aggression and economic discrimination against all Central American countries"; and (vi) "that no foreign military bases be installed in Central America and that military exercises in the Central American area with the participation of foreign armies be suspended". Two days later Reagan responded by saying that the proposal constituted a "first step" in the peace process but that it did not "go far enough", adding that in his opinion achieving peace "would be extremely difficult" as the Nicaraguans "are being directed by outside forces".

In October 1983 the Nicaraguan government made a further multilateral proposal, comprising four draft treaties, of which the first two were between Nicaragua and the United States, banning "the establishment of any foreign military bases in the region" and guaranteeing the passage of US vessels and aircraft in Nicaraguan waters and airspace; under these treaties the United States would be required to end all its military manoeuvres in Central America within 30 days and close all military bases in Honduras and El Salvador within 90 days. The third treaty covered all five states, banning arms trafficking, covert and overt actions to overthrow other governments and the provision of "logistic support of training camps for anti-government forces of another nation", while the fourth treaty was an accord on El Salvador involving "all nations interested in resolving the present conflict". The whole proposal required the United States and other Central American countries to recognize Nicaragua's "inalienable right to its independence and self-determination", and was rejected by the US administration the day after it was made.

In December 1983 Stone held a meeting in Panama with representatives of the FDN, Arde and M–3V in Panama, and agreement was reached on the presentation of a joint offer to the Sandinista government to cease military operations if the government would take what they termed "credible steps towards democracy". The government, however, said that it would not consider entering discussions with "traitors and assassins" and d'Escoto added: "We do not talk to puppets, we would rather talk to the puppeteers." (The meeting had apparently been part of a US effort to achieve a measure of unity between the contra groups—see also section 3.1.5—despite the existing mutual hostility; at a news conference in Tegucigalpa at the end of the month Fagoth Müller accused Pastora of having "close and direct links with Sandinism" and of being a "fifth columnist", deliberately trying to prevent unity within the contras.)

6.3.2: The Manzanillo Talks

Between June and November 1984 eight sessions of talks were held in Manzanillo (Mexico) and Atlanta (Georgia) between Stone's replacement, Shlaudeman, and Víctor Hugo Tinoco, the Nicaraguan deputy foreign minister. The content of the talks was kept secret, and there was no public agenda, but they were initiated after a visit to Managua by Shultz in June, during which he had told Ortega that the normalization of relations between the two countries depended on the following conditions: (i) the cessation of Nicaraguan support for the FMLN; (ii) the withdrawal of Cuban and Soviet advisers from Nicaragua; (iii) the reduction of Nicaragua's military potential; and (iv) respect for pluralistic democracy and human rights in Nicaragua. The State Department had said that the visit should not be seen as an attempt at bilateral negotiations but as a contribution to the Contadora process.

The United States suspended the talks just before the ninth round was due to begin in January 1985, because of what was termed Nicaragua's "effort to portray the conflict in Central America as a bilateral issue between itself and the United States". After his announcement at the end of February 1985 that 100 Cuban military advisers would be asked to leave Nicaragua, Ortega said he hoped that this action would encourage other Central American governments "to subscribe to the Contadora proposals" and would prompt the United States to return to bilateral talks with Nicaragua. Vice-President George Bush responded by condemning Nicaraguan acquisition of Soviet military transport (helicopters, tanks and armoured vehicles), adding: "The tyrants are not shy about supporting communism and subversion. Why should democratic countries hesitate in their support of freedom?"

Just before the congressional vote in April 1985 on aid to the contras (see section 5.2.5) Ortega offered a ceasefire if Congress rejected the resumption of aid to the contras. Shultz replied that acceptance of this deal would mean "unconditional surrender by those who are fighting for democracy". In mid-May Ortega agreed to a suggestion from Archbishop John O'Connor of New York that he and Reagan should meet at a summit, saying that he would make "all possible efforts to promote peace" and criticizing the Reagan administration for prosecuting "an illegal and immoral war of aggression"; in June he again offered to lift the state of emergency if the United States would cease to send aid to the contras. Reagan replied that he would consider negotiations (prior to the June vote on aid to the contras), but no progress was made on this proposal.

In the last week of October 1985 Shlaudeman and Carlos Tunnermann Bernheim (the Nicaraguan ambassador in Washington) held two meetings, but no agreement was reached on the resumption of talks. In response, the Contadora and Lima Groups submitted a draft resolution on Central America to the UN General Assembly calling for the direct resumption of bilateral US–Nicaraguan negotiations and an end to all military manoeuvres by foreign powers in the region; however, on Dec. 3 Honduras, El Salvador and Costa Rica refused to endorse it.

In April 1986, during the debate in Congress over a $100,000,000 aid package to the contras (see section 5.2.5), Ortega proposed "a reciprocal arrangement" under which Nicaragua would withdraw all foreign military advisers and halt aid to "irregular forces" in the region if the United States would end its military pressure on Nicaragua and its military manoeuvres. Ortega also warned that if the aid package were approved by Congress his government would start to expand the EPS to maintain a manpower ratio of 10 to 1 over the contras, and would seek further foreign military assistance.

6.3.3: Discussions with Miskito Leaders

In October 1984 the Nicaraguan contra leader Rivera accepted a government amnesty in order to open talks with Sandinista officials on the possibility of a ceasefire by Misurasata. He made the following conditions: (i) that the government should give Misurasata formal recognition as the representative organization of the indigenous peoples of the Atlantic Coast (i.e. rather than the new organization Misatán formed in July—see section 4.3.3); (ii) that any Miskitos in prison on political charges be released immediately; (iii) that the government commit itself to negotiating with Misurasata on autonomous status for the indigenous people; and (iv) that freedom of speech and expression be recognised. After his presidential election victory in November Ortega said that the government would consider granting limited autonomy to the Miskitos and that plans were underway to guarantee their linguistic, cultural and political freedoms, provided that any measures involved did not affect national integration. Because of his overtures three leading members of Misurasata broke with Rivera in January 1985, saying they would totally "repudiate and disauthorize" his actions (which were also condemned by other contra leaders) and believed that he was being manipulated by the Sandinista government.

Talks between Rivera and the newly-elected government were scheduled to open in Bogotá (Colombia), but were postponed indefinitely in early January 1985 when Rivera was wounded in an EPS ambush while on a trip into Nicaragua (apparently to explain his initiative to Miskitos still in the country). Rivera then said that in order for talks to reopen Indians should be allowed to return to a number of Atlantic coast villages (recently evacuated by the authorities to create a free-fire zone in the north of the country) and that they should be allowed to receive Red Cross relief supplies. It was also reported that the Indians were calling for the control of their traditional lands, a share of the profits from mineral and other natural resources, the creation of an indigenous military force and the repatriation of all Miskitos now in Honduras, whether as refugees or as guerrillas.

The Bogotá talks finally opened in May 1985, but collapsed after the government accused Misurasata of breaking an earlier agreement to avoid military engagements and insisted on negotiating steps to avoid new confrontations, whereas Misurasata charged the government with bad faith and deliberately trying to disrupt the talks. It was, however, expected that the government would invite all Miskitos to return to their traditional settlements.

6.3.4: Contra Proposals

Contra leaders met in San José on March 1, 1984 (apparently without the approval of the Costa Rican government), and called for the opening within 20 days of a dialogue with the government, organized and co-ordinated by the Church and involving other Central American governments. The communiqué issued under the title "Document of the Nicaraguan Resistance concerning National Dialogue", however, showed that there had been no great developments towards unity, as it was signed by Cruz, Calero, Chamorro Rapaccioli, Fagoth Müller and Robelo, but not by Rivera nor Pastora, and as it contained only a statement of common goals; the question of unity was seen as particularly important to the US administration in the weeks prior to the congressional vote on aid to the contras. The CD was not involved in the ultimatum, although its leader, Cruz, was later reported to have joined the contras.

An article published in *The Guardian* (April 24, 1985) gave the views of some of the main opposition leaders on the contra proposals. Within the CD Virgilio Godoy of the PLI and Jarquín of the PSCN said that the CD had for too long been dominated by pro–US politicians wanting to recreate a pro–US capitalist system, while Jarquín commented: "The war justifies Sandinista emergency measures and it is polarising the people. More and more people are seeking a military solution. We need a respite to preserve some room for political negotiations." On the other hand, Emilio Rapaccioli of the Conservative Party, maintained: "There is no room for the Sandinistas in Nicaragua. They must go." Within the government Borge accused the CD and *La Prensa* of receiving money from the Foundation for Democracy (funded by the US government) and said of the CD leaders: "Their heart is in Miami. They would sell their country. We will never negotiate with these people."

6.4: NEGOTIATIONS ON EL SALVADOR

6.4.1: Attempts to Open Political Dialogue (1981)

The first proposal for negotiations in El Salvador was made several months before the FMLN January 1981 offensive, when in October 1980 US ambassador White tried to arrange discussions between the government (with the agreement of the Salvadorean military command) and the FMLN–FDR, with church mediation. The offer was rejected by the FMLN–FDR, apparently in the hope that the "final offensive" would bring decisive victory. In April 1981 Archbishop (acting) Rivera y Damas travelled to Washington to meet Bush and William Clark (deputy secretary of state), to Panama to meet FMLN–FDR leaders, and to Europe to gain support there for his initiative (which was also backed by the Pope) in favour of talks. Although President Duarte had given preliminary agreement to the proposal, it was rejected by the US administration, apparently in the hope that the FMLN would be defeated militarily. In a subsequent letter to Bush, Rivera y Damas declared: "The United States must clearly indicate it is in favour of a political solution through negotiations or such negotiation will not occur in El Salvador. In addition to declaring its support for dialogue/mediation/negotiation, the US role is essential in pressing the military to accept a political solution."[1]

In June 1981 the FMLN–FDR expressed its willingness to enter negotiations without preconditions, but in July Enders said that the United States rejected a negotiated settlement with the guerrillas, and was committed to the existing plans for El Salvador's political future (i.e. through elections rather than the formation of any government—even provisional — including FMLN –FDR members): "We should recognize that El Salvador's leaders will not and should not grant the insurgents through negotiations the share of power the rebels have not been able to win on the battlefield. . . . The search for a political solution will not succeed unless the United States sustains its assistance to El Salvador. . . . The point is that a political solution can only be achieved if the guerrillas realize they cannot win by force of arms. . . . Our economic assistance . . . must continue to offset the guerrillas' efforts to prolong the war by sabotaging the economy."

Echoing this stance, Duarte told the UN General Assembly in September 1981 that the government "completely excludes any negotiations or dialogue with organized armed sectors", although the guerrillas would be allowed to contest the March 1982 elections as a political force if they laid down their arms. Zamora replied that while the FMLN–FDR did not reject elections, it considered that it would be "political and physical suicide" to abandon their weapons and rely on the mercy on the Salvadorean army. Moreover, Castillo (speaking in New York) said that the FDR could not join the elections because of the lack of a free press, since the elections would not be conducted democratically because of pressure from the armed forces and as electoral fraud was inevitable because of the composition of the electoral commission. The FDR position on this issue was backed by Majano, who described the elections as "madness", and said that the guerrillas could not be expected to participate "if there is not dialogue first", and by Rivera y Damas, who asserted that the elections could have no meaning in the current climate of violence and the general lack of confidence in the government.

In late 1981 the FDR announced its plan for a political solution, consisting of (i) the immediate opening of a dialogue to lead into negotiations; (ii) negotiation among all parties, with international mediation; (iii) a mutually agreed timetable for negotiations; (iv) an undertaking that the Salvadorean people be kept informed of the progress made in the negotiations; and (v) no preconditions be set by any party. In December the five FMLN leaders (Carpio of the FPL, Cienfuegos of the FARN, Schafik Handal of the PCS, Villalobos of the ERP and Roca of the PRTC) sent an open letter to Reagan reiterating "our disposition to undertake [negotiations] at any time, without pre-conditions placed on any of the parties in the conflict", and charging his administration with "sustaining at a peak of power the most repressive elements of the Salvadorean army".

6.4.2: The Apaneca Pact

After the conclusion of the Apaneca Pact in August 1982 (see section 1.4.16) there were reports that Costa Rica might act as a mediator in negotiations, when in September the Costa Rican foreign minister, Fernando Volio Jiménez, met Magaña, and President Monge talked with Ungo. In addition the FMLN–FDR was reported to have dropped its demands for access to the national press, guarantees of personal safety for left-wing sympathizers in the country and an end to the state of siege. In the first week of October Ungo issued a peace plan signed by the FMLN–FDR leadership calling for "an early direct dialogue without previous conditions", with members of the executive, the Assembly and the armed forces under the auspices of a good offices group, and possibly also including representatives of other groups such as the church, trade unions, political parties, businessmen and university or professional bodies. The initiative was welcomed by the church and moderate political organizations, but the government insisted that the guerrillas must first lay down their arms. D'Aubuisson was a prominent opponent of talks, making several attempts to hold a vote in the Assembly to block any further negotiation attempts, saying it would be "a most vile and absurd policy" if the government "were to sit down to talk, much less negotiate, with those who have planted mourning and destruction on the Salvadorean people".

In February 1983 the political commission established under the Apaneca Pact published its findings under the title "Bases for Peace in El Salvador", which stated that "the democratic process . . . is the sole path for achieving peace", and affirmed the commission's "firm determination to establish respect for the various ideological concepts, in order to achieve a pluralistic, democratic and equitable society that, through strict respect for human rights, will promote social improvement". In late September 1983 the commission (chaired by Francisco Quiñónez Avila) held talks in Bogotá with two FDR and two FMLN leaders, but the attempt failed within 24 hours as the FMLN–FDR refused to meet the condition that they participate in the 1984 elections.

6.4.3: Stone's Peace Efforts

In June 1983 Richard Stone (the US Special Envoy to Central America—see section 5.1.2) was authorized by Reagan to explore the possibility of meeting guerrilla leaders with a view to bringing the two sides together (despite Magaña's reiterated refusal to negotiate, made during a visit to Washington the same month). Although the appointment of Stone appeared to be a new departure, the main thrust of his task was still to get the guerrillas to take part in the current Salvadorean electoral process rather than seek any new, mutually acceptable formula.[2] A meeting with FMLN–FDR leaders scheduled for early July was cancelled as they insisted on witnesses being present and Stone objected to the people they suggested, while the FMLN –FDR leaders protested over a joint White House-State Department statement which asserted that the purpose of the meeting was to persuade the more moderate members of the FDR to enter elections (as this statement prejudiced the principle of an open agenda).

A meeting was finally arranged for the end of July 1983 by President Betancur of Colombia, involving Stone and Zamora, but afterwards Zamora said that while he welcomed Contadora mediation he rejected any suggestion that Stone could be a mediator as the United States was an involved party: "Stone is another soldier of US intervention . . . [and] if we have talked with him it is because we are willing to try all alternatives, including talks with our enemies, . . . to bring peace to Central America." The two men met again in Costa Rica at the end of August, when Monge, Ungo and two FMLN members (Mario Aguinada and Cdr Mario López) also attended. The resultant communiqué recorded that discussions had been held on the basis of an "open agenda" and that the parties had "agreed to maintain communication". Afterwards Zamora commented: "The United States has the key to opening the door for a political solution in El Salvador. The Salvadorean military is not going to start to travel the road of a political settlement unless the US administration gives the green light."

6.4.4: FMLN–FDR Initiatives in 1984

In January 1984 the FMLN–FDR called for the establishment of a broad-based provisional government, to prepare for general elections, which would (i) end the state of siege; (ii) release political prisoners; (iii) abolish the security forces (except the army), the death squads and Arena; (iv) purge the army and integrate FMLN combatants into it; (v) launch an investigation into past human rights abuses; (vi) implement an emergency reconstruction plan; and (vii) introduce a nationwide literacy campaign. At the end of May the call for the formation of a provisional government was repeated, on the grounds that Duarte had not been "elected by all the people and will not have control over the country's territory" and would therefore be obliged to reach a "negotiated political settlement" to avoid being "a doormat for the US occupation forces". In the same month Monge met separately with Duarte and FDR leaders, and it was reported that both sides had agreed to his mediation, that talks would open in San José in early July and that the FDR had agreed to recognize Duarte as the government's legal spokesman (although it disputed the legality of the elections), but had rejected the possibility of a ceasefire as a precondition for negotiations.

In the first week of June 1984 the FDR placed an advertisement in some San Salvador newspapers declaring their "readiness to begin a dialogue without preconditions". Duarte responded by saying that the FDR must first prove its control over the guerrilla wing by dismissing Villalobos, that the FMLN must lay down its arms and that he would negotiate only to end the war, not to share power. Later in the month FDR leaders met Rev. Jesse Jackson (then a contender for the US Democratic presidential nomination) in Panama City, and agreed to go to San Salvador for talks on a cease-fire if Jackson could obtain assurances from the Salvadorean goverment that the armed forces would not try to arrest or "intimidate" them. The initiative failed, however, when Jackson met Duarte, who said that the guerrillas' proposal contained "nothing new".

In September 1984 it was reported that the government had recently extended its informal contacts with the FMLN–FDR through the offices of the church and with the support of many senior officers (including Col. Blandón), and that it was examining possibilities for talks under pressure from the UPD (which had given strong support to Duarte in the election—see section 1.4.17).

6.4.5: The La Palma Talks (1984)

In an address to the UN General Assembly on Oct. 8, 1984, Duarte announced that he was inviting the guerrilla leaders to a meeting on Oct. 15 at the town of La Palma (in a guerrilla-held area of Chalatenango, near the Honduran border) and that he intended to ask the Assembly to approve the offer of an amnesty for political crimes. His invitation was accepted by the FMLN –FDR, which requested unsuccessfully that President Betancur also attend; when the talks opened those present included Duarte, Vides Casanova, Julio Adolfo Rey Prendes (minister of the presidency), Ungo, Zamora, Cienfuegos, Cdr Facundo Guardado of the FPL, Nidia Díaz (of the FMLN–FDR), Rivera y Damas and other church representatives and Colombian, French and Swiss diplomats. (Despite threats from the ESA the government and FMLN–FDR members attended unarmed; Guardado replaced Villalobos, who had been invited but had refused to come when the government declined to send a helicopter for him.) The invitation was welcomed by the National Association for Private Enterprise (ANEP) and the US embassy, although both warned that the rebels should be given only the chance to share in the existing political process and not offered a share of power; ANEP withdrew its support from the initiative before the second round.

Duarte opened the meeting by presenting a seven-page set of proposals, which was largely a reiteration of his policy on negotiations since taking office in June, offering a new amnesty and laws allowing all political parties to register, but making no mention of a ceasefire. The FMLN–FDR drew up a list of 29 demands (see appendix 4), incorporating their previous proposals on human rights, decrease of army activity against civilians and social and economic reforms, and after the talks were over issued a statement, declaring:

> With the start of the dialogue, we have made important conquests in the political field and we have opened a space for the organization, mobilization and political expression of the popular masses. . . . Dialogue has to begin while our rifles fight and deliver hard blows to the puppet regime. . . . The dialogue in La Palma is the beginning of a complex and difficult process in the context of a war which is being prolonged and deepened by the interventionist policy of the Reagan administration.

On the government side, Duarte said "we cannot offer miracles, nor can we offer peace from morning to night", and Rey Prendes said that a ceasefire had not been discussed as "it would imply that the guerrillas control parts of the national territory, where the reality is that they are permanently on the move". At the conclusion of the five-hour talks Rivera y Damas read a statement which said that the aim of both parties was peace "in the shortest possible time" in the context of "democratic pluralism and social justice", and announced that a peace commission would be formed of four members from the government, two from the FDR and two from the FMLN and that the next round of talks would be held in November.

The La Palma talks brought no immediate diminution in the general level of armed activity, and shortly afterwards the army launched a new offensive in Morazán (see section 3.3.5), while the FMLN on Oct. 18 called for a total boycott of transport throughout the country in a show of strength, as both parties were keen to demonstrate that they were not talking from a position of weakness. In a newspaper interview printed in early November 1984, Zamora stated:

> The army hardliners were tranquilized into accepting talks by the reassurance that the guerrillas were losing the war and were very weak. Now this has been demonstrated to be untrue, and they will react against the dialogue. . . . [The right-wing politicians] were caught off guard by La Palma, but they will wake up soon. We need much more security at future talks. . . . Our objective in El Salvador is freedom of political expression. If that can be achieved without power-sharing in the short term, then we are prepared to consider a change of means. . . . We have offered to negotiate on concrete matters of security: for instance, that there would never be foreign bases in El Salvador, nor nuclear missiles, as well as on questions regarding the sources of armaments and the training of the security forces. We have absolutely no interest in El Salvador becoming a surrogate power for the Soviet Union.[3]

The second round was held just within the time limit set on Nov. 30, 1984, at Ayagualo (20 km south of San Salvador), but neither Duarte nor Ungo attended. Announcing the date of the meeting in one of his weekly sermons, Rivera y Damas warned his hearers that "we cannot delude ourselves that peace is coming as a Christmas present". The only agreements reached during the 12 hours of talks were one to allow free passage of vehicles and persons on the highways for two weeks from Dec. 22 (in recognition of Christmas) and another to meet again early in 1985. The church representatives had requested a Christmas truce, and Rivera y Damas blamed the FMLN–FDR for the failure to agree on such a truce; nevertheless, a few days later Ungo announced a unilateral ceasefire on the part of the guerrillas, which was in the end observed by both sides. In fact the second round merely emphasized the major differences still remaining between the two sides, with armed activity resuming immediately, and Duarte called the guerrilla position "nothing serious", adding: "It was only to say no to dialogue and no to the possibility that the country can find peace. . . . I have made it clear that I am not going to step outside the constitution. They have first to accept the constitution."

A measure of the frustration with the progress of the talks after initial optimism was indicated by the government's agreement at La Palma to build a bridge over the Torola river (in Morazán, just south of Meanguera, and forming an unofficial border between army- and guerrilla-controlled territory), in return for a guerrilla undertaking not to destroy it. (So far the FMLN had blown up about 60 bridges in the country since 1981, and the town of Meanguera had not had any electricity since 1981.) Only days before the bridge was due to be opened, some soldiers drove up to it and guerrillas opened fire on them; a few days later the FMLN blew up the bridge.[4]

In January 1985 the Catholic Church made renewed efforts to reopen the talks (see also section 2.4.5), the Pope offering his services as a mediator. The FMLN–FDR rejected this offer, while Duarte declared that he was unwilling to resume talks unless the left showed itself interested in what he described as "sincere dialogue". It therefore soon became clear that the government would not entertain the possibility of talks until after the March legislative elections. At a news conference in May a guerrilla delegation said that it had written to Duarte proposing a preliminary private meeting in the capital at the end of the month, to be followed by top-level peace talks in June at the town of Perquín (in guerrilla-held territory); Ungo warned the government not to treat dialogue as "a game" but as something "important and necessary", but nothing came of this proposal. It was reported that in private interviews both sides conceded that their differences were too great for anything useful to be gained from further talks at present.

Zamora blamed the breakdown of the process on the influence of the US administration, which, he said, still hoped for a military victory against the FMLN: "The American military advisers in El Salvador are against a dialogue with us, and the State Department sees it only as a tactful method to legitimize Duarte internationally."

Later in 1985 and in early 1986 there were a variety of abortive moves on the part of the FMLN–FDR, the government, the Church and the National University to renew talks. These included a proposal made on March 4, 1986, by Duarte, for a three-point peace plan covering simultaneous negotiations between the Salvadorean government and the FMLN and the Nicaraguan government and the contras on the grounds that "an understanding between Nicaragua and El Salvador is vital in order to achieve peace in our country". Two days later the FMLN–FDR described this proposal as "absurd" and "a servile act of co- operation with President Reagan's policy".

6.4.6: Abortive Attempt to Resume Talks (1986)

In preparation for a third round of talks a private meeting was held on April 26, 1986, in Lima (Peru) between Julio Rey Prendes (minister of culture and communications), Zamora and Héctor Oquelí Colindres (of the MNR). This meeting signified a desire for talks on both sides, despite the fact that neither had changed their basic stances. Duarte issued an invitation to a third round on June 1, and within two days the FMLN–FDR had accepted, while continuing to refuse to recognise the current government as legitimate. The FLMN–FDR suggested that discussions take place in the capital in the form of a public debate with Duarte and members of the senior command of the armed forces, but both terms were rejected, and Rey Prendes reiterated the government's insistence that the guerrillas lay down their arms and join the political process. In July the FMLN– FDR dropped its demand for the integration of its own fighting forces into the army and offered to release their most prestigious prisoner, Col. Omar Napoleón Avalos (captured in October

1985), in exchange for a number of non-combatant political detainees. In August it agreed to attend prior discussions in Mexico on Aug. 20–26 under the mediation of Rivera y Damas.

It was agreed in Mexico that the third round be held in Sesori (San Miguel), opening on Sept. 19, between Rodolfo Castillo Claramount (the foreign minister), Rey Prendes and Ricardo Soriano (of the National Rural Workers' Union) for the government, Aronett Díaz de Zamora (of the MPSC), Samayoa and Jorge Villacorta (of the MNR) for the FMLN–FDR, and representatives of the armed forces, with Rivera y Damas again acting as mediator.

The initiative collapsed, however, at the preliminary talks held in Panama on Sept. 12–14, 1986, when the government refused to agree to an FMLN–FDR demand for the demilitarization of an area of 300 sq km around Sesori during the talks. The guerrillas refused to attend, and although Duarte travelled to Sesori as originally scheduled, he rejected a further FMLN–FDR proposal made on Sept. 19 for new preliminary talks on Sept. 29.

Notes

1. Quoted in Bonner, *op. cit.*, p. 285.
2. See Bonner, *op. cit.*, pp. 288–89.
3. *The Sunday Times*, Nov. 4, 1984.
4. *The Times*, Dec. 18, 1984.

6.5: THE CONTADORA GROUP

6.5.1: Formation of the Group and Initial Meetings

The regional peace efforts made by Mexico, Venezuela, Colombia and Panama in 1981–82 (see section 6.2.1) were combined in early 1983, at the instigation of Mexico, with the formation of the Contadora Group, named after the Panamanian island where the foreign ministers of the four countries met for the first time on Jan. 5. A few days later the Group issued a statement calling on all foreign powers to withdraw their military advisers from the region, and for economic initiatives to benefit the region, similar to the San José agreement of 1980 (see section 2.1.7). The ministers also made it clear that they saw the origins of the conflict in the economic, social and political inequalities in each country, rather than primarily as part of the East–West conflict. As a result the Contadora Group received only qualified support from those states most closely aligned with US policy, and at his inauguration in August 1983 Gen. Mejía Victores of Guatemala claimed: "The Contadora Group has nothing to do with Central America. . . . The Nicaraguan government represents a threat not only to Guatemala, but to the entire continent."[1]

The ministers reconvened in Panama on April 11, 1983, to review the January declaration, and, according to President Betancur of Colombia, to make it "more pertinent, more pervasive and more penetrating". A new set of proposals was drafted, expanding the January statement, calling for (i) the withdrawal of all foreign advisers; (ii) the cessation of arms sales to places suffering from armed conflict; (iii) the implementation of a plan for economic reactivation; (iv) the resolution of internal problems by political means and with the participation of all the political groups in each country; and (v) the inclusion of representatives of the region's various ethnic minorities at peace talks. During the meeting the Group persuaded the OAS to suspend its discussions on the region and to give a measure of support to the Contadora process, and afterwards the members embarked on a tour of the five countries, declaring their intention to continue to search for peace.

The third round of talks, held on April 20-22, 1983, was also attended by representatives from Guatemala, Honduras, El Salvador, Nicaragua, Costa Rica and the Dominican Republic, and was dominated by concern over the possible outbreak of a war between Nicaragua and Honduras. The main achievement was the drafting of an agenda for negotiations to be held in May on either a multilateral or a bilateral basis, covering the topics of (i) arms supply routes; (ii) a controlled plan for arms reduction; (iii) arms trafficking; (iv) the presence of foreign military advisers; (v) activities in the region designed to destabilize the internal order of any of the countries; (vi) verbal threats and aggression; (vii) acts of war and border tensions; and (viii) the inculcation of human rights and individual guarantees. (At the end of April President Figueiredo of Brazil expressed his support for the Contadora initiative.)

The meeting scheduled for May 27, 1983, was brought forward to May 11 because of the tension created by Reagan's April 27 speech (see section 5.1.3) and d'Escoto's plea to the UN Security Council on May 9 (see also section 6.1.2). Discussions were based not on the agenda drafted in April, but on a Mexican–Costa Rican proposal announced on May 9, to the effect that UN Secretary–General Pérez de Cuellar should "use his good offices to further regional détente and find a peaceful and negotiated solution to the zone's problems, including the sending of observers". It was agreed on May 15 that 11 civilian observers should be sent to inspect the border between Nicaragua and Costa Rica (although these observers drew no substantial conclusions); the proposal for the despatch of an armed peace-keeping force to the region did not succeed as it was supported only by Venezuela. The Group organized a meeting between the foreign ministers of the five Central American countries on May 28–30, 1983, but the ministers simply restated their governments' positions on the regional conflict and no progress was made towards negotiations.

The Group's efforts received considerable support in Western Europe, and at their meeting in Stuttgart on June 17–19, 1983, the heads of government of the European Community states endorsed the Contadora process and stated that they were "convinced that the problems of Central America cannot be solved by military means" and were "ready to continue contributing to further development in the area in order to promote progress towards stability". During a visit to Washington in June, the Spanish Prime Minister, Felipe González, urged the United States to adopt a more positive attitude towards the Group (having described the US involvement in the region as "fundamentally harmful"); he was told by Reagan: "We must not listen to those who would disarm our friends and allow Central America to be turned into a string of anti-American Marxist dictatorships. The result could be a tidal wave of refugees—and this time they'll be 'feet people' not 'boat people'—swarming into our country seeking a safe haven from communist repression to our south."

The ministers met in Panama on July 14, 1983, to draft the agenda for the Contadora presidential summit of July 16–17. The presidents (de la Madrid of Mexico, Betancur of Colombia, de la Espriella of Panama and Herrera Campíns of Venezuela) stated: "The conflicts in Central America confront the international community with a choice of supporting and strengthening the path to political understanding . . . or passively accepting factors which could lead to armed confrontation of greater danger." The programme drawn up by the presidents proposed that commitments should be made:

(1) To put an end to all existing warlike situations;
(2) to a top-level freeze on existing offensive weapons;
(3) to a start to talks on agreements to control and reduce the present inventory of armaments with adequate supervisory mechanisms;
(4) to prohibit the existence of foreign military installations in their territories;
(5) to give previous notice of troop movements near the border, whenever those contingents are in excess of the number stated in the agreement;
(6) to carry out, as needed, joint border patrols or international supervision of borders, by observers chosen by common agreement by the interested parties;
(7) to form joint security commissions in order to prevent, and if necessary to settle, border incidents;
(8) to establish internal control mechanisms to prevent the supplying of arms from the territory of any country in the area to another country;

(9) to promote a climate of detente and trust in the area, avoiding declarations which might endanger the indispensable climate of political confidence required; and
(10) to co-ordinate systems of direct communicatons among the governments, in order to prevent armed conflicts and to generate an atmosphere of reciprocal trust.

In July Fidel Castro of Cuba expressed his support for the Contadora efforts (see section 5.3.4).

6.5.2: The Programme for Peace in Central America

The Contadora ministers met again on July 28 and Sept. 7, 1983, with the Central American foreign ministers also present. On the second occasion they proposed the establishment of three working groups covering political, security and economic and social issues "to accelerate the analysis and discussion of the subjects on the agenda, as well as to oversee the implementation of determined solutions". They also drafted a 21–point programme for peace in Central America, designed to ensure the "peace, security and stability of the region", adherence to the "principles of international law", respect for "human, political, civil, economic, social, religious and cultural rights", the "establishment or in some cases improvement of representative and pluralist democratic systems" and the promotion of "national reconciliation". The main proposals contained in the programme were as follows:

(1) The initiation of negotiations on arms reduction and control and on the number of active armed fighters;
(2) the banning of the installation of foreign military bases and of any form of foreign military intervention;
(3) the conclusion of agreements on the elimination of the presence of foreign military advisers;
(4) the introduction of measures to hinder arms traffic between the countries or from other countries designed to destabilize Central American governments;
(5) a commitment to refrain from fostering or supporting acts of terrorism, subversion or sabotage in the region and from giving military or logistic support to anyone trying to overthrow a government in the region;
(6) the establishment of direct means of communication between the countries;
(7) the continuation of humanitarian aid programmes to refugees; and
(8) the adoption of economic and technical co-operation programmes.

Stone expressed the US administration's support for the programme a few days later, and in November the White House spokesman, Larry Speakes, said that the President believed it "provided the best basis for a lasting solution to the problems of the region".

The 21-point programme did not produce any immediate easing of tension in the region, and on Oct. 21–22, 1983, the ministers issued a statement warning of the "danger of war", since "the process of democratization and efforts towards national reconciliation have been delayed or interrupted" and "violations of human rights multiply while foreign involvement proliferates dangerously, particularly in the military sphere". At their meeting on Nov. 13, 1983, the ministers prepared a progress report for the OAS, which three days later passed a resolution offering "the firmest support" for Contadora, and reaffirming the obligation of all countries in the hemisphere "not to interfere either directly or indirectly or for whatever reason in the internal or external affairs of any other state".

It was originally intended that the Contadora and Central American foreign ministers would meet on Dec. 16, 1983, to sign a draft peace agreement based on the 21-point programme, but the meeting was cancelled. Three days previously the Guatemalan, Honduran, Salvadorean and Costa Rican ministers had met for talks, and had apparently expressed their anxiety over recent Nicaraguan peace proposals (see section 6.3.1), which they feared would leave Nicaraguan military capability untouched while forcing the closure of US bases in their own countries.

6.5.3: The Act for Peace and Co-operation in Central America

A preliminary agreement was reached on Jan. 7–8, 1984, by the nine foreign ministers on a considerably modified version of the 21–point programme, although a counter-proposal submitted on the second day of the meeting by Costa Rica, Honduras and El Salvador to change it still further (including a demand for a head-count of all foreign military advisers in the region) was not accepted. This preliminary agreement formed the base for the 15–point Act for Peace and Co-operation in Central America issued on June 10, under which the signatories would:

(1) Not allow their own territory to be used by foreign irregular forces;
(2) stop terrorist activities or destabilization attempts in the region;
(3) expel all foreign military advisers;
(4) limit their acquisition of defence material;
(5) allow for the verification and control of their arsenals;
(6) ban the installation of foreign military bases;
(7) establish and improve the institutions of representative and pluralist democracy;
(8) guarantee full respect for human rights and make national reconciliation possible;
(9) provide guarantees for those taking up amnesty offers;
(10) open the election process to all citizens and establish the autonomy of the judicial system;
(11) collaborate on the regional refugee problem;
(12) negotiate a regional stance on foreign finance;
(13) promote inter-regional trade;
(14) undertake joint investment projects; and
(15) establish fairer economic structures.

The Contadora ministers issued a statement from Panama City on April 9, 1984, noting (i) "the actions of irregular forces, supported and supplied by communications centres located in neighbouring countries, which are seeking to destabilize the region"; (ii) that "operations are being carried out, such as the mining of ports [i.e. Corinto], which impair the economy, disrupt trade and hinder freedom of navigation"; and (iii) "the increasingly open presence of foreign troops and advisers, an increase in arms build-ups, and the proliferation of weapons and military actions and exercises, all of which help to intensify tension and deepen mistrust". In an attempt to ease these tensions the Group formed the Action Committee for the Social and Economic

Development of Central America (Cadesca) as a "means of channelling international aid for the internal and integration efforts of the Central American countries".

At first it seemed likely that all countries except Nicaragua would favour the draft treaty, with the Guatemalan foreign minister, Fernando Andrade Díaz Durán, announcing in August, 1984, that his government accepted it "without addition or qualification" (despite opposition to Contadora by the MLN, which wanted a political, military and economic boycott of Nicaragua). Then, on Sept. 21, the Sandinista government announced its readiness to sign the treaty in its present form, and called on the United States to ratify it; the US State Department responded by describing the Nicaraguan announcement as a "propaganda ploy" and a "hypocritical" move since, it maintained, Nicaragua was not committed to free elections as specified in the treaty.

Previously the US administration had spoken of bringing pressure to bear on Nicaragua to sign the treaty, especially through the Manzanillo talks, but after the announcement Shultz said that there were problems with the draft plan. The Honduran foreign minister, Paz Bárnica, stated on Oct. 3, 1984, that Honduras, El Salvador and Costa Rica wanted "certain changes" in the draft, and the US administration amplified its criticism, saying that it considered the verification procedure contained in the treaty to be inadequate; it also wanted a detailed timetable for the withdrawal of foreign troops and advisers and a tightening of the procedures stipulated for democratic elections. Meanwhile, at the UN General Assembly Daniel Ortega claimed that the United States planned a military intervention in Nicaragua to begin on Oct. 15 (the date scheduled for the signature of the treaty), and that heavy concentrations of contras and CIA mercenaries had been seen along Nicaragua's borders with Honduras and Costa Rica.

At the debate on Central America in the UN General Assembly on Oct. 24, 1984, the Mexican and Nicaraguan representatives attempted to force the United States either to accept the Contadora draft or to declare publicly its opposition to it. The Contadora member–countries drafted a resolution urging all states "in particular those with ties and interests in the region, to respect fully . . . the Contadora Act and the commitments undertaken by virtue of their accession to its additional protocol". (US signature of the protocol would have been tantamount to signing the actual treaty.)

In October and November 1984 the foreign ministers of Honduras, El Salvador and Costa Rica met to discuss the changes they wanted to the draft, the chief of which were (i) the elimination of the provision prohibiting international military manoeuvres in the region; (ii) an increase in the authority of the proposed verification panel and the formation of an "ad hoc disarmament panel"; (iii) the imposition of an immediate temporary freeze on the acquisition of military equipment by the Central American countries (apparently in response to the MiGs crisis—see section 5.3.5); and (iv) the removal of a clause (originally inserted at Nicaragua's insistence) providing that the limit on the military development of each country would take into account that country's security interests (i.e. allowing Nicaragua to arm in line with the perceived threat of a US invasion). The new changes did not alter the previous commitment laid upon all parties to attend a further round of negotiations to set limits on each others' military inventories.

At the beginning of January 1985 the Contadora ministers met again in

Panama, not to work on the revised draft of Honduras, El Salvador and Costa Rica, but to return to the objections made to the original draft, saying that the changes went beyond the scope of foreseen "refinements". In a new development, however, Monge announced that Costa Rica would not attend the meeting until the Group took action on his government's complaints against Nicaragua; these complaints arose from the arrest on Dec. 24, 1984, of a Nicaraguan student, José Urbina Lara, who had spent four months at the Costa Rican embassy in Managua as a refugee from the military service law, and who was subsequently sentenced to five years' imprisonment for draft-dodging and collaboration with the contras. At the beginning of February 1985 the Costa Rican government announced that it would not attend the Group meeting on Feb. 14–15 unless Urbina Lara were released, and so was accused by Nicaragua of wanting to sabotage the Contadora process on behalf of the US. When Honduras and El Salvador announced on Feb. 13 that they would boycott the meeting in solidarity with Costa Rica, it was abandoned.

At the beginning of March 1985 Ortega announced that Urbina Lara had been released and flown to Colombia and that the Nicaraguan government had therefore "removed the pretext for halting Contadora"; after this move, and the conciliatory Costa Rican measure of expelling Calero from its territory, the talks resumed on May 14–16 (during which the Contadora members condemned the US economic embargo against Nicaragua—see section 5.2.5). Nicaragua proposed that the Honduran and Nicaraguan governments jointly disarm the contras, but although Honduras agreed to the provision on the removal of "destabilizing forces", it still did not acknowledge the existence of contra groups on Honduran territory; moreover, Nicaragua blocked a proposal that Contadora officials should mediate between the government and the contras (not recognizing them as a legitimate opposition force while under arms). The other discussions concentrated on the membership of ad hoc commissions to investigate border disputes and on improving regional security communications, but there were divisions over the timing and the scale of military reduction and verification mechanisms.

The next meeting (the 14th, as the 12th and 13th had been boycotted) opened on June 18, 1985, but the agenda (focusing on verification and control issues) was rejected by Tinoco (for Nicaragua), saying that it should be set aside in favour of the discussion of "specific problems affecting regional security"—i.e. the approval by the US Congress of $27,000,000 to the contras (see section 5.2.5). Nicaraguan delegates withdrew from the meeting the next day, complaining that the Group was ignoring new elements of the war in Central America, and Tinoco commented: "It makes no sense to discuss theoretical agreements for the future while every measure that can lead to war is being implemented."

A communiqué issued after a secret Group meeting on July 21–23, 1985, stated that the Group had "managed to unblock the negotiating process", and a plea was made to the United States to resume the Manzanillo talks. The Group met again in Cartagena (Colombia) on Aug. 23–25, when it was joined by the recently formed Lima Group, comprising the foreign ministers of Argentina, Brazil, Peru and Uruguay, and discussed a new draft treaty, which was presented to the Central American foreign ministers on Sept. 12. The countries were given until Oct. 7 to study the draft and until Nov. 20 to sign it, but on Nov. 11 Nicaragua announced that it would not subscribe as the draft did not ban US military manoeuvres in the region. Ortega proposed instead that a new protocol be inserted "directly solely at the US government", calling on it to "cease its aggressions in all forms against Nicaragua".

The Group announced that the deadline would be extended until Dec. 20, 1985, and that if no progress were made the Contadora process would be finished. In the first week of December, however, Augusto Ramírez Ocampo (Colombian foreign minister) said that the negotiations had been suspended for five months at the request of Nicaragua. The Nicaraguan suggestion had been made on the grounds that the inauguration of new governments in Guatemala, Honduras and Costa Rica in the first four months of 1986 could lead to a change in the regional policy of those countries. (Ramírez also noted that the current "deep confrontation" between the United States and Nicaragua "damages and deteriorates the process of negotiation".)

In the meantime the Contadora and Lima Groups convened at Caraballeda (Venezuela) on Jan. 11–12, 1986, and drafted the "Caraballeda Message for Peace, Security and Democracy in Central America", which was adopted on Jan. 15 by the Central American foreign ministers as the "Guatemala Declaration". The principal proposals of the Message were: (i) an end to the support of unconventional forces and insurrectionist movements in the region; (ii) the suspension of international military manoeuvres; (iii) the gradual phasing out of foreign military advisers and installations; (iv) unilateral pledges of commitment to non-aggression by the five Central American states; (v) the resumption of negotiations leading to the signing of the peace agreement; and (vi) promotion of regional and international co-operation to alleviate pressing economic and social problems. In addition, the Message called on the United States to resume bilateral talks with Nicaragua.

Meeting again at Punta del Este (Uruguay) on Feb. 28, 1986, the two Groups issued a document which included a proposal to form a civilian international commission to monitor the Nicaraguan–Costa Rican border. It was agreed on March 12 (when Costa Rican and Nicaraguan representatives were also present) that the commission should be permanent and on both sides of the border, and should comprise members from the two interested countries and from the Contadora and Lima Group countries.

After talks with the Central American foreign ministers the two Groups issued the "Panama Compromise" on April 7, 1986, which contained an undertaking to sign the draft treaty on June 6, with the assent of all the Central American foreign ministers except d'Escoto (reiterating his country's objection of November 1985 to initiating demilitarization without a simultaneous commitment from the United States to cease assistance to the contras). Five days later President Ortega pledged Nicaragua's willingness to sign, and Jorge Abadía Arias, the Panamanian foreign minister, announced that in a letter dated April 14 from the US ambassador the US government had agreed "to cease all its support for the Nicaraguan contras at the same time that Nicaragua signs the Contadora peace accord".

The crucial factor in the signing of the draft treaty was the giving of guarantees on the principle of non-intervention; after the Nicaraguan government had announced on May 10, 1986, that it was not ready to sign further negotiations on arms control and international military manoeuvres were held. The countries failed to reach agreement, specifically on Nicaragua's insistence on the immediate cessation of foreign military manoeuvres and distinction between offensive and defensive weapons, with only defensive weapons being permitted to remain. The "Declaration of Esquipulas" issued on May 24 after a summit meeting of the five presidents at the Guatemalan town, restated the countries' willingness to sign the treaty, but recognized the outstanding problems. On June 2 President Cerezo announced an indefinite postponement of the June 6 deadline.

On June 6 the Contadora and Lima Groups presented the Central American ministers with a revised draft (which they described as their "last"), which was accepted by Nicaragua but rejected by the other four countries. The revisions included prohibitions on (i) the use of national territories for attacks on third countries; (ii) membership of "military or political blocs"; and (iii) assistance to "irregular or guerrilla groups trying to topple legitimate regimes".

The two groups reconvened in Bogotá on Aug. 8, 1986, and agreed to "renew their efforts for peace", but expressed less optimism at a meeting in New York on Sept. 30, when they issued a document called "Peace is still possible in Central America", observing that the regional crisis was "more serious every day", and "each time the risk of war much greater".

6.5.4: US Attitude to the Contadora Process

Officially the US administration supported the Contadora process. After meeting Ortega at the inauguration of President Julio Sanguinetti in Uruguay at the beginning of March 1985, Secretary of State Shultz commented: "I don't know that anything has changed, although perhaps there is a recognition all round that the Contadora process has to be the centre of negotiations, and the sooner everyone realises that and gets the process started, the better." It was, however, widely reported that privately the administration did not favour the Group's efforts, and Senate papers later showed that US pressure had persuaded Honduras, El Salvador and Costa Rica to halt the signing of the treaty in October 1984.[1] In 1984 the US publication *Newsweek* recorded one US government official as saying: "On the surface we're going to support Contadora; in reality we're not going to let it interfere with US goals."

Although Philip Habib, after his appointment in March 1986 as US special envoy to Central America (see section 5.1.2), maintained that the treaty could be workable, the Defence Department, National Security Council staff and Casey (CIA director) were all reported to be far more guarded over its viability. After the Punta del Este meeting of February 1986, Elliott Abrams (assistant secretary of state for inter-American affairs) described the position of the Contadora and Lima Groups as "erroneous"; while conceding that the proposed $100,000,000 aid package for the contras (see section 5.2.5) was incompatible with the Contadora Group's stance, he claimed that only armed force would make the Sandinista government negotiate.

Note

1. *Newsnight*, BBC, April 12, 1985; *Central America Bulletin*, Vol. 4, No. 7, July 1985, p. 4.

APPENDICES, SELECT BIBLIOGRAPHY AND INDEXES

APPENDIX ONE

Platform of the FDR of El Salvador (April 1980)*

The economic and social structures of our country—which have served to guarantee the disproportionate enrichment of an oligarchic minority and the exploitation of our people by Yankee imperialism—are in deep and insoluble crisis. . . .

The decisive task of the revolution on which completion of all its objectives depends is the conquest of power and the installation of a *democratic revolutionary government*, which at the head of the people will launch the construction of a new society.

Tasks and Objectives of the Revolution

The tasks and objectives of the revolution in El Salvador are the following:

(1) To overthrow the reactionary military dictatorship of the oligarchy and Yankee imperialism, imposed and sustained against the will of the Salvadorean people for fifty years; to destroy its criminal political-military machine; and to establish a *democratic revolutionary government* founded on the unity of the revolutionary and democratic forces in the People's Army and the Salvadorean people.

(2) To put an end to the overall political, economic and social power of the great lords of land and capital.

(3) To liquidate once and for all the economic, political and military dependence of our country on Yankee imperialism.

(4) To assure democratic rights and freedoms for the entire people—particularly for the working masses, who are the ones who have least enjoyed such freedoms.

(5) To transfer to the people, through nationalizations and the creation of collective and socialized enterprises, the fundamental means of production and distribution that are now hoarded by the oligarchy and the US monopolies: the land held by the big landlords, the enterprises that produce and distribute electricity and other monopolized services, foreign trade, banking, and large transportation enterprises. None of this will affect small or medium-sized private businesses, which will be given every kind of stimulus and support in the various branches of the national economy.

(6) To raise the cultural and material living standards of the population.

(7) To create a new army for our country, one that will arise fundamentally on the basis of the People's Army to be built in the course of the revolutionary process. Those healthy, patriotic and worthy elements that belong to the current army can also be incorporated.

(8) To encourage all forms of organization of the people, at all levels and in all sectors, thus guaranteeing their active, creative and democratic involvement in the revolutionary process and securing the closest identification between the people and their government.

(9) To orient the foreign policy and international relations of our country around the principles of independence and self-determination, solidarity, peaceful coexistence, equal rights and mutual respect between states.

(10) Through all these measures, to assure our country peace, freedom, the well-being of our people and future social progress.

The Democratic Revolutionary Government—Its Composition and Platform of Social, Structural and Political Changes

The *democratic revolutionary government* will be made up of representatives of the revolutionary and people's movement, as well as of the democratic parties, organizations, sectors and individuals who are willing to participate in the carrying out of this programmatic platform.

This government will rest on a broad political and social base, formed above all by the working class, the peasantry and the advanced middle layers. Intimately united to the latter forces will be all the social sectors that are willing to carry out this platform —small and medium-sized industrialists, merchants, artisans and farmers. . . . Also involved will be honest professionals, the progressive clergy, democratic parties such as the MNR, advanced sectors of the PDC, worthy and honest officers of the army who are willing to serve the interests of the people, and any other sectors, groups or individuals that uphold broad democracy for the popular masses, independent development and people's liberation. . . .

Immediate Political Measures

(1) A halt to all forms of repression against the people and release of all political prisoners.

(2) Clarification of the situation of those captured and disappeared since 1972; punishment of those responsible (be they military or civilian) for crimes against the people.

(3) Disarming and permanent dissolution of the repressive bodies [including Orden, the National Guard, National Police, Treasury Police and Customs Police]. . . . The current misnamed security bodies will be replaced by a civilian police force.

(4) Dissolution of the existing state powers (executive, legislative and judicial); abrogation of the Political Constitution and all decrees that have modified or added to it.

The *democratic revolutionary government* will decree a constitutional law and will organize the state and its activities with the aim of guaranteeing the rights and freedoms of the people and of achieving the other objectives and tasks of the revolution. In doing so, the *democratic revolutionary government* will adhere to the UN Universal Declaration of Human Rights.

The constitutional law referred to above will remain in force while the Salvadorean people prepare a new political constitution that faithfully reflects their interests.

(5) Municipal government will be restructured so as to be an organ of broad participation by the masses in managing the state, a real organ of the new people's power.

(6) The *democratic revolutionary government* will carry out an intense effort of liberating education, of cultural exposition and organization among the broadest masses, in order to promote their conscious incorporation into the development, strengthening and defence of the revolutionary process.

(7) The People's Army will be strengthened and developed. It will include the soldiers, non-commissioned officers, officers and chiefs of the current army who conduct themselves honestly, reject foreign intervention against the revolutionary process, and support the liberation struggle of our people.

The new army will be the true armed wing of the people. It will be at their service and absolutely faithful to their interests and their revolution. The armed forces will be truly patriotic, the defenders of national sovereignty and self-determination, and committed partisans of peaceful coexistence among peoples.

(8) Our country will withdraw from Condeca, from TIAR (Rio de Janeiro Inter-American Defence Treaty) and from any other military or police organizations that might be the instruments of interventionism.

(9) The *democratic revolutionary government* will establish diplomatic and trade relations with other countries without discrimination on the basis of differing social systems, but based instead on principles of equal rights, coexistence and respect for self-determination. . . . Close fraternal relations with Nicaragua will especially be sought, as the expression of the community of ideals and interest between our revolution and the Sandinista revolution.

Our country will become a member of the non-aligned movement and will develop a steadfast policy toward the defence of world peace and in favour of détente.

Structural Changes

The *democratic revolutionary government* will:
(1) Nationalize the entire banking and financial system. . . .
(2) Nationalize foreign trade.
(3) Nationalize the system of electricity distribution, along with the enterprises for its production that are in private hands.
(4) Nationalize the refining of petroleum.
(5) Carry out the expropriation, in accord with the national interest, of the monopolistic enterprises in industry, trade and services.
(6) Carry out a thorough agrarian reform, which will put the land that is now in the hands of the big landlords at the disposal of the broad masses who work it. This will be done according to an effective plan to benefit the great majority of poor and middle peasants and agricultural wage workers and to promote the development of agriculture and cattle raising. . . .
(7) Carry out an urban reform to benefit the great majority, without affecting small and medium owners of real estate.
(8) Thoroughly transform the tax system, so that tax payments no longer fall upon the workers. Indirect taxes on widely consumed goods will be reduced. . . .
(9) Establish effective mechanisms for credit, economic aid and technical assistance for small and medium-sized private businesses in all branches of the country's economy.
(10) Establish a system for effective planning of the national economy, which will make it possible to encourage balanced development.

Social Measures

The *democratic revolutionary government* will direct its efforts in the social arena towards the following objectives:
(1) To create sufficient sources of jobs, so as to eliminate unemployment in the briefest possible time.
(2) To bring into effect a just wage policy, based on: (*a*) regulation of wages, taking into account the cost of living; (*b*) an energetic policy of control and reduction of the prices charged for basic goods and services; and (*c*) a substantial increase in social services for the popular masses (social security, education, recreation, health care, etc.).
(3) To put into action a massive plan for construction of low cost housing.
(4) To create a unified national health system, which will guarantee efficient medical service to the entire population. Preventive care will be the principal aim.
(5) To carry out a literacy campaign that will put an end to illiteracy in the shortest possible time.
(6) To develop the national education system so as to assure primary education to the entire population of school age and substantially broaden secondary and university education. Quality and scientific-technical diversification will be increased at all levels, and free education will be progressively introduced.
(7) To promote cultural activity on a broad scale, effectively supporting and stimulating national artists and writers, recovering and developing the cultural heritage of the nation, and incorporating into the cultural assets of the broad popular masses the best of universal culture. . . .

*These extracts are taken from the document printed in Armstrong and Shenk, *El Salvador: The Face of Revolution*, pp. 254–59.

APPENDIX TWO

US State Department Report on the "Soviet–Cuban Connection in Central America and the Caribbean" (March 1985)

The US report called *The Soviet–Cuban Connection in Central America and the Caribbean*, released by the departments of state and defence in March 1985, began with the following quotation from President Reagan (from May 1984): "We Americans should be proud of what we're trying to do in Central America, and proud of what, together with our friends, we can do in Central America, to support democracy, human rights and economic growth, while preserving peace so close to home. Let us show the world that we want no hostile, communist colonies here in the Americas: South, Central or North."

The document then declared: "US policy in the area is based on four mutually supportive elements that are being pursued simultaneously: to assist in the development of democratic institutions and to encourage creation of representative governments accountable to their citizens; to address on an urgent basis the economic and social problems of the region by providing economic assistance to stimulate growth, create opportunity, and improve the quality of life of the people; to provide security assistance to enable the countries to defend themselves against Soviet-bloc, Cuban and Nicaraguan supported insurgents and terrorists intent on establishing Marxist–Leninist dictatorships; [and] to promote peaceful solutions through negotiation and dialogue among the countries of the region and among political groups within each country."

The introduction was concluded by another quotation from President Reagan of May 1984: "If we do nothing or if we continue to provide too little help, our choice will be a communist Central America with additional communist military bases on the mainland of this hemisphere, and communist subversion spreading southward and northward. This communist subversion poses the threat that 100 million people from Panama to the open border on our south could come under the control of pro-Soviet regimes.

"If we come to our senses too late, when our vital interests are even more directly threatened, and after a lack of American support causes our friends to lose the ability to defend themselves, then the risks to our security and our way of life will be infinitely greater."

On Cuba, in a chapter entitled "Cuba: The Key Soviet Proxy", the document stated: "To protect their military investment in Cuba, the Soviets are making a sizeable economic investment as well. . . . This substantial investment in Cuba gives the Soviet Union both military and intelligence capabilities in an area that is a lifeline for the US economy. The Caribbean and Gulf of Mexico maritime routes carry about 55 per cent of imported petroleum to the United States, as well as approximately 45 per cent of all US seaborne trade. Furthermore, in any NATO–Warsaw Pact confrontation, more than half of all NATO resupply would be shipped from Gulf ports and would have to pass by Cuba."

In a chapter on Grenada, entitled "Grenada: A Failed Revolution", the document claimed: "Bishop secretly planned to impose a single-party dictatorship while promising a pluralistic democracy. The Soviets and Cubans were party to the entire deception."

In the same vein the chapter "Nicaragua: A Betrayed Revolution", stated: "The Sandinistas had pledged to have free elections, political pluralism, a mixed economy and a non-aligned foreign policy. . . Since those hopeful early days, Nicaragua has moved not towards democracy, but towards a new dictatorship tied ever more closely to Cuba and the Soviet Union. . . . By words and deeds, the Sandinista leaders have demonstrated that they are, in fact, dedicated Marxist–Leninists." Emphasis was placed on the acquisition of military supplies by Nicaragua, with the assertion that the military build-up was in preparation for aggression: "The Honduran army is striving to modernize and professionalize, but it lags behind the rapid expansion of the Sandinista army. Costa Rica has no army. The Salvadorean armed forces are fully occupied with combating Sandinista-supported insurgents. Clearly, Nicaragua's military power threatens—and is not threatened by—its neighbours."

The chapter "El Salvador: A Democratic Revolution" defended the Duarte government: "El Salvador is, in fact, moving toward the goal of establishing a government that is accountable to its citizens. This is being carried out behind the shield of the much improved armed forces, whose initiative on the battlefield, combined with President Duarte's popular mandate, moved the guerrillas to accept President Duarte's call to participate in a dialogue with the government. Lacking broad popular support, the guerrillas continue to be a potent military force because of the extensive support they receive from Nicaragua, Cuba, other communist countries such as Vietnam and radical regimes such as Libya. The unification of the Salvadorean guerrillas was co-ordinated by Fidel Castro."

The chapter "Castro: Subversive Catalyst" states: "Acting to fulfil his own revolutionary ambitions as well as being an agent of Soviet influence, Fidel Castro is working closely with subversive elements throughout Central America and the Caribbean. In addition to El Salvador, Guatemala and Honduras have been targets of Castro's subversion. In Guatemala he has provided training and some financial support to three guerrilla factions, although he has not succeeded in unifying them to the extent he did in El Salvador. Honduran territory is used principally as a conduit of support for the Salvadorean guerrillas, but Honduras has also been a target of Cuban destabilization. . . . A disturbing aspect of the current Castro offensive is the apparent use of money generated by narcotics to supply arms for guerrillas. Several high-ranking Cuban officials have provided protection for planes and small ships carrying drugs. The drugs move northward from Colombia to the United States, at times via Cuba and on at least one occasion via Nicaragua."

The final section, headed "The Challenge and the Response", contained the following statement: "Ideology plays an important role in Soviet motivations, as the creation of assitional communist states validates the tenets of Marxism–Leninism and bolsters the Soviet Union itself. Most importantly, Kremlin leaders hope that ultimately the United States could become so preoccupied with turmoil in the Central American and Caribbean region that it would be less able militarily and politically to oppose Soviet goals in other key areas of the world.

"The Soviets are using Cuba and Nicaragua to exploit the instability and poverty in the area. There is a high degree of congruence in Soviet, Cuban and Nicaraguan foreign policy goals. These three countries are working in concert to train and support guerrilla organizations in countries throughout the area. Should these guerrillas succeed in coming to power, they undoubtedly will establish regimes similar to those of their patrons—one-party communist dictatorships maintained in power by military force and political and psychological intimidation."

APPENDIX THREE

The Central American Crisis—A European Response

(by the Transnational Institute, Amsterdam, October 1984)

Europe and Central America

Europe has its own interest in helping to prevent Central America from becoming a focus for conflict and East–West tension. Europe is linked to and interdependent with the United States in many ways. The United States plays a major role in the defence of Europe. It is in Europe's interest, therefore, that the United States should not become involved in Central America in ways which undermine the Atlantic relationship. The actions of the US government in Central America such as the mining of Nicaraguan ports and its refusal to admit the validity of the ruling of the International Court of Justice, its support for the contras and now its attempts to undermine the Contadora initiative, are seen by many Europeans as proof that the United States is prepared to disregard the principles of international conduct which it professes to uphold and which the NATO charter pledges it to observe, whenever it declares its national interests to be at state, however questionably or arbitrarily these may be defined.

On a wider scale, Europe has an interest in demonstrating that the West can contribute to substantive development that will satisfy people's basic needs. It is important to come to terms with the fact that, for the foreseeable future, the countries of Central America will be poor. It will be years before they recover the levels of income they enjoyed before the economic recession and the civil wars and insurgencies of the past five years. The poverty, dependence and indebtedness of their economies make economic, political and social choices difficult. There are no convenient surpluses to finance populist policies or to soften the clash of competing priorities and the conflict between different classes and interest groups. In such a situation, development, peace and social justice are interdependent and cannot be pursued separately. A durable peace can be established only if development is rooted in a reasonably just social order. In this sense, Central America is a microcosm in extreme form of the problems which beset many developing countries. Failure on the part of Europe to contribute to stable and constructive solutions to the crisis in Central America will be discouraging to those political forces in the developing world, and specially in Latin America, which look to Europe for a more disinterested and understanding approach to development problems.

We are making this concerted initiative in order to demonstrate our concern and alarm at the situation in Central America. In the past governments and political parties have taken positions on Central America but so far these have had little effect on the logic of confrontation which still seems to be gathering momentum in the region.

Recommendations

There are six ways in which Europe can make a significant contribution towards the resolution of the problems of Central America:

(1) Europe should give strong diplomatic and political backing to the Contadora Group to enable it to resist pressure from outside the region. Europe should follow the example of Canada by appointing representatives as observers to the Contadora Group.

(2) Europe should call unequivocally for the disarming and disbandment of the contras, using appropriate international institutions to achieve this end. This implies a unilateral action on the part of the US government which should withdraw all support from the contras and, more generally, support the provisions of the Contadora treaty, calling on its signatories not to allow their territory to be used by insurgents seeking to destabilize the governments of neighbouring countries. The establishment of secure and peaceful borders between Nicaragua and its neighbours is a crucial element in the Contadora process.

(3) Europe should agree on a substantial aid programme for all Central America, tied to stringent human rights conditions. The experience of European non-governmental organizations and government-funded agencies in Central America will be specially relevant to such a programme.

(4) Europe should insist that international financial institutions, such as the World Bank, deal even-handedly with all the countries in Central America.

(5) Europe should seek to commit the political weight of the UN and the resources and expertise of its specialized agencies to the peaceful resolution of the problems of Central America.

(6) The European Economic Community, and European countries individually, should use its/their own financial and commercial institutions and resources to encourage stable trading relations with Central America.

APPENDIX FOUR

FMLN–FDR Demands at the La Palma Talks (October 1984)*

(1) The arrest and trial of those responsible for the murder of Archbishop Romero.

(2) The arrest and trial of those responsible for killing the four US missionaries [i.e. those who ordered the killing, carried out by five former National Guardsmen].

(3) The arrest and trial of those responsible for the slaying of six FDR members in November 1980.

(4) The arrest and trial of those responsible for killing Hammer, Pearlman and Viera.

(5) The arrest and trial of those responsible for the slaying of the four Dutch journalists in March 1982, and those responsible for all political murders in recent years.

(6) Freedom for political prisoners and an accounting of those who have disappeared.

(7) Cessation of the bombing of the civilian population in zones controlled by the FMLN.

(8) Freedom of movement and organization for urban and rural workers.

(9) The right of workers to strike.

(10) Demilitarization of all work centres.

(11) Freedom for government employees to organize.

(12) A daily salary minimum this year of 18 colones, or $4.80.

(13) A 10 per cent general increase in wages for commercial, bank and industrial employees.

(14) A reduction in the prices of basic food products.

(15) A revival of the agrarian reform programme.

(16) Suspension of forced recruiting by the army.

(17) Increased funding for the National University.

(18) Sustaining a scholarship programme for the children of workers.

(19) Salary reductions for the president, deputies, high-ranking government officials and all military officers with the rank of major and above and a wage rise for common soldiers.

(20) The removal of US military advisers and an end to US military aid.

(21) No repression or persecution of market women and a plan to allow them to earn a better living.

(22) Lower prices for gasoline and other fuels.

(23) Access to radio, television, newspapers and magazines by leftists.

(24) Freedom of the press.

(25) Lower prices for electricity, water and other utilities.

(26) The elimination of public school costs to parents and limits on private college costs.

(27) A reduction in interest rates for small and medium-scale farmers.

(28) A reduction in interest rates for small businesses.

(29) A 100 per cent increase in taxes on income from utility services and large businesses.

*As broadcast by Radio Venceremos

LATE INFORMATION

In Nicaragua the newspaper *Barricada* reported in mid-December 1986 that economy minister Henry Ruiz had signed an economic agreement in Moscow covering aid for 1987 worth $300,000,000, mostly in the form of oil, raw materials and machinery.

In Honduras US and Honduran military sources stated in early November 1986 that a number of islands off the country's Pacific coast would be used to store supplies for contra airborne attacks on nearby Nicaraguan targets; such action contrasted strongly with assurances given by the Azcona government earlier in the year of no assistance to the contras (see page 249). At the beginning of December Nicaraguan EPS units carried out several forays across the Honduran border against contra bases, and in response President Azcona submitted a request to the US administration on Dec. 6 for the airlift of several hundred Honduran troops into the region. Shortly afterwards the Nicaraguan government claimed that the Honduran air force had strafed the Nicaraguan towns of Wiwili and Mura.

In Costa Rica the US ambassador Lewis Tambs (who had replaced Curtin Winsor—see page 250) resigned in December 1986. He denied current news reports that he had tried unsuccessfully to bring pressure to bear on the Costa Rican government to allow contras to make use of a US-built airstrip inside Costa Rica. President Azcona ordered that the airstrip be closed to prevent any such use. The airstrip was alleged to have been financed by the secret sale of US arms to Iran (see below).

In the United States the $100,000,000 aid package for the contras agreed by Congress in August 1986 (see page 249) was signed into law by President Reagan on Oct. 9, making $60,000,000 available immediately (largely for rifles, ammunition and grenade launchers), with the balance retained until mid-February 1987. It was anticipated, however, that in 1987 the Reagan administration would face greater difficulty in raising funds for the contras because of the political uproar occasioned by the revelation in November that unofficial arms supplies to the contras had been funded by the secret sale of arms to Iran (with investigations into the conduct of many administration officials continuing into the new year), and by the congressional elections of December which overturned the Republican majority in the Senate in favour of the Democratic Party.

The Contadora and Lima Groups reconvened in mid-December 1986 in an attempt to revive the peace process which had reached stalemate in June (see page 301). They expressed their "grave concern" over the recent escalation of contra activities (made possible by the renewed US aid—see above), the increase in what they termed foreign political intervention and the suspension of dialogue between the parties, and announced their intention of sending a delegation to Central America early in the new year, including UN and OAS representatives.

SELECT BIBLIOGRAPHY

General Historical Background

Ralph Lee Woodward, *Central America: A Nation Divided*, OUP, New York, 1976.

See also:
Salvador de Madariaga, *Latin America between the Eagle and the Bear*, Hollis and Carter, London, 1962.
   Dana G. Munro, *The Five Republics of Central America*, New York, 1967.
   Munro, *Intervention and Dollar Diplomacy 1900–21*, Princeton, 1964.
   Munro, *The United States and the Caribbean Republics 1921–33*, Princeton, 1964.
   Franklin D. Parker, *The Central American Republics*, OUP, London, 1964.
   Claudio Véliz (ed.), *Latin America and the Caribbean: A Handbook*, Anthony Blond, London, 1968.
   Oxfam Pack on Central America.

Guatemala

George Black, *Garrison Guatemala*, Zed Press, London, 1984.
   Thomas and Marjorie Melville, *Guatemala—Another Vietnam?*, Penguin, Harmondsworth, 1971.
   Stephen Schlesinger and Stephen Kinzer, *Bitter Fruit: The Untold Story of the American Coup in Guatemala*, Sinclair Browne, London, 1982.

Honduras

Honduras: State for Sale, Latin America Bureau, London, 1985.
   James A. Morris, *Honduras—Caudillo Politics and Military Rulers*, Westview (Boulder, Colorado), 1983.
   Paul Theroux, *The Mosquito Coast*, Penguin, Harmondsworth, 1982 (a novel set in the Mosquitia region of Honduras).

El Salvador

Manlio Argueta, *Una Dia en la Vida*, UCA Editores, San Salvador, 1980 (English translation *One Day of Life*, Chatto and Windus, London, 1984)
   Robert Armstrong and Janet Shenk, *El Salvador—The Face of Revolution*, Pluto Press, London, 1982.
   Raymond Bonner, *Weakness and Deceit: US Policy in El Salvador*, Hamish Hamilton, London, 1984.
   Frank Devine, *El Salvador—Embassy under Siege*, Vantage Press, New York 1981 (Devine was ambassador in San Salvador 1977–80).
   Joan Didion, *Salvador*, Chatto and Windus, London, 1983.
   James Dunkerley, *The Long War—Dictatorship and Revolution in El Salvador*, Junction Books, London, 1982.

Harry Mattison, Susan Meiselas and Fae Rubenstein (eds.), *El Salvador* (a photographic record).

El Salvador: Background to the Crisis, Central American Information Office (CAMINO), 1151 Massachusetts Avenue, Cambridge, Mass. 02138, USA.

Nicaragua

George Black, *Triumph of the People: The Sandinista Revolution in Nicaragua*, Zed Press, London, 1981.

George Black and John Bevan, *The Loss of Fear: Education in Nicaragua Before and After the Revolution*, Nicaragua Solidarity Campaign/World University Service, London, 1980.

Dianna Melrose, *Nicaragua: The Threat of a Good Example?*, Oxfam Public Affairs Unit, 1985.

Peter Rosset and John Vandermeer (eds.), *The Nicaraguan Reader: Documents of a Revolution under Fire*, Grove Press, New York, 1983.

Henri Weber, *Nicaragua: The Sandinista Revolution*, Verso, London, 1981.

Costa Rica

Leonard Bird, Costa Rica: *The Unarmed Democracy*, Sheppard Press, London, 1984.

Panama

Graham Greene, *Getting to Know the General—The Story of an Involvement*, Bodley Head, London, 1984.

Cuba

Peter Wyden, *Bay of Pigs—The Untold Story*, Jonathan Cape, London, 1979.

Grenada

Hugh O'Shaughnessy, *Grenada: Revolution, Invasion and Aftermath*, Hamish Hamilton with *The Observer*, London, 1984.

US Policy

Stuart Holland MP and Donald Anderson MP, *Kissinger's Kingdom? A Counter-report on Central America*, Spokesman, Nottingham, 1984.

Walter Lefebar, *Inevitable Revolutions: The United States in Central America*, Norton, Toronto, 1983.

Jenny Pearce, *Under the Eagle: US Intervention in Central America and the Caribbean*, Latin America Bureau, London, 1982.

Periodicals

Central America Bulletin, Central America Research Institute (CARIN), POB 4797, Berkeley, Calif. 94704, USA.

Central America Report, published by the El Salvador Committee for Human Rights and the Guatemala Committee for Human Rights, London.

Central America Update, Box 2207, Station P, Toronto, Ontario, Canada M55 2T2.

Centroamerica Al Dia (international press review), POB 248, Leuven 1, Belgium.

Costa Rica Digest, CUSO, Apdo. 100, San Pedro, San José.

El Salvador Bulletin, published by El Salvador Solidarity Campaign, London.

Inforpress Centroamericana, 9a Calle "A" 3–56, Zona 1, Guatemala City.

Latinamerica Press/Noticias Aliadas (English and Spanish editions), Apdo, 5594, Lima 100, Peru.

Multinational Monitor, POB 19405, Washington, DC 20036, USA.

SUBJECT INDEX

NAMES INDEX